Forgotten Fires

FRONTISPIECE. This 1903 photo, described as a "mock-up of starting a prairie fire," shows Blackfoot Indians near Calgary, Alberta. From the Provincial Archives of Alberta, Edmonton.

Forgotten Fires

Native Americans and the Transient Wilderness

by Omer C. Stewart

Edited and with Introductions by
Henry T. Lewis and M. Kat Anderson

University of Oklahoma Press : Norman

This book is published with the generous assistance of The Kerr Foundation, Inc.

Library of Congress Cataloging-in-Publication Data

Stewart, Omer Call, 1908–
  Forgotten fires : Native Americans and the transient wilderness /
Omer C. Stewart; edited and with introductions by Henry T. Lewis and
M. Kat Anderson.
    p.   cm.
  Includes bibliographical references and index.
  ISBN 0-8061-3423-2 (hc : alk. paper)
  1. Indians of North America—Fire use. 2. Indians of North America—
Agriculture 3. Indigenous peoples—Ecology. 4. Fire ecology. 5. Shifting
cultivation. 6. Traditional farming. I. Lewis, Henry T. II. Anderson, Kat,
1955–   III. Title.

E98.F38 S74 2002
577.2—dc21
                                                              2002020503

To Lenore Stewart,
beloved wife and companion of Omer,
devoted mother of Ann, Steve, Kate, and Carl,
and generous friend of many

Only to the white man was nature a "wilderness" and only to him was the land "infested" with "wild" animals and "savage" people.

Luther Standing Bear (1868–1939),
chief of the Oglala Sioux

Contents

List of Illustrations   xi
Introduction, *Henry T. Lewis and M. Kat Anderson*   3
An Anthropological Critique, *Henry T. Lewis*   17
An Ecological Critique, *M. Kat Anderson*   37
The Effects of Burning of Grasslands and Forests
     by Aborigines the World Over, *Omer C. Stewart*   65
       Introduction   67
       The Eastern Woodlands   70
       Prairies and Plains   113
       The Mountain West   217
Abbreviations   313
Bibliography, *Omer C. Stewart*   315
References Cited, *Henry T. Lewis and M. Kat Anderson*   339
Index   357

Illustrations

Blackfeet Indians starting a prairie fire, 1903   *frontispiece*
1. Yosemite Valley (1866 and 1961)   45
2. The full spectrum of human-nature interactions   47
3. Trajectories of ecosystem changes   52
4. Indigenous resource management at different levels of
   biological organization   53
5. Beating seeds into a collection basket   57
6. Digging bulbs and tubers with a hardwood digging stick   58
7. A basketmaker from Massett, British Columbia   59
8. Collecting long, straight branches for basketry   60

Forgotten Fires

Introduction

Henry T. Lewis and M. Kat Anderson

Native Americans were an integral part of America's forests. The forests and the people who lived there formed an inseparable whole that developed together over millennia. . . . Native Americans helped to create and sustain the ancient forests that Europeans found beautiful enough to set aside in national parks.

Thomas M. Bonnicksen,
America's Ancient Forests: From the Ice Age to the Age of Discovery

FIRES WARMED HEARTHS, heightened the palatability of meats and vegetables, aided nighttime fishing, hollowed out tree trunks for making dugout canoes, felled mighty oaks for earth lodge construction, and kept predators at bay. While the fires of hearth and home have most often been of interest to anthropologists, it is the fires of field and forest that are the major focus of this book. The use of fire as a land management tool was universal and of critical importance in how humans related to environments. Setting fires to influence vegetation patterns was one of the most portentous achievements of our species; it literally shifted our status from foragers to cultivators of nature. Its application to North American landscapes is most likely as ancient as the first human occupation over ten to twenty thousand years ago, and earlier still in other parts of the world.

Indigenous burning practices are a theoretically important dimension of human adaptation and a significant part of almost every habitat's historical ecology—a fact that makes indigenous burning a highly relevant subject to ecologists, conservation biologists, and land managers interested in restoring various areas to their pre-European settlement condition. Indigenous burning practices were so successful in altering pathways of vegetation change that most of North America does not fit the definition of a

3

pristine, uninhabited wilderness at the point of European contact. From the New Jersey pine barrens to the drier Douglas fir forests of the Pacific Northwest to the vast prairies of Canada and the United States, many vegetation types were profoundly affected by Native American burning.

The success of indigenous economies depended upon setting fires. In many areas of the West, for example, setting fires was integral to the maintenance of food, cordage, and basketry production systems, three essential cultural use categories that required enormous quantities of high-quality plant material to satisfy human needs. Furthermore, Native Americans thoroughly understood the necessity of "fighting fire with fire." Their deliberately set fires were often designed to preclude the kinds of holocaust fires that regularly devastate large areas today.

Indigenous peoples' detailed traditional knowledge about fire, although superficially referenced in various writings, has not for the most part been analyzed in detail or simulated by resource managers, wildlife biologists, and ecologists. Whether foraging peoples set fires in ways that differ significantly from natural fire regimes is a question that still requires further consideration (Lewis 1982b). Instead, scientists have developed the principles and theories of fire ecology, fire behavior and effects models, and concepts of conservation, wildlife management, and ecosystem management largely independent of native examples. Additionally, scientific understanding of indigenous land management systems has been severely hampered by the longstanding academic resistance to true interdisciplinary research that values qualitative ethnographic and ethnohistoric research as well as results from the experimental research in the "hard sciences."

At the same time, most anthropologists have by and large believed that hunter-gatherers, unlike farmers, were environmentally benign, incapable of influencing the productivity and availability of natural resources. Whether anthropologists actually observed burning practices being carried out in a few cases, were told by informants about such practices, or only learned of them from historical accounts, the idea that such people possessed a sophisticated technological knowledge about burning and realized the ecological consequences of what they did was neither understood nor contemplated. For the great majority of anthropologists, the importance of human uses of fire in vegetation management continues to be a nonissue with respect to the adaptations of so-called simpler societies.[1]

As an example of how anthropology students continue to be instructed on the importance of fire, Alice B. Kehoe, an acknowledged scholar of Native American cultures, sums up its importance to human evolution without comment on the varied and widespread practices whereby hunter-gatherers regularly set fire to a range of habitat types.

The greatest invention in the history of humankind was made in the Paleolithic: control of fire. This invention had a tremendous effect upon our development. Controlling fire enabled humans to live in cold regions, opening up huge areas of the globe to human expansion. Controlling fire gave humans an advantage over every other animal, for there *is* one behavior that distinguishes humans from all other creatures, and that is technology to control fire. Around a blazing campfire, humans were safe from hunting animals. Fire enabled people to render a great variety of foods edible, and took the stress of chewing raw foods off our teeth and jaws, allowing survival of the light, easily moved jaw needed for human speech. In time, fire made possible the smelting of metals and the combustion engine. Fire probably had a psychological effect, too: Humans knew they had tamed one of the terrifying forces of nature. As so many myths around the world tell it, for humans to control fire was a godlike act. By half a million years ago, this great leap in human capacity had spread throughout most of the human world; evidence for it has been found from China to England. (1998:89–90; emphasis in original)

Unfortunately, anthropologists in general still have not recognized the significance that culturally based habitat fires have had for human adaptations. The central importance of such fires in hunting-gathering strategies is least of all understood, other than noting that fires were sometimes set to drive or surround animals. The historian Stephen J. Pyne, however, has argued that Native Americans would have been seriously endangered had they not understood the effects of and used controlled fires:

It is often assumed that the American Indian was incapable of greatly modifying his environment and that he would not have been much interested in doing so if he did have the capabilities. In fact, he possessed both the tools and the will to use it. That tool was fire . . . without which most Indian economies would have collapsed. (Pyne 1982:71)

Over fifty years ago Omer C. Stewart recognized the long-term influences that Native Americans had on "natural" landscapes and the significance of indigenous burning for both the social and biological sciences. His stance was a radical departure from the opinions of ecologists and anthropologists of the time. Stewart adamantly criticized the dismissal of this ancient knowledge as a valuable source of ideas about ecology. He added that ecologists' observations of the natural environment and experiments spanned short periods of one to five years (Stewart 1963:118).

Indigenous knowledge, by contrast, spanned centuries or millennia and could reveal innovative ways to combat destructive insects, weeds,

and diseases; offer innovative uses of the native flora and fauna; and provide insights into advancing the fields of theoretical and applied ecology.
Periodically non-Indian people have recognized the tremendous value of
indigenous burning knowledge. For instance, several acting superintend-
ents of Yosemite National Park from 1894 to 1903 suggested to the Secretary of the Interior a return to the old Indian custom of systematically burning over portions of the forests of the park each year in the autumn.
Although the significance of fire is now widely recognized and acted upon
in national parks and other areas, the extent and importance of indigenous
fire regimes are still largely marginalized.

This book is Stewart's major work on hunter-gatherer uses of fire,
completed in 1954 and originally titled "The Effects of Burning of Grasslands and Forests by Aborigines the World Over." Although we have
changed the title (for reasons mentioned below), our goal has been to
leave the integrity of the manuscript largely intact, in part because it would
be almost impossible to update it, given what has been published about
indigenous peoples' uses of fire over the past twenty-five years. It is also
important to show how far ahead Stewart was in relation to anthropological discussions of "primitive man's" uses of fire, almost all of which ignored
the impacts that hunter-gatherers made on local and regional environmental systems. This book encompasses only Stewart's materials on North
America, primarily because his reports on other areas outside of North
America were so much more limited.[2] We have added anthropological
(Lewis) and ecological (Anderson) critiques of his work and its relevance
to contemporary studies in both fields today.

Stewart's manuscript is presented here much as it would have
appeared had it been published in the mid- to late 1950s, except for minor
editorial corrections (spelling, punctuation, grammatical errors, page numbers, dates of reference materials, etc.). We have treated it as a historic
document in itself, in terms of both what is presented and the overall
anthropological style of the mid-twentieth century. For instance, the reader
will note Stewart's references to hunter-gatherers as "primitive" and possessing "primitive technologies," along with his gender bias with respect
to "mankind" and other male terms referring to the human condition—a
kind of discrimination still found in anthropologists' descriptions of foraging societies more than ten years later with such male tropes as *Man
the Hunter* (Lee and DeVore 1966). In contrast, Stewart's subsequent
major publications such as *Peyote Religion* (1987) and *As Long as the River
Shall Run* (with Martha Knack, 1984) reflect the changes as anthropologists increasingly included women as a part of "mankind" three decades
later. We have also left his unconventional referencing system as it appears

in the original manuscript, whereas the references for the introduction and our respective critiques follow the format used in virtually all anthropological publications today. A few sources (e.g., Stewart's own field notes and those of colleagues) may be difficult to locate or access, but scholars wishing to track down resource materials can consult the original manuscript on file in the Omer C. Stewart Collection Archive, University of Colorado Libraries. Other materials relating to Stewart's work can be found in the Special Collections, Marriott Library, at the University of Utah.

When Stewart wrote the manuscript, only his own work and an important article by the Canadian anthropologist Gordon Day ("The Indian as an Ecological Factor in the Northeastern Forest," 1953) raised serious questions within anthropology about public attitudes and governmental declarations, which denigrated the burning practices of hunter-gatherers, pastoralists, and horticulturists across a range of environments throughout most of the world.

Stewart's interest in indigenous uses of fire began in the mid-1930s while he was an anthropology graduate student at the University of California at Berkeley. It emerged in the process of collecting ethnographic information on the "trait lists" of California Indians for his major advisor and mentor, Alfred Kroeber, as well as through seminars and personal contacts with the geographer Carl Sauer, who at the time was beginning to write articles about the importance of fire.[3] As Stewart says in his biography: "In 1935 my first old Pomo informant told me that Indians had intentionally set fire to all the fields and forests to keep down the brush so that they could more easily travel and could see game better and to produce more abundant vegetable food. My little monograph on the ethnogeography of the Pomo . . . started me on a research program to popularize Indian foresting methods" (Howell 1998:207–8).

Stewart's overall contributions to anthropology—which also included important studies of Peyote Religion, Indian land claims, and applied anthropology—have yet to be fully appreciated, but his twelve articles on Native American uses of fire have received the least attention. As discussed in our anthropological and ecological critiques, despite widespread evidence of Indian burning practices in the historical record, anthropologists knew far too little about ecology and presumed to know far too much about hunting-gathering strategies to accommodate what Stewart and Day were arguing. Paradoxically, it was this dimension of Stewart's scholarship that was best known and is still most frequently cited by nonanthropologists—specifically, by specialists in the fields of fire ecology, range management, and forestry.

Stewart's work is particularly provocative and seminal because he understood that Indian burning had significant ecological effects on the distribution, diversity, and relative abundance of plants and animals. He even went so far as to state that indigenous fire was the deciding factor in determining the types of vegetation covering about a fourth of the globe (Stewart 1963:124). This was a revolutionary idea: it both challenged the concept of wilderness without human effects and refuted the ecologists' static view of nature with the thought that ecosystems are ever dynamic. At that time the sciences of fire ecology and prescribed burning were in their infancy (Biswell 1989). Years later E. V. Komarek, a fire ecologist at Tall Timbers Research Station in Florida, recognized Stewart's pioneering work and dubbed him a "fire maverick" (Komarek 1963).

Stewart read widely in the biological sciences, including ecology and the fields of range management and forestry, placing his arguments regarding Indian burning within a broader context long before the academic climate changed to favor more interdisciplinary dialogues and studies. He urged anthropologists and ecologists always to consider "the human factor when calculating climate, soil, plant life and animal life which have interacted to produce any particular landscape at any given period" (Stewart 1963:125). Along with climatic, edaphic, and topographic factors, Indian influences were often decisive in determining particular plant assemblages. For example, from the very first a central hypothesis of Stewart's papers on indigenous uses of fire was his repeated claim that Indians used fires both to establish and to maintain grasslands. As discussed in the ecological critique, he directly challenged the then dominant view in ecology as presented in the works of Frederic Clements, a leading figure in North American ecology.

Essentially Stewart was pleading with anthropologists and ecologists to become meticulous historians or at least to understand that the land is partially a product of its human history (Stewart 1951:317). He warned that not to consider Indians as a legitimate and important disturbance factor was a dangerous oversight that would ultimately cloud ecologists' findings, theories, and concepts. For example, Stewart believed that without Indian burning there would be far less deciduous pine in the Southeast and more evergreen, far less Douglas fir in drier Pacific Northwest forests, far less birch and aspen in the taiga, and far less unbroken grassland in the midwestern prairies.

Proof of the accuracy of his interpretations has now been provided by the enormous amount of work done in the biological sciences since the 1950s. For example, it is well accepted that the prairies were shaped by both Indian and lightning fires (Knapp et al. 1998; R. C. Anderson 1990;

Axelrod 1985; Wells 1970a, 1970b). Another example is in the serpentine barrens of eastern North America, where controlled burning is now used experimentally to maintain the open prairies and fire-dependent pines with their diverse animal and plant life (Latham 1993). The landmark Leopold Report (Leopold et al. 1963) supported Stewart's emphasis on burning: the authors of that report recognized that many biotic communities, such as certain hardwood forests and oak savannas, are not fixed or stable entities and therefore must be actively manipulated to maintain wildlife habitat.

Pyro-dendrochronology studies around the country suggest that the high frequency of fires in sequoia–mixed conifer forests of the Sierra Nevada, the oak-hickory forests of eastern North America, and the lodgepole pine forests of the Rocky Mountains could not be explained by the contemporary ignition rate from lightning alone but only in conjunction with indigenous burning (Abrams 1992; Barrett and Arno 1982; Barrett 1981; Kilgore and Taylor 1979). Stephen Pyne, the acknowledged authority on the history of fire, and Thomas Bonnicksen, a renowned expert on fire and restoration ecology, have both presented major studies that emphasize the importance of understanding indigenous peoples' uses of fire (Bonnicksen 2000; Pyne 1982, 1991b, 1997b).

Stewart's vast list of references provides the reader with compelling evidence that the prehistoric Indians' effects, positive or negative, on the environment can no longer be ignored by anthropologists and ecologists. The document is a poignant reminder to the reader of our repeated failure to recognize the importance of ecologically based technological practices that occurred throughout the entire 10,000 years of the Holocene and even earlier and that are no less relevant today. The manuscript provides a benchmark, disclosing the far-reaching significance of Stewart's research and ideas for current resource management of wildlands.

When land managers, ecologists, and archaeologists understand the intricacies and mechanics of how and why Native Americans shaped ecosystems with fire, they will have a richer inventory of interpretations and management methods and will be in a better position to make informed, historically based decisions. If the goal of public land-managing agencies is to preserve some representation of the precontact structures and functions of certain ecosystems, then they can no longer ignore these anthropogenic effects and will have to consider the possibility of simulating some of these practices.

A wildlife biologist managing for great gray owl habitat in the Sierra Nevada could consider the reintroduction of the burning regimes of the Western Monos and Foothill Yokuts to maintain the owl's prime foraging habitat—montane meadows. Range managers conducting studies to restore degraded oak-hickory range habitat in the eastern woodlands could look at how the Illinois, Miamis, Menominis, and other tribes burned, altering the structure and function of oak habitat to meet their needs. A state or national park employee managing palm oases could investigate how the Mohaves, Pimas, Cahuillas, and other tribes of the Southwest extended the range and affected structure and function of the desert fan palm (*Washingtonia filifera*) stands with burning and planting. Similarly, parks and wildlife managers can benefit from the traditional ecological knowledge of burning practices formerly employed by Algonquian- and Athabascan-speaking tribes in Canadian boreal forest regions.

Stewart's efforts to get his manuscript published constituted a catalogue of frustrations. In late 1952, much encouraged after receiving a letter from the publisher Alfred Knopf in New York (who said that he personally wished to consider the manuscript), Stewart sent off a nearly completed but still rough first draft. Apologizing for its preliminary form, he wrote that he was anxious to get Knopf's initial reaction and appreciated any changes that the publisher might suggest for its improvement. In less than a week he was surprised to receive a scathing and paternalistic letter that rejected his manuscript out of hand, ostensibly on the basis of style and presentation.

> Your manuscript as it stands is in perfectly impossible shape and no reader could give the time that would be required to deal with it. If you were seeking a job, would you put on your oldest and dirtiest clothes, grow three days' beard, fail to wash for a couple of days, and then present yourself with the notion of telling your prospective employer that if he wanted to take you on, you'd go home, shave, put on a clean suit, bathe, wash, and become an altogether different person in appearance? After all, a book should be its author's—not its publisher's, and I think you owe it to a prospective publisher to put your work into the best possible shape you can before submitting it. To be sure, I asked you to send it on, but I surely thought you would wait to do so until you had it at least in presentable shape.

A week later, in slightly less gratuitous terms and at least commenting on the content of the manuscript, Knopf wrote: "Since it [arrived] we have gone over it rather carefully. But I am afraid that we can't see in it even the making of a book that would have sufficient appeal to justify its being included on the list of a general trade publisher. Consequently we can't even give you useful suggestions for revising and reworking the manuscript."

Six months after this summary rejection Stewart initiated an exchange of letters with the anthropologist A. Irving Hallowell at the University of

Pennsylvania, then editor of the Viking Fund Publications in Anthropology, inquiring about the consideration of his manuscript as a Wenner-Gren Viking Series monograph. It went no further than an exchange of letters, however; with the manuscript having increased to over seven hundred and fifty pages, size was probably a factor. Following further communications over the next two years and a final effort by Hallowell to gain funding from the Wenner-Gren Foundation, the Viking Fund withdrew as a potential publisher.

Stewart was increasingly caught up in a labyrinth of research, writing, and especially legal representations on behalf of Native American land claims, and several years passed before the manuscript was submitted for a third time. In the early 1960s it was sent to a specialized publishing venue, Tall Timbers Research, Inc., in Tallahassee, Florida, which published occasional monographs and annual symposia on the ecology of fire. This initially promising possibility derived from correspondence with the institute and a paper that Stewart presented there in 1962, which subsequently appeared in the 1963 *Annual Proceedings, Tall Timbers Fire Ecology Conference* under the title "Barriers to Understanding the Influence of Use of Fire by Aborigines on Vegetation." This, as it turned out, was the last substantive piece he was to write on hunter-gatherer uses of prescribed burning.

The book manuscript was well received, but it was again faced with the problem of inadequate funding; the institute deferred editorial work leading toward its publication. In what was to have been an interim period pending publication, the manuscript was filed and held as a part of the institute's collection of unpublished papers. A number of years later, after follow-up inquiries, Stewart was informed that the manuscript had been misplaced. After several more years had passed, he was notified that it had again been located and would be reconsidered. Much, much later—expressing considerable regret for the amount of time that had passed—the editor returned the manuscript to Stewart twenty-five years after it had been received by the institute, with no further mention of its being published.

Though Stewart remained interested in the ecology of fire, answered numerous inquiries, and generously provided other researchers with copies of his published articles as well as the loan of his manuscript and even basic source materials, he wrote nothing more on the topic. Regrettably, he influenced neither colleagues nor students at the University of Colorado in following up on this aspect of his work; given anthropologists' general indifference and continued lack of understanding of the technological means and ecological consequences involved, this is perhaps not surprising. Instead anthropologists and nonanthropologists elsewhere (none of whom were colleagues or former students), for disparate reasons and with varied backgrounds, became interested in indigenous uses of fire (cf. Lewis 1993).

Finally, though the manuscript had not been updated, Stewart submitted it a third and final time, on this occasion to the University of Oklahoma Press, only six months before his death on New Year's Eve in 1992. With more than thirty-five years having passed since it was originally written, the University of Oklahoma Press reviewers considered it too out of date to be published in its original form. Nonetheless, the two reviewers emphasized that despite being dated in terms of publications that began to appear in the early 1970s the manuscript contained important materials that had never been seen before and was important as a historical document in terms of ecological and anthropological theory and the questions Stewart had raised almost forty years earlier.

The importance of indigenous burning practices is nowhere more evident than in the semi-arid environments that were influenced by Native Americans, especially when contrasted with the effective neglect of such areas now and the enormously destructive fires that occur there. Pyne (1991b) has referred to semi-arid (or Mediterranean-type) regions as "pyrophytic environments," such as those found in much of the American Southwest, California, and central Oregon as well as in the Mediterranean Basin, South Africa, parts of Chile, and very large areas of southern and western Australia. All are characterized by a range of plant community types that over thousands upon thousands of years became more dependent on human rather than natural fire regimes.

Many years ago the geographer Carl Sauer wrote about the extreme dangers of government practices aimed at fully achieving fire exclusion and fire protection. Such practices, he argued, resulted in unrestricted accumulations of fuels in increasingly over-aged stands of forest and chaparral. His concern was that the "longer the accumulation, the greater . . . the fire hazard and the more severe the fire when it results"; he correspondingly urged the reintroduction of controlled burning (Sauer 1956:56). Half a century later the major conflagrations that so concerned him and others are still regularly repeated in California, and most recently in northern New Mexico, just as in other semiarid regions of the world.

Based on historic and ethnographic evidence, some of the most comprehensive interpretations of how indigenous peoples used fires are those reported for California (Anderson 1993b, 1996a, 1997b, 1999; Shipek 1989, 1993; Timbrook et al. 1982; Bean and Lawton 1973; Lewis 1973), central Oregon (Boyd 1986), and comparable semi-arid regions of Australia (Pyne 1991a; Flood 1990; Hallam 1975, 1989). In terms of how people have understood and acted upon environmental systems, the contrasts between the similar beliefs and practices of the two indigenous "primitive peoples" (Indians and Aborigines) and those of the two exogenous "modern societies" (American and Australian) are striking. Australian children today are taught about the singular danger of fire and how it must be kept out of the environment. Aboriginal children were told in the past—and in some remote areas still are—about the many advantages of fire, were regularly shown how to use it, and learned about the disadvantages and dangers that occur when environments are not periodically burned (Kimber 1993).[4]

In learning about the extreme hazards of "bush fires," Australian schoolchildren today are provided the historical examples of "Black Friday" and "Ash Wednesday." They can tell you that the former represents a number of particularly terrifying days in 1939 and the latter an equally horrific period in 1983, both of which involved the massive destruction of property and considerable losses of life when wildfires swept through parts of Victoria and South Australia (with seventy-one people killed in 1939 and seventy-five in 1983). Australian schoolchildren may also know of the numerous other "black days" in their country's recent history when wildfires engulfed large areas of scrub and forest lands and threatened the margins and suburbs of towns and cities.

What they are not taught are the ecological lessons that derive—or should derive—from holocaust fires. By contrast, a form of ecological instruction was integral to the knowledge passed down to Australia's Aboriginal children for thousands of years before the arrival of Europeans. This aspect of traditional knowledge, woven into the epic stories of the Aborigines' "Dreamtime," was and still is ecologically far more relevant than the historical parables taught to schoolchildren today. Briefly stated, Aboriginal children were taught that periodic light fires brought about and maintained a diversity of habitats at variable stages of growth; that these habitats were more manageable and safer for humans as well as other species and provided a greater variety of resources for both humans and animals; and that (along with ritual practices, hunting, harvesting, and the cultivation of plants) the deployment of habitat fires was central to people's responsibilities in both using and taking care of their environments as outlined in the Dreamtime.

The environmental conditions and social-cultural factors that led to the worst wildfires in Australia's recent history directly parallel those that contributed to the Oakland Hills fire in California in 1991 and to the repeated chaparral fires of southern California throughout the 1990s and the first years of the twenty-first century. In May 2000 the Los Alamos fire of northern New Mexico was among the worst recorded for the American Southwest but only paled by comparison with those that erupted two years later in southern Colorado and northern Arizona. As the work of Stewart and others has shown, all these fires have occurred in areas known to have been regularly and safely burned by Native Americans. Like Australia's recurrent conflagrations (the most recent of which happened in New South Wales in late 1997, 1998, early 2000, and summer of 2001–2002), they represent extreme examples of wildfires in their most horrific conformations. In what Pyne (1991a) has called the "urbanized bush" (the suburban fringes of metropolitan centers) real estate developments have pushed into over-aged stands of pyrophytic brush and trees that—in the absence of reducing fuel accumulations, as formerly done by indigenous peoples—are extremely dangerous places to live.[5]

Notwithstanding repeated warnings by concerned fire ecologists and many fire-control officials, the dominant and widely accepted view is still that fire is the essential problem, rather than the extremely dangerous accumulations of fuel. Despite the development of enormously sophisticated fire-fighting tools and techniques, over the past one hundred years forest and brush fires have become increasingly destructive and difficult to control. The apparent lesson that unchecked amounts of fuel will inevitably result in hazardous fires is neither understood by the public nor sufficiently acted upon by government agencies. Rather than periodically reducing and safely removing fuel loads through prescribed burning—and educating people accordingly—fire prevention is all too frequently limited to instructing people how to "be careful with fire," as if the irreducible problem were the careless use of matches rather than the neglect and mismanagement of over-aged forests and derelict stands of brush.

Unfortunately, efforts to reduce fuels are not undertaken due to "environmental concerns" or, where controlled fires have been strongly recommended to governments, because appropriate agencies have been prevented from significantly reducing hazardous accumulations due to political factors, threats of litigation, and public pressure. Efforts to prevent prescribed burning are often presented to the public in terms of "wilderness values" and catch phrases suggesting that by not disrupting natural processes we can "protect the ecology," "save endangered species," and not upset "the delicate balance of nature." All of these comments are made in reference to environments that are significantly different in appearance from those first described by Spaniards in California and English settlers in Australia. Indigenous knowledge, however much steeped in traditional mythological meaning, was immeasurably more enlightened than the modern myth that fire exclusion protects environments against fire, an idea that Native Americans and Australian Aborigines would have found both ludicrous and irresponsible.

Over the past twenty years an increasing number of researchers, many of them variously motivated by the published works of Omer Stewart, have demonstrated that indigenous peoples employed strategies of burning to increase and maintain biodiversity while at the same time preventing the accumulations of fuel that result in such highly disruptive and extremely dangerous fires. In the overall context of using fire as a tool to facilitate hunting-gathering strategies, fire protection was only one of many recognized consequences and advantages that derive from managing the relative productivity and local distribution of resources. In northern Australia, where indigenous burning regimes are still maintained, Aborigines describe a kind of environmental ethic: "taking care of," "cleaning," or "sweeping" one's country with fire (Jones 1980).

Life would have been extremely problematic had hunting-gathering peoples ignored the underlying conditions that otherwise feed and energize wildfires. It is impossible to conceive how Native Californians could have maintained their relatively high population densities had they been reduced to living in the relatively unproductive, high-risk habitats of today's stands of chaparral, parklands, and forests. By acts of omission modern society has made a very different cultural imprint on environments once managed by indigenous peoples; many people today mistakenly assume these environments to have been an "untouched wilderness," while arguments for the significance of fire in the adaptations of foraging societies are still unfamiliar to most anthropologists.

As in other biomes, wildfires in semiarid parts of North America and Australia were undoubtedly less frequent and certainly less disruptive when fire-managed by indigenous populations. An understanding of how the elimination of burning regimes can have adverse consequences for human adaptations was succinctly stated in 1983 by an older Aborigine in northern Australia who regularly used fire for "taking care" of his home country. The comment came in response to the question of what he thought about the fires that had occurred only a few months earlier, the "Ash Wednesday Fires" in South Australia and Victoria. His reply was that it was a "crime," a crime that habitats were so badly neglected and poorly managed that fires of such great intensity occurred: "If people don't take care of their country, if they don't burn it, keep it clean, then it grows and grows, and when it does burn it's a really hot fire. I take care of my country. We don't (have) fires like that" (Lewis 1989a:940).

Today the tragedy or "crime" is not that scientists and government technicians do not know what the essential problem is; the tragedy is that (for reasons noted above) appropriate government agencies are overly cautious or severely constrained from taking adequate preventive measure. Nonetheless, the message of fire prevention is still primarily about fire exclusion, not educating the public about the importance of preventing fire by using fire while emphasizing the fundamental dangers of allowing the unrestricted buildup of fuels. It is apparently also the case that many scientists and most government officials still find it difficult to accept the idea that "primitive people" did what "modern societies" are only now in earnest attempting to do. As the following text clearly shows, Omer Stewart understood this decades before the rest of us.

Our "References Cited" and Stewart's "Bibliography" are provided in separate sections. Stewart used a different system of citations, referring to sources by numbers (arranged alphabetically by name) rather than by name within the text itself. We have left his bibliography in its original form, which includes some citations (specifically those on areas outside of North America) that do not appear in the following text.

Notes

1. For instance, in more than twenty-five years of publication, the editors of the prestigious *Annual Review of Anthropology*—described as the "serial ethnography of anthropology"—have neither published nor apparently sought a review article on the technology and ecology of hunter-gatherer, pastoral, or agricultural uses of fire.

2. Readers interested in Stewart's limited comments on indigenous uses of fire in Australia, South America, and southern Africa can consult the original manuscript on file at the University of Colorado Libraries in Boulder.

3. Stewart's initial publication on Native American uses of fire (1951) appeared not in an anthropological journal but in *Geographic Review* (of which Carl Sauer was an editor at several stages).

4. Richard Kimber's article "Learning about Fire: Western Desert Aborigines" (1993) is the only one specifically concerned with how children learn to use fire. Since burning requires understanding of cause-effect relationships, it is safe to assume that appropriate knowledge and examples of the technology and ecology of fire were passed down from generation to generation along with other forms of knowledge.

5. Efforts by state agencies in Australia to broadly replicate Aboriginal fire regimes have been consistently frustrated by the opposition of environmental groups to any controlled burning, with the result that combustible growth continues to accumulate and intensify any fires once started.

An Anthropological Critique

Henry T. Lewis

READERS OF THIS book may be forgiven for asking why it was not published half a century earlier, at least within a decade of its having been completed in the mid-1950s. As noted in the introduction, Stewart's manuscript was first rejected by a publisher, then failed to get funded by another, and in the end was filed away by a third for over two decades. The fact that it concerned practices that were contrary to accepted beliefs about fires, forests, and the popularized myths of Smokey the Bear should not have been a problem for the anthropologists who reviewed the manuscript, even if they did not understand what hunter-gatherers were up to. It should have been enough that Stewart and Gordon Day (1953) did and that the two of them understood what Native Americans accomplished with fire, especially since they clearly explained the practices and outlined the broader environmental consequences that follow from burning particular kinds of habitats at various times of the year.

Anthropologists in the middle of the twentieth century were certainly not deterred from writing about "primitive customs" that middle- and upperclass Americans found morally or socially offensive any more than they are today. Quite the contrary: as scholars in "the science of mankind," cultural anthropologists prided themselves on interpreting the ostensibly unusual behaviors of "exotic peoples," whether it involved detailed accounts of headhunting, cannibalism, witchcraft, genital mutilation, the sacrificial offering of human flesh, or the "sex life of savages." With respect to indigenous uses of fire, however, practices that also contravened the accepted norms of Euro-American and European societies, Stewart found little willingness by fellow anthropologists to consider this a subject worthy of study, teaching, or publication.

Stewart vs. Steward

Though it was not his intention, in two important respects Stewart became a maverick in anthropology. First, as noted, his work on hunter-gatherer uses of fire was new and difficult for anthropologists to accept and understand; Stewart's and Day's publications on the subject failed to alter the view of almost all anthropologists that hunter-gatherers made little or no impact on their environments. Another topic that identified Stewart even more as a dissident, however, may have had reverberations that influenced the way his studies on indigenous uses of fire were accepted and evaluated by his peers. This concerned the activities of anthropologists on Indian land claims. Stewart played an extremely important role on behalf of Native American claimants against the U.S. government and a number of anthropologists contracted as expert witnesses by the Justice Department.

Appearing in twelve land claims cases for Native American litigants, Stewart challenged and successfully rebutted the evidence provided by some of the leading figures in American anthropology at the time. The most prominent of those he faced was his former professor from his days as an undergraduate student at the University of Utah, Julian Steward. Having already provided testimony in two cases, Stewart was asked by Kroeber in 1953 to assist with the strategy and preparation in a claim made for all California Indians. Kroeber had been one of the first anthropologists to undertake such work and was an important influence on Stewart in deciding to represent Native American land claims. Given the economic and legal implications, the California claim was an extremely important precedent for the cases that followed. In addition, Kroeber and Stewart worked with several other associates from the University of California, most notably Samuel A. Barrett, S. F. Cook, Edward F. Gifford, and Robert F. Heizer.

On the other side, Julian Steward acted as a witness for the defense, the U.S. Department of Justice; because of his earlier studies in eastern California, the government considered him to be especially important for contesting the claim made by the Northern Paiutes to the traditional ownership of Owens Valley.[1] Omer Stewart's expertise came from having worked widely with a number of indigenous groups throughout the West and having an encyclopedic knowledge of the anthropology and history of the region. At the same time, he concentrated on empirical evidence, while Steward relied heavily on his own highly contested theory of cultural evolution. The most contentious of the courtroom confrontations were those between Stewart and Steward regarding the Owens Valley Paiutes. This was all but certain to generate resentments and recriminations, particularly since

Steward was being challenged by a former student, someone he would have considered a subordinate and, by his actions, an ingrate.

In addition to Steward, the Department of Justice obtained expert advice from other leading anthropologists—notable among them Ralph Beals, Harold Driver, Walter Goldschmidt, Abraham Halpern, and William Strong. Like Stewart, they were former students of Alfred Kroeber; unlike Stewart, they provided testimony against Native American claimants. In the hearings that followed, several students of Julian Steward and of the others supporting the government position also made representations for the Department of Justice. Stewart challenged each one in turn and, in the end, won all of the twelve cases in which he participated—successes that, according to Richard Stoffle (1992), were to have negative impacts on his career. His achievements on behalf of Native American litigants did not endear him to those he bested in court.

Though scholarly debates over theory, and even facts, are the stuff of anthropological journals and intellectual discourse, Stewart's specific work on Indian land claims was neither directly attacked nor acknowledged as a part of the history of anthropology, much less an important part. In terms of getting recognition from within the discipline, it was somewhat of a pyrrhic victory for Stewart; in terms of what he considered it appropriate for anthropologists to do in practical ways, he saw it as a form of applied anthropology in the truest and best sense.

As various comments made in his biography show (Howell 1998), the animosity between Omer Stewart and Julian Steward preceded the land claims cases and increased tremendously in the context of the courtroom confrontations. Stewart was extremely critical of his former professor's attitudes toward Native Americans. As Stewart states in his biography:

> Julian liked the romance of Indian lore, but didn't care much for the Indians. He believed that it was wholly up to them to adjust to our society. When he was working for the Bureau of Indian Affairs, and at the Smithsonian, virtually all contact he had with the Indians was through his secretary. As he saw it, his duty was to funnel government policy to reservation agents. This was an odd attitude for an anthropologist and one that always bothered me.
>
> Over the years that I testified in Indian claims cases, I went head-to-head with Julian three different times: I testified for the Indians and he for the government. I was fairly accomplished at debating and all three decisions were in favor of the Indians. (Howell 1998:164)

The confrontations with his former student angered Steward, particularly regarding the Northern Paiutes' claim for Owens Valley, the area in which he had done some of his most important work and which was a mainstay of his theory of cultural evolution (Steward 1951). In that particular court case Stewart used Steward's own research data to contradict his testimony, specifically by introducing maps into the proceedings that Steward had made to define the territories separating the Shoshonis and Paiutes. Again, in Stewart's words: "In court, Julian asserted that the tribes did not define their territory, each simply made some use of the land on an irregular basis. When confronted with his own map his response was that he had changed his mind. It galled him to realize it was his evidence that won our case" (Howell 1998:165).

Richard Stoffle, a former student and friend of Stewart's, has been more direct still in his assessment of what he sees as Julian Steward's adversarial role in Stewart's career. As Stoffle wrote in his "Epitaph for Omer Call Stewart":

> Omer's data led him to conclude that there were levels of social organization in the Great Basin that were far more complex than those postulated in Julian Steward's new theoretical model. Steward concluded that Omer had broken ranks, thus committing an unforgivable heresy. Despite Omer's attempts to explain away the theoretical disagreement by reference to field data, Steward set about to destroy the young scholar. Omer had an excellent academic record and was one of the most promising anthropologists in the country, yet Steward *blackballed* Omer, making it impossible for him to be employed in any of the major anthropology departments. Omer suspected that Steward also intervened as a professional reviewer of manuscripts to suppress Omer's heretical views. Many of Steward's students continued the battle against Omer's ideas. (Stoffle 1992:xi; emphasis in original)

Further on, Stoffle adds:

> Julian Steward viewed Great Basin Indians as living fossils representing an earlier stage of human evolution. Omer viewed Great Basin Indians as humans who had been moved by his [Mormon] Church to make way for his family to farm. . . . The confrontation between theory and data came when both Julian Steward and Omer Stewart testified during the United States Indian Land Claims hearings. Steward took an anti-Indian position when he moved to stop the hearings before they started. According to Omer, Steward felt his model demonstrated that the Indian people never used the land in the highest and best way, so they deserved to relinquish the land to Euro-Americans who represented a socially more advanced stage of evolution. Their debate was formalized in the adversary proceedings of

the court. There, Omer's concern with documentable facts held sway over the generalizations provided by Steward and his students. Omer won every case for the Indian groups he represented. Steward and his students lost all the cases in which they were involved testifying against Indian interests. (Stoffle 1992:xii–xiii).

In a recent publication, *Julian Steward and the Great Basin* (Clemmer et al. 1999:174), Sheree Ronaasen et al. maintain that Stewart in fact was not adversely affected since he was offered a position at the University of Colorado. When Stewart was hired at the University of Colorado in 1945 there was no anthropology program at Boulder, however, and the major confrontations occurred a decade later (Howell 1998:138–40; Stoffle, personal communication, 1999). It is also the case that he had come highly recommended to university administrators by Kroeber and Clyde Kluckhohn, both of whom were well known and widely respected beyond the discipline and internal travails of anthropology.[2]

Scholarly reviews and academic references are protected by rules of confidentiality, so there is no precise way of knowing how or even if actions were taken against Stewart's access to publication. The matter of his inability to get this manuscript published, first by Knopf and then by Viking Fund, only suggests adverse influence. Whatever the case, Stewart received relatively little recognition for his contributions to anthropology and Native American land claims from within the discipline. Steward, in contrast, is recognized as a major figure in the history of anthropology, yet his attitudes and actions in contesting Indian land claims were until recently not publicized, let alone criticized.[3]

Given anthropologists' combined apathy and resistance to considering hunter-gatherer uses of fire important in influencing environments, the post-trial recriminations may have constituted only one more obstacle, coming at a time when feelings against Stewart would have been most acrimonious. Stewart's later works on other topics—particularly his much later publication *Peyote Religion* (1987)—were accepted and well received. The recognition he did gain was primarily from within the subfield of applied anthropology, which is itself viewed by most anthropologists as outside the mainstream of the discipline.[4]

In addition to the courtroom confrontations, the two protagonists were intellectually at odds over how Native American hunter-gatherers were seen on the one hand, by Stewart, to have directly influenced and altered natural systems and on the other, by Steward, as merely reacting to environmental imperatives. This was particularly evident in their respective views of ecology and, in turn, their perceptions of ethnographic fact and evolutionary theory. Their antithetical perspectives on how hunter-gatherers related to natural environments were inevitably linked to their differences and confrontations over Indian land claims.

JULIAN STEWARD'S CULTURAL ECOLOGY

Stewart's earlier publications on Indian uses of fire (1951, 1954, 1955a, 1955b, 1955c) and the article by Gordon M. Day (1953) were far more germane to the interdisciplinary field of ecology than any written during the middle of the century by other anthropologists concerning human-environmental relationships. As formulated by Julian Steward (1955), cultural-environmental studies in anthropology had been grouped under the rubric of "cultural ecology." While his approach had challenged the older anthropological view that cultures and environments were separate spheres of study, anthropologists made very limited use of the perspectives that had been developed in plant and animal ecology.[5]

Steward had proposed that the aim of cultural ecology was to show how environments influenced human behaviors, maintaining that population numbers and human settlement patterns "correlated with the fertility of the natural environment" (1955:48). In many ways this position differed little from environmental determinism, the inevitable consequence of Steward's view of cultural ecology as merely "a heuristic device for understanding *the effect of environment upon culture*" (1955:30; emphasis added). In advocating this he ignored one of the most basic tenets of ecology, which maintains that all organisms influence *and* are influenced by their environments.[6]

Stewart's and Day's publications about American Indian uses of fire were thus direct contradictions of Steward's assertion that foraging societies merely responded to environmental conditions. Though at least one writer in cultural ecology would subsequently acknowledge the importance of "reciprocal causality" (Hardesty 1977), in terms of hunting-gathering adaptations, ecological anthropology continued to focus almost exclusively on how foraging societies adapted to environmental factors rather than offering a more balanced view that would have included how they acted upon them as well. Even Steward's strongest critics (e.g., Harris 1968; Vayda and Rappaport 1968) ignored the means whereby hunting-gathering people both altered and maintained environments.

In *Theory of Culture Change* (1955), Julian Steward stressed that anthropologists should study the "cultural core," what he designated as "the constellation of features which are more closely related to subsistence activities and economic arrangements"—the various social and cultural means

whereby humans adapted to but seemingly did not influence environments. With his emphasis on subsistence activities and economic arrangements as the focus of ecological studies in anthropology, Steward's "cultural ecology" was more appropriately a part of the subdiscipline of
economic anthropology. Following Steward's preemption of what ecology
was supposed to mean for understanding human adaptations in the 1950s
and 1960s, anthropologists did little to contribute to or draw upon the interdisciplinary field of ecology.[7]

Given that for hundreds of thousands of years hunter-gatherers had
been among the most effective of predatory omnivores, not to have included
the use of habitat fire as an integral part of the "subsistence activities" that
made up the "cultural core" was an extraordinary oversight; not to
acknowledge that such influences even existed was more incredible still.
Even in those parts of the world in which foragers have been unable to
employ fire on a broad scale to alter the relative abundance and distribution of plants and animals—such as arctic regions and equatorial rain-
forests where little or no habitat burning is reported to have been carried
out—humans have invariably been the dominant or "keystone" species with
respect to influencing a range of environmental systems.

In contrast to Julian Steward's largely one-dimensional conception of
cultural ecology, ecologists in the biological sciences would never accept
the premise that one set of influences in an organism's relationship to its
environment was important while the other was not. As noted, Stewart repri-
manded fellow anthropologists for not considering how hunting-gathering
societies influenced ecosystems; most of them, he said, "have assumed
that though natives adjusted to their environment, they did not change the
physical world sufficiently to warrant careful investigation" (1954:248).
What must have caused him the most disappointment was that the
assumed ineffectiveness of foraging technologies continued to be unques-
tioned by anthropologists. Unfortunately, to a high degree the idea that
hunting-gathering technologies are essentially benign with respect to ecological systems still persists, and far too many anthropologists have still
not "revised their thinking on this matter."

Anthropologists have been very slow in accepting the idea that hunter-
gatherers manipulated the relative abundance and local distribution of
plant and animal resources. The fact that foraging peoples did not merely
imitate natural fire regimes, establishing cultural fire regimes that are significantly different in terms of the seasonality, distribution, and impacts,
entails questions still further removed from consideration (Lewis 1982a).
Even in the few cases where anthropologists have noted in passing the
setting of habitat fires, the idea that hunting-gathering peoples possessed

an elaborate technological knowledge about the use of fire, managed the abundance and sustainability of selected resources, and understood the ecological consequences of what they did was never seriously contemplated until the late 1960s. The Australian Rhys Jones (1969) was the first person following the works of Stewart and Day to write about hunter-gatherer uses of fire, in that instance Aborigines in Tasmania. Other works followed in the early 1970s, and today a number of anthropologists (and others) publish studies on Native American uses of fire that are still peripheral to mainstream anthropology.[8]

For the most part, indigenous uses of fire are neither mentioned in ethnographic description nor considered to be of practical much less theoretical importance. For example, a researcher on southern Africa, who asked that we not use his name, stated that he had frequently observed Bushmen setting fires but did not think that informants actually thought much about what they were doing—"they just set fires as they went along"; he then admitted, however, that he had never asked about such practices. In the mid-1980s an eminent Australian anthropologist who had spent a number of years working in the Northern Territory, where burning is still regularly carried out by Aborigines, simply denied to me that it was done, except "occasionally by people who didn't know any better." For the majority of anthropologists, the use of fire continues to be a nonissue with respect to the adaptations of foraging societies.

For instance, A. B. Kehoe (1992), in providing a comprehensive overview of Native Americans, makes not a single reference to Stewart's or Day's works or any other mention of hunting-gathering or farming uses of fire—this at a time well after numerous studies had been published on the topic, particularly on hunter-gatherer uses of fire in the New World. And, in what is coopted and staked out as "The New Ecological Anthropology," none of the work done by Stewart and subsequent researchers on indigenous uses of fire is noted (Kottak 1999). Whereas their work might have been included in what the author says about the "old ecological anthropology" as having "pointed out that natives did a reasonable job of managing their resources and preserving their ecosystems" (Kottak 1999:25), it is simply ignored as a topic that has contributed to studies on how humans have interacted and in some parts of the world continue to interact with environments.

Reflecting the lack of perspective on hunter-gatherer uses of fire, introductory texts usually mention fire only in terms of its domestic importance, very seldom in terms of how fires were and in some places still are used to affect natural environments. For instance, one textbook author, while describing Neanderthals as "efficient hunters," sums up their uses of fire as being "not only for warmth but also for cooking and perhaps for protection against dangerous animals," later adding that further along in human evolution "Cro-Magnons used fire for cooking as well as for heat" (Scupin 1998:26, 30). Two other textbook writers acknowledge that some foragers make "modest efforts" to affect resources "by burning forests and grasslands" (Peoples and Bailey 1997:119). The resistance to accepting prescribed burning as more than "modest efforts" to manipulate resources derives directly from some of anthropology's most deeply entrenched and untested assumptions applying to the "Agricultural Revolution."

FIRE AND THE ORIGINS OF AGRICULTURE

In terms of some of the most basic ideas about cultural evolution, hunter-gatherer uses of fire almost have to be ignored, since to acknowledge their importance in influencing the distribution and increasing the abundance of natural resources amounts to a kind of theoretical heresy. The assumption that hunter-gatherers are ecologically inept, or at least environmentally benign, has been central to the perception that the origins of agriculture constituted a "revolutionary change" in how humans related to the environment. Leslie White (1949:371), most prominent among others in this respect, emphasized that it was only with the onset of farming that humans established "control over the forces of nature," assuming that prior to the beginnings of agriculture people could not have influenced the local availability, distribution, and abundance of either plants or animals. As maintained by the renowned archaeologist Robert Braidwood, "[Agriculture] amounted to a revolution just as important as the Industrial Revolution. In it people first learned to domesticate plants and animals. They began producing their food instead of simply gathering or collecting it" (1975:92).

Despite the fact that anthropologists had overwhelmingly rejected simplistic nineteenth-century evolutionary schemes about stages of "savagery" and "barbarism," all of which were seen to lead to "Western civilization," the broad characterization of hunting-gathering technologies as being "simple," and therefore ecologically ineffective, persisted. For example, whereas the cultural anthropologists Felix Keesing and Roger Keesing were not committed to particular theories of evolution, they grouped and presented existing cultures in terms of a linear, evolutionary framework. In the process they portrayed foraging societies as environmentally passive, living in some kind of idyllic relationship with nature, a view fully in keeping with Julian Steward's perceptions of hunter-gatherers as merely responding to natural forces. "At this technological level, man adjusts to an environment, changing his patterns of living to follow the cycles of an ecosystem. He has a oneness with the world of nature that modern men, and even Neolithic people, have lost" (Keesing and Keesing 1971:136).

Whereas research and understandings in the biological sciences concerning the importance of fire have changed enormously since the middle of this century, within the field of study that Stewart hoped most to change there still remains an amazing nescience regarding the significance of fire in the adaptations of foragers, farmers, and pastoralists. Even some of the most comprehensive studies of hunting-gathering societies have, for whatever reasons, ignored the use of fire as a part of the technological and ecological strategies underlying such adaptations. Unfortunately, the majority of studies concerned with the relationships between foragers and their respective environments continue to ignore practices of prescribed burning or only note that habitat fires are (or were) used, without considering the practical consequences and theoretical implications involved.[9]

Although many prehistorians now acknowledge the importance of hunter-gatherer uses of fire, best represented by a number of articles in an important book on the origins of farming by David R. Harris and Gordon C. Hillman (1989),[10] for anthropologists in general the most significant difference between foraging and farming systems concerns how these two forms of adaptation affect (or do not affect) the availability, distribution, and abundance of plants and animals. In a statement that represents precisely what Leslie White wrote more than fifty years ago, one writer notes: "Collecting food—as compared to producing food—involves the exploitation of wild plants and animals that already exist in the natural environment. . . . [With the origins of agriculture] humans gained a measure of control over their food supply [and] humans were now able to produce food *rather than having to rely solely on what nature produced for the environment*" (Ferraro 1992:131, 136; emphasis added).

In an introduction to the uses of animals in ancient Israel, Odad Borowski (1998:23) characterizes the essential difference between the adaptations of pastoralists and those of foragers: "Domestication is a totally different approach to animal management than hunting-gathering, since *it requires a decisive action for people to manipulate nature rather than merely to take advantage of it*" (emphasis added).

Although archaeologists are keenly aware of the variations in and uses of other types of tools, they have either ignored or been unaware that fire constitutes a multipurpose tool that can result in a range of reasonably predictable consequences. At the same time, no studies have considered in what respects the fire regimes of foragers and farmers both differ from and are similar to each other—nor how both are significantly different from natural or lightning fires (Lewis 1982a). Maintaining that fire is a "natural disturbance" or merely a "simple technique" is imperceptive in the extreme.

For the most part, prehistorians continue to refer to fire in the singular, as if it were but one of several "primitive tools" used by hunter-gatherers. This ingenuous view overlooks the most ecologically effective and technologically powerful tool available to foragers, farmers, and pastoralists. As noted by one writer in giving a highly qualified recognition of the use of fire: "One can think of plant cultivation as a single point along a continuum of human/plant interactions. At the least intrusive end is the simple harvesting of crops, which can have an effect on a wild plant population; *the use of fire and other simple techniques* also encourage particular wild plants" (Miller 1992:39, emphasis added).

SIGNIFICANCE AND CHANGE

In the almost fifty years since Omer Stewart's first publication on Indian burning practices, government views and related practices concerning fire, both natural and human-made, have undergone dramatic changes. Nonetheless, the importance and meaning of the burning practices once employed by Native Americans are still not well understood by government agencies or widely known by the general public—little more, in fact, than when Stewart's first article appeared half a century ago.

Had Stewart's manuscript been published in the mid-1950s, it is unlikely that it would have done much to change professional, much less public, thinking about the importance of Indian practices in influencing North American environments. With prescribed burning prohibited and viewed as dangerous, the notion that "primitive societies" might have been able to reduce or even preclude the worst effects of wildfires was inconceivable. In what was undoubtedly a reference to Stewart's earlier papers— and fairly typical of the disdain and ethnocentrism toward Indian uses of fire, collectively denigrated as "Paiute Forestry"—a writer for the California Division of Forestry noted scathingly: "It would be difficult to find a reason why the Indians . . . should care one way or another if the forest burned. It is quite something else again to contend that the Indians used fire systematically to 'improve' the forest. Improve it for what purpose? . . . Yet this fantastic idea has been and still is put forth time and again . . ." (Clar 1959:7).

Stewart's publications had already provided an abundance of reasons why Native Americans did "care one way or another if the forest burned," just as they did for most nonforested areas. We know that they "used fire systematically to 'improve' the forest" in order to increase the abundance, density, and distribution of resources upon which they depended as well as to reduce fire hazards. Since the late 1950s this "fantastic idea" has been demonstrated "time and again" in historical records and in ethnographic studies. Yet, though a considerable number of publications now exist— and original research on traditional ecological knowledge of fire can still be carried out in a few areas of North America—there has been an absence of studies in the biological sciences that have used historic and anthropological examples (ethnographic analogues) in any substantive way as a significant component of environmental restoration efforts. At the most, indigenous practices are noted but not considered as part of restoration programs.

From several hundred references, many involving more than one example of indigenous burning practices, Stewart compiled a comprehensive list of reasons why Native Americans set fires. These in turn were cross-referenced to show their geographical and cultural distributions. In addition to Stewart's own interests in why hunting-gathering peoples set fires, similar questions appear frequently in the citations themselves— from the earliest reports of Spanish explorers, angered because grasses had been fired near campsites with an absence of forage for their horses, to short notations by ethnographers in the 1930s, many of whom seemed puzzled by what burning meant and either asked or simply inferred why fires were set.

For explorers and settlers, these questions were undoubtedly related to the historical fact that habitat fires were also widely used by Euro-Americans. Such practices included clearing land to initiate agriculture; the burning of wheat and barley stubbles following harvests; the firing of pastures and rangelands by cattle and sheep ranchers at the onset or end of the growing season; the setting of grass fires along traplines by fur trappers; the burning of slash and stumps by loggers to clear detritus and regenerate tree growth; the setting of fires alongside rail lines by railroad companies to reduce fire hazards; the burning of understory growth in long-leaf pine forests in the southeastern United States to enhance tree growth, reduce fire hazards, and contain pests; the annual firing of cemetery grasses in prairie towns; the setting of fires by "gentlemen hunters" to improve habitats for grouse and other game birds; and fires set by prospectors who did not want to be inconvenienced by brush and trees. The difference was that fires set by hunters and gatherers were frequently antithetical in terms of Euro-American goals and values and sometimes caused problems for explorers, endangered settlements, threatened crops, or could be used as a weapon of war.

Thus, for Euro-Americans it was not that burning per se was bad—far from it. Rather, it was that the burning was done differently and considered to be inappropriate or misguided in contrast to the ways in which fires were used by explorers and settlers before and during the nineteenth century. It was not until the early part of the twentieth century that habitat burning became the primary concern of governments and was simply seen as wrong—whether it was the burning of accumulated undergrowth within a forest, the firing of dead and overage brushfields, the reduction of fire hazards, the maintenance of prairie grasslands through fall or spring burning, the improvement of habitats for game, or the overall maintenance of biodiversity by Indians or others. A highly simplified, legally proscriptive view of burning came to dominate government policy during the last century. By the late 1940s the U.S. Forest Service had thoroughly "educated" an urban-dominated population with a modern fable of fire in the popular myths and totemic imagery of "Smokey the Bear."

As Stewart's work here and elsewhere shows, he was well aware of the major ecological consequences of indigenous uses of fire and knew that hunting-gathering strategies were far more sophisticated and complex than was assumed by most anthropologists. As demonstrated in this book, Stewart commented upon the knowledge that Native Americans had about the consequences of what they did as well as the natural processes involved. Nonetheless, he touched only indirectly on what they understood about causes and consequences. There were several reasons for following this approach, which derived from his background of study and research in anthropology.

Stewart's presentations of his evidence on North American Indian uses of fire were fully in keeping with his approach to anthropology as a whole. For reasons partly related to his rejection of Mormonism, and what he considered to be its "vague interpretations," Stewart considered theory just another form of dogma that threatened "his belief in the science of anthropology" (Howell 1998:89). He was concerned, rather, with presenting empirical examples, "facts," which, in the case of hunter-gatherer uses of fire, were found repeated again and again within and between geographic and cultural areas. The same antitheoretical approach had characterized his work on Native American land claims, particularly his criticisms of Julian Steward's use of theory. His antipathy to theory fitted comfortably with the work that he had done as a graduate student for Alfred Kroeber in carrying out culture area surveys, first in California, then in Nevada, and for several months in Utah, Arizona, and Colorado between 1935 and 1938.

"Culture element surveys" were designed by Kroeber to "revolutionize comparative ethnology in western North America" (Driver 1962:17). In brief, they involved the statistical study of "trait distributions" covering every cultural-linguistic group from the Rocky Mountains to the Pacific Coast and from Mexico to Alaska. These studies received little attention, however, and were generally rejected by other anthropologists. Kroeber's explanation for the failure of the program, attributing it to the "current folkways" of other anthropologists, illustrates some of the major problems involved.

> The twenty-five monographs published in the Culture Element Distribution Series of the University of California have had rather little note taken of them by the anthropological profession. . . . [Archaeologists] showed least reluctance toward enumerative and quantitative treatment. Ethnologists and social anthropologists proved, on the whole, averse to quantitative expression, averse to questionnaires, in principle, averse to presence and absence of data, averse to single informants per tribe or band even when the number of bands runs into the hundreds. The whole procedure was not according to their current folkways; mostly they would have none of it for themselves; and in general they criticized the approach less than they ignored it. (Kroeber 1952:263).

Thirteen fieldworkers, surveying over 250 groups, were involved in the project over a period of four years. According to Harold Driver, most "did not approve of quantification in ethnology and knew little about it" but undertook the work because it provided funding, though none "dared to express such an opinion to Kroeber" (1962:17). Stewart, unlike Driver and most other students, was not a critic of Kroeber's aims and methods and, according to his wife, Lenore, was fully and enthusiastically committed to the program. Speaking about this to his biographer, he stated: "We gained a terrific amount of knowledge" (Howell 1998:37).

Out of interviews that involved asking questions of informants on an enormously large number of topics—with lists that could amount to over 4,000 questions for a given culture area—Stewart developed interests that subsequently led to his work on Indian land claims, on the Peyote Religion, and in applied anthropology. From the first of his interviews he progressively accumulated information on Native American burning practices. Neither detailed ethnographic descriptions nor extensive studies involving the ecology of fire were available in the 1940s and 1950s. Stewart's original field data derived from his work on culture area surveys, and the bulk of his examples came from secondary, mostly historical or archival sources. Though Kroeber ceased work on culture surveys after the 1930s, in Stewart's case they provided the basis and stimulus for his studies on Indian uses of fire, fully establishing the fact that habitat burning was a universal feature in almost all hunting-gathering societies.

Commenting on his 1954 publication "The Forgotten Side of Ethnogeography," Stewart emphasized to his biographer the importance of making people aware of how much Native Americans had influenced natural systems:

> Although ethnogeography purports to explore the mutual relation of people and the environment, most studies remained limited in scope by recognizing only the manifestations of a people's adaptation to a given geography. An abundance of evidence of the degree to which the aboriginal population had influenced and altered the environment was being systematically overlooked to the detriment of all science. I was typically blunt in my assessment of what I believed to be the shortsightedness of other anthropologists, including Kroeber, and hoped to suggest some of the resources available, as well as stressing the importance of making our knowledge available to others. (Howell 1998:149)

For anthropologists, this book comes at a time when the focus of studies on indigenous burning practices is changing from the approach followed by Stewart to those undertaken in the 1970s, 1980s, and 1990s and still newer directions being followed today. The first phase is represented by the publications of Stewart and of Gordon Day (1953). The second phase of studies has involved publications that began to appear in the late 1960s: ethno-historical reconstructions and overviews of what Native North Americans (as well as Australian Aborigines) did within particular regions or original ethnographic research much more focused on local practices.

Studies dealing with regions and specific groups differed from Stewart's writings (including the following chapters) largely in terms of attempting to deal with the connections among traditional ecological knowledge, technological practices, and environmental consequences. These studies were able to benefit from a much expanded body of studies on the ecology of fire, providing researchers with new contexts for understanding that were not available to Omer Stewart and Gordon Day in the 1940s and 1950s. The subsequent more focused ethnographic studies from the 1970s to the 1990s were increasingly based on interviews with older informants ("oral traditions") about practices that for the most part were no longer employed or were very much attenuated. These studies are most characteristic of research in North America.[11]

In contrast, in the same period a large proportion of studies in Australia were and continue to be carried out on the ongoing practices of indigenous burning in more remote parts of the country where fires are still employed by Aborigines on a fairly regular basis.[12] Though the plants and animals of Australia and those of North America are significantly different, there are important technological and ecological parallels in the ways that indigenous people on both continents have understood and affected local resources.[13] Studies based both on oral traditions and on direct observation have focused on fire technology—how, when, where, and where not to use fire—along with a people's knowledge about the perceived consequences of initiating, maintaining, and changing fire regimes in particular kinds of habitats.

More recent studies represent a third and most significant phase. These are best described as "ethnoecological" in that they take a more holistic, more comprehensive view than concentrating research on the technology of burning and the specific consequences involved. Indigenous burning is not studied as a discrete technological feature analytically separate from other aspects of how hunter-gatherers relate to and influence plant and animal communities but, rather, as an integral part of the overall system of technological causes and ecological effects. The broader focus in these studies is on technology, not merely fire technology, and on overall ecological consequences, not merely the ecological consequences of fire.[14]

Stewart's works and those published in the past two to three decades were necessary precursors in drawing attention to the ecological importance of indigenous burning practices; both provide important background materials for researchers undertaking ethnoecological studies and for ecologists who wish to add a historical dimension to studies of prescribed burning. Together, all three phases of the work on indigenous uses of fire can lead to a general consensus within and between the social and biological sciences as to the theoretical importance and varied applications of indigenous ecological knowledge.

With a minimum population estimated at 10 million within the boundaries of what is now the United States (with more extreme estimates as high as 60 to 90 million), making up the 800 to 900 tribes recognized and unrecognized by the U.S. and Canadian governments as having lived there for at least 10,000–15,000 years, there is no question that there were sufficient numbers of people living throughout a range of environmental zones to have made significant impacts on the "American wilderness" found by Europeans. Humans primarily set burns at times that differ from the seasons in which lightning fires occur, which means that Native Americans did much more than simply adapt themselves to nature, as Julian Steward maintained. Whether they only burned forest clearings, stream sides, and ridge lines (as the evidence shows for temperate rainforest regions) or set large-scale fires across most prairies (as evidenced on the Great Plains), Native Americans played decisive roles in assuring that cultural rather than natural fire regimes dominated many pre-Columbian environments and variously influenced others.

Research over the past thirty years has clearly demonstrated the significance of indigenous burning practices and the important ways that hunting-gathering technologies have differed from natural fire regimes. To quote Pyne (1991b:505):

> The patterns of Indian burning did not . . . merely recapitulate natural fire. . . . At first blush it seems impossible that relatively small numbers of semi-nomadic hunters, foragers, and swidden cultivators could have exerted much influence over their environment. But fire, properly used, has a multiplicative effect. It propagates. It compounds and magnifies the effects of other processes with which it is associated. It can create, but even more powerfully, it can sustain. Intelligent beings armed with fire can apply it at critical times for maximum spread and effect. The consequences, of course, varied with environments and tribal histories, but by and large the effects were to replace woody vegetation with grassy vegetation, to keep forests (especially pine and oak) in a seral stage, and to reduce understories.

To emphasize the point still further, neither a dependence on the random and unpredictable occurrence of lightning fires nor mere imitations of such regimes could have sustained hunting-gathering adaptations for long. Whereas hunter-gatherers normally set fires at safer, more favorable times of the year, lightning fires typically occur in environmentally disruptive periods. The intentional setting of fires at preferred times, in selected places, and under optimal conditions added considerable degrees of predictability to adaptations that depended upon a range of habitats at various stages of ecological succession. In the absence of prescribed fires, survival would have been extremely tenuous, and the land could not have supported the relatively large populations found throughout much of North America.

Even where lightning fires occur with very high frequency—such as California, the American Southwest, and semiarid parts of Australia—indigenous people neither could nor would have depended upon the distribution of natural fires. To assume that lightning ignitions, even in these most fire-adapted environments, are sufficient for human purposes is most naive, furthering the misguided idea that hunter-gatherers could only exploit what nature provided. Setting fires in specific places, at designated times of the year, and under conditions that best sustain resource habitats and serve human goals is far more important than whether there is an abundance (or poverty!) of lightning fires that might somehow inadvertently serve human goals. In terms of what we now know about the ecologies of natural and prescribed fires, the important question is no longer why hunter-gatherers would have set the fires but, rather, why on earth they would not have done so.

It is far more reasonable to assume that in fact the most intense and elaborate uses of prescribed burning by indigenous peoples occurred in those environments most heavily affected by lighting fires, in order to ameliorate the undesirable impacts of natural fires. Since mainstream anthropology ignored such questions, until recently scientists in other ecological disciplines were not sufficiently challenged to contemplate, much less debate, the importance of indigenous fires for maintaining and changing "wilderness areas." Today, however, consideration of the significance of aboriginal burning practices is increasingly prominent in biological ecology.[15] Thomas M. Bonnicksen, a widely respected forest scientist, provides the kind of interpretation that Stewart hoped anthropologists would make following his studies forty to fifty years ago: ". . . Paleoindians and modern Indians not only increased the frequency of fires, but they also changed the size and behavior of fires, the time of the year when they burned, and even the places they burned" (Bonnicksen 2000:147).

Stewart's book is now being published during a much more favorable period when prescribed uses of fire are widely advocated and applied by national, state, and private agencies, even though controversy and litigation abound. The broader understanding and appreciation of the pyrotechnical practices once employed by America's indigenous peoples must inevitably aid the proponents of controlled burning. Stewart's manuscript is important to those who advocate prescribed burning for three reasons: (1) the sheer number of historic and ethnographic examples that he provides for over 200 cultural ("tribal") traditions; (2) the examples from a number of bio-regions, encompassing a range of habitat types, involving people of many different linguistic and cultural traditions; and (3) the comparability between the technological practices and environmental impacts discussed here and the techniques used and conclusions derived by ecologists. The cumulative record on Native American uses of fire—as well as that for Australia and other regions—clearly refutes assumptions that the burning practices of hunting-gathering societies were anecdotal, unsystematic, or, at best, little more than imitations of natural fire regimes.

This book thus comes at an important time in terms of work to be carried out in both anthropology and the biological sciences: first, for what it has to say to anthropologists about the technological and ecological sophistication of indigenous knowledge and practice; second, for its direct relation to the practical concerns and public pressures that face fire ecologists and resource managers today; and, third, in showing what such practices can mean to contemporary Native American cultures in terms of what is ecologically most traditional and most modern. All these factors are important for ecological restorationists, who must convince government agencies, and in turn the public, of the necessity of using controlled and prescribed fires to reduce fuel loads, restore rare and endangered species, and reestablish and maintain biodiversity while simultaneously lessening the horrendous costs and extreme hazards that all too frequently derive from wildfires.

When the setting of small-scale fires by environmental users—foresters, ranchers, farmers, and restorationists—becomes almost as common as it was a century and a half ago, anthropological textbooks may inform students about the full importance of fire in human evolution, especially how it simultaneously separated humans from and engaged them in the environment. At the same time, we hope, anthropologists will have revised the history of their discipline to acknowledge the importance of Omer Stewart as an original and prescient thinker.

NOTES

1. Until recently, Julian Steward's role on Indian land claims had received relatively little attention. The most detailed critique of the respective positions of Steward and Stewart on Indian land claims is that by Ronaasen et al. (1999).

2. Stewart originally taught as one of two anthropologists in the Department of Social Sciences at the University of Colorado and served once as head of that department (1952–54). Anthropology did not become a separate unit until 1957, at which time he became the first chair.

3. In *Julian Steward and the Great Basin* (Clemmer et al. 1999) several authors offer critiques of Steward's work in terms of his place in American anthropology. Particularly critical of Steward's contributions are the chapters by Ned Blackhawk, Richard Clemmer, Sheree Ronaasen et al., Elmer Rusco, and Deward Walker.

4. Omer Stewart's major recognition, which included an important acknowledgment of his work on Native American land claims, came in 1983, when he was accorded the prestigious Malinowski Award by the Society of Applied Anthropology.

5. The only other exception was Barth's (1956) use of the idea of ecological niche, an innovative application of a concept from the biological sciences that he used for understanding human-environmental and human-human interrelationships in northeast Pakistan.

6. Paradoxically, Julian Steward described Indian uses of habitat fires in the Basin-Plateau and acknowledged their importance for influencing environments. Stewart includes a quotation of Steward's on Indian burning practices and says that the two of them "apparently came to the same conclusion" (see the section on the Great Basin and Plateau): that Native Americans changed the natural landscape by repeated firings, probably intentional as well as accidental, which burned off seedlings and created grasslands where climax vegetation would have been brush or forest (Steward 1940:478).

7. Geertz (1963) was highly critical of the limitations represented by the concept of cultural core and argued that there must at least be the equivalent of an "environmental core."

8. For important publications that include a significant number of articles on Native American uses of fire, as well as lengthy lists of references, see Blackburn and Anderson (1993) and Boyd (1999). References and reviews of the literature can also be found in Bonnicksen (2000) and Bonnicksen et al. (2000). Further references can be found in Williams (1994).

9. Some of the more striking examples of this omission can be seen with the collection of papers from the several "International Conferences on Hunting and Gathering Societies" (cf. Burch and Ellanna 1994; Ingold et al. 1988), in which prescribed uses of fire have never been included as a specific topic or even as an important part of individual symposia papers.

10. See the respective papers therein by Cane (1989), Hallam (1989), Harris (1989), Shipek (1989), and Yen (1989).

11. For important publications that include a significant number of articles on Native American uses of fire, as well as lengthy lists of references, see Blackburn and Anderson (1993) and Boyd (1999). References and reviews of the literature can also be found in Bonnicksen (2000) and Bonnicksen et al. (2000). Further references can be found in Williams (1994).

12. For a comprehensive overview, see Pyne (1991a); for a recent analysis and survey of the literature on Aboriginal burning, see Bowman (1998).

13. Comparative studies of hunter-gatherer uses of burning in different parts of the world are still somewhat limited. For a few that exist, see Lewis (1982a, 1991a) and Lewis and Ferguson (1988).

14. See Anderson's "An Ecological Critique" in this volume for an extensive list of publications in this area.

15. Bonnicksen (2000) and MacCleery (1994), both of whom are forest ecologists, provide overviews and discussions of the importance of Native American uses of fire, while Bowman (1998), also a forest ecologist, has critiqued studies carried out in Australia.

An Ecological Critique

M. Kat Anderson

Historical Ecological Contexts

THE STEREOTYPE OF the environmentally benign North American Indian espoused by anthropologists (discussed in the anthropological critique) was readily adopted by foresters, wildlife managers, range managers, environmentalists, and plant ecologists during the first half of this century (Worster 1977:217; Muir 1944:54). Until very recently Western scientists, through deductive reasoning, not with scientific proof, concluded that Indian burning had little or no ecological or evolutionary effects on wildland environments (Parsons et al. 1986; Houston 1982). Omer Stewart was one of the first anthropologists to note that few ecologists directly inquired into aboriginal activities and their possible influence upon landscapes (Stewart 1963:119).

To many ecologists during Stewart's career, the pre-Columbian landscapes appeared untouched. Except for the earthen mounds made by the Mississippian culture in the Midwest, Southeast, and Northeast, the terraced settlements of the Anasazis in the Four Corners region, the network of irrigation canals of the Hohokam people of the Southwest, and the cleared agricultural fields of the Iroquois and other agriculturally based tribes, nowhere did the human alteration of the land overpower the "naturalness" of the place.

The prima facie idea that indigenous subsistence patterns and impacts were fairly analogous to those of other animal species that left no indelible marks on the vegetation prevailed in the fields of ecology, resource management, and environmental studies until fairly recently (Winterhalder and Smith 1981; Harlan and de Wet 1973). Thus, during the time when Stewart was writing this manuscript, most ecologists, range managers, and foresters were routinely *underestimating* the extent to which native peoples managed and influenced wildlands (N. C. Johnson 1999; Blackburn and Anderson 1993; Pyne 1982).

With little or no indigenous influence, all wildlands could truly be called "pristine" by the earliest ecologists and environmentalists. The field of plant ecology evolved a body of thought, concepts, and principles, largely derived from the study of these so-called *natural* systems. The "virgin" midwestern landscapes were to become the outdoor laboratories of such early ecologists as H. C. Cowles, W. S. Cooper, and F. E. Clements (Cowles 1899; Cooper 1913; Clements 1904).

For decades most plant ecologists preferred to work in pristine ecosystems to unravel the inner workings of nature and thus followed a binary premise: lands that were altered by agriculture, transmission lines, grazing, or mining were left unresearched, whereas pristine grasslands and untouched old-growth forests were vigorously studied. They used the wilderness—forest, bog, or prairie—as a study area to develop and test new ecological theories. The irony is that some of these "virgin" ecosystems evolved with the presence and influence of Indians over thousands of years. The mesophytic oak forest margins in the Great Lakes region that Cowles included in his designation of "mature, climax" forest were in fact an expanded artifact of former Ojibwa burning practices. Many of the plains prairie borders that Clements included in his "climatic climaxes" were due to the firing techniques of the Sioux.

A corollary that supported the idea that Indians were environmentally benign was the view that nature was "naturally abundant and diverse." The apparent ease with which the Navajos shot deer with bows and arrows, the Western Monos dug vast seed grounds in open, parklike forests, or the Cheyennes dug tubers with digging sticks in rich, diverse meadows made a deceivingly simplistic impression on the minds of most non-Indians. American Indians were frequently depicted as indolent, in a paradisiacal world where toil is unnecessary due to nature's vast biological wealth (Perry 1999). Furthermore, ecologists and land managers believed that humans' agricultural crops were inherently more unstable, more susceptible to insects and diseases and extremes of weather, than nature's (Worster 1977:234).

Early theories in ecology supported this "Garden of Eden" image. Nature was perceived as ordered and, through the process of succession, constantly increasing in fertility and steadily improving toward a climax state. Climax vegetation in the 1950s was defined as a "steady state system" with maximum species diversity and biomass production (Whittaker 1973). According to Daniel Botkin, the climax forest epitomized the concept of the "balance of nature" (Botkin 1994:71). Indigenous hunter-gatherers did nothing to disrupt this progression, as their activities were part of the ecosystem and of a scale and intensity unable to affect ecosystem change—

like those of the other animals. Sometimes they were viewed as the first conservationists, yet their actions did not upset the balance of nature and did not leave permanent marks (Johnson 1952).

The forces that degrade and rejuvenate ecosystems, such as insects, floods, fires, diseases, tree windfalls, and detritus accumulation, were frequently not factored into this idyllic image. Early ecologists in fact viewed plant communities as climatically and edaphically determined, and perturbations had little influence on shaping the pattern of vegetation in different areas. For example, esteemed ecologist Frederic E. Clements said in reference to the midwestern prairies and northwestern and eastern forests: "The general habit of migration among the animals [bison] further insured that serious effects from overgrazing and trampling were but local or transitory, while the influence of fires set by the Indians was even less significant in modifying the plant cover. As to the forests, those of the northwest were still primeval and in the east they were yet to be changed over wide areas by lumbering and burning on a large scale" (Clements 1936:253).

Stewart consistently challenged Clements, arguing that the midwestern prairies were anthropogenic in origin and that Clements had underestimated indigenous influences in all parts of the country, wrongly regarding biotic associations to be wholly determined by climate.

Throughout the manuscript, Stewart did not present his views and findings in an interdisciplinary vacuum. He explored the value of indigenous burning as a context for integrating disciplines (the natural and social sciences and the humanities) and gave indigenous, place-based forms of knowledge and knowledge derived from Western scientific sources equal weight. He conducted voluminous reading in the fields of ecology and resource management, enabling him to converse with ecologists and place his arguments about human impacts in the context of mainstream ecological thought.

While some early ecologists viewed fire as beneficial in specific plant communities, Indian-set fires were often not distinguished from lightning fires (Daubenmire 1959; McDougall 1949:111). Prescribed burning was just beginning to be used by some land managers in the 1940s, solely as a silvicultural tool. Fire was not perceived as a natural part of the ecosystem to be reinstated but rather was used only to produce desired results such as clear slash or to thin overcrowded stands of conifers (Robbins and Myers 1992:5).

Most kinds of disturbances were viewed by ecologists and land managers as inherently destructive forces threatening valuable tree resources, protective watershed cover, and wildlife that must be suppressed (Weaver and Clements 1938:244–45; Sterling 1905; California State Board of Forestry

1892). F. E. Olmsted (1911:43, 46), district forester for California, said: "We are told that the present virgin stands of timber have lived on and flourished in spite of these Indian fires. Hence, it is said, we should follow the savage's example of 'burning up the woods' to a small extent in order that they may not be burnt up to a greater extent bye and bye." He goes on to conclude: "As for the 'old Indian fires,' in California alone they have reduced over 2,000,000 acres of valuable timber lands to non-productive wastes of brush; they have damaged the mature stands of virgin timber which we now have to the extent of reducing their original volume by at least thirty-five per cent; and they have practically eliminated most of the young growth in their paths up to thirty years of age."

The field of plant ecology followed a paradigm that stated that "systems conserved and isolated from direct disturbance will maintain themselves in the desirable state for which they were originally conserved" (Pickett et al. 1992:68). Under this guiding conceptual framework, resource managers promoted a static approach to land management for decades, supporting the view that land acquisition and protection were enough to maintain unique and valuable habitat types. Thus, the earliest land managers viewed national and state parks and wilderness reserves as refuges to harbor and protect plant and animal species and were bent on excluding all fires from parks and wilderness areas (Marshall 1998:92–93).

The idea that the ecological integrity of ecosystems is always self-sustaining justified wilderness protection as a sufficient strategy to preserve nature. Stewart's manuscript is prescient because it implicitly challenged the idea of virgin, uninhabited wilderness. Only in the last decade have historians, geographers, ecologists, and social scientists come to these same conclusions that the wilderness idea may be a false Western construct and that indigenous influences have helped shape the forest, shrubland, and prairie in many areas (Cronon 1995; Denevan 1992; Gómez-Pompa and Kaus 1992). A special feature of *Ecological Applications* has recently been devoted to the topic of traditional ecological knowledge and land management practices of indigenous peoples (Ford and Martinez 2000).

During Stewart's lifetime, many historians such as Wallace Stegner and Frederick Jackson Turner continually used the terms "frontier," "New World," and "pioneer," reinforcing the wilderness idea (Stegner 1961). Even today some geographers, ecologists, and environmentalists still think that the proportion of Indian influence was small relative to the vastness of wild nature on the North American continent (Vale 1998; Snyder 1995).

One of Stewart's pioneering contributions is that he elevated indigenous interactions with nature as an important part of the land's ecological history. This was a novel idea in academia a half-century ago. His manuscript stresses that many of the landscapes that early explorers, settlers, and missionaries found so remarkably rich were in part engendered and regularly renewed through the land management practices employed by Indians. Many vegetation types were not climax systems at the time of Euro-American contact but, rather, were mosaics of various seral stages or fire subclimaxes, intensified and perpetuated by Native American uses of seasonally scheduled burning. In a very real sense, the most productive and carefully managed "natural habitats" were Indian artifacts. He argued that landscapes such as the new Jersey pine barrens, the tall-grass prairies of the Midwest, and the Appalachian balds were Indian-modified landscapes.

Stewart stressed the significance of the cultural use of fire as the most effective, efficient, and widely employed vegetation management tool of Native American tribes, a view that is more and more widely accepted as we understand the tremendous and integral role of fire in the maintenance of indigenous economies and the maintenance of many ecosystems throughout the continent (Bonnicksen 2000; Anderson 1996b; Gruell 1991; Bonnicksen and Stone 1985).

If ecologists and environmentalists were to endorse the premise that Indians shaped the ecology of certain plant communities with fire, they would have to rethink the tenets upon which their wilderness philosophies are based and would have to face up to the removal of Native Americans from wilderness areas as in at least some instances a grave ecological *faux pas* that would ultimately undermine the unique habitat types and the biological diversity that they sought to preserve. They would also have to reevaluate the assumption that land use and conservation are always incompatible or that human tinkering with nature is inevitably destructive.

Stewart, in contrast, understood that present-day changes on the land had a historical basis and removal of Indians from their roles in traditional burning created additional ecological consequences, such as the overstocking of forests with a shift to more shade-tolerant and fire-sensitive species, the encroachment of woody vegetation onto meadows, prairies, and grasslands, and the invasion of western juniper into big sagebrush communities (Stewart 1955a, 1955b). Despite his conclusions, most scientists would not understand the importance of indigenous influences in the years to come. For instant, Harold Heady, grassland ecologist and professor emeritus of the Department of Environmental Science, Policy and Management, University of California at Berkeley, in a paper presented in 1972 at the Tall Timber Fire Ecology Conference concluded: "Indian burning in California is historically fascinating but of marginal consequence in helping us to understand present day grassland changes" (Heady 1972).

Native Americans do not speak in a technical jargon respected by scientists that includes the use of scientific names of species and a set vernacular that accompanies different scientific disciplines. Their knowledge is also based upon trial and error and keen observation without empirical study through well-designed quantitative experiments. Therefore, their knowledge has been passed off as folklore, which assumes a priori that it does not qualify as "real" science (La Barre 1942:200). The experts, in contrast, learn knowledge through lectures and textbooks and through the design of carefully controlled and statistically sound experiments. In this book Stewart gives the reader example after example of professionals and scientists who discredit indigenous ingenuity, skills, and actions in shaping the ecology of landscapes. Unlike native dwellers on the land, most ecologists did neither hunting nor gathering of the food they required. Thus indigenous lifeways remained inaccessible and unfathomable. For instance, references in the historical literature to indigenous burning of areas for hunting purposes to lure, capture, or drive wildlife or for wildlife habitat enhancement are numerous. Yet in a paper presented to the Society of American Foresters in 1959 L. T. Burcham, then assistant deputy state forester of California in range and watershed management, wrote without reference to any documentation to support his assertions: "Use of fire in hunting was circumscribed by a great amount of ritual which tended to limit its application; and no evidence has yet been found to indicate its widespread use for hunting in brush or forested lands" (Burcham 1959).

Many of the reasons for setting indigenous forest fires would ironically be identical to the objectives of the forester, entomologist, or range manager: to thin forests and reduce insects and diseases for ecosystem health and to increase the palatability, diversity, and quantity of grasses and forbs for animals important for meat production. In truth, judicious gathering, hunting, and wildland management necessary to maintain productive landscapes took complex, multidimensional knowledge.

CONTEMPORARY ECOLOGICAL CONTEXTS

Since the writing of this book many changes have occurred in the fields of plant ecology and resource management. The evolving body of concepts, theories, and research findings in the ecological sciences, by and large, provides a far more favorable intellectual climate for Stewart's work and ideas than in the 1950s.

Today fire is recognized as one of the major ecological factors that plays a role in the maintenance of many plant communities (Pyne et al. 1996; Anderson 1990; Collins 1990; Barbour et al. 1980; Cooper 1961). Many studies in the last two decades have shown the direct ecological benefits of fire. Certain bunchgrasses and forbs exhibit enhanced flowering and seed germination rates after fires (Keeley and Keeley 1989). Certain fire regimes will promote enhanced soil productivity (DeBano et al. 1979). In addition to soil arthropods, bacteria, and fungi, fire is a mineralizing agent in forests and other vegetation types that can speed up nutrient recycling, returning sites to high productivity (Kutiel and Shaviv 1992; St. John and Rundel 1976). While fire can accelerate nitrification and thus nutrient loss, research is demonstrating that in some cases the increase of leguminous forbs and shrubs that fix nitrogen rapidly replaces this lost nutrient (Ellis and Kummerow 1989). Recent studies indicate that grassland ecosystems, in the absence of fire, become choked with detritus; productivity and reproduction fall drastically, unless old material is recycled (Knapp et al. 1998; Knapp and Seastedt 1986). Pathologists, entomologists, and fire ecologists have proven that prescribed fire can effectively reduce insects and diseases of trees and shrubs (Abrahamson and Hartnett 1990; Hardison 1976).

Fire is now a universally accepted management tool in natural resource management and conservation biology (National Research Council 1992; Biswell 1989). Prescribed fire stimulates natural recovery of trees requiring bare mineral soil seedbeds such as loblolly pine (*Pinus taeda*) and California black oak (*Quercus kelloggii*) (Kauffman and Martin 1987). Fire has been correlated with the maintenance of biodiversity in various vegetation types (Huston 1994:413), including virtually all shrubland types (Christensen 1985). Conservation biology and fire ecology studies have also shown that frequent fire is necessary to the health, restoration, and maintenance of habitat for many endangered biota, such as a fungus feeding moth (*Chytonix sensilis*), the northern spotted owl (*Strix occidentalis*), the red-cockaded woodpecker (*Picoides borealis*), and the Kirtland's warbler (*Dendroica kirtlandii*) (McCabe 1995:167; Weatherspoon et al. 1992; Connor and Rudolph 1989; Costa and Escano 1989; Watts and Stulver 1980; Anderson and Storer 1976). There is a recent recognition that some of the diminishment of this biodiversity may be directly tied to past fire suppression policies of federal and state governments (Costa and Walker 1995:87; National Research Council 1992).

Not just species but whole ecosystems are also endangered. Ecosystem decline is linked with contemporary land uses that cause degradation, fragmentation, and outright loss of habitat (LaRoe et al. 1995; Noss et al. 1995). Fire suppression is another major cause of decline in certain ecosystems such as oak savannas, aspen forests, and montane meadows. Oak savannas in central North America, for example, are being encroached upon by tree and shrub species and are not regenerating due to absence of fire (Packard 1988; Nuzzo 1986). Strings of montane meadows that contain unique plant and animal life are shrinking throughout the West. Native Americans prehistorically set fires in the meadows and the ecotone areas surrounding the meadows to decrease the encroachment of more wet-tolerant lodgepole pine or other conifers into meadow areas, thus maintaining and perhaps in some cases enlarging meadow areas (see figure 1; Anderson 1996b). Communities of aspen (*Populus tremuloides*) are also dwindling throughout the western United States due to fire suppression, being replaced by more shade-tolerant conifers. Aspen groves burned at short fire return intervals in the past, due to Native American burning (Kay 1997:4). Thus fire is also being viewed by certain ecologists and restorationists as an essential process in restoring some endangered ecosystems such as oak-hickory woodlands, oak barrens, and prairie grassland in Ohio and Illinois to their presettlement condition (Packard and Mutel 1997; Noss et al. 1995:44).

One of the most significant, even paradigmatic, shifts in ecology since Stewart's writing of this book is the changing view of disturbance (fire is just one of many perturbations). This has involved dismantling the "balance of nature" model and replacing it with a nonequilibrium paradigm whereby the dynamics of natural communities are found to have multiple persistent states and are subject to physical disruptions from a wide range of natural and human forces and events (Dale et al. 2000; Pickett et al. 1992). There are still serious weaknesses with this new paradigm, however, in that hunter-gatherers are for the most part perceived as a shadow ecological force neither fully understood nor adequately appreciated. Many ecologists, biologists, and geographers still perceive hunter-gatherers as "opportunist omnivores"—they were not capable of alteration and manipulation of the environment until they entered the fields of animal husbandry and agriculture (Coe 1980:278), or their fire management was confined to small areas around village sites and did not have the capability to create vegetation mosaics and other landscape-level impacts (Kayll 1974:485).

A further important divergence in ecology is the recognition that most disturbances produce heterogeneous and patchy effects (White and Pickett 1985:4). Today ecological studies from all over the world, in both aquatic and terrestrial ecosystems, have borne out that disturbances have an ecological role in forest, shrubland, grassland, and wetland development and maintenance. In many instances moderate to medium disturbance promotes biological diversity, such as small mammal activity increasing the abundance and diversity of geophytes (Lovegrove and Jarvis 1986), wave action contributing to intertidal rock biodiversity (Sousa 1985), fires maintaining biologically rich grasslands (Risser 1988:177), and the alternate

FIG. 1 A & B. Early view of Yosemite Valley (above), taken in 1866; and view recorded a century later (below), in 1961, which reveals extensive encroachment of shade tolerant conifers into meadows, probably due in part to reduction in the frequency of fire in the absence of management by Indians. Photos courtesy of University of California Board of Regents and Yosemite Museum, Yosemite National Park: 1866 photo taken by C. E. Watkins from Union Point (RL16347); 1961 photo taken by Robert P. Gibbens from the same location.

filling and draining of lakes, marshes, and estuaries from the recurrent changes in water level of major rivers, supporting vast populations of diverse aquatic life and waterfowl (Mitsch and Gosselink 1993). Some scientists suggest that pyrodiversity leads to heterogeneity of vegetation (Martin and Sapsis 1992).

Disturbance is a recurrent feature of virtually every ecosystem (Christensen 1988). In fact, it is now accepted that perturbations are *required* for the rejuvenation of many plant populations and ecosystems. While heightened species diversity, abundance, and densities have been associated with disturbance, clear connections between indigenous disturbance regimes and the practical aspects of land use—in making a living—are only now beginning to be unraveled by scientists. New in-depth ethnoecological studies conducted by anthropologists and ethnobiologists in the last two decades that involve direct fieldwork with native people have disclosed to a much greater extent how integral fire is to the overall success of indigenous economies (Peacock and Turner 2000; Marshall 1999; Turner 1999; Anderson 1993b, 1997b, 1999). This is where much of the detailed ecological knowledge, though fragmented, rests—*within* the living native cultures.

According to J. H. Connell's intermediate disturbance hypothesis, disturbances that occur at intermediate intensities and frequencies promote the greatest biological diversity (Connell 1978). Researchers have hypothesized that Native American disturbances, in at least some instances, also occurred at intermediate intensities and frequencies, promoting a heterogeneous mosaic of different vegetation types and heightening the variety and abundance of plant species useful to their cultures (see figure 2; Delcourt and Delcourt 1997).

A strong counterforce causing scientists to reevaluate the substantial indigenous role in shaping landscapes is the catastrophic fires that have plagued the arid West in the last several decades (Sampson et al. 1994). It is now recognized that there are serious forest health problems in the West caused by a disruption of historic fire cycles and timber harvest practices of the period 1900–1990 (Covington et al. 1994). In a recent statement to the United States Senate, former U.S. Forest Service chief Jack Ward Thomas acknowledged the Indian role in setting fires and creating a forest mosaic: "Prior to the 1880's, low intensity fires, both lightning caused and those set by Native Americans, burned periodically through summer and early autumn. In the extensive, dry forests where ponderosa pine, and in some areas, western larch were the predominant species, fires burned every 5 to 30 years. . . . We have the basic knowledge to begin treatment of the forest health problem in the short-term by restoring high risk sites to some semblance of their historic conditions" (Thomas 1994).

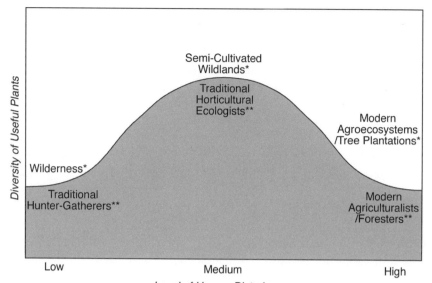

FIG. 2 The full spectrum of human-nature interactions. Tree plantations and large-scale agriculture, which both cause profound alterations in the natural environment, fall at one end of the spectrum of interaction, and wilderness (requiring little or no human intervention) falls at the other end. In between there is a continuum of cultivation systems in wildlands involving horticultural techniques (e.g., burning, pruning, sowing, weeding) used by many Native American tribes. These cultivation systems have characteristically involved use and even disturbance but rarely push the habitat beyond its capacity for natural regeneration; in fact there is growing evidence that both biodiversity and the abundance of plants and animals useful to humans commonly reach high levels in this middle part of the spectrum.

Like Stewart some forty years earlier, Thomas now not only acknowledges the Indian role but supports the idea that history matters in our ability to assess the present health and condition of forest ecosystems and that knowledge of the history of natural systems is an essential component of scientific analysis.

During the early 1950s, when Omer Stewart was in the midst of writing the manuscript, the scientific methods for how to anticipate, reconstruct, and measure former human impacts on wildland vegetation certainly were largely undeveloped. Today that has changed. Scientists and practitioners are beginning to pull in findings from diverse disciplines and develop new methodologies to uncover the vegetation and land use histories of specific sites (Arno and Sneck 1977).

More accurate reconstructions of interactions between indigenous people and the natural environment in North America have recently materialized through interdisciplinary research that combines knowledge in the realms of the social, physical, and biological sciences and the humanities. This field, called "historical ecology," relies upon the compilation, analysis, and interpretation of findings from plant ecology, paleoecology, history, archaeology, pyro-dendrochronology, ethnography, ethnobotany, and other disciplines to identify specific biotic resources, ecosystem types, and whole biomes that are likely to have been significantly influenced by prehistoric indigenous management practices (Crumley 1994; Merchant 1993; Hammett 1992; Jorgensen 1989). For instance, nature keeps a historical record of environmental changes in the land in the growth rings of trees, plant remains in a preserved packrat's nest, plant and animal fossils and charcoals in the soil, and plant pollen laid down in layers in bog sediments. Scientists with sophisticated equipment, molecular dating methods, and other special techniques can retrieve this information—incorporating it into a comprehensive framework for interpretation—to give us a clearer window to the past (Stahle 1996; Pearsall 1989; Piperno 1988; Faegri and Iversen 1975).

New techniques such as fire scar and pollen studies, historical photograph interpretation, and archaeobotanical research have given scientists a better idea of the role of fire, and specifically Native American fires, in shaping ecosystems (Egan and Howell 2001). For example, recent pyro-dendrochronological studies around the country suggest that the high frequency of fires in sequoia-mixed conifer forests of the Sierra Nevada, the mixed conifer forests of the Sandia Mountains of New Mexico, and the oak-hickory forests of eastern North America could not be explained by the contemporary ignition rate from lightning alone, only in conjunction with indigenous burning (Baisan and Swetnam 1997; Abrams 1992; Kilgore and Taylor 1979). The fire history work of Stephen Barrett and Stephen Arno, among others, and the historical photographic interpretation studies of George Gruell suggest that Indian-caused fires substantially augmented lightning fires over large areas in the Rocky Mountains; particularly in the lower-elevation seral stands of ponderosa pine (*Pinus ponderosa*), Douglas fir (*Pseudotsuga menziesii*), and western larch (*Larix latifolia*) (Gruell 1983; Barrett and Arno 1982; Barrett 1981).

Interdisciplinary studies (unavailable to Stewart in the 1950s), while few in number, have added rich dimensions and clarified complexities in unraveling the pervasive Indian role in shaping landscapes with fire. For example, biologist James Cornett in using paleontological, genetic, and anthropological techniques has disclosed the tremendous role Native Americans have played in the dispersal of the desert fan palm (*Washingtonia filifera*) into the Southwest and the manipulation of the structure, function, and composition of the groves with indigenous fire (Cornett 1985, 1989a, 1989b). Along the northern California coast, Indian-set fires modified the grassland to fire-resistant species, expanded the coastal prairie vegetation type, and increased the productivity of the soil. Forest ecologist Susan Bicknell used a variety of methodologies, including vegetation and soil sampling, opal analysis, pollen analysis, charcoal analysis, and ethnohistoric literature reviews to prove that soils from areas currently occupied by coastal scrub, bishop pine forest and woodland, mixed evergreen forest, redwood forest, and riparian woodland were once prairie. She has concluded that the reduction in these vegetation mosaics is in part due to absence of frequent burning by Native Americans and that the lightning fire regime alone would not be sufficient to keep extensive areas in coastal prairie in precontact times (Bicknell et al. 1992; Bicknell 1989).

Using an integrated research approach, Ronald Myers and Patricia Peroni (1983) have revealed a long-standing history of anthropogenic fire in Florida, possibly as early as 12,000 b.p. They summarized and correlated archeological studies that reveal early settlement and resource use patterns (Sears 1982; Purdy 1981) with studies that record changes in the pollen records from Florida lakes and differences in soil characteristics (Kalisz 1982; Watts and Stulver 1980; Watts 1975), together with early ethnohistoric accounts of aboriginal fire (Pyne 1982; Núñez Cabeza DeVaca 1972).

The State of Our Knowledge Regarding Indian Fire Regimes and Resulting Impacts

Despite the thousands of fire-related studies, new technologies for detecting historical fires, and interdisciplinary research approaches developed since the 1950s, there are still many unanswered questions. While Stewart viewed Indians as the determining factor in engendering many landscapes, plant ecologists are still in wide disagreement as to the *degree* of importance of Indians as an integral disturbance factor in different vegetation types. The topic is fervently debated, with few areas of complete consensus. For example, are the Appalachian balds and the New Jersey pine barrens cultural artifacts; a product of soils, climate, lightning, and topography; or combinations of both?

Conventional ecologists view indigenous influences as transient, restricted in extent and usually near settlements, and frequently without genetic consequences (Norse 1990:28). For instance, some ecologists in the Northeast believe the indigenous influence extending beyond agricultural fields to be minimal and not permanent, restricted mainly to floodplains and meadows and leaving the old growth forests largely untouched. While some fires were set by Indians, these were of a scale and intensity similar to lightning fires, making impacts slight and part of the natural order. Old-growth forests are viewed as products of lightning fire, windfalls, soils, and topography (Leverett 1996:5; Stahle 1996:321–22; Russell 1980, 1981, 1983).

Other ecologists view indigenous influences as widespread, with genetic consequences, and permanent (insofar as the plant community will not go back to some prehuman state of nature). If we look at the Northeast as an example, according to some ecologists, the pre-European settlement forests were influenced by Indian burning as well as lightning, and the cumulative effects were substantial in shaping these landscapes. Indian-set fires shortened the fire-free interval, creating vast oak-dominated forests and changing vegetation structures. Indian-set fires also produced type conversions, shifting forests to grasslands or savannas and encouraging suitable habitat that extended the range of bison (Abrams 1992; Patterson and Sassaman 1988; Cronon 1983; Pyne 1982).

Other scientists, while they recognize the pervasive influence of indigenous burning, are reluctant to mimic the details of past structure, function, or composition during the Indian era or to build "a set of desired conditions" for fear that they will stem from a highly inferred and perhaps false range of variability. Instead these plant ecologists and resource managers seek to ensure that natural forces (e.g., lightning fire, hydrologic function, nutrient cycles) will continue to operate in the landscape and to determine the fire regime and ecosystem structure, rather than attempting to recreate historic conditions (SNEP Science Team 1996; Graber 1995; Kilgore 1973).

What is astonishing is that after almost half a century of fire and anthropological research since the writing of this book there is so little knowledge of how indigenous fire regimes differed from lightning fire regimes in different plant communities of the United States and so little attempt to simulate indigenous fire regimes. Many land management agencies have not worked out what role alteration of fire regimes by Native Americans should play in setting fire management policy (Christensen 1991). Whether Indian ignitions should be considered natural is still a hotly debated issue (Kilgore 1985); in Yellowstone National Park and many other wilderness areas only lightning-caused fires are considered "natural" and allowed to burn (Brown 1991). Prescribed burning is now conducted on public lands to reduce fuel loads and simulate the natural lightning fire regime in attempts to counteract the damage done by decades of fire suppression, but the human manipulations during the Indian era are virtually ignored. In areas where fire exclusion strategies have altered fuel conditions, fire behavior may be considerably different than on pre-European contact landscapes (Christensen 1991). Additionally, prescribed burning programs often do not cover enough acreage and are hampered by both strict air quality standards and increasing fire risk to human safety and property. Some scientists now argue that the wildfires are more severe and occur on a larger scale than the wildland fires in aboriginal times and that therefore the wildland ecosystems are also at risk (Martin and Sapsis 1992; Bonnicksen and Stone 1985). N. C. Johnson (1999:434) states: "The lesson here is that sudden departures from long-established human-ecological interactions can lead to yet another ecological transformation. This new ecological condition may bear little resemblance to a primeval state that disappeared when prehistoric people arrived."

If land managers, ecologists, and archaeologists understand the intricacies and mechanics of how and why native people shaped ecosystems with fire, it will enrich their inventory of management methods, and they will be in a better position to make informed decisions about the reintroduction of human-set fires based on Indian practices (Anderson and Moratto 1996).

Many of the plant communities that have been managed with fire suppression tactics are extremely biologically impoverished, containing a mere fraction of the biodiversity that existed at the point of Euro-American contact. While some prescribed burning has been reintroduced into these areas, in many drier Douglas fir forests of the Pacific Northwest, the mixed conifer forests of the Cascades and Sierra Nevada, and ponderosa pine forests of the Southwest stand structures are much denser, and the forest understory has shifted from grasses and herbs to shade-tolerant forbs and tree litter (Skinner and Chang 1996; Sampson et al. 1994). Rich, diverse southwestern desert grasslands have been encroached by woodlands, most notably juniper (*Juniperus* spp.) and mesquite (*Prosopis* spp.) (McPherson 1995; Parker 1945; Leopold 1924). Other research suggests that many longleaf pine (*Pinus palustris*) sites have been replaced by south Florida slash pine (*Pinus elliottii*) or sand pine-scrub vegetation (Frost 1993; Myers and Peroni 1983). Many of these vegetation changes are in part a result of shifts in the fire regimes, likely due to a decrease in Indian burning.

While Stewart asserted that Indians were instrumental agents of environmental change in a multitude of vegetation types, the profound implications of this assertion for the science of ecology have not been fully realized. Today in most ecology and conservation biology books and articles disturbance is still defined as natural or created by modern humans—without a separate detailed distinction of *indigenous* disturbances.

Why should one make this distinction? Because Indian manipulations may have occurred long enough in an area to be considered part of the

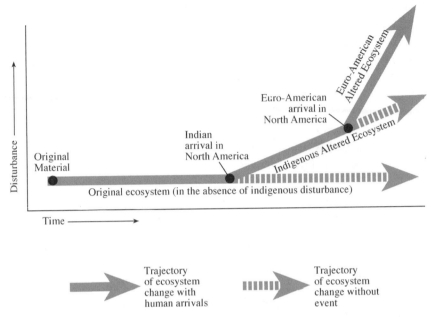

FIG. 3 Ecosystem change. Like other species, humans represent an ecological force within an ecosystem—influencing its trajectory in ways that are often highly culture-specific.

normal environment of a vegetation type. The disturbance regime descriptors (such as distribution, frequency return interval, season, severity, etc.) in some cases were different enough from the natural disturbance pattern to create new pathways of vegetation change and ecosystem development (see figure 3). Ecological effects from indigenous burning might register at every level of biological organization from the organismal to the landscape scale. If, for example, Indian-set fires were more frequent and in a different season than the natural lightning fire regime of a geographic area, this could affect genetic variation, individual life spans, and adaptations at the species or organismal level; and it could affect whole landscapes by changing the diversity and mosaic pattern of plant communities and alter the relative proportion of pyrogenic and nonpyrogenic vegetation (see figure 4).

   Part of the problem has been that true interdisciplinary research that compares and correlates Native American settlement patterns with plant and animal resource use and management and the paleoecological record has not been done for most parts of the United States; if conducted, it would probably give us much more substantial data for interpretation. For

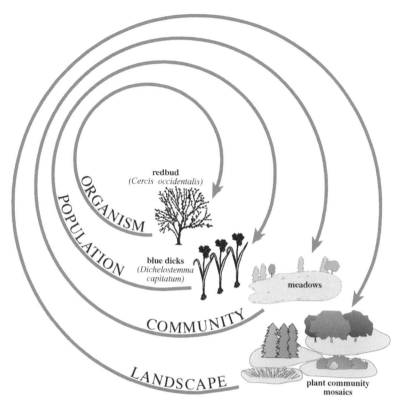

FIG. 4 Indigenous Resource Management at Different Levels of Biological Organization. Tribes across North America managed their natural environment at various
scales. The tribes of the central and southern Sierra Nevada of California, for
example, managed individual redbud trees at the organism level by pruning or
spot burning to promote long, straight branches for basketry; they managed
populations of blue dicks, relished for their edible underground corms, by tilling
and replanting cormlets; they burned around and within meadows to keep surrounding trees from encroaching and promote the growth of numerous plant
species for medicines, foods, and basketry; and they burned many areas, creating shifting mosaics of different plant community types at the landscape scale.

example, archaeological evidence showing fluctuations in prehistoric human
population density along with fluctuations in botanical resources from the
pollen record can indicate former environmental manipulations by Native
Americans (Anderson and Carpenter 1991:1). Often a prehistoric shift in
species dominance in a vegetation type is attributed to climate change or
other factors, with no thought as to what Native Americans were doing in
the region during that shift.

Many research studies (e.g., archaeological, ethnobotanical, fire scar) are still done along strict disciplinary lines—but even these have not been gathered, cross-referenced, and synthesized to gain a more complete picture of Indian-nature interactions in different geographic regions. Ecologists are urged to consider both the large corpus of ethnobotanies (published and unpublished) assembled for many tribes and the plant remains from archaeological contexts in understanding extinct subsistence and environmental systems (Cowan 1978:263) as well as other kinds of studies conducted in the social sciences.

Another reason why so little is known about whether a fire is lightning-caused or anthropogenic is that the state of our technologies, sampling techniques, and methods of analysis still, for the most part, does not enable us to distinguish the *cause* of the fires. While shifts in climate correlated with shifts in the types of pollen, increases in charcoal, and fire scars left on tree stumps all can provide evidence of fire, in most cases scientists can not decipher whether they were caused by Indian-set fires or lightning fires. Furthermore, the frequencies of fire scars in many areas can be accounted for by lightning fires alone, such as at many sites in Arizona and New Mexico (Swetnam and Baisan 1996).

An additional problem is that many of the light surface fires do not show up in the fire scar records (for example, in the drier Douglas fir forests of the Pacific Northwest) because mature trees have very thick bark and are well insulated from the heat and do not have the thick needle mat that burns easily. The fires have a tendency to smolder through the trees and not burn so severely (Carl Skinner, pers. comm. 1998): thus light surface fires set by Native Americans may not show up in the fire scar record. Uneven fire scarring has been noted in other biotypes as well (McBride and Lewis 1984).

Early and pervasive logging practices in many vegetation types have left few old trees or stumps that can be dated and analyzed for their fire history. For example, few fire scar studies have been done in the Northeast that disclose pre-European settlement burning frequencies because it has been difficult to locate trees or stumps that are even 400–500 years old (Guyette and Cutter 1991; Buell et al. 1954). Most of the precontact fire scar work has been done in Ontario, Canada (Guyette and Dey 1995; Guyette 1995a, 1995b, 1995c). According to Jim Clark (pers. comm. 1996; Clark and Royall 1995, 1996; Clark 1990, 1995), most fire scar studies date from long after the collapse of the Indian populations and the beginnings of subsistence agriculture and more intense land use. There are not enough old trees to reconstruct presettlement times. Furthermore, in many parts of the eastern United States there has been poor faunal and floral preservation because of the region's excessively acid soils and high annual rainfall. Particularly scarce are food remains at many archaeological sites, making it hard to determine the extent of environmental manipulation (Dragoo 1976).

ETHNOECOLOGICAL RESEARCH AND ECOLOGICAL RESTORATION:
AVENUES FOR RECREATING AND REEXPERIENCING HISTORIC LANDSCAPES
AND TRADITIONAL WAYS OF RELATING TO LANDSCAPES

With increasing knowledge that the planetary biosphere is being degraded, the power and limits of scientific insight and application have been reassessed. New disciplines (such as conservation biology and restoration ecology) that combine methods of science with the values of nature recovery and protection have emerged to cope with the present biodiversity crisis (Jordan et al. 1987; Soulé 1986). With recognition of the decline of forest and range health, scientists and resource managers have created a new type of management called ecosystem management. This new management approach encompasses whole watersheds or landscapes, rather than single species, and involves managing for biological values such as ecological integrity and total native diversity (Grumbine 1994). Under this new management approach, whole systems are managed for a variety of purposes rather than simply for production of a single resource type like "food" or "timber." It differs from older approaches in that managers are concerned with how human activities affect ecosystem processes and structural elements as well as outputs.

Within the social sciences the emerging field of ethnoecology, a subdiscipline of ethnobiology, encompasses the study of the biological bases for plant and animal harvest and use among native peoples and the limitations and ecological consequences of human actions on the natural environment (Ford 1981; Bye 1979). Ethnoecological studies are multidisciplinary in nature and utilize methods from anthropology, ecology, and biology to elucidate the current and historical interrelationships between human cultures and plants, animals, fungi, and other living organisms (Cox 1989). Additionally, the methods and concepts of historical ecology are more and more being used as a framework for ethnoecological research (Ford 1978:43).

Only very recently have ethnoecologists begun to consider the linkages between the practical aspects of indigenous land use (e.g., collecting non-wormy acorns, disease-free berries, and abundant understory herbs for food) and the necessary harvesting and management regimes to ensure proper quantities and qualities of the resource supply. Thus they ask indigenous informants questions that attempt to reveal the types and variables of harvesting and resource management (e.g., season, frequency, intensity,

and extent), which are directly tied to creating specific ecological consequences as perceived and stated by Native Americans during the interview
process (Anderson 2001; Turner et al. 2000; Loewen 1998; Fowler 1996).
The information is then evaluated within a Western scientific framework,
through interviews with scientific experts in entomology, mycology, botany,
ornithology, and other disciplines and through review of published scientific
papers to explore the potential ecological effects of indigenous harvesting
and management practices. What is important about this approach is that
it defines specific ecological outcomes linked with harvesting and management techniques.

While many of the citations in Omer Stewart's manuscript reflect reasons
for indigenous burning that are unrelated to ecological effects (e.g., animal
drives, ease of travel, increased visibility, clearing underbrush that could
hide enemies), producing specific ecological consequences probably was
the most significant reason for Native Americans to burn. Many of these
purposes are underrecorded in the earlier historical and ethnographic
literature but have been uncovered in recent ethnoecological studies in
various parts of North America (L. M. Johnson 1999; Marshall 1999;
Anderson 1993b, 1996a, 1997b; Turner 1991, 1999). Some of these purposes
include increasing abundance and densities of edible tubers, greens, and
mushrooms; decreasing insects and diseases of wild foods and basketry
material; increasing the quality and quantity of medicinal plants; increasing
the quantity and quality of material for basketry and cordage; decreasing
detritus; increasing epicormic branches for household items, granaries,
fish weirs, clothing, games, hunting and fishing traps, and weapons; recycling nutrients; decreasing plant competition; and maintaining specific
plant community types (see figures 5–8).

Frequently the indigenous manipulation of landscapes occurred to
promote specialized growth characteristics of plant populations affecting
not only the quantity but also the *quality* of the plant part, including the
size, shape, color, length, diameter, taste, nutritional value, and other para-
meters. Therefore, there are usually strong links among (1) the quality
and quantity of the plant material growing in the natural environment, (2)
the ease of manufacturing or preparation, and (3) the level of functionality
of the finished product.

The function of a coiled basket made in California, for example, may
be to hold water or to cook soup. The quality of the plant materials will
affect the ultimate function of the basket. Foundation materials must be
able to absorb water and swell to make the basket leak-proof, while lacing
materials must exhibit flexibility and not break under tension. The length
of sewing strands is also important, longer material being preferred (the

FIG. 5 Beating seeds of wildflowers and grasses with a shallow basket into a collection basket for food was just the first in a series of management steps.
Afterward areas were burned to reduce plant competition and recycle nutrients; some of the seed was saved and broadcast in the burned area. This
practice is recorded for tribes of the Plateau, Great Basin, Southwest, and
Pacific Northwest. Photograph of Cecilia-Joaquin, Central Pomo, courtesy
of the Smithsonian Institution. Neg. #75-14715.

FIG. 6 The digging of bulbs and tubers with a hardwood digging stick, replanting propagules, and burning-over areas to increase numbers, densities, and size of subterranean organs of wild plants for food were common practices throughout the West. These had subtle yet significant effects in shaping the ecology of many ecosystems. Photograph of Rosa Charles and Billy George (Wintu couple), courtesy of the Santa Barbara Museum of Natural History. #JPH-CA-WT-201.

less often new material is added, the tighter and finer the stitching, which helps maintain the basket's impermeability). All materials must exhibit no insect or disease damage. Young shrub growth that rapidly elongates from a perennial shrub after being exposed to disturbance displays many of the above desirable characteristics. Since these characteristics do not occur readily on wild shrubs, Native Americans frequently augmented these growth forms with management in the form of pruning and burning (Anderson 1991, 1999).

Fɪɢ. 7 A basketmaker from Massett, British Columbia, weaving a close-twined basket.
Some basketry materials required periodic burning to decrease detritus, recycle nutrients, and keep woody vegetation from encroaching, such as beargrass
(*Xerophyllum tenax*), a plant whose leaves were used (and continue to be used)
in basketry by many Northwest Coast tribes. Photograph #CSA854 courtesy
of the Field Museum, Chicago, Illinois.

Next the ethnoecologist moves beyond the descriptive stage by
attempting to *quantify* the ecological effects of indigenous harvesting
regimes and horticultural practices on plant productivity and vegetation
dynamics. This involves enlisting the expertise of plant ecologists and stat-
isticians in the design of ecological field experiments (Anderson and
Rowney 1999; Anderson 1993a). The experimental approach has the
advantage of focusing on specific questions and/or hypotheses relating to
the effects of indigenous practices on specified features of individual
plants, populations, or plant communities. Results from these experiments
could be used to develop guidelines for harvesting populations of native
plants in a sustainable manner and to develop management regimes that
are reintroduced to create patch sizes, edge/area ratios, connectivity, and
contiguity similar to those of the historic period to maintain populations
of diverse species important to Native American tribes (Anderson 2001).

FIG. 8 Long, straight branches needed for basketry do not occur naturally in large
        numbers and thus were collected from shrubs or trees maintained for this pur-
        pose by burning or pruning by tribes throughout California and the Southwest.
        Photograph of a Karuk weaver, courtesy of the Smithsonian Institution. #75-
        16219

Through well-designed long-term experiments, researchers will be
able to distinguish between natural variation and low-level effects of indigenous perturbations on native plants at the organism and population levels.
Ecological data will also reveal whether or not a variable—such as flower
production, acorn production, or availability of young shoots for basketry—
is enhanced or decreased from its reference state before the disturbance.
Biotic measures and criteria for success of the restoration and continuous
management of native plant populations could be thus established from
Native American perspectives.

A major thrust of restoration ecology is to restore ecosystems to a
semblance of their *historic* structures, composition, and functions prior to
major Euro-American settlement and development. Ecological restoration
can be defined as "[t]he practice of reestablishing the historic plant and
animal communities of a given area or region and the renewal of the
ecosystem and cultural functions necessary to maintain these communities now and into the future" (Dave Egan, editor of *Ecological Restoration*,
pers. comm. 2001).

Restoration of ecosystems and the application of new land management strategies are based on reconstructing the "historical ranges of variability" within the ecosystem. According to J. B. Haufler (1999:24): "Under this approach, the desired amount and description of each successional stage within an ecologically defined unit, such as a habitat type, can be defined based on an understanding of historical disturbance regimes that affected each ecological unit and resulting stand conditions." Haufler goes on to say that "[t]he primary assumption of this approach is that the native species of a region adapted to and occurred within the historical range of ecosystem condition, and that by maintaining ecosystems within this range, the needs of all species will be met."

Like resource managers and agriculturalists, Native Americans in various regions of North America manipulated ecosystems through heuristic exercises in ecology (Harper 1987:36). Restorationists are beginning to work with ethnoecologists and other scientists who utilize methods in historical ecology to reconstruct these practices and then apply these regimes to various sites in order to recreate more authentic historical landscapes (Egan and Howell 2001). In certain ecosystems native species evolved under both natural and indigenous disturbance patterns; thus maintaining a full range of similar conditions under management offers the best assurance against losses of biodiversity (Seymour and Hunter 1999).

By discovering how and why Native Americans managed for diverse plant and animal species and simulating their practices in experiments, ethnoecologists and restorationists will be making a substantial contribution to the development of ecosystem management protocols for different wildlands. Both restorationists and ethnoecologists bridge Western science and indigenous knowledge systems involving real-world applications. These new fields have tremendous application to broader academic and policy concerns about the linkage of indigenous knowledge, biodiversity, restoration, and natural resource sustainability.

Weaknesses in Stewart's Manuscript

Stewart considered fire to be axiomatic: if it *could* be used by Native Americans, it *was* used. The reader is given a false impression that Indians burned everywhere, which is clearly not the case. Given the diverse habitat types in North America, the uneven indigenous occupation in some types, and the inflammability of some kinds of vegetation in different climates, indigenous influence with fire was neither uniform nor equally effective across landscapes. The subalpine forests of the high Adirondack and New England Mountains; the drier desert regions of Arizona, New Mexico, and southern California; and the red cedar swamps and coastal Sitka spruce/ western hemlock forests of the Pacific Northwest do not burn readily. Furthermore, there are also areas that were off limits to burning by Indians. For example, the Skykomish chiefs of the Pacific Northwest ordered people not to fire brush where red elderberries (*Sambucus callicarpa*) grew, because the deer ate the ripe ones (Gunther 1973:47), and stands of saskatoon berries or serviceberries (*Amelanchier alnifolia*) were purposefully not burned by native people in the boreal forests of western Canada (Lewis 1982b:41). Other areas such as the Black Hills that were sacred or were not visited by tribes may have been shaped very little, if at all, by Indian burning.

Perhaps it is more reasonable and accurate to view Indian interventions in North American landscapes as part of a continuum or spectrum that would encompass a full range of human modifications from very little or no Native American influence (true wilderness) to fully human-created (anthropogenic) ecosystems. Eastern woodlands such as hemlock forests, the drier desert regions of the Southwest, and subalpine flora of the Sierra Nevada would qualify as true wilderness at one endpoint, while the agricultural fields of the Iroquois, the dry coastal prairies of the northwest coastal tribes of California and Oregon, and the palm oases of the Cahuilla in southern California are almost entirely anthropogenic at the opposite endpoint. Other landscapes fall somewhere in the middle of the continuum, reflecting some degree of indigenous influence.

Another major shortcoming of Stewart's manuscript is that he divided the continent into broad vegetation types and made generalizations about their fire history without distinguishing the many different plant communities within each broad type. Thus his vague reference to "fire type forests" of the Pacific Northwest or the southeastern Coastal Plain belies what is a much more complex picture. Within broad vegetation types such as the "eastern deciduous forests" there is an elaborate mosaic of vegetation subtypes that occur under variable topographic, climatic, and soil conditions, which in turn affect the species composition, vegetation structure, and the role of fire in each respective subtype. For example, indigenous burning probably greatly influenced the oak-chestnut and oak-hickory associations but had very little influence in the hemlock-northern hardwood forests— both of which are part of the classification "eastern deciduous forests."

This complexity also exists in other broad regions such as the Pacific Northwest: the wettest, foggiest forests (red cedar swamps and coastal Sitka spruce/western hemlock forests) burn extremely rarely—once every 400 or 500 years—while fire intervals in mixed coniferous forests in southern Oregon and northern California are much shorter, every 5 to 22 years

(Wills and Stuart 1994; Norse 1990). Fire effects span the full spectrum from creating treeless grasslands, to patchy underburns in drier seral forests, to enormous stand replacement fires in climax temperate rain-forests and lodgepole pine forests (Agee 1993; Norse 1990; Franklin 1988).

Stewart concludes that the role of Indian-set fires "may have been an equal role with lightning," citing the number and locations of historical strikes for some areas and concluding that these were not sufficient to burn and shape vast vegetation types. This conclusion is also not supported with concrete evidence, as comparative data for acreage burned under historical indigenous versus lightning fire regimes are lacking. A. R. Taylor (1974), for example, estimates that 37 percent of all ignitions in the Pacific states are from lightning but acreage burned per year is a more important indicator of the influence of lightning than number of ignitions.

CONCLUSIONS

In the highest windy passes of the Sierra Nevada one can still find mortar-cup depressions in granite outcrops formerly used by Native Americans for processing foods. Ten-thousand-year-old spear points lodged between the ribs of giant bison lie buried in clay near present-day Folsom, New Mexico. Medicine wheels (circles in stone) lie undisturbed in the Bighorn Mountains of present-day Wyoming. Rock paintings enrich the cliff faces of the lower Pecos River in what is now southwest Texas. A clay pipe rests at an ancient Mohawk village called Otstungo in what is presently New York. These and many of the other stories in stone provide evidence of former Native American occupation in North America. The archaeologists' radiocarbon methods have turned up dates as old as 12,000 to 15,000 years for human settlement.

Subtle to the untrained eye of the outside observer, yet more indelible and wide-reaching than the stories in stone, are the signatures of indigenous land use and management left on the vegetation of North America. Few Westerners identify parklike oak forests, lush tall-grass prairies, or fertile desert fan palm oases with ancient Native American burning practices. Yet the wielding of fire as a horticultural tool enabled Native Americans systematically to alter the natural environment on a long-term basis and at varying scales from individual shrubs to whole bioregions. Fire not only warmed hearths and kept predators at bay; it increased forage for wildlife, curtailed insects that plagued food crops, and promoted long, straight shoots for basketry.

One lone anthropologist, Omer Stewart, recognized that indigenous fire management practices had *significant* ecological consequences on

The Effects of Burning of Grasslands and Forests by Aborigines the World Over

The Effects of Burning of Grasslands and Forests by Aborigines the World Over

Omer C. Stewart

INTRODUCTION

PLANT SCIENTISTS ARE not all as extreme in their views as Donald Culross Peattie, who wrote: "Each tree has its place; each is, or it was in days of virgin innocence, adjusted to its environment and held with its neighbors in a precise ecologic balance." His "days of virgin innocence" were those before modern industry and agriculture disrupted the "precise ecologic balance." They were before Europeans invaded this hemisphere. Most botanists and ecologists ignore the American Indian as an important ecological force. Especially the nonagricultural, hunting and gathering Indians of the United States are omitted from accounts of the environmental conditions affecting "natural vegetation." This is unfortunate and leads to error. For at least 10,000 years, probably for 25,000 years, and possibly for 100,000 years, Indians have occupied the New World. Their influence on the vegetation has been important.

We cannot know exactly how the aborigines influenced and modified the plant life of America during the full time of their occupancy of the country. The picture of prehistoric life revealed by archaeology is too fragmentary. We will not be far wrong, however, if we project back into the earliest periods of the Indian's prehistory some of our knowledge of his historic activities. It can be assumed that many of the practices of primitive hunting and gathering peoples, like many of their tools, have continued for thousands of years. The natives observed by the first Europeans profoundly altered the balance of plant life. Their ancestors had undoubtedly been doing so during their entire history on the continent.

Such assertions are not made lightly. We know, for example, that Plains Indians in historic times stampeded great herds of bison over embankments by means of grass fires. At the extinct-bison-bone quarry near Folsom, New Mexico, where nineteen projectile points were found associated with skeletons of twenty-three extinct *Bison taylori,* we have evidence of a great slaughter that occurred over 10,000 years ago. It is possible that Folsom Man used fire to stampede bison, as did his descendants in the same area.

There is evidence that fires set by Indians were of the utmost importance in determining the pattern of the vegetation from the time mankind first peopled the Western Hemisphere. The methods of using fire and the actual examples of their effect will come, of course, from historic records.

The evidence suggests that few Europeans have ever seen in America vegetation areas that were not at some time burned over. Exceptions are found only in places where vegetable matter was too scant to carry fire from one plant to another. If there was anything to burn, Indians set fire to it. The effect of fires would vary from place to place. How burning would modify the vegetation balance would depend upon many other natural conditions. Topography, moisture, wind, and the plants set afire would all interact to determine the relative influence of the fires. How often the vegetation might be burned varied.

Fires set by Indians were not the only ones that seemed to determine what plants grew in any particular area. Lightning causes forest fires today, and scars on giant redwoods prove it has done so for ages. But fires from lightning are too irregular and too limited in distribution to approach in effectiveness fires started by man.

In spite of this evidence, fire has been almost ignored as one of the important ecological variables determining vegetation. Particularly neglected have been man-made fires. This work is written specifically to try to remedy that neglect. I will try always to consider topography, soils, and climate—rainfall, evaporation, wind, heat—whenever evaluating the influence of burning upon the vegetation of any area. If I appear to overemphasize fire as a determining factor, I do so because of my desire to make up for its having been neglected by most botanists, foresters, plant ecologists, and geographers in the past.

The most significant point of view supported by this study is that tall grass of the prairies is not climax vegetation. Short grass of the plains is probably not climax vegetation. Furthermore, pure grasslands on deep, rich soil are not climax vegetation, but result from burning. That Indian burning established prairies, or at least maintained them, appears to be true beyond question. That short-grass plains would be brush-covered were it not for the action of fire appears probable. Grass fires continuing to the present, cultivation, and overgrazing deprived the plains and prairies of a chance to demonstrate what vegetation might have developed without Indian burning. Enough small samples and some experiments strongly support the view that all extensive grasslands would be covered with woody vegetation were they not periodically burned over. On the moister tall-grass prairies, true forests would grow. On the drier high plains, bushes, brush, and scrub trees would first appear. Such an evaporation-reducing cover could easily modify the soil and climate so that drought-resistant trees would grow.

Fire appears to be the essential ecological ingredient for the formation and maintenance of grasslands. Without a fairly intense fire, woody growth of some type takes over. Overgrazing will allow brush to replace grass, even if burning is continued, because fires then will not destroy the woody growth. A lack of historic perspective has led some to include burning as a cause for replacement of grass by brush. It is said that burning destroys grasslands and aids brush to take over, but this is unwarranted. Since burning maintained the grasslands in presettlement days, certainly burning now would not destroy the same grasslands by allowing brush to cover them. Overgrazing, whether burning is stopped or not, is responsible for the change. Brush or trees would probably invade the grass without overgrazing if burning were stopped.

Another important problem touched by this work is the burning of forests. There existed many excellent forests in America when it was first settled. Yet until European occupation changed Indian habits, frequently, almost annually, fires passed through those forests. Nevertheless, the trees were large; the forests were open and healthy. Indian burning destroyed much of the underbrush and allowed grass to grow between the trees without killing the trees. Pasture and timber were preserved in good balance. Since burning has been stopped, grass in forests has decreased; brush has increased. Brush growing high among the trees makes modern forest fires, which occur in spite of all efforts to avoid them, much more destructive to timber than were the periodic forest fires in aboriginal times. Grazing changes the old plant balance, but the condition of forests during Indian times suggests a careful study and experimentation to determine whether or not we should return to periodic burning of forest lands.

The original stimulation for this research came from my professor of geography, Carl O. Sauer, and professor of anthropology, A. L. Kroeber, at the University of California at Berkeley. They encouraged me, but I must take personal responsibility for the interpretations and conclusions arrived at. This work does not exhaust the subject. It is based entirely on published sources. More experimental controlled burning and fully documented vegetation changes since European settlement will add much to our knowledge of the subject.

An opportunity to search the ecological literature and to prepare the manuscript for publication was provided by the regents and administrative officers of the University of Colorado through a faculty research fellowship from January to March 1951. The fellowship freed me from teaching for one quarter, so that I could devote full time to research. Much of the library work was done in 1940 as part of my duties as supervisor for Works Progress Administration Official Project 665-08-3-30, Unit A-15, University of California, Berkeley. The research and writing was interrupted for four years by World War II and readjustment following that. A grant-in-aid for typing the manuscript received from the Council on Research and Creative Work, University of Colorado Graduate School, which stimulated and provided the means for early completion of the project, is gratefully acknowledged.

THE EASTERN WOODLANDS

Indians burned the forests of the eastern United States to such an extent that the general vegetation first observed by Europeans was not at all what could be expected from an evaluation of soil and climate. Thousands of square miles of the Indian-fire-forest, frequently called "virgin forest," have been maintained to the present time against floral competitors by the same means used by the Indians. This clear, well-documented fact has been ignored by most ecologists, botanists, and foresters. One example will demonstrate this. It is an "answer" given to a hypothetical "question" in the U. S. Department of Agriculture Yearbook for 1949 entitled *Trees* (579, p. 20):

> Q. Why did the Indians start fires in forests?
> A. Tradition says that they did so to drive game, but we have no positive proof that they did this as a regular custom over any area. The Indians had no matches and they used small campfires that they tended carefully; so, it is improbable that they set many fires.

I do not know what Mr. Bergoffen, author of the "Question and Answer" section, considers "positive proof" or "regular custom," but he was clearly mistaken. Contrary to his offhand impression, Indians burned for a number of reasons, "to drive game" being only one. Even when we have reviewed the full written account of Indians starting forest fires, there is much more to learn. Vegetation itself constitutes a historical record. Trees can tell a story of forest fires extending back a thousand years. Only when information from all sources is considered in relation to climatological and geographical data is the importance of forest fires started by

Indians fully appreciated. A knowledge of the effect of fires in woodlands has a very real bearing on an understanding of the influence of grass fires.

Before presenting what I see as proof that Indians burned forests extensively and frequently, I should explain why I believe that all eastern woodlands were regularly burned. It is based upon the "culture area concept." Anthropologists have shown that practices typical of part of a culture area are usually present throughout the entire culture area. When the samples are widely scattered, as they are in the case of woodland burning, over a region of uniform environment and cultural similarity, the samples are assumed to represent the whole area. The eastern woodlands culture area has been divided into subcultures on the basis of local specialization of some elements. However, vegetation burning does not appear to have varied within or between subculture areas but rather corresponds to the basic technological traits for the culture area as a whole.

It would be expected, in any event, from our knowledge that peoples within a limited area and possessing a common basic culture respond similarly to a uniform environment. Although there are some variations in the forest types of the eastern United States, from the point of view of Indian adjustment to living in them, their uniformities far outweigh their differences. References to Indian burning are well scattered, although more numerous, or at least better reported, in some regions such as Virginia. That some sections should be represented more fully than others results solely, I believe, from the chances that determine historical reporting and subsequent summarizing in the available literature. We can reasonably assume that over the whole area burning was as common as in the best-reported area.

Records of Indian burning in the eastern woodlands date back to the time of the first English settlement along the Atlantic sea coast. Fourteen authors can be cited to substantiate the view that the Virginia Indians set fire to vegetation to drive game; improve the pasturage for game; clear brush so that game could be more easily seen; increase wild seed production; increase yield of berries and other wild vegetable food; clear brush to make seeds, nuts, and berries more easily accessible; clear aged forest to allow for early succession growth; clear land for planting crops; keep woods open to facilitate travel; and, finally, by simply allowing campfires to escape and ignite surrounding vegetation.

Maxwell (358) brought together most of the information on Virginia, and I quote from him extensively. Flannery (174, p. 14), Friederici (185, pp. 91–96), Swanton (501, pp. 317–20), and Birket-Smith (46, pp. 160–61, 330–31) also present several references to Indian fires in the woodlands. In 1953 Gordon M. Day assembled 150 titles, many concerned with fire, for his excellent article on "The Indian as an Ecological Factor in the Northeastern Forest."

Our earliest reference for this area is dated 1609 and was written by Spelman (470, p. cvii):

> Ther maner of ther Huntinge is thiss [where] they meett sum 2 or 300 togither and hauinge ther bowes and arrows and euery one with a fier sticke in ther hand they besett a great thikett round about, which dunn euery one sett fier on the ranke grass gandg which ye Deare seinge fleeth from ye fier, and the menn cumminge in by a litell and little incloseth ther game in a narrow roome, so as with ther Bowes and arrowes they kill them at ther pleasuer takinge ther skinns which is the greatest thinge they desier, and sume flesh for their prouision.

Strachey (499) in 1612 and Captain John Smith in 1624 also described hunting with fire. Smith (467, vol. 1, p. 365) wrote: "At their huntings in the deserts they are commonly two or three hundred together. Having found the Deere, they environ them with many fires, and betwixt the fires they place themselves. And some take their stands in the midsts. The Deere being thus feared by the fires, and their voyces, they chase them so long within that circle, that many times they kill 6, 8, 10, or 15 at a hunting."

A reference to burning in order to maintain pasturage and keep woods open for travel comes from Alvord and Bidgood (11, pp. 47–48) as reported by the first English travelers into the Virginia piedmont in 1650:

> The Virginia piedmont across which their journey took them is a rolling or hilly country sloping gently to the east. At the time when the explorers entered this practically unknown land, it offered a pleasant variety of forest and grass lands, intersected by narrow meadow and swamp tracts in the stream "bottoms." Here, as almost everywhere, the Indians followed the custom of burning over the country in the fall, so that the level uplands and long gentle slopes were kept as open grazing country, pasture for deer, elk and buffalo. The poorer, stonier, and steeper ground was covered with forests of deciduous growth, and the bottoms, where not cleared by the Indians for their fields, were covered with a practically impenetrable tangle of well-nigh tropical luxuriance.

Michel (362, pp. 41–42) mentioned the "openness of the forest" of Virginia in 1701 and then described the fire drive, which "helps not a little to clear the forests and pastures." Beverley (40) described encircling game with fire in Virginia in 1722. Lawson (305) reported that the Shawnees used fire for hunting in the Carolinas in 1718, and Brickell (60, p. 361) described hunting in North Carolina in 1737 as follows:

When they are disposed to hunt in the Woods, they generally go out in great Numbers together, and several Days Journies from home. They always begin these Hunting matches at the approach of Winter, when the Leaves, are fallen from the trees, and become dry, or when Skins and Furs are best in Season. It is then they burn the Woods, by setting fire to the withered Leaves, Bent and dry Grass, which they do with matches made of the Black Moss that hangs on the Trees, which is sometimes above six Feet long. This Moss when dead becomes black (though of an Ash colour before) and will then hold Fire as well as the best Match in Europe. In places where this Moss is not to be found (as towards the Mountains and Heads of the Rivers) they make Lentels of the bark of Cypress, which serves as well.

Thus they frequently leave their Houses and retire into the Woods for four or five Months together, viz. November, December, January, February, and March, at which time the Skins are in Season, and set Fire to the Woods for many Miles together to drive out the Deer and other Game into small Necks of Lands, and other places where they fix their Guards, by which means they kill and destroy what they please, especially such as strive to escape the Fire and get through the passes they have made for that purpose.

Catesby (76a) also mentioned the Indian custom of periodic burning of vegetation by Indians in Carolinas in 1731. The history of the survey of the dividing line between Virginia and North Carolina in 1728–29, by William Byrd (71), is of especial interest because it documents Indian carelessness with campfires, as well as adding a note regarding hunting with fire. Of southwestern Virginia he wrote:

The atmosphere was so smoky all around us that the mountains were again grown invisible. This happened not from haziness of the sky, but from the firing of the woods by the Indians, for we were now near the route the northern savages take when they go out to war with the Catawbas and other southern nations. On their way, the fires they make in their camps are left burning, which catching the dry leaves which lie near, soon put the adjacent woods in a flame.

Sometime after that another fire was observed of which he spoke:

As we marched along we were alarmed at the sight of a great fire which showed itself to the northward. . . . [W]e could not see a tree of any bigness standing within our prospect, and the reason why fire makes such a havoc in these lonely parts is this: The Woods are not there burnt every year, as they generally are among the inhabitants, but the dead leaves and trash of many years are generally heaped up together, which being at length kindled by the Indians that happened to pass that way, furnish fuel for a conflagration that carries all before it.

Anthropologists who have studied the southern part of the eastern woodlands have confirmed the reports of earlier writers. Fowke (184, p. 72) said the valleys of the James and Potomac were burned each fall "to prevent timber from growing and thus diminishing the area of their hunting ground." Speck (468a, p. 23) describes the game drive by means of fire of the Yuchis, who lived along the Georgia-South Carolina border. Swanton (501, p. 693), Birket-Smith (45, p. 213, and 46, pp. 160–161), Day, and Flannery (174, p. 14) made general statements to the effect that Indians of the Atlantic Coast, especially Algonquins, used fire to drive game. Birket-Smith and Day refer to the southern and northern Atlantic states.

The direct evidence for Indian burning of forests of the northeastern United States is as strong as that for the southeastern. We are dependent, as in the South, upon early historic accounts, for the Iroquois and Algonquins of north Atlantic States were nearly all displaced before modern ethnographers studied them. The earliest, an anonymous account in "Brief Relations of New England, 1607–1622" (62, p. 283), tells of hunting deer "by making of several fires, and setting the Countrey with people, to force them into the Sea . . . and then there are others that attend them in their Boates with Bowes and weapons of severall kindes, wherewith they slay and take at their pleasure."

Morton's (375, pp. 36–37) description of New English Canaan of 1632 indicates the extent of burning and a reason, other than hunting, for setting fires:

> The Savalges are accustomed, to set fire of the Country in all places where they come; and to burne it, twice a yeare, viz at the Spring, and the fall of the leafe. The reason that mooves them to doe so, is because it would other wise be so overgrowne with underweedes, that it would be all a coppice wood, and the people would not be able in any wise to passe through the Country out of a beaten path.
>
> The meanes that they do it with, is with certaine minerals stones, that they carry about them: in baggs made for that purpose of the skinnes of little beastes which they convert into good tether; carrying in the same a peece of touch wood (very excellent for that purpose of their owne making). These minnerall stones they have from the Piquenteenes (which is to the Southward of all the plantations in New England) by trade and trafficke with those people.

The burning of the grasse destroyes the under-woods, and so score-cheth the elder trees, that it shrinkes them, and hinders their grouth very much: So that hee that will looke to finde large trees, and good tymber, must not depend upon the help of a wooden prospect to finde them on the upland ground; but must seeke for them, (as I and others have done) in the lower grounds where the grounds are wett when the Country is fired: by reason of the snow water that remaines there for a time, untill the Sunne by continuance of that hath exhaled the vapoures of the earth, and dried up those places, where the fire (by reason of the moisture) can have no power to doe them any hurt: and if he would endevoure to finde out any goodly Cedars, hee must not seeke for them on the higher grounds, but make his inquest for them in the vallies, for the Salvages by this Custome of theirs, have spoiled all the rest: for this custome hath bin continued from the beginninge.

And least their firing of the Country in this manner; should be an occasion of damnifying us, and indaingering our habitations; wee our selves have used carefully about the same times; to observe the winds and fire the grounds about our owne habitations, to prevent the Dammage that might happen by any neglect thereof, if the fire should come neere those howses in our absence.

For when the fire is once kindled, it dilates and spreads it selfe as well against, as with the winde; burning continually night and day, untill a shower of raine falls to quench it.

And this custome of firing the Country is the means to make it pass-able, and by that meanes the trees growe here, and there as in our parks: and makes the Country very beautiful and commodious.

Wood (571, pp. 16–17), telling of conditions in Massachusetts in 1634, mentioned the rapidity of growth of underbrush after burning had stopped:

And whereas it is generally conceived, that the woods grow so thicke, that there is no more cleare ground than is hewed out by labour of man; it is nothing so; in many places, divers Acres being cleare, so that one may ride a hunting in most places of the land, if he will venture himselfe for being lost: there is no underwood saving in swamps, and low grounds that are wet, in which the English get Osiers, and Hasles, and such small wood as is for their use. Of these swamps, some be ten, some twenty, some thirty miles long, being preserved by the wetnesse of the soil wherein they grow; for it being the custome of the Indians to burne the wood in Novem-ber, when the grasse is withered, and leaves dryed, it consumes all the underwood, and rubbish which otherwise would over-grow the Country, making it unpassable, and spoile their much affected hunting: so that by this means in those places where the Indians inhabit, there is scarce a bush or bramble, or any cumbersome underwood to bee seene in the more champion ground. Small wood growing in these places where the fire could not come, is preserved. In some places where the Indians dyed of the Plague some fourteene yeares ague, is much underwood, as in the mid way betwixt Wessaguscus and Plimouth, because it thath not been burned; certaine Rivers stopping the fire from comming to cleare that place of the countrey, hath made it unuse-full and troublesome to travels thorow, in so much that it is called ragged plaine, because it teares and rents the Loathes of them that passe.

De Vries (134, pp. 99–100) told of smelling smoke far off the coast of Delaware on December 2, 1633, as a result of forest fires set by Indians "in order to hunt," and Winthrop (565, vol. 1, p. 38) described the dangers from "burning grass" in Massachusetts in 1630. Van der Donck (517, vol. 1, p. 150) gave three different reasons for Indians setting fires in New York in 1656. These are as follows:

The Indians have a yearly custom (which some of our Christians have also adopted) of burning the woods, plains and meadows in the fall of the year, when the leaves have fallen, and when the grass and vegetable sub-stances are dry. Those places which are then passed over are fired in the spring in April. This practice is named by us and the Indians, "bush burn-ing," which is done for several reasons; first, to render hunting easier, as the bush and vegetable growth renders the walking difficult for the hunter, and the crackling of the dry substances betrays him and fright-ens away the game. Secondly, to thin out and clear the woods of all dead substances and grass, which grow better the ensuing spring. Thirdly, to circumscribe and enclose the game within the lines of the fire, when it is more easily taken, and also, because the game is more easily tracked over the burned parts of the woods.

Lindstrom (321, p. 213) gave a good description of the use of fire to encircle and kill "a great multitude of all kinds of animals" in Delaware in 1691, while Loskiel (334), speaking of Delaware for 1788, and Kalm (275), speaking of New Jersey for 1749, described woods burning to improve growth of pasture, indicating that the early settlers in the Middle Atlantic states continued the Indian custom of burning forests to keep them open and thus maintained their value for grazing. Kalm said that "the govern-ment of Pennsylvania have lately published an edict, which prohibits this burning; nevertheless every one did as he pleased, and this prohibition met with general censure." Burnaby (70, p. 750) in 1760 reported that laws against forest fires existed in "New England, New York or New Jersey; a restriction absolutely necessary . . . as a check upon that very destructive practice taken from the Indians, for fire-hunting . . . [such] fires did not only contract itself inwardly, but dilated also outwardly, and sometimes continued burning for several weeks till rain, or some accidental circumstances put it out."

The quotations above establish beyond question that the Indians of the Atlantic seaboard used fire for hunting and also to keep the forests open. To strengthen the deduction that such was a general culture trait for all Indians of the eastern woodlands culture area are statements from Weld (545) and Dwight (150), written in 1800 and 1822 respectively, concerning burning over the county in the vicinity of Buffalo, New York. Dwight (p. 60) says, "The object of these conflagrations was to produce fresh and sweet pasture, for the purpose of alluring the deer, to the spots, on which they had been kindled."

Morgan (371), the first ethnographer to study carefully all aspects of the life and customs of an American Indian tribe, wrote in 1851 that it was a general Iroquois practice to set fire to the woods to drive game. Another anthropologist, Willoughby (560), wrote as follows:

> We are apt to picture the country when first seen by Europeans as thickly covered with primeval forests and as having few open spaces and fields. This was probably true of the more remote uninhabited sections, but does not apply to all tribal lands, especially those of the southern half of New England. These were burnt in the fall and spring for the purpose of killing the undergrowth and keeping the fields and woodlands open. It was principally in the swamps where the fire did not penetrate that nature took its course.

The accounts of forest burning west of the Allegheny Mountains start with Hennepin's (239, vol. 1, pp. 145–47). This French missionary-explorer and companion of LaSalle described how, in 1683, Indians hunted with fire near the present Indiana-Michigan border.

> Having past through great Marshes, we found a vast Plain, on which nothing grows but only some Herbs, which were dry at that time, and burnt, because the bliami's set them on fire every Year, in their hunting wild Bulls [bison], as I shall mention anon. . . . When the Savages discover a great Number of those Beasts together, they likewise assemble their whole Tribe to encompass the Bulls, and then set on fire the dry Herbs about them, except in some places, which they leave free; and therein lay themselves in Ambuscade. The Bulls seeing the Flame round about them,

run away through those passages where they see no fire; and there fall into the Hands of the Savages, who by these Means will kill sometimes above six-score in a day.

The next reference dates from over a century later, 1819, after pioneers from the English colonies had established themselves in the area. Of the general region between the Alleghenies and the Mississippi, Wells (546, p. 335) wrote:

> The Indians . . . burn the woods, not ordinarily for the purpose of taking or catching game . . . but for many other advantages attending that practice. If the woods be not burned as usual, the hunter finds it impossible to kill the game, which, alarmed at the great noise made in walking through the dry grass and leaves, flee in all directions at his approach. Also the Indians travel much during the winter, from one village to another, and . . . hunting . . . which becomes extremely painful and laborious from the quantity of briers, vines, grass, etc. To remedy these and many other inconveniences, even the woods were originally burned so as to cause prairies. . . .

Mr. Bourne (54, p. 32) of Chillicothe, Ohio, also wrote in 1819: "The fires were . . . kindled by the Indians for the convenience of traveling . . . to enable them to approach game. . . . Also to insure a good crop of grass for the next summer."

The early settlers of Ohio seem to have continued the Indian custom of using fire for hunting, for we find the statement below in Finley's *Life among the Indians,* published in 1857 (171, p. 384–85):

> These plains are, for the most part, thin land, and interspersed throughout with bogs, or low, wet places, and often covered with water for half a mile. Our traveling now being more pleasant, my friends conversed with me about the country, and I learned that this tract of land, lying between Portage river and the Maumee, which was all plains, interspersed with groves of timber, covered a large extent of country, and was used every fall for the ring hunt. This is made by setting fire to the leaves and grass in a circle of fifteen or twenty miles; and the fire drives all the game into a pound, where they are shot down in immense quantities. Sometimes as many as five hundred deer have killed on one of these occasions. The raccoons climb the trees in the groves of timber, and are caught in great abundance. One of our party said he had killed as many as fifty in one day. These are most generally shot with the bow and arrow. The product of the hunt is equally divided among the individuals who compose the party.

Shaler (450, p. 324), writing of "the relative humid districts of Michigan" in 1891, said:

> The native Indians of this part of the country were in the habit, through carelessness or design, of firing the prairie grasses every spring. Such fires swept like a whirlwind over the plains and were rarely interrupted in their ravages by broad rivers or by swamps. They would extend into the margins of the forest, and if the vegetable mold was not very retentive of moisture would result in the destruction of all young trees in the wood. In pine woods such fires would destroy all the vegetation with which they came in contact.

An entry by McClure (345, p. 59) in his diary regarding eastern Ohio from 1748 to 1820 confirms that Indians of the interior burned for the same reasons and with the same effect as those along the Atlantic seaboard. "The woods were clear from underbrush, and the oaks and black walnut and other timber do not grow very compact, and there is scarcely anything to incommode a travler in riding, almost in any direction, in the woods of the Ohio. The Indians have been in the practice of burning over the ground, that they may have the advantage of seeing game at a distance among the trees. We saw this day several deer and flocks of Turkies."

Although Indians had been driven away from Kentucky about fifty years before the territory was settled, Shaler (450, p. 324) quotes Senator Underwood, "who was a most intelligent observer," regarding the "habit which the aborigines had of firing the grasses in the open ground."

Flint (176, p. 284), who visited in Kentucky in 1818, also believed "the Indians . . . set fire to dried grass and other vegetables with the design of facilitating their hunting." Hussey (265, p. 8), writing in the Kentucky Geological Survey in 1884, supported this idea with the statement that "[i]t is well understood that the aborigines of this country were accustomed to burn over the surface of the prairies." Two references to interior tribes in the southeastern woodland area complete the review of direct evidence about the aboriginal practice of burning forests. The earliest, published in 1849, comes from the famous British naturalist Sir Charles Lyell (343, vol. 2, p. 69), reporting upon his *Second Visit to the United States of America*. Speaking of the vicinity of Tuscaloosa, Alabama, he said: "These hills were covered with longleaved pines, and the large proportion they bear to hardwoods is said to have been increased by the Indian practice of burning the grass."

The other reference is part of a myth recorded by the ethnologist James Mooney (368, pp. 317, 468) and printed in 1900. The fact that burning leaves in the fall is described in the tribal folklore suggests it was an ancient custom. The myth contains the statement: "When the Cherokee went out in the fall, according to their custom, to burn the leaves off from the mountains in order to get the chestnuts on the ground, they were never safe, for the old witch was always on the lookout, and as soon as she saw the smoke rise she knew there were Indians there and sneaked up to surprise one alone." And, in a footnote, he added: "To burn the leaves— The burning of the fallen leaves in the autumn, in order to get at the nuts upon the ground below, is still practiced by the white mountaineers of the southern Alleghenies. The line of fire slowly creeping up the mountain side upon a dark night is one of the picturesque sights of that picturesque country."

Even were no additional evidence available of burning eastern woodlands, most scientists would have to conclude that it was a practice characteristic of the whole region. The direct statements presented indicate that the great tribes of the major linguistic and cultural groups—Algonquin, Iroquois, Muskogee—east of the Mississippi River regularly set fire to the vegetation and allowed the fires to burn over the landscape. In spite of the strength of this direct evidence, indirect evidence that fire had played a frequent and decisive role in the eastern woodlands is even stronger. Although many early observers indicated that they fully appreciated the great importance of fire, as did Lyell (343) in the quotation above, it appears to be a fashion of recent years to ignore or minimize the role of fire, especially man-made fires, in determining the type of forests discovered by early European explorers and to discount its continuing influence.

The early English explorers sensed what has been established by modern science. Many of the writings of the first settlers show that they recognized that the whole eastern woodlands region was perfectly suited by soil, temperature, and moisture for the luxuriant and rank growth of trees and brush. With few exceptional spots, wherever trees are not kept back by cultivation or other human activity, a veritable jungle quickly takes over the land. But the Europeans did not find on the eastern coast of the United States a thick forest filled with underbrush, characteristic of an untouched forest produced by adequate rainfall. In the introduction of his study of burning by Indians in Virginia Maxwell (358, p. 37) had this to say:

> The Indian is by nature an incendiary, and forest burning was the Virginia Indian's besetting sin. The few trees and poles which he took for use, and the thousand destroyed to make his cornfields, were a small drain on the forests in comparison with the millions which his woods fires consumed.

It is not known how long he had been burning the valleys and mountains before the white men came to Virginia, but the custom was general at the time of the first settlement, and it was, apparently, of long standing, though there is no positive evidence of it, that the lesson of destruction was being learned from western Indians who, by the agency of fire, were changing forests into treeless prairies. If any considerable regions of Virginia, except swamps too damp to burn, had escaped repeated visitations by fire, the early explorers failed to make note of them. Complete destruction of forests by fire had already occurred over tracts aggregating hundreds of square miles, and undergrowth had been injured or destroyed almost everywhere in the regions early explored. In many localities the mature trees alone remained, and they were frequently so thinned and depleted that the woods resembled parks rather than forests, as is abundantly set forth in contemporaneous writings. Over very large tracts, at the period of discovery, the forests had apparently reached the last stage before their fall. No small wood was coming on to take the place of the old trees, and with the death of the mature timber many regions would have been treeless.

A writer (Philip Alexander Bruce [66]) on Virginia's economic history sums up the evidence contained in the early records by saying: "Freedom from undergrowth was one of the most notable features of the original woods of Virginia."

Captain John Smith (467, vol. 1, p. 365), writing in 1624, provided the first witnessed report: "Near their habitations is but little small wood or old trees on the ground, by reason of their burning of them for fire, so that a man may gallop a horse among these woods anyway except when the creeks or rivers shall hinder."

The open nature of the woods of the Virginia coastal plain were noted by several other early visitors to the area. In 1612 Strachey (499) declared that "at no point was it impossible for horse and foot to pass" and that horses could be ridden at full speed among the trees without risk of collision with the trunks. Andrew White (548, p. 18), traveling up the Potomac River in 1633, also described the absence of forest understory: "On each bank of solid earth rise beautiful groves of trees, not choked up with an undergrowth of brambles and bushes, but as if laid out by hand, in a manner so open that you might drive a four-horse chariot in the midst of the trees."

In 1649 William Bullock (69, p. 3) published a similar impression following a trip to Virginia: "The body of the country from the rivers is generally woody, but not like ours in England, for they are so clear from underwood that one may be seen above a mile and a half in the woods, and the trees stand at that distance that you may drive carts or coaches between the thickest of them, being clear from boughs a great height. Strawberries and grapes grow there in abundance."

The abundance of wild strawberries is also an indication of the openness of the woods, because strawberries do not grow in woods sufficiently dense to shut out most sunlight. Ralph Hamar in 1614 was also impressed by the abundance of berries (cited in 358, p. 90), as were several other writers. Williams (559) in 1650 left the following graphic description of Virginia wild berries. "No shrub or underwood chokes your passage, and in its season your foot can hardly direct itself where it will not be dyed in the blood of large and delicious strawberries."

Exploration of the interior of Virginia was not undertaken for almost a half-century after the settlement of the coastal plain, which was about a hundred miles wide. When the English did venture into the hills and mountains, "they found that the Indians had been as industrious with their forest fires there as in the lower country" (358, p. 91). Lederer's account (307, p. 35), written in August 1670, is one of the first reports of the back country: "We traveled through the Savannah among vast herds of red and fallow deer which stood gazing at us, and a little after we came to the promontories of spurs of the Appalachian mountains."

Michel (362, p. 41) in 1701 attributed Indian "fire hunting" to the open forests he observed: "The forests are very convenient to ride or hunt it. The trees are far apart, with no undergrowth on the ground, so that one can ride anywhere on horseback. The game is easily discovered, because of the openness of the forest." Beverley, a historian, while not an eyewitness himself, doubtless talked with persons who had been, for he wrote in 1722 of the conditions in the mountains of Virginia at the time of exploration (40, p. 62): "They found large level plains, and fine savannahs three or four miles wide, in which were an infinite quantity of turkeys, deer . . . and buffaloes. . . ."

Fontaine's *Journal* (180, p. 271) of 1716, regarding a region just east of the Blue Ridge in southwestern Virginia, indicates that similar open grasslands were present there: "We saw . . . several fine tracts of land, and plains called savannahs, which lie along by the riverside, much like our low meadow lands in England. There is neither tree nor shrub that grows upon these plains, nothing but good grass. . . . These places are not miry, but good, firm ground." In 1910 Maxwell (358, p. 94) added his own views regarding the reasons for the "savannahs."

The promptness with which forests take possession of cleared ground in Virginia is proof that the meadows and savannas described by Lederer,

Beverley, Fontaine, and others had not been long exempt from periodic fires that kept seedling trees out. In Virginia the present-day woods quickly spring up at the first opportunity, and the following extract from Beverley (40, p. 108) shows that they did the same thing two hundred years ago: "Wood grows at every man's door so fast that after it has been cut down it will in seven years' time grow up again from seed to substantial firewood, and in eighteen or twenty years it will come to be very good board timber."

Of special interest for an understanding of the role of fire in the eastern woodlands region and for a fair evaluation of its influence on the prairies and plains of the Middle West is the Shenandoah Valley. Difference in climate between the Shenandoah and the area east of the Blue Ridge is indicated by Shantz and Zon (454, fig. 2) by two subdivisions of their southern hardwood forest. The Shenandoah is included within the chestnut-chestnut oak-yellow poplar region. Virginia east of Blue Ridge is designated as part of the oak-pine forest region. Livingston and Shreve (327, p. 258) specify the climatic difference by the summer precipitation-evaporation ratio, which they consider an extremely important determinant of vegetation. The P/E ratio at Lynchburg, Virginia, is 0.87, while it is 1.24 at Norfolk, Virginia. On the basis of present vegetation and moisture available for plant growth as expressed by the precipitation-evaporation ratio, the Shenandoah is somewhat dryer and would support less rank growth than the coastal region of Virginia. By the same indices, however, the Shenandoah Valley has an excellent climate for forest growth.

Maxwell (358, pp. 94–96), recognizing the special significance of the Shenandoah Valley, devoted a separate section of his report to it. The following is from the introduction to his sub-section entitled "Treeless Tracts in the Shenandoah":

It is one of the finest regions in the United States, and it was doubtless a favorite hunting ground for Indians since time immemorial. No portion of Virginia was more terribly burned. In some parts of the valley, the lower portion in particular, Indian fires had done their worst before white men came.

The exact date of the region's first exploration, if Spotswood's was not the first, is not known. The falls of the Potomac, fourteen miles above Washington, seem to have been the limit of exploration about the year 1700. The Shenandoah Valley is known to have been a highway for Indians traveling north or south, and camps of natives were in the valley, at certain times at least, until after settlements by white men began, about 1730; but the valley probably had no resident tribes subsequent to the Iroquois conquest about 1672. The worst burning doubtless occurred before that time. An area now occupied in part by the three counties—Frederick, Berkeley, and Jefferson—was treeless. The burnt lands extended across the present State of Maryland, and into Pennsylvania, and in those States were long called "The Barrens," and occasionally are still so called, on account of the stunted timber which once grew there. The area of the treeless region in the Shenandoah Valley exceeded 1,000 square miles in one body. Grass covered the region except for an occasional fringe of trees along the streams where fires would not burn. When the Indians no longer set their fires, trees began to creep back, and the early settlers were obliged to clear away the young growth to open their farms.

In W. H. Foote's *Sketch of Virginia* (181), he says: "A large part of the valley from the headsprings of the Shenandoah to the Potomac or the Maryland line, a distance of about 150 miles, embracing ten counties, was covered with prairies abounding in tall grass, and these, with scattered forests, were filled with pea vines. Much of the beautiful timber in the valley has grown since the emigrants chose their habitations."

Although Shaler (450, p. 324) in 1891 mentioned the fact that a large prairie formerly covered the Shenandoah Valley and said it "had been deforested by Indians, probably by means of fire," it is no longer so marked on vegetation maps, and the fact that it was a prairie is not now recognized. Fowke (184, p. 72), three years after Shaler, in 1894, and as part of an archaeological report, further added: "These various tribes hunted and fought over all this region. Each year, before going into winter quarters, they set fire to the dry grass in order to prevent timber from growing and thus diminishing the area of their hunting grounds. For this reason the country was almost devoid of trees, except along the streams and to some extent in the mountains, the forests which now exist having sprung up since Spotswood's day [1716]."

The greater extent of the Shenandoah grassland resulted from its topography, which allowed fires to spread more widely without interruption by streams or elevations. The example is clear. Given the appropriate topography, fires set by Indians can reduce a forest to a grassland, even when climate and soil are admirably suited to forest growth. If moisture is sufficient, trees will quickly reclaim grasslands when fires are no longer set.

The indirect evidence is the presence of "lower" vegetation, in this case grasses, occupying land that can easily support trees. There is no doubt that the human factor was the critical determining element that made open woods and extensive grasslands in Virginia where natural conditions favored dense woody growth. Thus finding such open woods and prairies is indirect evidence of Indian burning.

Early references to the northern woodland vegetation are not as numerous as for Virginia; nonetheless they do add to our knowledge of the effect of Indian burning of forests. Lindstrom (321, pp. 213–14) had this to say of Delaware in 1691: "There indeed grows a great deal of high grass, which reaches above the knees of a man. . . . There is also no thickly grown forest but trees stand far apart, as if they were planted."

Following this, Lindstrom described the Indian fire-hunt at the "time of the year the grass . . . is as dry as hay." Burnaby (70, p. 750) gave this description of the Indian use of fire to drive game: "The trees included within the circle, although not absolutely burnt down, were so dried and injured, that they never vegetated any more; and as the fire did not only contract itself inwardly, but dilated also outwardly, and sometimes continued burning for several weeks till rain, or some accidental circumstance put it out; it is incredible what injury and devastation it occasioned in the woods."

Weld (545, p. 317) in 1800, speaking of western New York state, reported that various "opinions have been entertained respecting the deficiency of trees on these extended tracts of lands in the midst of a country that abounds so generally with wood." Regarding the same area, Dwight (150, vol. 4, pp. 57, 60–63), twenty-two years later, not only confirmed the presence of extensive grasslands in the forests at that time but afforded a very convincing argument regarding their origin, which I quote:

> The grounds are also termed "Openings"; as being in a great degree destitute of forests. . . . These grounds are of a singular and interesting appearance. The trees, growing on them, are almost universally oaks. . . .
>
> The origin of the peculiar appearance of these grounds is probably this. The Indians annually, and sometimes oftener, burned such parts of the North American forests, as they found sufficiently dry. In every such case the fuel consists chiefly of the fallen leaves; which are rarely dry enough for an extensive combustion, except on uplands. . . . Of this nature, were always the oak, and yellow-pine grounds; which were therefore usually subjected to an annual conflagration. The beech and maple grounds were commonly too wet to be burned. Hence on these grounds the vegetable mold is from six inches to a foot in depth, having been rarely or never consumed by fire; while on the oak and pine grounds it often does not exceed an inch. That this is the effect of fire only, and not of any diversity in the nature of the trees, is evident from the fact, that in moist soils, where the fire cannot penetrate, the mold is as deep on the oak, as on the maple grounds. The mold is combustible; and by an intense fire is wholly consumed.

The object of these conflagrations was to produce fresh and sweet pasture, for the purpose of alluring the deer, to the spots, on which they had been kindled. Immediately after the fires, a species of grass springs up, sometimes called fire grass, because it usually succeeds a conflagration. Whether it is a peculiar species of grass, I am unable to say not having seen it since the days of childhood. Either from its nature, or from the efficacy of the fire, it is remarkably sweet, and eagerly sought by deer. All the underwood is at the same time consumed; so that these animals are easily discovered at considerable distances, a thing impracticable where the forests have not been burned. You will remember, that to supply himself with timber for a weekwam [sic], and with wood for fuel, was the only use, which an Indian could make of a forest; and that the earth furnished him with nothing but a place for his residence, his garden, and his game. While, therefore, he destroyed both the forest and the soil, he converted them to the most profitable use for himself. . . .

Thus, in time, these plains were disforested, to the degree, in which we now see them; and were gradually converted into pasture grounds. It ought to be observed, that they were in all probability burnt over, for ages after they were disforested, I presume, down to a very late period. In a dry season of autumn, the grass would furnish ample fuel for this purpose.

That this is the true cause of the singular appearance of these plains, can scarcely be doubted, when the following facts are compared.

That the Indians customarily burned, every year, such parts of the forests, as were sufficiently dry to admit of conflagration:

That these were the only grounds, which except in rare cases, could be successfully burned:

That, wherever they have been for a considerable length of time free from fires, the young trees are now springing up in great numbers; and will soon change these open grounds into forests, if left to the course of nature. Such, particularly, is the fact on the first of these plains, near the Genesee River and still more strikingly in Bloomfield and Charleston, where the fires have been longer intermitted:

That in various places the marks of the fire are now visible on the trunks of the remaining trees; particularly near the ground. These marks I suppose to have been impressed at a comparatively late period, and by fires kindled in the grass:

That on the borders of these very plains, trees, of exactly the same species, are now growing in great numbers, and in the usual regular succession, of all ages and sizes, within the nearest neighbourhood of those on the plains; and that this diversity, perfectly explicable on this supposition, is inexplicable on any other:

That there can be no account given, why the vegetable should be so thinly spread over these plains, except that it has been continually consumed by fire, since it exists in the usual quantity in the forests, composed of the same trees, on moister ground, bordering these plains on every side:

And, that all the phenomena over, if I mistake not, are explained by the cause alleged.

Should it be asked, why there are no such grounds in New-England, in which country also Indians lived, and hunted: I answer,

1st. The New-England oak, and yellow pine forests, have not been subjected to fire for many years.

2dly. No accounts of their ancient appearance have come down to us.

3dly. The whole of Southern New-England, except the mountains, and swamps, was almost wholly covered with oak and pine forests. All, therefore, being capable of any annual and easy conflagration, there was no inducement to burn any single part frequently. Yet, beside the well-known fact, that the Indians kindled the forests yearly for the above named purpose, there are now remaining many proofs of such fires.

4thly. That within my own remembrance there were, in the township of Northampton, spots, desolated in a similar manner. These, although laid waste in an inferiour degree, were yet so far destroyed, as to be left in a great measure naked. Now they are completely covered with a thick forest. I suppose these grounds, however, to have been frequently burnt by the English inhabitants; who foolishly followed this Indian custom, in order to provide feed for their cattle in the spring.

These plains have, until very lately, been considered as of little value, when compared with the maple and beech land; which here is called by way of distinction from them, timbered land. From numerous experiments, made on them within a short time, it appears however, that the wheat, sown on them, not only grows luxuriantly, and yields a rich crop, but is heavier, by several pounds in the bushel than that, which grows on the maple lands. It is also whiter, and better; and commands therefore, a higher price. It is hardly necessary to observe, that these facts have rapidly raised the plains in the public estimation.

The eastern section of the woodlands cultural and vegetation zone, being settled earlier, stimulated fewer articles "explaining" the presence of the "barrens," "prairies," or "openings" in what was clearly a potential forest environment than did the western section. Most of the grasslands of the Atlantic coastal plain and Appalachian piedmont had disappeared, becoming either cultivated fields or forests, before pioneers from that area migrated over the mountains to establish new homes in Ohio, Kentucky, and Tennessee. The extensive areas without trees greatly impressed the first settlers west of the mountains because they did not know that the forest region they were leaving had formerly been interspersed by similar large savannas. A century had removed from the landscape, and from the memories of the original farmer-families who supplied the vanguard of migrants, all traces of the open woods and extensive grasslands described by the first English observers of the Atlantic seaboard.

Professor Carl O. Sauer in his study of the *Geography of the Pennyroyal* (434, pp. 123–30) for the Kentucky Geological Survey in 1927 convincingly summarizes the evidence indicating that the "barrens" of Kentucky, which seemed so strangely out of place to the earliest settlers, were in reality the result of fires set by Indians. Sauer (434, p. 123) concludes that the word "barrens," as used in Kentucky, was used as "the result of a dilemma of language rather than as a judgment of fertility." "Barrens," the English word that gained currency in Kentucky, was really synonymous with "prairie," the French word used in Illinois to designate the large treeless tracts encountered in these areas. Sauer cites Filson's map of 1784 and Elihu Barker's map of 1792 and quotes from the report of 1797 by Gilbert Imlay, land commissioner in the "Back Settlements," to establish the fact that the first trained observers in Kentucky recognized and reported that the "barrens" were not treeless because of the sterility of the soil. Imlay (268, p. 35) mentions "extensive plains, which stretch upwards of one hundred and fifty miles in a south-west course, and end only when they join the mountainous country." The overall size was about the same as the Shenandoah Savanna, mentioned above.

Sauer (434, p. 125) gives credit to Brown, who wrote in the *Western Gazetteer,* for providing the following: "In 1817 the grassy lands south of Russellville, fifteen by ninety miles in extent, were stated to be: 'prairies . . . rich, finely watered, and . . . sufficient to maintain an immense population.'"

Sauer also quotes Timothy Flint (178, p. 347), who reported in 1832 on the extensive "barrens" between the Rolling Fork of the Salt River and the Green River, and "still larger tracts" between the Green and Cumberland Rivers, on which, Flint said, "the soil is generally good."

Smaller than the Kentucky grasslands, those discovered in Ohio were nonetheless the cause of wonder and speculation. In 1818, in the first volume of the *American Journal of Science,* Atwater (19, p. 117) describes the seven-mile-long, three-mile-wide Pickaway Plains of south central Ohio as being: "elevated above the Sciote river, [and] almost perfectly level, [the plains] are covered with a great quantity of grass, some weeds and plumbushes; and in the most elevated places, there were a few trees."

Atwater also mentioned the Sandusky Plains of north-central Ohio, saying that prairies and "barrens" were present in all states west of the Allegheny Mountains. He reiterated that "barrens are found on a level country," which he took as evidence that their treelessness resulted from the soil's having recently been under the waters of Lake Erie. Atwater's article stimulated several others in the *American Journal of Science*. The first, by Wells (546, pp. 331–37), appeared in a later number of the same volume. Wells identified himself as a surveyor who has "often visited and observed with attention . . . prairies on the Allegheny mountains, in the states of Ohio, Indiana, and Illinois, and . . . in the prairie country of Missouri and Mississippi. . . ."

Wells refuted Atwater with topographic and geologic evidence and said prairies "were occasioned by the combustion of vegetables," supporting his view with the statement quoted above. Bourne (54, pp. 30–34) also replied to Atwater, mentioning the grasslands of the same woodland states as Wells and expressing an opinion similar to that of Wells. Bourne wrote: "I think it must be evident to everyone who will view the barrens attentively that their present appearance was caused by fire. . . ."

He supports his conclusion in saying (p. 33):

When the white people settle on the barrens . . . fires are seldom seen, a young growth of trees, healthy and vigorous soon springs up.

That the barrens are frequently burned; and that when the burnings cease, a . . . vigorous growth of trees soon springs up, are facts which can be attested by the most respectable people of this country.

Marsh (355, pp. 136–37) in 1867 expressed a similar view from an analysis made of the same area:

In many parts of the North American States, the first white settlers found extensive tracts of thin woods, of a very parklike character, called "oak openings," from the predominance of different species of that tree upon them. These were the semi-artificial pasture grounds of the Indians, brought into that state, and so kept, by partial clearing, and by the annual burning of the grass. The object of this operation was to attract the deer to the fresh herbage which sprang up after the fire. The oaks bore the annual scorching, at least for a certain time; but if it had been indefinitely continued, they would very probably have been destroyed at last. The soil would have then been much in the prairie condition, and would have needed nothing but grazing for a long succession of years to make the resemblance perfect. That the annual fires alone occasioned the peculiar character of the oak openings, is proved by the fact, that as soon as the

Indians had left the country, young trees of many species sprang up and
grew luxuriantly upon them.

Shaler (450), in his general work on the *Origin and Nature of Soils,*
also rejected the idea that the prairies and barrens of the eastern woodlands were determined by conditions of the soil. Michaux (361, p. 268),
who traveled in America in 1802, made the earliest statement I discovered
in print to the effect that the Kentucky barrens were being overgrown by
forests. He said many were "kept up as meadows by the custom that is still
practiced of annually setting them on fire."

James Flint (176, p. 284), in his *Letters from America, 1818–1820,*
reported similarly:

> In the neighbourhood of Salt River and Green River, in Kentucky, there
> are extensive tracks of barren wastes. Small hazel bushes from two to
> three feet in height abound in these; and the quantity of nuts produced
> exceeds anything of the kind which I have ever seen. The soil of these
> wastes seems to be very similar to that of the adjoining woods; and on
> account of the trees diminishing gradually in size, from the forest toward
> the waste, it is sometimes impossible to discover a line where the one
> stops and other begins. This, together with the fact told by an old settler,
> that some small saplings which stood on his farm twenty years ago, are
> now become tall trees, leads me to adopt the opinion entertained by some,
> that the wastes or barrens owe their characteristic form to the Indians,
> who set fire to dried grass and other vegetables with the design of facili-
> tating their hunting.

Sauer (434) quotes Davenport (129) of 1830, Darby and Dwight
(125) of 1833, and Fisher (173a) of 1853, all in the *Gazetteer,* documenting the fact that the Kentucky barrens were becoming wooded. The lit-
erary naturalist John Muir (376, p. 251), after a walk through the area in
1867, also testified to changes taking place: "Entered a sandy stretch of
black oak called 'Barrens,' many of which were sixty or seventy feet in
height, and are said to have grown since the fires were kept off, forty
years ago."

Early scientific reports confirmed the impressions reported above.
Owen (387, pp. 83–84), in the first volume of the Kentucky Geological
Survey, 1854–55, had this to say about the "barrens":

> At the present time the so called "Barrens" of Kentucky are, to a consid-
> erable extent, timbered with the above varieties of oak, black Hickory,
> and occasionally Butternut, *Juglans cathartica*; Black Walnut, *Juglans
> nigra*; Dogwood, *Cornus florida*; Sugar-tree, *Acer saccharinum.*

The old inhabitants of that part of Kentucky all declare that when the country was first settled it was, for the most part, an open prairie district, with hardly a stick of timber sufficient to make a rail, as far as the eye could reach, where now forests exist of trees of medium growth, obstructing entirely the view.

They generally attribute this change to the wild fires which formerly used to sweep over the whole country, in dry seasons, being now, for the most part, avoided or subdued, if by accident they should break out. No timber appears capable of surviving the scorching effects of such fires, but the thick-barked black-jack oak, which, here and there resisting its ravages, stood solitary monuments of its hardy nature, and the blasting influence of the prairie fire.

It is probable, however, that some other influence contributed to suppress the growth of timber in the Barrens of Kentucky, since wild fires were equally liable to occur in the heavy timbered land of adjacent formations.

Owen suggested that the limestone soils were less favorable to tree growth. In 1884 the botanist Hussey (265, pp. 8–11) brought out the role of topography as a factor in the formation and maintenance of barrens.

My collections were made in the western part of Barren county, or that part west of the Louisville and Nashville Railroad, in the Cave region, and in the county of Edmonson. Icy observations in Barren county would lead me to the conclusion that the traditions which are current as coming from the settlers are true; that is to say, that when the whites first came to these parts, it was, indeed, a barren region, destitute at least of trees. On the more level parts of this county the trees are yet small in size and few in species. The size of the trees alone would settle the question as to the length of time in which the present forest has stood, especially when taken in connection with the absence of the remnants of an older forest in the matter of fallen trunks and stumps. On the line of sandstone-capped hills seen rising between the line of the railroad and Green river are to be found larger trees than any in the more level portions of the county, showing that when the rest of the county was bare of trees, there were some crowning these hills. The limited number of species found in Barren county would itself be conclusive of the question of the recent introduction of forest growth into this region. The most of the oaks are of the following species: *Quercus, coccinea, rubra, nigra*—the latter species very numerous. *Alba* is found, but not abundant; also *imbricaria* and *obtusiloba*, about the numerous sinkholes. I saw no poplars, no tulip trees, linn, beech, black walnut or butternut.

Hussey also considered the question of soil type as a cause of grasslands, but rejected it in favor of fire. He said:

> The reason of the deficiency of trees on the prairies has been held by some
> to be the absence of the nutriment in the soil which they required, or the
> fineness of the soil, which was supposed to be unfavorable to the growth
> of timber trees. The latter view, taken in connection with the fact that the
> knolls on which the clumps of trees are generally found are composed of
> more porous material, as sand or gravel, seemed to receive confirmation.
> But the fact that all kinds of trees do grow well when planted and pro-
> tected in prairie soil, upsets both these theories without further refutation.
> The soil is not too finely divided; it does not lack the necessary constituents.
> Not taking into consideration how a country may have been deprived of
> a forest—whether by the ravages of insects, a succession of unfavorable
> seasons, or by a conflagration alone, or connected with one or all of the
> foregoing causes, or by any other cause—when once deprived of a forest,
> annual fires would likely prevent its restoration while they were continued.
> If the fires were purposely kindled, and at a certain time, so that the villages
> could be protected against their ravages, the inhabitants would do it by
> clearing away the dead grass from the vicinity of their dwellings. In fact,
> the grass would perish to the roots around their villages from being tram-
> pled upon and burnt out by the fires in and about their habitations. It is
> not beyond supposition that the aborigines themselves, for various reasons,
> might scatter the seeds of trees intentionally or accidentally, from the
> mast with which they must have provided themselves for winter consump-
> tion. They would occupy the knolls, if such there were, for their villages.

Shaler (450, p. 324) pointed to Kentucky as an example for all grasslands of the forest area east of the Mississippi River and explained the
process by which forests became prairie and how prairies were maintained
in a forest-growing environment. He wrote in 1891:

> Evidence that this timberless character of the plains east of the Missis-
> sippi River has been brought about by the spread of fires is afforded by
> the conditions which existed in Kentucky during the latter part of the last
> century. While the Indians used this region as a hunting ground, the district
> between Louisville, and the Tennessee line, extending thence westerly
> along the southern border of Kentucky to the Cumberland River, was
> mostly in the condition of prairies. Except near the streams and on the
> margin of this so-called "barren district," the forests were scarred by fire.
> There were no young trees springing up to take the place of the old and
> thickbarked veterans of the wood, which from the hardness of their outer

coating could resist flame. When these mature trees died they had no succession, and so the prairie ground became gradually extended over the area originally occupied by forest. After the Indians were driven away about 50 years elapsed before the country was generally settled, and in this period the woods to a considerable extent recovered possession of the areas of open ground. The periodic firing of the grass having ceased, seeds were disseminated from the scattered clumps of wood, and soon made them the centers of swiftly spreading plantations.

Sauer (434, p. 130) offered the following summary in 1927:

These various accounts suggest the following association of events: the suppression of fires through settlement, the deterioration of the wild sod through grazing and its destruction by the plow, the spread of forest from valley sides and upland copses, and the gradual immigration of more numerous forest species. Today the land that is not cultivated is well covered with trees. Knolls on the plains, swampy flatwoods, worn pastures, and abandoned fields are the forest sites of the present. The rapidity of forest invasion in the past century indicates that the checks upon it previously were not those of climate or soil. For the second time man appears to have changed fundamentally vegetational formation of the area.

One study made since Sauer published his comprehensive report contributes significant data, of almost experimental character, to our understanding of the chain reaction accompanying removal of trees from an area in the eastern woodlands. The example, described by Hursh and Connaughton (264, pp. 864–66), in 1938, follows:

... ample evidence is available to demonstrate that [forests] have a marked effect on the local or environmental climate. . . . Opportunities for comparing the climate of similar contiguous areas of large size differing only in the presence or absence of forest are rare. However, one exists in eastern Tennessee, where in relatively recent years an area of 7,000 acres, in Copper Basin, once heavily forested, has been completely denuded by smelter fumes. Surrounding this island of absolutely complete denudation is a zone of 12,000 acres which supports a stand of perennial grasses. This is in turn surrounded by a hardwood forest of approximately the same composition as that which originally occupied the basin.

The authors kept records for two years, 1935 and 1936. Average temperature was three to four degrees higher in the treeless area. Wind velocity was seven to ten times greater in winter and thirty-four to forty times greater in summer on denuded area than in forest. Seventeen to twenty-five percent less moisture was measured on open land than in the forest. These data suggest that grasslands would be more easily maintained than originally formed because the increased wind and greater dryness would favor the burning of the grass. The reverse would also be true. As trees covered the grasslands, increased moisture and decreased wind would improve the chances for continued and better tree growth. The principle must be remembered if the ecology of the prairies and plains is to be understood.

The southeastern section of the eastern woodlands, although providing few direct statements of Indian forest fires, offers the most decisive evidence of the effect of frequent Indian fires of any area in America. We know that the aborigines must have burned over thousands of square miles of the woods of the southeastern states during a period of thousands of years because of the type of forests that were discovered by the first Europeans in the area.

Fortunately, for an understanding of the ecology of the region, forests survive until the present because the practice of burning also survives. I refer to one of the largest forest areas of America, which Shantz and Zon (454, fig. 2 and p. 14) designated "Longleaf-Loblolly-Slash Pines (Southeastern Pine Forest)." In their text, they devoted twenty lines to describing it, a coverage equal to that for mangrove thickets. The major portion of their statement follows:

> This forest occupies a belt which extends through the Coastal Plain from extreme southern Virginia to the Everglades in Florida and Trinity River in Texas. It is made up of ten different species of pine, of which, however, the longleaf pine is the most abundant and occupies extensive areas. The forest, besides furnishing at present a large part of the timber cut of the country, is the source of the naval stores (turpentine and rosin) of the United States.
>
> Although the region is one of heavy precipitation (from 40 to 60 inches), with a growing season covering from 6 to 12 months in a year, the sandy soil and the rapid evaporation make the vegetation resemble in many respects the pure forests of western yellow pine. The longleaf pine forests had the same open parklike character and the ground is covered with coarse grasses or low shrubs.

By attributing to "the sandy soil and the rapid evaporation" the "open parklike character" of the southern pine forest, Shantz and Zon have completely ignored human influences; until recently most botanists, foresters, and ecologists have done likewise. Today, however, no one acquainted with the literature regarding this forested area can do so. Shantz and Zon published the statement above in 1924. They would undoubtedly write differently now.

The real awakening regarding the role of fire in the longleaf pine region occurred in 1931 and 1932. Those years are chosen because two important articles were published that shocked many into an awareness that the woodland fires carried out by Indians and continued by whites to the present had far-reaching and decisive influences on the area. Others had noted this previously, and the idea was included in the book *Plant Ecology* by Weaver and Clements (542) in 1929. Although this became the foremost text in its field, the full implication of their notice was appreciated fully by neither the authors nor the teachers and students who used it. Weaver and Clements wrote (542, p. 512): "The extent of this great pine belt has naturally led to the assumption that it is climax in nature, but its ecological character, as well as actual successional studies at widely separated points, leaves little or no doubt that it is essentially a fire sub-climax."

An indication of the failure of Weaver and Clements to convincingly establish their view of fire's importance in the southern pines comes from Vestal (521, p. 233), who reviewed *Plant Ecology* in *Ecology* in 1931. Vestal frankly stated his doubt that fire played the dominant role in the formation of longleaf pine forests that Weaver and Clements attributed to it. The shock came a few months later in 1931 in an article entitled "The Forest That Fire Made" by S. W. Greene (217, p. 583), which appeared, surprisingly enough, in *American Forests*, the monthly journal of the American Forestry Association. The long comment by the editor (217, p. 583) that preceded the article indicated something of the feeling on the subject.

> . . . the author raises questions that will be warmly controverted. His conclusions that the longleaf forests of the South are the result of long years of grass fires and that continued fires are essential to the perpetuation of the species as a type will come as a startling revolutionary theory to readers schooled to the belief that fire in any form is the arch enemy of forests and forestry. . . .
>
> Mr. Greene . . . is not a forester. For the past fifteen years, he has represented the Bureau of Animal Industry at the Coastal Plains Experiment Station at McNeill, Mississippi, in the study of the effect of ground fires upon forage. . . . For a number of years his work has been in cooperation with the United States Forest Service in its study of the influence of fire upon forest growth. His conclusions . . . have been arrived at through study and observation at first hand. . . . *American Forests* does not vouch for the accuracy of Mr. Greene's conclusions.

A long quotation from Greene best illustrates his "revolutionary theory":

> Fire was the only effective tool that primitive man had for the clearing of forest land and it has remained throughout the ages as the prime force for

land clearing, which must still go on to open up the most fertile soils for cultivation and grazing and push the forests back to less productive soils.

All fires in the woods are by no means forest fires that destroy useful timber, even though they are uncontrolled, and not all foresters are fanatics on the subject of fires. . . . As early as 1855 a trained ecologist (Hilgard), working in the longleaf pine area of southern Mississippi, discovered that ground fires in the forest were understood by the natives and were applied for a useful purpose which he mentioned in one short sentence. Secrets of nature were so commonplace to woodsmen that they were considered hardly worth mentioning and so the story of "The Forest That Fire Made" is just coming to general notice although "The Fire Made Forest" itself was the most amazing physical characteristic of the South when traversed by De Soto and his men from 1539–42 and has remained as such for centuries.

Longleaf pine (*Pinus palustris*) stretched in unbroken, almost pure stands, from Virginia into eastern Texas, a distance of more than 1,200 miles and De Soto and his men traveled the length and breadth of it, for here was a highway free of underbrush, where a deer could been seen through the timber as far as the eye could reach. . . .

No forest of such extent in pure stands and of such commercial value has been found on the face of the earth. Here was a poser, indeed, for the ecologist to ferret out the force of nature responsible for so favoring a single species of tree. . . . In a region of heavy rainfall and mild temperature, one would expect a forest growth of great variety with a jungle undergrowth of vines and shrubs. . . . There was no lack of a variety of seed trees of other species. . . . It was noticeable that other species crowded out longleaf only in the absence of annual grass fires. . . . Fire then was a good clue and when approached from every angle the scent of fire became constantly stronger. But how could fire stop everything else yet encourage longleaf?

A peculiar habit of growth of longleaf possessed by no other pine gave the clue. . . . It forms a bundle of leaves in the grass and for a period of five, ten and no one knows how many years, it builds a root system and stores its reserve food there. If fire causes it to shed its needles it merely calls on the reserve food supply in the roots to form a new set and goes on growing. No one knows what determines the start of its upward growth but when it is ready it sends up a husky shoot and makes a rapid growth, often three feet or more in one year. . . .

The longleaf pine has two serious enemies—the hog and the brown spot needle disease. Hogs root the seedlings up and can live on the stored food material in the roots. However, hogs had no effect on the virgin stand for there were no hogs until the Spaniards introduced them. The needle disease is caused by a fungus which is often a very serious enemy of the young seedlings underneath a "rough" of dead grass. Burning the dead grass in winter is an effective means of control.

The picture now clears up. Where seed trees are available all that is necessary to get a pure stand of longleaf without a hardwood undergrowth is to have frequent grass fires. Indians and lightning could and did set fire to the dead grass and strawfall and the material was ready to burn expanses hundreds of miles in extent any time after frost and in the summer if it had not burned the previous year. Fires offered no threat to the life or property of the Indian for they were not forest fires but merely grass fires that cleared the undergrowth of grass and hardwoods, making travel easy as it does today. No roads or fields were in the way and fire could go across or around the head of small streams until it reached large river courses or was rained out. In the year 1773 the famous botanist William Bartram traveled with the Indians over much the same trail as De Soto from South Carolina to the Mississippi River and gave detailed descriptions of the longleaf pine country. He speaks repeatedly of the open pine forests, describes Indians chasing deer on horseback through the woods and says of Indians setting fires . . . which happens almost every day throughout the year, in some part or other, by the Indians, for the purpose of rousing game, as also by the lightning. The very upper surface of the earth being mixed with the ashes of burnt vegetables, renders it of sufficient strength or fertility to clothe itself perfectly with a great variety of grasses. The cattle were as large and fat as those of the rich grazing pastures of Moyomensing. . . . Thus two hundred years after De Soto, the Indians were still burning the grass and the white men, no doubt continued the practice directly after them.

Greene states his case strongly and convincingly. The surprise is that the influence of fires in the southern woods was not recognized and documented earlier. No anthropologist, to my knowledge, has recognized the great importance of fire set by Indians in determining the type of vegetation formed in the Southeast. Only statements regarding Indians using fire to drive game could I find in over two thousand pages on southeastern Indians published by Swanton, the recognized authority on the area. Certainly, if Greene's theory is correct, some recognition should have been given the Indians as an ecological force by the specialists in Indian cultures and history. Does Greene stand alone? Without mentioning the article "The Forest That Fire Made" or Greene, H. H. Chapman of the Yale School of Forestry presented the same idea in 1932 in an article entitled "Is the Longleaf Type a Climax?" in *Ecology* (82, p. 331). He notes: "The conclusion that the species owed its existence and survival to fires and would disappear were it not for the continuance of fire was definitely stated by Mrs. Ellen Call Long in 1880 and by Dr. Roland M. Harper in 1911–13. . . ."

Chapman, who had been experimenting for fifteen years, presented the results of his experiments to substantiate the thesis that fire is essential to the maintenance of the longleaf pine. His experiments indicated that burning at two to three year intervals was better than annual burning. The statement of Michaux (361, p. 301), made in 1802, takes on more meaning in the light of the results of modern experiments. He wrote of the Carolinas and Georgia: "Seven-tenths of the country are covered with pines of one species, or *Pinus palustris*. . . . These trees are not damaged by the fire that they make here annually in the woods, at the commencement of spring, to burn the grass and other plants that the frost has killed."

Michaux added that the oaks that came up among the pines were "only fit to burn." Of course, Weaver and Clements (542) had recognized that fire was important in the southern pines before Greene and Chapman published their studies. Tracy (512) had clearly described the open woodlands of the Gulf coast "with very little undergrowth" in 1898, but he did not mention fire. Ashe (18) recognized in 1915 that fire was an essential factor in the production of loblolly pine in North Carolina. It has only been since Greene's article, however, that data have been amassed to give complete and irrefutable evidence that longleaf forests were fire-made and are still fire-maintained. In addition to the references cited, I have reviewed thirty-five articles all reporting results of controlled experiments that support the general thesis presented by Greene (217).

Professor H. H. Chapman, who became dean of Yale's School of Forestry, continued his experimentation and wrote thirteen articles explaining the best methods for producing longleaf pine. In a second article in 1932, published in the *Journal of Forestry*, Chapman (81, p. 603) concluded that "if complete fire protection must be enforced . . . the longleaf pine will disappear as a species. . . ."

In 1935 Hardtner (230), a successful lumberman in Louisiana, added his support to the idea that regular burning of forests is beneficial. He presented evidence that pigs did great damage to seedling longleaf pine. Another practical forester, Simerly (464), added his voice in 1936 in support of controlled burning to clear ground and reduce danger of harmful forest fires by clearing off underbrush. In 1938 Haig (225, pp. 1045–47) quoted a number of early travelers to show that openings had long existed in the south and added: "Indeed almost every forest climax of North America displays a fire subclimax, usually occurring over a considerable area." Heyward (244) in 1939 also reviewed the earlier literature and stated: "Forest fires are more common in the region of longleaf pine . . . than in any other portion of the United States."

Not all experimenters obtained favorable results. Gemmer et al. (194), for example, in 1940 reported that longleaf seed germinated better in "rough" (i.e., grass or brush) than on burned-off soil. Pessin and Chapman (395), in 1944, refuted Gemmer with results of a carefully controlled experiment. They obtained best germination and growth from seeds planted in ashes.

Watson (531) also reviewed nearly all previous studies and concluded that controlled burning of forests was, in summary, good for trees because it reduced disease; good for grazing because cattle gained more weight if grazed on land that had been burned over the year before; burning was good for the soil; burning of forests made for better hunting; burned forests produced more turpentine and rosin; and controlled burning greatly reduced the danger of destructive forest fires.

Ten years of reporting on research that had been carried on for over twenty-five years and had convinced dozens of scientists and practical foresters that fires had brought about the longleaf forest and that fire was a very useful silvicultural tool for longleaf forest management did not, however, persuade the U.S. Forest Service to relax its campaign to stop all prescribed burning of forests everywhere in the nation. Consequently, there took place in the pages of the *Journal of Forestry* in 1941 a sharp debate over "Controlled Burning" between Chapman and Wheeler (84).

The facts presented by Chapman changed not at all Wheeler's faith in the value of complete fire exclusion. Chapman (86) reported in 1943 the conclusive results of a test carried on for twenty-seven years that demonstrated that burning greatly aided longleaf pine by reducing competition from hardwoods and by reducing the damage from brown-spot disease. In 1944 Siggers (463), in a U.S. Department of Agriculture bulletin, added additional evidence on the value of fire in hindering brown-spot. That same year Chapman (87) pointed out that the climate of the southeastern states was really most favorable to hardwoods and that if the more valuable pines were to survive fire must be used.

Wakeley and Muntz (529) were new supporters of controlled burning in 1947 with the results of their experiment that showed that longleaf pine that had been burned twice were taller at the end of 11\F1/2 years than were trees the same age that had not been burned. Most experimentation had been done in Louisiana and Mississippi, but, also in 1947, Squires (474) reported from Florida that controlled burning was desirable for a number of reasons. The same year, Chapman (90) added to the record from the Yale Experimental Forest in Louisiana the information that longleaf pine survived better than hardwood brush in even the hottest type of fire made possible by a great accumulation of dry grass and shrubs.

In 1947 Chapman (89) also pointed out that areas formerly and densely stocked with pine were taken over by inferior hardwoods because of complete fire protection and that pines would not sprout under hardwood cover. Bruce (63) was another name added in 1947 to the roster of advocates of burning in the management of longleaf forests. His controlled experiment, carried on for thirty-two years in Louisiana, demonstrated that annual burning, considered excessive by some, produced an excellent stand of marketable timber.

In 1948 another article by Chapman (92, p. 505) reported that because of the "reluctance of foresters to accept the fact that fire rotation . . . is indispensable in permitting the pine to survive competition and disease and establish itself . . . millions of acres of longleaf lands now devastated could have been reproduced to fully stocked stands of the most valuable pine in the South."

Morriss and Mills (373) reported in 1948 that 26,000 acres had been successfully stocked by controlled burning in three-year cycles, whereas a nearby plot was "practically denuded by annually burned wild fires." Yet the value of controlled burning had not diffused to all foresters, as indicated by Zobel's (581) report of the elaborate fire-fighting program needed to protect an army camp on a reservation on which complete exclusion of woods burning was attempted.

Articles by Bruce and Bickford (64) and Pomeroy and Barron (401), published in 1950 and containing additional evidence in favor of controlled burning, indicate that the struggle for a fair evaluation of the use of fire as a silvicultural tool in southern pine forests has produced results. That fire may be helpful in producing excellent forests of the type first discovered by Europeans is being finally recognized. In view of the heated exchange between Chapman and Wheeler (84) in 1941, a decided change is indicated by an article in the Department of Agriculture Yearbook (579, p. 517) for 1949, by Arthur W. Hartman, entitled "Fire as a Tool in Southern Pine." The work of H. H. Chapman is cited approvingly, and the methods for controlled burning are outlined. The benefits to be derived from the use of fire in longleaf pine regeneration and management are set forth.

My review of the experimental work done in the southern pine area is presented here so that there can be no doubt that fires, used for millennia by Indians and continued for centuries by whites, were the determining factor in producing and maintaining pines in a hardwood forest area. If Indian burning of vegetation could maintain an open, parklike pine forest in an area of abundant rainfall and good soil, what might be the effect of fire in an area of much less rainfall? There are lessons to be learned in the eastern woodlands to be applied elsewhere.

In addition to learning about the growth habits of the longleaf pines, we can learn about the role of fire in producing grass. Since Indians have said that they set fires to improve pasturage, significance is added to their claims when modern experiments indicate that burning does improve grass yield. It is also significant that the use of fire does not actually reduce the forage yield, especially considering the regularity with which burning is condemned and accused of reducing repasturage and lowering soil ferti-lity. An example of such condemnation is found in the U.S. Department of Agriculture Yearbook for 1938 (577, p. 615) and also the Yearbook for 1948 (578, p. 18) in which Edwards writes that "[b]ecause of the persistence of the practice of burning of the woods, the timber forage declined."

In 1939 Wahlenberg, Greene, and Reed (528) published their findings regarding the status of grazing in the southern states. They found that Indian burning had prepared the woods for grass growing and that when regular burning was stopped in particular areas the amount of cattle feed was reduced simply because it was covered by hardwoods. Terry (505, p. 246) made the following statement in 1941:

> But we must concede that the early pioneers, in burning off the leaf-litter and ground cover, did attain their object. They increased the amount of grass for their stock to feed on. . . . And if burning is continued year after year, destroying and preventing reproduction, the forest will become more and more open and the grasses will grow rank and form a sod. . . . In time nothing will be left of the forest but an open grove of over-mature, decadent trees, and they will finally disappear.

Controlled experiments by Biswell and Lemon (47), the findings of which were published in 1943, demonstrated that burning is necessary for grass reproduction in the southern forests. They wrote: "Winter, spring, and early summer burning of forest range lands in the wiregrass type of the Southeast greatly stimulates seed-stalk production of many of the impor-tant native forage plants. Clumps of many native grasses will live for years without producing seed stalks, but if burned will produce in abundance."

Grass clumps not burned produced no seed stalks, they found. Clumps burned in winter produced twenty-five seed stalks. Careful observations recorded by Biswell et al. (48) and Lemon (309 and 310), published between 1944 and 1949, leave no doubt that burning improves forage for grazing and that cattle grazed on burned-over forest land gain better than those grazed on unburned forest. These modern experiments with cattle verify the Indian observations regarding wild game and add justification for the continuation of the ancient aboriginal practice of frequently setting fire to the southern forests in order to maintain them as pastures.

The other aspect of the problem is that of the soil. Not only on the prairies and plains, where condition of the soil is put forth as the determining factor in grassland formation, but also in the southern pine areas, type of soil is invoked as the cause of grasslands. For example, McGuire (348) in 1834 wrote that the prairies of Alabama were there because the land had but recently risen above the waters of the Gulf. Soil scientists like Coffey (108) and Hilgard (245) say that to a large degree type of soil is a decisive influence on the type of vegetation growing on it.

Ecologists will admit, as do Weaver and Clements (542, p. 173), that "vegetation has played a remarkable role in the formation" of soil. Their research reports, however, so greatly emphasize the part played by soil in determining plant growth that one gets the impression that they forget in their actual work their own statement that vegetation plays a part in soil formation. An example may be the words of Wackerman (526, p. 731), who wrote in 1929 of the prairies in Arkansas and Louisiana, saying that the "natives long resident in the country, say that the prairies have grown noticeably smaller within memory." Yet he attributed their presence to poor drainage of the soil.

Heyward (243, pp. 23–27) offers data of vital importance to an understanding of the relationship between soil and vegetation. He found, in 1937, that "[t]he greatest percentage of longleaf pine forest soils is morphologically more similar to grasslands soils than to forest soils."

Heyward thought this unusual phenomenon was due directly to the effect of frequent fires. Of equal importance were Heyward's data establishing the fact that in the southern woodland "ten years protection from burning changes the character of the soil." Billings (43, p. 448) reviewed the literature on the subject, especially the analyses conducted in Switzerland and Estonia as well as in the United States, which agreed with his own findings, and in 1941 presented quantitative correlations showing that plant cover determines type of soil. In spite of these findings and many others regarding the fertility of frequently burned prairie soils, in 1946 Wilde (557, p. 153), writing on "forest soils and forest growth" and referring specifically to the Atlantic Coastal Plain of America, said: "Aside from the fire hazard, burning of forest floor is objectionable because it results in a total loss of the most valuable fertilizer ingredients, nitrogen. . . . These ill effects of burning have been emphasized by many writers."

It should be noted that such ideas have been emphasized without sound experimental support. The studies by Heyward (243) and Billings (43) mentioned above and others, including that of Bruce (65) in 1951, provide sound facts with which to refute the facile deduction that burning harms the soil.

The Indians said that they burned off the fields and forests to improve the availability of game, and early travelers did observe all types of wild animals and birds in greater abundance on the open grasslands than in the thick forests. The proponents of complete forest fire prevention have taken the opposite side. The wildlife organizations have been convinced that all forest and grass fires damage wild life and reduce the number of game animals. Sportsmen have been sold the idea that absolute fire prevention is best.

Neither Indians nor country folk in the southern states have agreed with this, and the latter have clung to aboriginal notions that woodland fires improve hunting. Knowing the popular belief that has been built up by extensive, well-financed, long-term publicity against fires, it is surprising to find Stoddard's (494, p. 346) research in 1931, thoroughly documented, establishing that periodic controlled burning in the southeastern upland has a "demonstrated value" in game management. Not only grazing game are aided; mention is also made of increased populations of wild turkey, quail, and other wild life in burned-over areas, as compared to areas protected from fire.

The southeastern portion of the eastern woodlands vegetation and culture area is unique in providing modern experimental data to verify the correctness of the Indians' theories presented to justify their culture pattern of periodic setting of fire to grasslands and forests. Experimental studies have further demonstrated that the southern pine forest as a type must have been established by Indians, by means of fire, and that its continuation depends on continued frequent burning. The peculiarities of the major southern pine tree, the longleaf, which have allowed it to become dominant because of the intermittent burning over extended periods, raise an important question that foresters have only partially answered. In 1931 Vestal (521, p. 236) briefly raised the question when he expressed the doubt that fire determined the composition of southern pine forests, adding, however: "Furthermore, if fire is a constantly recurring condition in a certain climate, then it is a feature of that climate, and as expectable as rainfall, though far more irregular."

Unfortunately, neither foresters, botanists, nor ecologists have placed fire on an equal footing with moisture, wind, elevation, or soil as an important causative factor to be carefully evaluated, past and present, in order to understand the vegetation of a region, large or small. Professor Chapman (91, p. 193) restated this general thesis in 1947 but greatly diminished the force of his otherwise excellent pronouncement by minimizing the extent of vegetation burning by Indians. He said:

Natural areas [in the southeastern state] . . . consist first of such old growth as might be capable of preservation, and which should be burned over every two to five years to perpetuate the conditions which Ponce de Leon found in his first trip, and to secure naturally grouped reproduction. . . . If fire is kept out, the whole character of the longleaf forest undergoes a complete change.

The forester in his praiseworthy desire to improve upon nature for the production of desired species, quality, and volume, may frequently fail dismally in the outcome by actually going against the most deep-seated natural laws—laws which gave rise to different species and attuned them each to a niche in the environment. These niches are the result of the recurrence of fire, wind, insects, and disease; as well as the fertility and moisture content of soils, climate, and the inflammability of ground cover and brush.

It was undoubtedly because Chapman did not know that forest and grass burning was a general American Indian habit that he weakened his statement by adding: "Actually we started out in this country with the entire continent as a great natural area, modified only slightly by man by the Indian habit of burning the woods."

Here Chapman falls into the all but universal error of ecologists, which is to assume that the influence of aboriginal burning was limited to small areas. If Chapman had known that the northern part of the eastern woodlands had been subjected to fires as had the southern part, if he had known that plains and prairies had been constantly fired by Indians, if he had known that the mountains and valleys of the West had been regularly subjected to fire, I doubt that he would have said the continent had been "modified only slightly . . . by the Indian habit of burning." Chapman himself provided the evidence that Indian fires in the southern pine forests made the forests what they were when discovered. We have seen that Indian fires made Virginia and Kentucky landscapes what they were. Yet to be represented is the ample evidence that Indian fires made prairies and plains what they were when viewed by Europeans. The facts from all areas must be used for a full understanding of the forces that determined the vegetation in all other areas.

Chapman's error in properly evaluating the full influence of Indian burning of fields and forests appears to stem from another failure, also very common among ecologists—the failure to appreciate the length of time humans have occupied the New World. That this is true of Chapman is clear from his article (93, p. 10) entitled "Lightning in the Longleaf," published in 1950. He realized that the growth habits of the longleaf pine were so unusually well adapted to surviving frequent fires that he made the suggestion that here was a species of plant that had made a fundamental genetic, probably evolutionary, adjustment to fire. This appears to be a valid conclusion, for there is no doubt of the longleaf pine's excellent adaptation to survive frequent burning and rapidly producing large and healthy trees. The weakness in Chapman's argument is in attributing to lightning fires exclusively the burning to which the longleaf had to adjust.

Although there is an almost complete lack of knowledge of the time required for plants to accommodate themselves to particular environmental conditions, Chapman's conclusion that the longleaf adjusted to "lightning fires, starting millions of years ago" and continuing to the present, appears weak because it does not take into consideration the comparative influence of lightning fires in other areas. If lightning fires were to have a special, unusual influence in the southern pine forest as compared with other forests, one would expect to find an exceptionally large number of fires started by lightning in that area. Chapman (93, p. 10) said that between 1940 and 1947 there were 613 fires attributed to lightning in the forests of Alabama, Florida, Louisiana, Mississippi, and Texas. That is a very small number compared with 4,410 lightning fires for California for only one year, 1947, which is close to California's yearly average of 4,829 lightning-caused fires for 1943–47. There are more fires, from all causes, in the southern states than there are for all the rest of the nation. For 1930 the South had 90 percent of the 190,000 forest fires. Yet Wackerman (527, p. 63) reported that only 1 percent of the fires in the South were caused by lightning. On the other hand, 41.5 percent of California's recorded forest fires from 1911 to 1920 were started by lightning. Compare the 1 percent of the fires caused by lightning in the southern states with these figures from the 1949 Department of Agriculture Yearbook (579, p. 25):

Rocky Mountains: 70 percent of fires started by lightning
Northwest: 50 percent of fires started by lightning
California: 23 percent of fires started by lightning.

With these data it is difficult to justify the unusual development of fire resistance in the longleaf pine as a response only to lightning fires. But is it necessary to postulate that "millions of years" were necessary for the evolution to take place? Would not "thousands of years" be enough? No one knows. By guessing that ten to twenty-five thousand years would have been sufficient time for the remarkable adaptation of the longleaf pine, we can assume that the adjustment was to man-made fires. The Vero and Melbourne (Florida) sites, at which human skeletons were found in association with mastodon bones, suggest that the southeastern section of the eastern woodlands area has been inhabited as long as any in the New World. If it were thought that a hundred thousand years were required for evolutionary development of longleaf pine peculiarities, it could be taken as support for the authenticity of the Abilene flints, placed in the third interglacial.

In any event, the recognition that man has occupied the New World for at least 10,000 years, that he has been here for probably 25,000 years and possibly for 100,000 years, and admitting the probability that during his entire history here he has set fire to vegetation, we can account for such adaptations as that made by the longleaf pine as resulting from the plant's response to man-made fire. This time perspective permits an understanding of many ecological adjustments otherwise impossible to comprehend.

Although less spectacular than for the southeastern pine forest, the modern evidence for ancient forest fires in the oak-pine division of southern hardwood forest is also impressive. Weaver and Clements (542, p. 511), in the textbook *Plant Ecology*, appear to attribute this whole oak-pine forest to fire. Under the subhead "The Maple-Beech Forest" they say:

> The general effect of fire in the maple-beech association is to develop or maintain a sub-climax of oak-hickory. This is essentially a pre-climax. . . . To the north and east, however, where pines occur in abundance, the rule obtains and a burn subclimax of one or more species of jack pine or similar scrub pines develops. Along the contact with the pine-hemlock forest, this is regularly the jack-pine proper, *Pinus banksiana*, where it is present, but the most significant communities of this type are found from the New Jersey pine barrens south and westward along the coast to Texas.

Clements (103, p. 65) published in 1934 another statement regarding New Jersey: "Explicit testimony to the paramount role of fire was also discovered in the so-called 'plains' of New Jersey. . . ."

Clements found further evidence of fire in the grass and heath bands of the Great Smoky Mountains. Eyre (164) presented confirmation for this view in 1938 in a detailed analysis of a method for regenerating a jack pine forest by use of machines but concluded that fire is the normal way to maintain this pine in the deciduous forest zone. Lutz (342) in 1934 and Moore (369) in 1939 also wrote that fire was important in the management of New Jersey pine forests.

The most recent and detailed presentation of data supporting the value of controlled burning of the oak-pine forest is a series of papers by S. Little and his associates (323, 324, 325, 326). From 1945 to 1949 Little et al. reported the results of their own experiments and reviewed the work of others. The first article reported that controlled burning was beneficial, especially in preparation of the seed bed for pines. A five-year experiment of controlled burning indicated that there was no damage to the soil from fires. The fact that controlled burning reduced the fire hazard loomed large, for they said that the most conscientious preventive measures were unsuccessful if underbrush was allowed to accumulate. They found records of "severe burns, commonly occurring at intervals of fifteen to forty years . . . [from] 1800 to present." In 1948 they wrote of the area of Lebanon State Forest, basing their information on twenty years of experience and twelve years of testing. They recommended winter burning at one- or two-year intervals to reduce fire hazard and to favor "reproduction of pines instead of the less desirable hardwoods." Their 1949 report listed eighteen publications that indicate the importance of fire in maintaining pine forests in many regions of the United States besides New Jersey and reiterated their conclusion that prescribed burning was necessary to maintain or restore the most valuable pine forests.

Speaking of the southeastern end of the oak-pine forests in Arkansas and Louisiana, Chapman (85) recommended use of fire to assure pine growth in a hardwood area, much as Little did for New Jersey. The oak-chestnut section of the southern hardwood forest, as defined by Shantz and Zon (454, fig. 2), covers most of the Appalachian Mountains and Kentucky, Tennessee, and eastern Ohio. This forest, as well as that called oak-pine, is designated as "burn preclimax" by Weaver and Clements (542, p. 511) in their statement cited above. The quotations noted above for this region were concerned with the ancient "barrens" that formerly existed within the oak-chestnut forest area and that were instead extensive grasslands caused and maintained by being burned over very frequently by the Indians.

Surrounding the grasslands were oak-chestnut forests, which quickly invaded and dominated the barrens when fires were suppressed. My thesis, which is that Indians burned everywhere, not only on the grasslands, is supported by the statement of Weaver and Clements to the effect that the whole oak-chestnut forest is maintained as pre-climax by fire. An equal amount of burning could cause a prairie where topography favored rapid spread of fire while maintaining open woodland on rough terrain. Although the reduction in burning-over in the oak-hickory forests was sufficient to allow trees to invade the grasslands, the Indian practice of burning woodlands has continued to the present, enough to keep the region from producing the maple-beech forest of which it is climatologically capable.

It is enlightening, therefore, to realize that Tennessee is also in the region having the greatest number of forest fires annually in the United States. Evans (163) reported that for 1942 the southern states, including Tennessee, had 28,500,000 acres of forest burned-over, which equaled about 30 percent of the total forests in the area. Gustafson (223) made an intensive survey of a timber area in eastern Kentucky from 1942 to 1944. He sampled 500,000 acres of forest and determined the dates of fires by analysis of burn scars on trees. He found that conifers were injured less than hardwoods but concluded that even light controlled burning did some damage to trees. Gustafson discovered that "[n]early 9 out of 10 acres of the area studied had been burned at least once in the ten years 1935 through 1945; practically all of the sample area had been burned in the last 40 years."

Gustafson found that most of the area was burned at least once in the five years preceding his study, and in 1942 alone 62 percent of the area was burned. If Tennessee and Kentucky, the areas for which I have found detailed reports, are typical, it is understandable why the oak-chestnut forest is maintained in a pre-climax status.

One other study of the oak-chestnut forest area should be cited. Blizzard (49) published an article in 1931 concerning the spread of deciduous trees into the prairies of Long Island, New York. Blizzard described the grasslands as follows (p. 208): "The grasslands of *Andropogon scoparius* on Long Island . . . are a bit of prairie similar to parts of the Great Plains of Central United States. The absence of trees on these Hempstead, L. I. plains Harper attributes to recurring fires."

Blizzard found records showing that the grass plain was more extensive in 1825 and quoted Silas Wood in 1800, who wrote: "By neglecting the Indian practice of annual burning, in a few years the young timber and underbrush increased so as to injure the feed in the woods."

Silas Wood had discovered an ancient Hempstead record that showed that "[i]n 1667, the town court appointed two men to warn the inhabitants to meet to fire the woods at such time as they should think fit."

Blizzard's main contribution was to point out the method of forest invasion of grassland. *Juniperus virginiana* was the only tree he found invading the sod directly. Usually bayberry bushes became established first, destroying the grass by shade and preparing the habitat for trees. His paper relating the Long Island prairie to those of the "Great Plains" gains importance from one by Schmidt (440) that appeared in 1938.

Schmidt studied the distribution of reptiles and concluded that formerly the prairie of the Midwest extended "eastward between the Ohio and the Great Lakes to western New York and Pennsylvania" and possibly to the Atlantic. Since Schmidt considered the change from grasslands a result of marked climatic change, he placed the prairies in the area back in the period immediately following the last glacier. The presence of plains-prairie reptiles in the northeastern forests may also indicate that grasslands were extensively maintained until comparatively recent times by Indian burning.

Hoffman's (250, vol. 1, p. 174) statement, written in 1835, regarding the oak-hickory region of Jackson County, Michigan, suggests that formerly more prairies existed there.

Today, for the first time, I saw the meadows on fire. They are of vast extent, running far into the woods like the firths of a lake; and as the wild grass, which they supply in the greatest profusion, furnishes the new settler with all the hay he uses for his stock, they are burnt over thus annually to make it tender. These fires, traveling far over the country, seize upon the large prairies, and consuming every tree in the woods except the hardies, cause the often-mentioned oak openings, so characteristic of Michigan scenery. It is a beautiful sight to see the fire shooting in every direction over these broad expanses of land, which are kindled at a variety of points. The flame at one moment curls along the ground, and seems to lick up its fuel from below, while at the next it tumbles over like the breakers of the sea upon the dried grass, and sweeps it as a wave of fire from the ground. I found myself repeatedly surrounded by the fire, while riding hither and thither, watching its progress: but was only on two occasions exposed to any inconvenience—once when my horse sank in the mire to the saddle-girths, so that I had to dismount in a morass covered with high weeds, to which the flame was approaching, and another time when I found myself in a small patch of woodland, which crackled and roared like Tophet itself.

Another interesting footnote to Blizzard's (49) article is one by Wood-man (573) in 1941. Blizzard reported on the action of the town court of 1667 in providing for controlled burning of the area. Woodman described the million-dollar disaster in Massachusetts in April 1941, which resulted from the failure that year of one town to provide funds to have the meadows carefully burned. When the meadows were not cleared of old, dry grass as usual by trained fire wardens, a wild fire caught the extra accumulation of grass on a dry, windy day and burned through the town.

Woodman did not say how long the annual grass burning had been going on before its fateful interruption in 1941, but the implication is that we have in Massachusetts a direct continuation of the original practice of grass burning. Too few records of such modern intentional grass and woods burning are published, but those available demand attention. False conclusions about the potential natural vegetation that the climate of an area might support can result if modern burning is ignored.

Lutz's (341) analysis of "The Vegetation of Heart's Content, a Virgin Forest in Northwestern Pennsylvania," published in 1930, indicated that fires had played a decisive role there as well. Since his evidence shows that the woods had been ravaged many times by fires set purposefully by

Indians and settlers, his designation of Heart's Content as a virgin forest seems unwarranted. Lutz wrote: "From data at hand it appears that fires have swept through portions of Heart's Content many times during the life of the present stand. This evidence comes from three sources: the literature, the soil, and the trees themselves. . . . That Indians, who originally lived in the forest, set many fires cannot be doubted."

Lutz referred to publications by C. A. Hanna, W. A. Whitehead, B. Moore and N. Taylor, and C. S. Sargent, in addition to a number I have cited, to establish the fact that Indians had burned the region for hunting, to improve grazing, to encourage growth of huckleberry bushes, and for other reasons as well. Although forest fires resulting from lightning are known in the area, being responsible for 4 percent of the fires reported over a period of six years, Lutz attributed to those set by man the decisive influence observed. He said it was "surprising that no greater apparent damage" was done by them and thought there was formerly less destruction because frequent fires kept the brush out of the forest. Lutz believed that the climate of the Heart's Content area would support a hemlock-beech forest; consequently, he sought an ecological reason for the presence of this famous white pine forest. He found that "[f]ire seems to be the only agency which would have exerted the widespread influence which was necessary to provide for the establishment of a considerable proportion of white pine on relatively heavy soils such as occur at Heart's Content."

Most of the forest became established after a very destructive fire about 250 years ago, as indicated by the large number of trees of that age. Two other years (1749 and 1872) are of note because tree-ring analysis shows that many were fire-scarred those years. The literature reveals that they were excessively dry years, marked by remarkably destructive fires throughout the North Atlantic states. Morey (370) in 1936 confirmed Lutz's evaluation regarding Heart's Content and added that Cook Forest of white pine was also a fire-forest. Cline and Spurr (106) in 1942 and Hough and Forbes (258) in 1943 further supported the view that fire was essential for maintaining white pine forests in Pennsylvania.

The importance of fire in white pine production is not limited to its growth in areas suited to hardwood dominance. That fire should be considered essential for the regeneration of white pine in Maine and southeastern Canada, areas marked on vegetation maps by Shantz and Zon (454) and Fernow (in 210, p. 68) as "Pine Forest," will come as a surprise to many. In 1935 Maissurow (351) proposed this in an article appearing in the *Journal of Forestry* titled "Fire as a Necessary Factor in the Perpetuation of White Pine." Maissurow based his theory upon observations made in Quebec about 150 miles north of Ottawa. He said: "White pine did not reproduce under the canopy of the virgin forest, and being only a temporary element of forest association perpetuated itself through hundreds and thousands of years primarily through the medium of forest fires."

Although logging started in the region of Maissurow's observations in 1876, the oldest stands of forest date from 1700. At present the white pine is reproducing on the burned-over areas following the lumbering operations.

In the following year Cary (75) seconded Maissurow on the basis of information from Maine, Michigan, and Wisconsin pine forests. That white pine forests in these areas originated after fires was suggested to Cary by their being so even-aged and because of the scars from previous fires. Michigan and Wisconsin forests began after fire between 1650 and 1700, long before the area was lumbered. Cary observed that pure stands of white pine were not over a hundred years old. Furthermore, forests of pines over 450 years old were being replaced by hemlock and hardwood.

In 1941 Maissurow (352) contributed another article on the role of fire in pine forests, this one based on studies made in northern Wisconsin. Because it conforms so closely to my own ideas, the following quotation from Maissurow could have been used as an introduction to this report on the eastern woodlands. "[There is] a tendency on the part of forest ecologists and foresters to disregard or minimize the importance of fire as a necessary factor in the perpetuation of certain species and types."

Maissurow observed that a mixed hardwood forest—sugar maple, yellow birch, basswood—would be the climax forest for northern Wisconsin. He also said:

> Forest fires have, in the last five centuries, burned through 95% of the virgin forest of northern Wisconsin. These fires were not conflagrations of catastrophic proportions which destroyed the primeval forest and changed its climax formations into subclimax types of the present era, but rather periodic and ecologically normal events in the life of the forest. . . .
>
> Fires have been necessary factors or agents in the perpetuation of a number of species, such as yellow birch, hemlock, pines and intolerant hardwoods. . . .
>
> Fires . . . have often resulted in the formation of grass or shrub subclimaxes and understocked, open and silviculturally worthless stands. . . .
>
> The terms "virgin" and "primeval" . . . in their application to the old forests of this region is rather meaningless . . . for practically all "virgin" stands are . . . rehabilitated burned areas.
>
> Although fire may be looked upon as a factor inimical to the normal development of the forest, it has been and is, from a broad ecological viewpoint, a normal, beneficial and necessary factor in the perpetuation of virgin forests.

If Maissurow and Cary are correct, the question remains as to whether the northeastern pine forest, which extended for a thousand miles from northern Minnesota through southern Ontario and Quebec to the Gulf of St. Lawrence, resulted from fires started by lightning or from fires set by Indians. No references were found saying that the tribes occupying this area set forest fires. This absence, however, is interpreted as a failure in reporting (or discovery of documents on my part) rather than an indication that the Algonquin Indians of this region were different in this respect from their linguistic kin to the southeast and west, who did use fire.

This interpretation appears necessary in view of the great extent of the territory and in view of the relative unimportance of lightning in the area. The agricultural yearbook for 1949, *Trees* (579), says that lightning is seldom the cause of forest fires east of the Rocky Mountains. An article in the *Journal of Forestry* (42:292) in 1944, summarizing the data on lightning-caused fires in Maine from 1926 to 1940, concluded that an average of only 4.7 percent of the area of forests burned annually in that region resulted from lightning-caused fires. The annual average acreage burned was 669, with the range from 0 to 5,000 per year. The number of fires annually varied from 2 to 45 per year for the 15-year period. Plummer (399, p. 27) said that "fires are seldom caused by lightning" in the Appalachian Mountains. In contrast to the northwestern states, where as much as 72 percent of all fires are attributed to lightning, 99 percent of forest fires in the northeastern states are thought to have been caused by humans.

Charcoal in peat bogs in New Brunswick, estimated to be several thousand years old, as Plummer (400) says, "indicates the occurrence of forest fires in the far distant past," but even such fires could have been man-made. Thus the great area burned and the relative infrequency of forest fires caused by lightning strongly suggest that Indian fires were a primary factor in the formation of jack, red, and white pine forests of the northeastern United States and southeastern Canada.

In summary, regarding the effect of fires set by Indians in the eastern woodlands, I have demonstrated that Indians used fire throughout the area for hunting, clearing brush, improving pasture, and several other reasons. Dozens of early travelers and settlers testify to such extensive grass and forest fires that it must be concluded that in aboriginal times the whole of the eastern woodlands, from the Mississippi River to the Atlantic, was periodically, perhaps annually, set on fire.

The indirect evidence that Indians burned-over the eastern woodlands comes from an analysis of the vegetation. All parts of the region have types of trees either dependent on fires, as is the longleaf pine, or maintained by fire. Fire-forests established by Indian burning are maintained to the present by the continuation of frequent burning-over by present inhabitants. Fires established and maintained extensive grasslands in a forest environment when the flames were aided by topography.

Prairies and Plains

The Indian practice of burning vegetation impressed the first European explorers who visited the great grasslands in the center of North America. The extensive "seas of grass" were in themselves remarkable, while waves of flame rolling across them provided an even more unforgettable spectacle. It was inevitable that fires would be considered a cause of the grasslands by those who saw the frightening, consuming prairie fires, whipped by hot summer winds. It was only after settlement that geologists and climatologists proposed that the prairies and plains resulted from purely natural geographic conditions. In 1818 Atwater (19), mentioned previously, was one of the first to discount the "popular opinion" that prairies were caused by Indian burning. He said that grasslands resulted from conditions of soil formed under water. Whitney (555) in 1858 and Lesquereaux (313) in 1865 were other early advocates of soil as the primary cause of prairies, and modern soil scientists have continued to regard soil as the deciding factor in prairie-plains formation.

Although Dana (124) in his *Manual of Geology* in 1862 listed "degree of moisture" as "the most influential of all causes . . . of prairies," climate as a causative or determining agent in the origin and continuation of grasslands was not generally emphasized until the present century. Only after the exact measurement of rainfall, evaporation, temperature, and wind velocity had been recorded for a number of years could the correlations between climate and vegetation types be made. Transeau in 1905, Clements (100) in 1916, Livingston and Shreve (327) in 1921, and Koppen (290) in 1923 published their model works setting the pattern for designating climatic causes for the existence of prairies and plains.

In the last quarter-century ecologists have attempted to evaluate all environmental factors that contribute to the vegetation of any area and have applied themselves energetically to measuring the various conditions present on prairies and plains. Since ecologists have considered soils, climate, competition between plants, plant competition with animals, and, finally, actions of humans in their various influences on the vegetation, their conclusions should give us all the information we need to determine the origin and persistence of grasslands. Two inadequacies in most ecological research have led ecologists to underestimate or misinterpret man's role in determining the vegetation of the plains and prairies. The first is a limited time perspective; the second is a limited geographic perspective. Most modern ecological studies have concentrated on intensive analyses of very small areas for only a few years, and those incorporating two or three years are considered conclusive. A hundred years is thought long enough for any possible significant change to be evident. My thesis is that we must consider the plains and prairies in the light of at least 25,000 years of human prehistory, while projecting trends thousands of years into the future, if we are to properly evaluate man's part in the formation of grasslands.

Furthermore, with regard to the human factor in past environments, American Indians have been all but ignored. Since ecologists have based their conclusions regarding grasslands on a number of regionally limited, short-term analyses of plains and prairie grasslands, they have made questionable deductions that would have been avoided if they had included the presence of grasslands in forested areas in their calculations. I believe it necessary to consider what fire did in moist eastern woodlands forests to understand properly what it could do in the drier plains and prairies.

Available information leads me to the conclusion that the extensive grasslands that we call prairies and plains owe their existence to fire set by Indians and continued by accident or design to the present. Natural grasslands resulting entirely from climatic or edaphic conditions are limited both in area and in number. Excessive moisture, extreme elevation or latitude, very thin soil covering bedrock, and alkali or salt all produce very specialized grassy areas. America's great middlewestern grassland is not such a specialized area. Grass was the principal vegetation covering deep, rich soil stretching across several climatic zones and extending from Mexico far into central Canada. The uniformity making the area a unit was its grassy nature, its slight topographic variation, and the fact that it was periodically subjected to fire.

Most writers mentioning grass fires set by Indians specify their use in game drives. Although this is by far the most frequent purpose stated in the literature, statements were also found giving other reasons for prairie fires: to improve pasture; burn off brush; collect insects; increase yields of grass seed and wild berries; clear land for agriculture; stimulate growth of wild tobacco; aid in warfare; facilitate travel; kill or drive away snakes; and, finally, because Indians did not always extinguish campfires. It will be recognized that the reasons for firing plains and prairies are about the same as those given by Indians for starting forest fires in the eastern woodlands.

Oviedo (386), writing in 1534, furnished the earliest statement as to burning of vegetation in the New World, but it is general, saying simply that wherever the Spanish settled they continued the Indian practice of using fire to clear the land. More pertinent to the discussion of prairie fires is the document of Cabeza de Vaca (72, p. 92), printed in 1555, which describes his experiences as a slave to the Iguaces Indians of southeastern Texas in 1528. He wrote: "Those from further inland have another remedy, just as bad and even worse, which is to go about with a firebrand, setting fire to the plains and timber so as to drive off the mosquitoes, and also to get lizards and similar things which they eat, to come out of the soil. In the same manner they kill deer, encircling them with fires, and they do it also to deprive the animals of pasture, compelling them to go for food where the Indians want."

The next quotation refers to the northern prairies, those of Illinois, and comes from Hennepin (239, vol. 1, p. 154). He mentioned the Illinois tribe explicitly and wrote in 1683 that "the Bulls and other Beasts had been driven from the Banks of the River by means of Fire."

Father Vivier (522) in 1750, writing of the vicinity of St. Louis, said:

> Both banks of the Mississippi are bordered throughout the whole of its course by two strips of dense forests, the depth of which varies, more or less, from half a league to four leagues. Behind these forests the country is more elevated, and is intersected by plains and groves, wherein trees are almost as thinly scattered as in our public promenades. This is partly due to the fact that the savages set fire to the prairies toward the end of autumn, when the grass is dry; the fire spreads everywhere and destroys most of the young trees. This does not happen in places nearer the river, because, the land being lower and consequently more watery, the grass remains green longer and less susceptible to the attack of fire.

Le Page du Pratz (312, p. 218) in 1758 also described burning prairies during the fall along the Mississippi and specified that it was done to aid travel and to produce new grass that would attract game. Charlevoix (95, p. 68) wrote of Indian uses of fire on the upper Mississippi:

> In the Southern and Western Parts of New France, on both Sides the Mississippi, the most famous Hunt is that of the Buffaloe, which is performed in this Manner: The Hunters range themselves on four Lines, which form a great Square, and begin by setting Fire to the Grass and Herbs, which are dry and very high: Then as the Fire gets forwards, they advance, closing their lines: The Buffaloes, which are extremely afraid of Fire, keep flying from it, and at last find themselves so crowded together that they are generally every one killed. They say that a Party seldom returns from hunting without killing Fifteen Hundred or Two Thousand. But lest the different Companies should hinder each other they all agree before they set out about the Place where they intend to hunt.

Carver (74, p. 287), who traveled on the upper Mississippi River in 1766–68, left a similar description of a fire-drive: "The Indian method of hunting the buffalo is by forming a circle or a square, nearly in the same manner as when they search for the bear. Having taken their different stations, they set the grass, which at this time is rank and dry, on fire, and these animals, who are extremely fearful of that element, flying with precipitation before it, great numbers are hemmed in a small compass, and scarcely a single one escapes."

Catlin (77), one of the first systematic recorders of Plains Indian customs, wrote in 1842 as follows:

The prairies burning form some of the most beautiful scenes that are to be witnessed in this country, and also some of the most sublime. Every acre of these vast prairies (being covered for hundreds and hundreds of miles, with a crop of grass, which dies and dried in the fall) burns over during the fall or early in the spring, leaving the ground of a black and doleful colour.

There are many modes by which the fire is communicated to them, both by white men and by Indians—par accident; and yet many more where it is voluntarily done for the purpose of getting a fresh crop of grass, for the grazing of their horses, and also for easier traveling during the next summer, when there will be no old grass to lie upon the prairies, entangling the feet of man and horse, as they are passing over them.

Over the elevated lands and prairie bluffs, where the grass is thin and short, the fire slowly creeps with a feeble flame, which one can easily step over . . . where the wild animals often rest in their lairs until the flames almost burn their noses, when they will reluctantly rise, and leap over it, and trot off amongst the cinders, where the fire has past and left the ground as black as jet. These scenes at night become indescribably beautiful, when their flames are seen at many miles distance, creeping over the sides and tops of the bluffs, appearing to be sparkling and brilliant chains of liquid fire (the hills being lost to the view), hanging suspended in graceful festoons from the skies.

But there is yet another character of burning prairies . . . that requires another letter, and a different pen to describe—the war, or hell of fires! where the grass is seven or eight feet high, as is often the case for many miles together, on the Missouri bottoms and the flames are driven forward by the hurricanes, which often sweep over the vast prairies of this denuded country. There are many of these meadows on the Missouri, the Platte, and the Arkansas, of many miles in breadth, which are perfectly level, with a waving grass, so high, that we are obliged to stand erect in our stirrups, in order to look over its waving tops, as we are riding through it. The fire in these, before such a wind, travels at an immense and frightful rate, and often destroys, on their fleetest horses, parties of Indians, who are so unlucky as to be overtaken by it; not that it travels as fast as a horse at full speed, but that the high grass is filled with wild pea-vines and other impediments, which render it necessary for the rider to guide his horse in the zig-zag paths of the deers and buffaloes, retarding his progress, until he is overtaken by the dense column of smoke that is swept before the fire-alarming the horse, which stops and stands terrified and immutable, till the burning grass which is wafted in the wind, falls about him, kindling up in a moment a thousand new fires, which are instantly wrapped in the swelling flood of smoke that is moving on like a black thundercloud, rolling on the earth, with its lightning's glare, and its thunder rumbling as it goes.

In the *Handbook of American Indians* (Hodge [249], vol. 1, p. 581), summarizing the knowledge of American aborigines up to 1907, is found the statement: "Indians used . . . firebrands and prairie fires for game drives."

With this comment, which implies that the practice was general among tribes included in the "Plains Indian Culture Area," I will consider the area in detail by states, so that the local conditions can be evaluated more carefully. Although many articles have been written that treated the grasslands as a unit or in two or three major divisions, it appears to me essential to review the information available for many smaller areas before presenting conclusions for the entire grassland. Many studies of vegetation are concerned with particular states; consequently, the same geographic unit will be followed generally, yet numerous exceptions will appear when either the references or other conditions require it.

ILLINOIS

There are more theoretical discussions of the vegetation of Illinois than of any other grassland state. This has probably come about because Illinois prairies appear to be an intrusion into the eastern woodlands area, having climatic conditions similar to those of woodlands. Gleason (207, p. 77) calls this extension "the Prairie Peninsula," a phrase made popular by Transeau (513) in 1935 by his using it for the title of an article in the journal *Ecology*. Interest in Illinois prairies has also been great because of the early and numerous references to their having been burned.

The earliest statement of grass fires in Illinois was recorded in 1683 by Hennepin (239), quoted earlier. Those also quoted from Vivier (522) of 1750, and Le Page du Pratz (312) for 1758, although less clearly localized, probably referred to Illinois as well. Fordham (182, p. 234) was one of the first American settlers to describe prairie fires. In 1818 he wrote of Edwards County, southeastern Illinois:

> The Northern Arm of the Long Prairie is more like an immense river, studded with islands of wood, and bounded by dark forests. . . . The surface . . . is gently undulating, completely free from brushwood, and its soil is still more rich than that of the Bon Pas Prairie. . . .
>
> Since I began to write this letter I have been interrupted by a tremendous fire in the Prairie, which driven by a strong South wind threatened our habitations. . . .
>
> It was the most glorious and most awful sight I ever beheld. A thousand acres of Prairie were in flames at once. . . . The flames reached the forests, and rushed like torrents through. . . .
>
> There are five large fires visible tonight, some many miles off.
>
> The prairies are fired by the hunters to drive out the deer. Two or three years after a place is settled, the grass is eaten down and will not burn.

Bourne (54) and Wells (546), both writing in 1819 and already quoted above, mentioned Illinois as one of the areas having prairies because of Indian burning practices. In 1825 Loomis (332) expressed a similar view, as follows:

> I have observed that on the western edges or borders of all the large prairies a thick growth of young timber is springing up, whereas on their eastern borders no underbrush is found within many rods of the open lands. The heat and fury of the flames driven by a westerly wind far into the timbered land . . . destroying the undergrowth of timber, and every year increasing the extent of prairie in that direction, has no doubt, for many centuries added to the quantity of open land found throughout this part of America.

Ellsworth (157) in 1837 also stated his belief that Illinois prairies resulted from frequently being burned, and Jones (276, p. 90) in 1838 explained how this was accomplished:

> This yearly burning consumes all the new trees and shrubs, and leaves the ground entirely unencumbered. The old trees, likewise, are annually diminishing in number. Scarcely a tree but is marked with fire, and when once the bark is penetrated by the fire, and the wood of the tree seared, the fire takes a readier and deeper hold thereon, until at last it overpowers and destroys it, and the tree falls with a startling crash, and generally consumes before the fire dies out, unless a violent rain extinguishes it, and leaves

it for food for the next annual passage of the devouring element. I have beheld many a line of ashes, making the spot where the entire trunk of a massy oak was consumed the previous autumn.

That fire was the essential factor in maintaining the grassland of Illinois is shown by Gerhard's (197) description of the methods used in 1857 to extend the forests:

> The first efforts to convert prairies into forest land were usually made on the part of the prairie adjoining the timber. A range of farms, which girded the entire prairie along its circumference having been established, three furrows were plowed all around the settlements in order to stop the burning of the prairie for the whole distance of the circuit in the neighborhood of these farms; whereupon the timber quickly grows up spontaneously on all the parts not burned, the groves and forests commencing a gradual encroachment on the adjoining prairies, so that one after another concentric circle springs up inside the preceding, and thus the entire prairie is steadily narrowed from all sides until it is finally occupied, forming a vast region covered with timbers and farms.

Englemann (159, p. 389) also remarked that forests were invading Illinois prairies in 1863, since regular burning had stopped. He said that the Indians had burned to facilitate hunting, to kill insects and snakes, to remove dry stalks, and to secure better pasture. Although Winchell (561) in 1864 denied that Indians caused prairies by frequently burning them, he did record that it was a common practice. Fendler (169, p. 154) disclosed that in 1866 he had observed the process of prairie formation in Illinois, Missouri, and Texas. He said: "Fire I consider by far the most powerful and principal agency that gave prairies and savannahs their existence, extending them in course of time."

Fendler believed that the American prairies formed as did the llanos of Venezuela, which he had seen develop in a humid forest climate. In 1867 the early American geographer Marsh (355, p. 134) expressed his belief that "only by the annual burning of the grass, by grazing animals, or by cultivation" were trees prevented from covering the prairies of the Mississippi valley. Caton (78, pp. 96, 100), in refutation of Lesqueraux's (314) theory that prairies resulted from conditions of the soil, wrote in 1869: "I entirely concur in the popular opinion that among the most important of the causes which have produced [the prairies] is fire. . . . The opinions of the first settlers . . . are entitled to respect . . . they universally attribute the absence of trees from the prairies to the periodical fires which swept over them. . . ."

Sargent (432), in a letter to Hartman published in 1897, expressed the same idea as follows: "[Indians] . . . burnt the prairies every year to improve the feed for [buffalo] and so prevented the spread of tree growth. This is proved by the fact that since the removal of Indians, great regions of Indiana, Illinois and Iowa which were formerly prairie are now covered with forest."

Wissler (567, p. 50), referring to several early travelers' accounts, in 1910 expressed his belief that the Indians of Illinois, as well as those of other prairies, hunted by firing the grass. Perrot (394b, p. 120) in 1911 also stated that the Indians of Illinois employed fire to encircle buffalo, and John Muir (378) attributed the treeless condition of Illinois grasslands to prairie fires.

From the statements presented above there can be no doubt that Indians frequently burned over much of Illinois and that forests very quickly invaded many prairie areas as soon as the grass fires stopped. Modern ecological studies of Illinois and neighboring prairie states began to appear about 1900 in the reports of Clements, Transeau, Gleason, and Shimek, to cite the best-known. Nearly all botanists and ecologists mention fire as a contributing factor in prairie formation and maintenance. I believe, however, that the role of fire has been generally grossly underestimated, especially in the "Prairie Peninsula." The development of soil sciences appears to have greatly contributed to the failure to appreciate the full force of fire.

Soil as a deciding factor in prairie formation was proposed by Atwater (19) in 1818 and strongly supported by Winchell (561) and Lesquereaux (313, 314) in the 1860s. Marsh (355) in 1867 and Shaler (450) in 1891, although soil scientists, maintained that fire was extremely important, if not essential, in the origin and continuation of prairies. The modern authorities on soils, beginning with Hilgard (245) in 1906 and continuing with Coffey (108) in 1912, Hulbert (262) in 1930, and Marbut (353) in 1935, and the U.S. Department of Agriculture Yearbook (577) *Soils and Men* in 1938, all but ignore fire as an ecological factor contributing to the existence of prairies. To soil scientists the vegetation is determined by the soil, even in Illinois. Hilgard (245, p. 513), for example, wrote as follows:

> North of the Ohio River the materials of the geological formations are not nearly as much varied as they are south of the same; consequently the vegetative features are also much more uniform. It must be remembered that from the Alleghenies nearly to the Mississippi, the states of Ohio, Southern Michigan, Indiana and Illinois are largely covered by drift deposits overlying the older formations, except that along the Ohio and Mississippi rivers lies the calcareous loam of the Loess or Bluff formation.

Within the states mentioned, however, not only are the older underlying formations very generally calcareous, but calcareous sand and gravel form a large proportion of the drift deposits, which in most cases overlie the rocks. Hence we find from the Alleghenies to the Mississippi a predominance of the oak forests which characterizes calcareous soils, as in the better class of uplands in Mississippi and Tennessee; interrupted only here and there by sandy belts or ridges bearing inferior growth, among which, again, the blackjack and post oaks, with short-leaved pine, are conspicuous. But in a large portion of Illinois, as well as in Western Indiana, the oak forest is interrupted by more or less continuous belts, and sometimes by a wide expanse, of black prairie, generally treeless or bearing only clumps of crab-apple and haw, and underlaid more or less directly by the carboniferous limestones, whose disintegration has materially contributed to the black prairie soils; which are noted for their high and long-continued productiveness. . . .

The black-jack and post oak are not nearly as frequently found on the prairies of Illinois as on those of Mississippi and Alabama; but where they occur they assume a similar habit, including the occurrence of the dwarfed, apple-tree-shaped form on the low ridges with heavy yellow clay soil, that sometimes intersect the prairies.

Hilgard seems unconcerned with the problem of diverse vegetation on the same type of soil or the radical changes in plant cover that have taken place in historic times. The question of soil as a factor in grassland formation is here reviewed later, but reference may be made again to recent studies by Heyward (243) and Billings (43) that indicate that the vegetation determines the soil type as much as or more than the soil determines the vegetation. Their studies indicate that soil responds quickly to vegetation changes.

Among the modern botanists, Gleason stands out as one of the most outspoken advocates of fire as the essential factor in prairie formation and maintenance. Although his later articles consider the vegetation of the "Middle West," many of his data come from Illinois. In 1912 Gleason (205, p. 48) reported on a careful analysis of "An Isolated Prairie Grove" in Champaign County, Illinois. He determined that the grove had survived because of topography, which had allowed water to collect to form a slough that had protected the trees from prairie fires. From that and other forest relicts, he concluded that Illinois had been at one time forested but that prairie fires had removed trees except where they were protected by special natural conditions.

In a second article a year later, Gleason (206, p. 175) reported on a more extensive investigation, including the evaluation of circumstances permitting the survival of isolated groves in eight Illinois counties, all having been indicated on old survey maps made about 1820. He also quoted a number of early accounts that documented the Indian practice of burning prairies. Although Gleason would not "hazard an opinion as to . . . first date of first prairie fire or its possible cause," he did state he had "no record of a prairie fire produced by lightning." He said further that "it is definitely known that the Indians habitually started fire, and the prairie fire as a phytogeographical factor dates back to the entrance of the Indians or to the origin of this habit."

Gleason noted that the prevailing winds were from the west and recorded the fact that tree belts along streams were narrower on the west than on the east side as a result of having prairie fires blown into them from the west. He stated his conclusion that "it seems evident that prairie fires have been the deciding factor in determining the distribution of forests in the Middle West. With prairie fires, the forests have been driven back or destroyed, except in those areas where the favor of morainic or fluviatile topography has enabled them to resist the encroachments of the prairies."

Gleason (207) continued his study of the prairies and wrote "The Vegetational History of the Middle West" in 1932. Much additional information regarding Illinois is included. For example, "In Champaign County 1.7 percent and in Piatt County 1 percent of the forest area is in isolated groves apart from any river system" (p. 79); and "[l]arge areas of barrens were converted into forest as by magic, when fires that had maintained them were stopped and oak sprouts became trees" (p. 78).

Gleason found evidence that forests had advanced one to two miles in thirty years in Macon and Moultrie Counties. He found also that northwestern Illinois, now heavily forested, had been 80–90 percent prairie (p. 82). He thought the prairies had spread far eastward of historic prairies during the dry, xerothermic climate following the Wisconsin glaciation and that the forests had begun occupying the prairies and were moving westward when the process was reversed by the Indian fires (p. 84). Gleason wrote of the "Prairie Peninsula" as follows: "The eastern migration of the prairie proceeded as a wedge-shaped extension between the coniferous vegetation at the north and the deciduous forests at the south and reached limits considerably beyond the eastern margin of modern continuous prairies. Numerous relic colonies formerly occurred . . . in eastern Indiana, northwestern Ohio and southern Michigan."

There is no reason to end the "Prairie Peninsula" in Ohio, for we saw in the earlier section of this work that grasslands extended into New York and New England and into Kentucky and Virginia, if "relic colonies" of prairie vegetation are evidence. One should recall also Blizzard's (49) study of the Long Island prairie. Although Vestal (521, p. 233) in 1931 questioned the dominant role of fire in southern pines, as mentioned earlier in this work, his own research in Illinois, reported in 1918 (519 and 520), showed that burning was a very important factor in the formation and maintenance of prairie vegetation within a forest. He observed small "prairies" invading forests along railroad rights-of-way. After the cuts and fills of railroad construction are made, he said, whether forests or prairies occupy the bare earth depends on drainage, exposure, rainfall, "and the destructive effects of burning or of mowing, both of which are common on rights of way."

Vestal's recognition that fire contributed to the maintenance of grass along railroad rights-of-way is remarkable in view of several botanists to be mentioned later who ignore this and, consequently, make dubious deductions. H. C. Sampson's (431) publication in 1921 of "An Ecological Survey of the Prairie Vegetation of Illinois" applies to Illinois principles of climatic determination of vegetation first applied by Transeau (513) in 1905 and carefully worked out, also in 1921, by Livingston and Shreve (327) for the nation as a whole. Sampson seems to ignore the articles mentioned above by Gleason and Vestal that preceded his, for he also minimizes fire as an ecological factor in prairie formation. For example, he wrote (p. 525): "To sum up, climatic factors are important in determining the general boundaries of distribution of the prairie, while edaphic factors are important in determining the origin and character of the prairie associations within these boundaries. The edaphic factors become more and more prominent toward the edges of the prairie, as in eastern Illinois. When a prairie association is once established, biotic factors and prairie fires are important in checking invasion by forest vegetation."

Sampson's view was also expressed in the following quotation (p. 574): ". . . prairie fires and grazing are an effect rather than a cause of the prairies. As shown above, this may be true also of the prairie soils in so far as they differ from forest soils. On the other hand, temperature, wind, humidity, rainfall, and topography were all important factors in causing the treelessness of the prairies, but no one of these factors considered alone will explain the prairies."

Sampson's argument fails if it is remembered that fire did produce and maintain prairies in the eastern woodlands under climatic conditions much more favorable to forest growth than those in Illinois. It also seems especially weak when it is remembered that forests "appeared like magic," as Gleason says, in many areas of Illinois, without changes in the five climatic factors Sampson lists, and with only a cessation of burning.

Sampson might have given prairie fires more credit for causing the prairies if he had remembered to consider the fact that grass fires continue to be common in Illinois. This oversight has important consequences, since Sampson's study rested heavily on the many "patches of virgin prairie along the railway rights-of-way" (p. 529). The regular burning or mowing of railway rights-of-way is such a common practice that its significance for the study of Illinois prairie cannot be overlooked. And, especially if one's examples of "virgin prairie" are regularly burned now, as they were in aboriginal times, burning cannot be passed over so lightly as it was by Sampson. His statement (p. 555) that "[a] recent fire in a small section of this prairie had destroyed most of the seedlings less than six feet in height" should have alerted him.

Waller (530), like Sampson a student and colleague of Transeau at Ohio State University, completely ignores fires as an ecological factor in determining the distribution of vegetation, as recorded by the first inhabitants in Ohio. Schaffner (438), also of the Ohio State University Department of Botany, in 1926 added his support to Transeau's "ratio of rainfall to evaporation" as the determining factor in grasslands formation. He accepted H. C. Sampson's report for Illinois and designated 60 to 80 percent ratio of rainfall to evaporation as the climate of true prairie. Illinois falls within the area of such a ratio.

Woodward (574) in 1924 reviewed the literature and presented his own ideas in an article entitled "Origin of Prairies in Illinois." His conclusions were as follows (p. 259): "Fires may have checked the invasion of forests into prairies, but prairies never originated by the destruction of forests by fires. Illinois Prairies are in [a] glaciated area . . . large areas in Illinois are still prairie because post-glacial time has been too short for the forests to invade such areas of level land."

H. C. Sampson, Waller, and Schaffner expressed views similar to Woodward's to the effect that Illinois prairies are survivals from the grasslands that took over the area following the retreat of the glaciers. This problem will be considered more fully later, but a statement here is appropriate. The denial of fire as the originator of Illinois prairies because glaciers had really removed the trees may be warranted, but it does not detract from the ecological importance of fire. It seems to make little difference whether fires removed trees that occupied Illinois following the glaciers or whether fires kept trees from spreading onto lands they would have occupied were it not for Indian use of fire.

Few of the students of prairie vegetation have thought of Indian burning of grass as beginning during the last glacial advance and continuing from that time until stopped following European settlement. There is good reason to believe that grass burning occurred as soon as grass growing followed the retreat of the last glaciers. The paramount importance of fire is suggested by Fuller's (190) evidence that the forests survived, during glacial advances, within fifty miles of the ice sheet and that trees grew in central and northern Illinois during the height of the Wisconsin glaciation. He believes that forests followed closely the retreat of the ice. If Fuller has correctly interpreted the geological evidence, something besides climate and soil must have kept the forests from Illinois or removed them. Fire could have done either or both. In spite of the high professional standing of the scholars who rejected fire as a necessary agent in Illinois prairie formation, Cowles (118) joined Gleason in 1928 in the judgment that fire was essential. He wrote:

> Fire and grazing may be factors also, for when they are eliminated trees frequently invade the adjoining prairie. Prairies are well suited for tree growth, for when trees are planted artificially they not only thrive but spread spontaneously. . . .
>
> [Near Chicago] trees are now encroaching on the prairie and are invading prairie soil.

Rice (418) gave additional testimony concerning the aboriginal use of fire and demonstrated the prevailing practice of using rights-of-way as samples of prairie. For her study of "The Effect of Fire on the Prairie Animal Communities," she used "strips of sub-climax prairie along the Illinois Central Railway, one mile west of Seymour, Illinois." She considered this a good experimental area because it was subject to "annual burning, following mowing . . . required by law." These conditions approach those of early settlement times, because, as she says (p. 392): "The Indians and early settlers burned the grasslands in late fall or early spring believing that the early appearance of green grass would attract game or give an abundance of early feed for their domestic animals."

F. E. Clements, who might be called the father of American ecology, has made what seem to me conflicting statements about the importance of fire in determining the vegetation of an area. His article (103) on "The Relict Method in Dynamic Ecology," published in 1934, reports "explicit testimony to the paramount role of fire" in the "plains" of New Jersey, but on the same page (65) states: "The most dramatic event of the period of desiccation was the falling back of the forest along the line of the isohyet of 40 in. running from central Missouri through southern Illinois and into Indiana."

Clements considers that prairie fires during the "period of settlement" inhibited the return of forests yet does not mention that fires set by Indians would have done the same. Also, he does not take into account relict "prairies" in Ohio, such as the one studied by Withrow (569), who reported her findings in the journal *Ecology* in 1932. Withrow found a typical prairie association dominated by *Andropogon scoparius*, *Sorghastrum nutans*, and *Silphium terebinthaceum* near Cincinnati. Scattered scrub oaks, small in spite of having "rounded out a good half century of life," were very unlike the forest trees that encircled the acre or so of natural grass. This small "prairie" was situated on a bluff, the rock being covered with a thin layer of soil. Consequently, Withrow concluded that "the grassland persists only in such areas as are edaphically unfavorable to forests." Nevertheless, according to the principles of "dynamic ecology" set forth by Clements, such a relict indicates that the "Prairie Peninsula" once extended continuously far beyond the isohyet of 40 inches, which he evaluates as being critical.

Although Transeau influenced the theories and methods of some students of prairies as early as 1910, according to an acknowledgment by H. C. Sampson, his own publication dealing specifically with grasslands, "The Prairie Peninsula," was published in 1935. Transeau (513) outlined various theories and summarized much evidence.

> To still others the Prairie Peninsula represents a pyrophoric victory of the Indians and pre-Indians attempting to enlarge native pastures, or to capture their grazing meat supply. . . .
>
> Fires favor persistence of prairie. . . .

Fire as an ecological factor seems to boil down to this: that in forest climates it retards development and may result in scrub, but it does not result in prairie. In a prairie climate it helps to maintain and perhaps enlarges the prairie.

But Transeau overemphasizes climate and falsely places fire in a secondary role in the persistence of prairies. One cannot ignore such data as those from Hursh and Connaughton (264), discussed in the section on the eastern woodlands, which demonstrate the effect of vegetation on local climate. With temperature, rainfall, and wind affected by the removal of forests as Hursh and Connaughton discovered, one must as carefully consider the possibility that the climate of the prairie peninsula has resulted from the removal of forests as that the prairies are treeless because of the climate.

WISCONSIN

Schoolcraft (443), who traveled on the upper Mississippi in 1820, added his statement regarding the burning of Wisconsin prairies by Indians to those of earlier explorers. Hoffman (250) in 1835 not only confirmed the

Indian practice of burning grasslands but theorized about its effect, while discussing the Prairie du Chien of southwest Wisconsin, as follows: "I forget whether I have before mentioned that the Indian name for prairie (*scutay*), which means also fire, would account for their origin with anyone who had had the opportunity of observing how the action of that element extends these grassy domains every season in one direction, while it leaves them to shoot up into a luxuriant growth of young forest in another."

Although many authors have combined Wisconsin with Illinois in their discussions of prairies, a number of recent studies treat specifically of Wisconsin. John Muir (378), for example, wrote the following in 1913: "The uniformly rich soil of Illinois and Wisconsin prairies produced so close and tall a growth of grasses for fires that no tree could live on it. Had there been no fires, these fine prairies, so marked a feature of the country, would have been covered by the heaviest forests."

Muir discussed Wisconsin "oak openings," and "park-like" forests, as well as "grubs," all of which he attributed to fire. Cottam (115, p. 272) summarized Muir's ideas as follows:

> Muir describes these "grubs" as oak and hickory plants that were prevented by the almost annual fires from becoming mature trees. Each year the plants would send up new shoots which would be killed by the autumn grass fires. The roots, however, would not die and would continue to send up the new shoots over long periods of time. Muir estimates that some of these grubs were over a century old.
>
> Muir also states that the arrival of the white man and the subsequent cessation of the annual grass fires permitted these grubs to grow up into trees, forming "tall thickets so dense that it was difficult to walk through them."

Gleason (207, p. 82) said that southwestern Wisconsin, now heavily forested, was 80 to 90 percent prairie at the time of settlement and attributed the change to the cessation of regular prairie fires. During the last decade several significant publications have appeared relative to prairie vegetation. D. White's (552) experiment on "Prairie Soil as a Medium for Tree Growth," reported in 1941, established the fact that seedlings grow better in a greenhouse if planted in soil from a forest than in soil from a prairie. Exhaustive analysis indicated slight chemical differences. Prairie soil seemed slightly deficient in available phosphorus and potassium. White's conclusion was, however, that the growth difference resulted from the two soils differing in mycorrhizae, i.e., "symbiotic associations of mycelium of certain fungi" (p. 405). Since soils respond quickly to vegetation, according to Heyward (243) and Billings (43), any initial disadvantage trees had on prairie soil would be overcome as forests became established. In fact, Wilde, Whitford, and Youngberg (558), also doing research in Wisconsin, reported a rapid change of prairie soil—"degradation," as they interpret the change—where burr oaks have invaded the prairie.

Another study by Chavennes (96), also published in 1941, documented the changes when Indian prairie fires were stopped. Her analysis of the maps and surveyors' notes made in 1829 and in 1854 of the prairie region of Wisconsin revealed marked changes taking place between the two dates. She wrote:

> The rapidity with which woods grow under protection was common knowledge, for though the prairie might be treeless when settled, trees set out for house protection and ornament or for woodlots grew thriftily, almost without exception. A striking example of this is described in the first [1854] annual report of the Wisconsin Geological Survey on a farm where grew "dense groves of young trees from six to ten inches in diameter, where 25 years ago not a single shrub could be found larger than a riding whip."
>
> The source of the new timber would lie in the seeds, roots and stumps sending up new growth after the inhibiting or destructive forces of the prairie fires were removed.
>
> Apparently this phenomenon was the chief cause of a 60 percent decrease in the prairie area of southwestern Wisconsin, which occurred between 1829 when Chandler marked it as nine-tenths prairie, and 1854 when the Geological Survey reported it was only one-third prairie, broken in part by groves and oak openings.
>
> But has there really been a marked increase in wooded territory at the expense of the prairie within historical time? Undoubtedly so, but it has not been accomplished by the natural processes of invasion alone. Before the advent of explorers, regiments and settlers, the successional processes between forest and prairie maintained themselves naturally, and the success of the slowly encroaching woodland seemed to depend chiefly on recurrent prairie fires set by the Indians. However, the men who preempted southern Wisconsin put an end to the fires and disturbed the natural prairie-woods balance. With the cessation of fires there was a tremendous acceleration of woodland growth in those areas where fence lines furnished an early protection. This prodigal increase in wooded area . . . was soon limited to woodlots and windbreaks, but not before the wooded aspect of the country had become quite pronounced.
>
> The landscape, rich in oak and hickory, maple and linden, is indeed a far cry to the time when the people who came to Wisconsin found one of the greatest drawbacks to travel was the lack of sufficient wood to build a campfire.

Although the quotation leaves no doubt that Wisconsin prairies were dependent on fire for their existence, it is surprising that Chavennes considers prairie fires part of the "natural prairie-woods balance." I would call Indian-set grass fires an unnatural, artificial weighting of the balance in favor of prairies. Curtis and Partch (123) added to our knowledge of competition between prairie and forests in their 1948 report, which showed that typical prairie plants appeared far beyond the traditional prairie zone "where fire or other agencies" prevent the establishment of woody species.

The most recent paper read dealing with Wisconsin prairie vegetation was that of Grant Cottam (115) printed in 1949. He made an exhaustive ecological study of Stewart's Woods, an old "oak opening" on the prairie about fifteen miles northeast of Madison, Wisconsin. The woods, now surrounded by fields, are maintained because they are in a small area of rough terrain. Cottam did not say so, but the ancient "oak-opening" probably survived the Indian-set prairie fires also because of the rough terrain. Cottam discovered that the parklike aspect of the "oak-opening" began to change into an oak wood about 1860 and has since become progressively a typical maple-elm-linden forest. What has changed in the environment of Stewart's Woods to allow such a remarkable modification in vegetation? Cottam believes the soil, climate, and topography are about the same as a century ago.

After reviewing the writings of Gleason, Transeau, Muir, and others relative to his problem, Cottam came to the conclusion that the oak-openings were remnants of more extensive forests and that presettlement fires "may have been responsible for the initial impetus that brought about the oak openings in southwestern Wisconsin" (p. 285). He states further that "the influence of fire on the perpetuation of oak openings can be demonstrated" by the effects of repeated ground fires in the University of Wisconsin Arboretum. Cottam (p. 287) states that "fires are known to have been common prior to settlement, being used by the Indians to drive game" and concludes that the "fire factor" offers the best explanation for the origin and maintenance of oak openings and the prairie flora accompanying them. For Wisconsin, as for Illinois, fire appears to be an essential condition for the existence of prairies.

MINNESOTA

Our record of Indians setting fire to Minnesota landscape goes back to the first French explorers of the Upper Mississippi, to whom I have referred, as well as Schoolcraft (443), Allen (10), and McGee (347), early American scholars interested in the same area. McGee in 1884 wrote that the Siouan Indians, who had occupied southern Minnesota and eastern Dakotas, set fires "to destroy the undergrowth in the interests of the chase" (p. 186). N. H. Winchell (562) in 1880 and W. Upham (515) in 1895, basing their opinions upon observation made during geological surveys, declared that Minnesota prairies had been caused by fire.

Recent, more exhaustive analyses of Minnesota vegetation that shed light upon the role of fire as an ecological factor come from Minnesota forested areas. Stallard's (476) 1929 study indicated that "annual or frequent burning" could maintain a prairie in Minnesota's northern forests. By inference, then, it may be concluded that Indian fires could easily have caused and maintained the prairies in the drier, hotter section of the state.

Also of interest, since it supports the view that Indians frequently set fires to all types of vegetation throughout the United States, is an article by Kittredge (285) published in 1934, concerning forest succession on Star Island, Minnesota. Kittredge did not mention that Indians set fire to forests, but he did say there had been an Indian village on Star Island. He said further that "the trees have preserved in the fire scars the record . . . of fires between 1803 and 1818 and in 1865, 1871 and 1872. . . . Apparently, however, no serious or extensive fire has burned over any large part of the island for more than fifty years."

During the two decades between Kittredge's two visits to Star Island, the forest vegetation changed markedly in amount and type. The succession from jack pine to maple-basswood dominance was evident; and by dating different aged trees, Kittredge decided the full succession would require six hundred and fifty years. During fifty years only, presumably since the Indians left Star Island, had the succession progressed uninterrupted by frequent fires. The only conclusion possible is that the Indians had burned frequently, thus maintaining large sections of the island in a pre-climax state, for the succession from jack pine to Norway pine to white pine to maple is now taking place under stable climatic and soil conditions.

A popular book by Holbrook (252) entitled *Burning an Empire,* which appeared in 1943, might appropriately be mentioned because Minnesota has had some of the nation's most disastrous forest fires. One is the Hinckley fire of 1894, the other the Cloquet fire of 1918. These and the other excessively damaging fires, by the dates they occurred, lend weight to the belief that Indians kept forests open and free of underbrush by frequently setting fires that did not destroy the mature trees. When the Indians were removed from an area or were prohibited from continuing their ancient practices, brush accumulated so that fires, which inevitably came, were much more destructive than at the time of settlement. Minnesota, being both a prairie and forest state, provides evidence that Indians burned fields and forests and that in both their fires were a decisive ecological factor.

IOWA

Like Illinois, Iowa has stimulated factual and theoretical articles about prairies. The first explorers of the Mississippi Valley reported prairie fires set by Indians of Iowa, as in other regions they visited. Maximilian Wied-Neuwied (556), who traveled up the Missouri in 1832, identified the Iowas near Council Bluffs as being responsible for "whole tracts covered with dead poplars, which had been killed by fires caused by the Indians in the forest and prairie" (p. 268). He also observed grass fires in the Ponca Indian area. Both Perrot (394b) and Wissler (568) included Iowa in the region in which they said Indians used fire to drive game.

Some early Iowa writers who were primarily interested in the history of vegetation did not identify the Indian tribes who set fire to the grass and forests of the region. Wells (546), who has been previously cited, wrote in 1819 that fire was the all-important force in the origin of prairies and may have been referring to the Iowas when he wrote (p. 335):

> Ordinarily, all the country, of a nature to become prairie is already in that state; yet the writer . . . has seen, in the country between the Missouri and Mississippi, after unusual dry seasons, more than one hundred acres of woodland together converted into prairie. And again, where the grass has been prevented from burning . . . or the prairie has been depastured by large herds of domestic cattle, it will assume, in a few years, the appearance of a young forest.

The reports of the Geological Survey of Iowa from 1858 to 1900 contain numerous statements regarding burning of prairies by Indians as well as interpretations of the relationship between the burning of grasses and the origin of prairies. Whitney (555), for example, in 1858 considered the nature of the soil the prime cause of the prairies, whereas C. A. White (549–51), writing from 1868 to 1871, and Macbride (344), writing from 1894 to 1900, both considered fire very important. White believed prairie fires were the determining factor. Gow (213) and Baker (22), also working about the turn of the century, placed fire as an important contributing agent in Iowa grassland formation.

No authority on prairie vegetation has been referred to more frequently than B. Shimek, botanist of the University of Iowa, whenever the question of origin of the prairies is considered by modern ecologists and botanists. Shimek's (457) famous paper "The Prairies," published in 1911, reviewed the historical literature on the subject so comprehensively that many writers since then have simply made reference to it to cover the earlier factual and theoretical publications on the subject. His selected and annotated bibliography of 146 titles arranged chronologically starts with "A1818-Atwater" and goes to "A1910-Gleason." Shimek states his "Summary of Conclusions" for Iowa as follows (p. 220):

1. Exposure to evaporation as determined by temperature, wind, and topography is the primary cause of the treelessness of the prairies.
2. The prairie flora persists on the exposed areas because it is xerophytic.
3. Rainfall and drainage, while of importance because determining the available supply of water in both soil and air, are not a general, determining cause, both frequently being equal on contiguous forested and prairie areas.
4. Soils and geological formations are of value only insofar as they affect conservation of water; the porosity of the former determining its power of holding moisture, and the latter often determining topography.
5. Prairie fires were an effect rather than a cause, and where acting as a cause were local.

Shimek's data and arguments appear reasonable and convincing; consequently, they have been widely accepted as definitive. He seems to consider fully and to weigh carefully all factors, including fire, before concluding, as do Transeau (513) and Livingston and Shreve (327), that prairies result from deficiency of moisture available to plants as indicated by the rainfall-evaporation ratio.

Two or three weaknesses appear to me in Shimek's argument. First is his use of data from small grassy openings in woods, hillsides, or ridges, etc., as examples for extensive, flat grasslands. As Withrow (569) found in Ohio, such small prairies may result from very special local conditions (e.g., shallow soil as in the example she studied), which do not apply to large Iowa prairies. Aikman (4, p. 587) discovered on Muscatine Island, Iowa, that there also "the development of the prairie . . . is due to an edaphic factor." Other faults are evident in Shimek's statement (p. 218):

> While there can be no question as [to] the extent and destructiveness of prairie fires, they must be looked upon . . . rather as an effect than a cause, for nowhere in Iowa or adjacent territory has there been any marked general encroachment of the forests on the prairie when the fires ceased. In much of the territory the rapid settlement and extensive cultivation of the prairies would have prevented any such encroachment, but in the hilly western part of the state, where the surface remained practically undisturbed, there has been only a slight extension of the borders of the groves. The oldest settlers in that part of the state agree that since the

cessation of prairie fires no new groves have appeared except where set out by man, and that the native groves have expanded very little.

The evidence I have presented for Illinois and Wisconsin, which showed great expansion of forests onto prairies, refutes his remark about "adjacent territories," and Wells's statement above casts doubt on Shimek's idea concerning Iowa. I would say further that slow and little expansion suggests greater possibilities in time, for Shimek himself records how a grove once established changes the whole aspect of the vicinity. Shimek's principal inadequacy is his failure to document the absence of present-day grass fires. Perhaps many of the plots he studied and described as examples of prairies that are treeless, due to inadequate moisture and excessive evaporation, were burned from time to time. In terms of what has been noted earlier, Shimek's statement (p. 185) that there exists "undisturbed prairie chiefly along railways" is highly inappropriate. His papers of 1925 (458) and 1948 (459) indicate more clearly than that of 1911 that he failed to appreciate the role of fire. He wrote (458, p. 3): "The purest remnants of the prairie are often found along the right of way of the older railways which entered the territory before the original prairie was broken, and they give the most striking illustration of the persistence of prairie where it remains undisturbed, even in such narrow strips as those here noted."

What Shimek failed to add is that because of fire hazards the law requires that rail line rights-of-way must be burned every year. If the "purest remnants of the prairie" are those annually burned, it must be concluded that burning is a fundamental condition of their existence. Although Shimek referred to C. A. White (551), he failed to see the implications in the burning practices that White reported on in 1871: "These together cover the ground every season; for the fires of one year do not at all impair or prevent their abundant growth the next. Stringent laws are enacted in the prairie States against the setting of fire to the prairies; yet each year's growth of grass, upon at least the larger ones, is somewhat almost invariably burned."

Shimek's "last words on a major problem of his lifelong studies," as indicated in an editor's note to his "Plant Geography of Iowa" (459, p. 159), published posthumously in 1948, reveal his bias against accepting fire as an important ecological factor and give added significance to the importance of Indian burning practices. More thorough documentation of the amount and reasons for Indians setting fire to vegetation refutes Shimek's view that there remains an "unverified story that Indians deliberately set fire to the prairies to secure pasture for the bison" (459, p. 164). My evidence does not leave "unverified" the practice of Indians setting fires to secure pasture. On the other hand, Shimek's studies confirm my belief that one must evaluate burning and its effect over very broad and diverse areas to assess properly its local influence. Shimek passed over the evidence provided by the growth of shelterbelts and woodlots artificially planted as unimportant.

It appears to me, however, that if woodlots develop forest conditions, as determined by their maintaining and reproducing themselves, it can be concluded that forests in Iowa, as in Illinois, would have spread over all such areas had not fire, and subsequently cultivation, inhibited forestation. Aikman and Smelser (5, p. 149) can be quoted in supporting this view:

> While the present conditions of plant growth within the [prairie] communities provide a sufficient basis for the explanation of their present structure, they do not provide a basis for the explanation of their original establishment. In the several prairie sites examined in central Iowa, the grasses are so well established and have built up the total nitrogen of the soil to so high a level that there is practically no evidence of the invasion of upland prairie by woody plants except in sites which are potentially forest but produce grass until the limiting factors of fire, cutting or overgrazing are removed. These areas of suppressed vegetation are often difficult to distinguish from typical prairie vegetation.

The uniqueness of Iowa's prairies is comparable to that of the open longleaf pine forests in the southeastern United States. Both have resulted from unusual circumstances. Just as there is no question that the longleaf pine forest needs fire for its survival, there appears to be no question that Iowa's tall-grass prairies also required fire for their survival during presettlement times. If my thesis that fire was the essential factor in prairie formation and persistence is correct it would have to take into account the work of paleobotanists, especially results obtained in analysis of pollen from peat bogs. On the other hand, if fire has had the influence I believe it has had, the paleobotanists must be more cautious in attributing to widespread climatic change the differences in relative amounts of pollen found at different depths of peat.

For example, Sears (447) interprets the variation in pollen profiles studied in northern Iowa as indicating a climatic change that was expressed in replacement of forest by grasses. Even if a change in general climate is accepted, the presence of Indians in the area and the probability of their setting fire to prairies and forests would require that consideration be given to their ability to upset or prohibit normal plant succession. Today the ratios of rainfall to evaporation in northern Iowa and southern Ohio are about equal (see 530), and presumably this ratio has been fairly uniform between the two areas for a long time. The general vegetation of the two areas varies greatly today and did so, according to Sears, in early post-Wisconsin glacier times. Why the variation? I say that the topography allowed Indian fires to have more widespread and decisive influence in Iowa than in Ohio, causing and maintaining extensive grasslands in Iowa but only small grasslands in Ohio. Thus an appreciation of the significance of fires set by American aborigines is necessary for the proper understanding of the history of vegetation in Iowa, as elsewhere, during the last 25,000 years. We cannot ignore the burning of vegetation by Indians as a significant ecological factor during and since the Wisconsin glaciation.

MISSOURI

Classified by Shantz and Zon (454) as part forest and part tall-grass prairie, Missouri presents a complex vegetational picture. I include it in the Prairie and Plains section because the historical evidence indicates that its forests were formerly less extensive and also more open than at present. Furthermore, it might be debated whether the ancient, open, parklike scattering of trees should be termed "forest," emphasizing the presence of woody growth, or whether extensive grasslands dotted with trees should be designated "prairie," thus stressing its herbaceous nature. However classified, the record of Indian firing of Missouri landscape, and its remarkable effect on the vegetation, is clear.

Two studies, Houck's (256) *A History of Missouri* and Sauer's (433) *Geography of the Ozark Highland of Missouri*, are particularly helpful, with quotations from earlier reports as well as the interpretations made by the authors. Father Membre, who accompanied La Salle down the Mississippi, said that the forests in what is now Missouri were so open and unobstructed that one could ride through them on horseback (Houck [256], p. 26). Father Vivier (522), already cited, characterized the high ground back from the river as "intersected by plains and groves, wherein trees are almost as thinly scattered as in our public promenades." He further attributed this condition to the fires set by "savages." Forty years after Vivier observed the country, Captain Foucher, Spanish commandant at New Madrid in 1790, told General Forman he could drive a coach-and-four through the open wood from New Madrid to St. Louis (Houck [256], p. 26).

Stoddard (493), reporting in 1812 on his visit to southeastern Missouri, described the countryside as "alternately divided into woodlands and prairies." He said (p. 213) that the trees on the high grounds are more scattered, and generally of a different species. The prairies are covered with grass. These were probably occasioned by the ravages of fire; because, wherever copses of trees are found on them, the ground about them is low, and too moist to admit the fire to pass over it; and because it is a common practice among Indians and other hunters to set the woods and prairies on fire, by which means they are able to kill an abundance of game.

Brackenridge (55) in 1814 found the territory from New Madrid to the Missouri "alternately prairie, and beautiful woods of tall oak, walnut . . . as though planted by art. . . . These prairies, it is well known, are caused by repeated and desolating fires." The ridges and mountain chain of the Ozarks, designated as within the oak-hickory forest by Shantz and Zon (454), were viewed by Schoolcraft in 1820 during a trip from Potosi to the north fork of White River. He described them as "nearly destitute of forest, often perfectly so" (cited in Houck [256], p. 25). That same year Bourne (54) included Missouri within his statement that "it must be evident to everyone who will view the barrens attentively, that their present appearance was caused by fire: The fires . . . kindled by the Indians for the convenience of traveling. . . to enable them to approach game . . . also to insure a good crop of grass for the next summer."

Also in 1819, Wells (546) wrote that prairies formerly came to the edge of the "second bottom" at St. Louis but that the forests were extending farther and farther from the river as the prevention of grass fires becomes more complete. Another reference to the prairie fires in the vicinity of St. Louis, which is well within Shantz and Zon's forest zone, comes from T. Flint (177, p. 239), who wrote in 1826 as follows:

> I have often witnessed in this country a most impressive view, which I do not remember to have seen noticed by any travelers who have preceded me. It is the burning of the prairies. It is visible at times in all parts of Missouri, but nowhere with more effect than in St. Louis. The tall and thick grass that grows in the prairies that abound through all the country, is fired; most frequently at that season of the year, called Indian summer. The moon rises with a broad disk, and of bloody hue, upon the smoky atmosphere. Thousands of acres of grass are burning in all directions. In the wide prairies the advancing front of flame often has an extent of miles. Many travelers, arrested by these burnings, have perished. The crimson-coloured flames, seen through the dim atmosphere, in the distance seem to rise from the earth to the sky. The view, before the eye becomes familiarized with it, is grand, I might almost say terrific; for nothing has ever given me such a striking image of our conceptions of the final conflagration.

Sauer (433, p. 53) states that "prairie fires are mentioned by almost every early writer as the cause of the prairies" and lists Duben (148) for 1824, Monks (365) and Featherstonhough (168) for 1844, and Swallow (500) for 1879, in addition to Stoddard (493) and Brackenridge (55), whom I have already cited. Sauer also referred to *American State Papers* (13) as follows: "An incident illustrating this early opinion was a refusal in 1830 by the United States of a grant of land to raise timber in south Missouri, on the ground that 'It is only necessary to keep out the fires to cover the prairies with timber by the operations of nature.'"

Featherstonhaugh (168, p. 354) left this graphic description of a grass fire in the Missouri Ozark Mountains:

> I was out until a late hour observing it. We were upon an elevated table-land, covered with dry autumnal leaves, grass, and sticks, upon which stood numerous dead and dry trees killed by previous fires. Not a quarter of a mile from the house was a narrow edging of bright crackling fire, sometimes not more than two inches broad, but much wider when it met with large quantities of combustible matter. On it came in a waving line, consuming every thing before it and setting fire to the dead trees, that, like so many burning masts, illuminated the scorched and gloomy background behind, and over which the wind—against which the fire was advancing—drove the smoke. Every now and then one of the flaming trees would come to the ground.

Wislizenus (566) in 1839, Fendler (169) in 1866, and Winslow (564) in 1892 were additional nineteenth-century authors who believed fire was a primary cause of Missouri prairies. In this century Houck (256), who published his *History of Missouri* in 1908, can be mentioned. On the basis of his historic research he believed that "fire, continued for ages by the Indians to clear the ground for hunting, had the effect of curtailing and destroying large vegetation." Sauer's (433) personal opinion of 1920 appears in this statement:

> Of the various influences that caused prairies on the uplands, man was chief. Indians and other hunters were wont to set fire to the grass in fall or spring in order to improve the grazing for the buffalo, elk, and other big game. Fires were also set to drive the game toward the hunters. Through this practice sprouts and tree seedlings were killed, and thus the grasslands were extended at the expense of the forests. . . . The practice of burning was continued by settlers for many years, principally to provide grazing for their stock. With settlement the forest began to reclaim the burned over tracts.

Although many ecologists and botanists, among them B. Shimek and F. E. Clements, reject the conclusions drawn by early settlers and travelers that fire was the fundamental factor in the existence of prairies, three very recent studies of the Missouri Ozarks confirm the correctness of the opinions first voiced by the French explorers and repeated by nineteenth-century writers. Steyermark (492), in his *Studies of the Vegetation of Missouri–I* published by the Field Museum in 1940, wrote (p. 388) that "the first woody plants to invade the prairie flora are sassafras and winged sumac." He found that black jack oak and post oak followed and that black oak invades prairies on broad level plateaus as well as those along railroad rights-of-way. To quote Steyermark again (p. 389): "This pioneering tendency of this scrub oak to penetrate the prairie habitat is shown by the black jackpost oak 'flats,' which, according to earlier records and reports made by travelers and settlers in the region, were originally level, open, treeless expanses."

Steyermark is one of the few plant scientists who recognize the need to document the continuation to the present of occurrences of fire as an important ecological factor. For example, he writes in a caption for a picture that it "illustrates encroachment of oaks into prairie habitat. . . . The area illustrated was unburned for many years." He also remarks (p. 412) that burning of the forest each autumn continues as an almost universal custom, the fire not harming the established trees. On page 403 Steyermark accepts statements of "old timers" regarding invasion of prairies by trees: "since it is well known, by records of scientific travelers throughout the Ozarks, and by reports of settlers and surveyors, that many portions of the upland Ozark plateau now forested were open prairie a hundred years or more ago."

Liming and Johnston (318) in 1944 and Koen (289) in 1948 told of the continued burning of the Ozarks, indicating that such burning maintains the openness of the forests. A study of prairie vegetation in north-central Missouri by Drew (141), which appeared in 1947, also contributes to our knowledge of the ecology of Missouri grasslands. He investigated "the 'virgin' prairie . . . about 20 miles east of Columbia, Missouri. . . . The 160-acre field represents an unplowed portion of original prairie." For 125 years it has been grazed and mowed. Furthermore: "Burning has also taken place frequently, as a result of both accidental firing and the setting of fires to burn off accumulated and unmowed, dead vegetation. Although trees, especially red cedars (*Juniperus virginiana*), have been observed by the owners in the past to invade the grasslands in considerable numbers, they invariably died out after only a few years."

Drew included in his study ungrazed natural prairies along railroad rights-of-way, adding that "these prairie relics have been cut intermittently for hay and have been burned over often." Drew's data allow for only one conclusion: "virgin" or natural prairie in Missouri is today, as it was in aboriginal times, burned-over prairie. Is the burning necessary?

ARKANSAS

The only grasslands in Arkansas so indicated by Shantz and Zon (454, fig. 2) are a few small areas scattered in the River Bottom Cypress forest. Although Wackerman (526) found that "natives long resident in the country say that the prairies have grown noticeably smaller within memory," he attributed their presence entirely to poor drainage of the soil. He did not mention whether they were ever set on fire. Although not now recognized as prairie country, the Arkansas Ozarks were undoubtedly formerly like the Missouri Ozarks—parklike forests, with large grassy areas interrupted by open stands of trees. In 1891 Winslow (563) wrote of the prairies of western Arkansas and attributed them to fires.

TEXAS

Texas is of special interest for several reasons. First, the earliest explicit statement regarding the Indian practice of setting fire to grass and timber is a report of Cabeza de Vaca's (72) experiences as a slave among Texas Indians, following a shipwreck in 1528. Second, the fact that woody vegetation has invaded great areas of grassland is abundantly documented. Third, the reasons for the recent domination of prairies by trees appear to me to be frequently misunderstood. Finally, Texas vegetation varies from wet forests to desert shrub. Little need be said of the longleaf–loblolly pine region of far eastern Texas. Zon (583) and Tharp (506, p. 28) reported that the area was burned yearly and that pine was invading the wet prairies as they dried. The ecological conditions of the Texas pine zone appear to be identical with those of the pine region of other southeastern states where fire in aboriginal and in historic times has been the factor determining whether pines or other trees dominate. Fire was also undoubtedly of major importance in the oak-pine and oak-hickory forests of Texas, as it was in similar vegetation east of the Mississippi River.

It is the plains-prairie zone of Texas, however, that provides data of greatest importance for the thesis advanced here. This is true in spite of the fact that in the ethnographic literature I found only one Indian tribe, the Iguaces or Yguaces, named by Cabeza de Vaca, specifically described as setting fire to Texas vegetation. Hartmann (235, p. 117) said that the Apaches fired grass to drive game, but they were not clearly placed in

Texas. Hartmann was writing of northern Mexico, but one can reasonably infer that the Apaches of Texas, as well as those in Mexico, used fire. All other references speak simply of the Indian practice of prairie burning, as if it were too well known to require elaboration and discussion.

From the general statement of Oviedo y Valdez (386), made in 1534, that Spanish settlers everywhere set fires to clear brush and renew grass, we can reasonably assume that the first Europeans in Texas perpetuated Indian custom. The earliest American published observation is that of F. M. Chapman (80) made in 1891. "Chapman made an interesting observation upon the prairies around Corpus Christi, Texas, where the arborescent vegetation has largely appeared during the last twenty years, and is yearly becoming denser and more extensive. This he understands is due to the introduction of cattle, which by grazing down the grass have prevented the fire from 'running' and thus destroying the tree-growth" (Christy [97], p. 95).

The next source, dated 1899, also mentions the coastal prairie in a publication titled *Grazing Problems in the Southwest*, a U.S. Department of Agriculture Bulletin from the Division of Agrostology written by Jared G. Smith (466). In it he noted (p. 32): "Dr. De Ryee, of Corpus Christi, states that the country between there and the Rio Grande was entirely open thirty years ago [1869]. . . . Now all of the open spaces have been filled with thorn-thickets."

Smith (p. 34) said that there was near Laredo a prairie thirty-five miles wide, "but it is only a question of a few years before the brush and cactus will have advanced from both directions to take complete possession of it."

Bray (59) wrote in 1901 of the south Texas Rio Grande plains as follows: some woody species, "with certain artificial barriers removed, the burning of the grass notably, are capable of waging a successful struggle against grass vegetation." O. F. Cook (110), also of the Department of Agriculture, wrote in 1908 of south Texas one of the most complete analyses of the problem of prairie-forest relationship. His view that the original forest clearing was done by Indians for agricultural purposes is partly confirmed by the archaeology of the region, which reveals advanced pottery makers preceding the pure hunters described by Cabeza de Vaca. He wrote: "The primitive Indian agriculture which accomplished the devastation of this region as of many others in Mexico and Central America was here, as elsewhere, a self-limiting process. Lands once cleared and abandoned were kept by fires from becoming reforested until the forests were all gone. That age of primitive agriculture ended in an age of grass and prairie fires, of wandering buffaloes, and nomadic hunters."

It is not essential for my argument that slash-and-burn forest clearing preceded the grass burning. Cabeza de Vaca's testimony establishes the fact that south Texas was burned by Indians and that it was an extensive grassland.

But Cook presents his case and my own so well that I quote him at length (110, pp. 1–16):

It is a matter of popular knowledge in south Texas that extensive regions which were formerly grassy, open prairies are now covered with a dense growth of mesquite (*Prosopis*), prickly-pear cactus (*Opuntia*), and many other shrubby plants of intermediate size. Testimony to this effect is definite and unanimous. It differs locally only in the number of years since the bushes began to grow—thirty years, or twenty, or ten—subsequent to the establishment of the grazing industry on a large scale, the annual burning of the grass by the cattlemen, and finally the fencing of the land for still more intensive grazing.

Many localities are only now being invaded by the woody vegetation. Very often the old mesquite pioneers, the scattered trees which made the "open mesquite country" of other decades, are still conspicuous among their much smaller progeny and the crowds of other camp-following species which now occupy the land to the almost complete exclusion of the grasses, upon which the herds of former days were pastured. A new order of nature is at hand in south Texas. The change has come so gradually that even those who have the most intimate acquaintance with the facts have not appreciated their significance, much less published them abroad.

Before the prairies were grazed by cattle the luxuriant growths of grass could accumulate for several years until conditions were favorable for accidental fires to spread. With these large supplies of fuel the fires which swept over these prairies were very besoms of destruction not only for man and animal but for all shrubs and trees which might have ventured out among the grass, and even for any trees or forests against which the burning wind might blow.

That such fires were evidently the cause of the former treeless condition of the southwestern prairies is also shown by the fact that trees are found in all situations which afford protection against fires. Along beaches and on naked sand dunes, in grassless river bottoms and abandoned channels of "slews," in deep swamps and in sterile rocky places the forest has maintained footholds. Nor is there any reason in the nature of the climate or the soil why trees should not thrive over the vast areas of open prairie land. Trees of many kinds have thriven well where planted in villages and about homesteads, in addition to the natural spread of the woody vegetation as soon as the fires cease.

Those who are acquainted only with northern regions of hills and valleys, heavy rains, and deep snows may find it difficult to believe that the burning of grass can destroy or prevent the growth of forests and keep vast regions in a treeless condition. One needs, perhaps, to have the mind prepared by actual observation of the destruction of forests by fires of grass. In humid countries dead grass is beaten down and decays during the next summer season. Forest fires in northern countries arise from accumulations of fallen leaves and other debris, but in the warmer parts of the world these conditions are generally reversed. The forests do not burn with their own fuel, but may be invaded and driven back by the adjacent grass. In this respect, as in several others, south Texas may be reckoned as part of the Tropics, in spite of the occasional "northers" of the winter season, which carry the temperature below the freezing point and thus exclude all the tender tropical types of perennial plants.

Settlers in south Texas early adopted the practice of burning over the prairies every year; partly to protect their homes against the fires, partly to give their cattle readier access to the fresh growth of grass. The fires were often set near the coast, the strong breeze which blows in from the Gulf spreading the flames over many square miles. While the grass was still abundant these annual burnings were able to keep the woody vegetation well in check, though no longer able to drive back the forest or even to prevent a slow advance.

In spots where the grass is thin, seedling mesquites and oaks escape the flames and in a year or two begin to shade the ground and gain more protection against the dangerous proximity of the combustible grass; and even though the tops are killed by later fires the roots may send up sprouts again and again to improve every chance of becoming established and joining branches with near neighbors to increase the area of shade. The lessened quantity of grass also makes it impracticable to burn the prairies over in the summer, as was customary in former decades. Burning has now to be done in the winter when the grass is dry, but the young trees are then in a dormant condition and are much less injured by fire than in the summer season of vegetative activity.

In the region between Houston and Victoria large tracts are being occupied by "oak runners." Farther south, the mesquite usually held sway alone for a considerable period before the smaller and less hardy types were able to advance against the gradually weaker fires. With the building of barbed-wire fences and the provision of permanent supplies of water by wells and reservoirs the cattle were greatly increased. About a decade ago [1898] there was a series of very dry seasons when the cattle left little grass to burn, often none at all. This was a time of notable prosperity for the bushes and cacti. Through many square miles of the Rio Grande Valley, and doubtless in many other parts, the victory over the grass was complete and final. There has been no burning since, nor ever will be, unless the bushes grow thick and accumulate dry wood enough to furnish the fuel.

The botanical explorers who have associated the South Texas region with the deserts farther to the west because they found it occupied by the same desert types of vegetation must revise their conclusions in the light of facts already accomplished and of others not long to be delayed. The mesquites, cacti, chaparral, and sagebrush are only an episode of the bionomic history of the region, not its original or normal condition or an index of its agricultural possibilities. They are merely the forerunners of the larger forest growth. If reforestation were to continue uninterrupted by fires or other forms of human interference the Gulf plains of Texas would again become covered with dense subtropical forests, and with the then impeded drainage would form vast swamps.

Tharp (506) in 1925, in his monograph on the structure of eastern Texas vegetation, divided south Texas into "Coastal Prairies" and "Oak Forest-Prairie Alternes." Shantz and Zon (454) in 1924 included in the same area "Creosote Bush," "Mesquite and Desert Grass Savanna," and "Tall Grass Prairie." All of this region appears to have been grassland in pre-conquest times. Tharp (506, p. 69) under the heading "Coastal Prairie" wrote: "This associes [association] occupies an area of approximately 10,000 square miles. . . . It is reputed formerly to have extended southwestward to the Rio Grande; but at present it is dominated by chaparral as far north as Refugio County." And again on p. 71:

> . . . it is generally conceded that active and relatively rapid invasion of prairie by woody plants is now going on. Testimony to this effect is to be had for the asking of any of the older inhabitants of the area and seems to be backed by field studies . . . where within the memory of men now living the original open prairie has been transformed into dense chaparral composed principally of *Acacia, Colubrina, Zizyphus, Eysenhardtia, Aloysia, Prosopis*, and *Celtis pallida*. Led in its invasion by *Acacia farnesiana*, this association seems to continue to impinge on the prairie from the south and west.

Tharp (p. 72) also records oaks as invaders of prairies and adds: "To what extent it is now actively spreading has not been ascertained, but with intensive pasturing and consequent elimination of prairie fires, mottes of it are unquestionably proceeding to attain to the dignity of trees." Referring to the Mexican-Spanish term for stands of growth in open country, "mottes" in Texas appear to be the same scrub growth called "grubs" on Wisconsin prairies, and in both places this scrub develops into trees when prairie fires are stopped. The south Texas prairies, which have been so greatly invaded in the last century, occur where rainfall varies, according to Tharp (pl. 2, p. 16), from below 25 inches to over 50 inches annually. Following Transeau's method of determining the annual precipitation-evaporation ratio, Livingston and Shreve (327, p. 333) designate these coastal prairies and former prairies in zones below 60 and above 110. Transeau's prairie peninsula in Illinois is mostly in the zone 60 to 80 (327, p. 333). Why do prairies occur in humid and semihumid areas? Because first Indians then Europeans burned over such areas.

There appears no room for postulating climatic change to explain the invasion of the coastal and tropic grassland by woody vegetation. Is the picture equally clear for other prairie regions of Texas? Most of the area designated by Shantz and Zon (454, fig. 2) as "Prairies" and "Desert Savanna" is in central Texas, extending westward to give way to the "Short Grass" plains of west Texas. The invasion by woody vegetation of central and west Texas grasslands may not have been as complete or as rapid as that of coastal and south Texas, but the pattern is remarkably similar. Jared G. Smith (466), who concentrated his research on west Texas, wrote in 1899 that there had been about 200,000 square miles of excellent pasture in the Southwest, mostly in Texas, when Europeans began occupying the area in 1860. From 1884 to 1899 the "carrying capacity has diminished fully 40 percent." Smith said further (pp. 7 and 8):

> At the time of the earliest settlement this Texas territory was for the most part treeless, excepting along streams and where the two bodies of "cross timbers" entered it on the north and where a wedged tongue of the east Texas timber belt penetrates the prairies south of Austin and San Antonio.
>
> Weeds and brush were kept in check by the fires set by the Indians in early spring to improve the pasturages. In this manner the encroaching of thorny shrubs, cactus and mesquite was prevented, and each grew only where protected or in scattered clumps at rare intervals in the open.

Smith (p. 17) quoted Bartlett's (1854) description of prairies 150 to 200 miles wide at 29E 30N (in the area of Austin), which were "gently undulating plains, without timber save along the margin of streams." Smith added that "now [1899] this same region is covered with brush and cactus."

Although mesquite was then spreading rapidly over the grassland, Smith said that "[i]n the early days, when the central prairies were sparsely settled, they were burned over each year, and the young seedlings . . . were killed to the ground." Shear (456), a colleague of Jared G. Smith in the USDA Division of Agrostology, studied the grassland of west Texas, New Mexico. and Arizona and in 1901 came to the same conclusion that overgrazing and cessation of grassfires allowed mesquite to invade and dominate grasslands. He wrote (p. 42) that Indians set "prairie fires . . . to improve the grazing" and added: "As soon as the prairie fires became less frequent the shrubby vegetation spread rapidly, especially the mesquite bean [that] now forms a scattered growth over a great portion of central and western Texas as well as throughout the lower altitudes of this whole region."

Bray (59), an early University of Texas botanist and ecologist, writing in the *Botanical Gazette* in 1901, provided further evidence of the marked change occurring on Texas prairies: "The energy and rate of encroachment of woody vegetation during the past half century lead one to believe that there is scarcely an area of consequence in the state that woody vegetation of some type will not occupy and cover more or less completely, granting of course that no artificial means are employed to check it."

And in the same article on page 289:

Regarding the establishment of woody vegetation, it is the unanimous testimony of men of long observation that most of the chaparral and mesquite covered country was formerly open grass prairie. This applied to the Rio Grande plain, as well as to the mesquite flats of the central provinces. Illustrations are everywhere at hand. At Austin, for example, many black land pastures have within a few years become covered by a perfect jungle of mesquite.

Apparently under the open prairie regime the equilibrium was maintained by more or less regular recurrence of prairie fires. This, of course, is by no means a new idea, but the strength of it lies in the fact that the grass vegetation was tolerant of fires and the woody vegetation was not. It was only after weakening the grass floor by heavy pasturing and ceasing to ward off the encroaching species by fire that the latter invaded the grasslands. Once the equilibrium was destroyed everything conspired to hasten the encroachment of chaparral—droughts, pasturing, trampling, seed scattering, and so on. As Smith pointed out, a mesquite tree once established became a center of infection in offering shelter for shrubby plants and shade-loving grasses, driving out the native prairie grasses. In brief, the efforts to exploit the wealth of grasslands for profit, namely stock raising, have been the main agency in transforming them rapidly into lands covered by a totally different and far less valuable vegetation.

Bray's 1906 bulletin (58) documents more fully the spread of mesquite, *Prosopis glandulosa*, not only over Texas grasslands but also across Oklahoma and into Kansas. Another Texas botanical ecologist, Tharp (506), a generation after Bray, even more clearly demonstrated the role of fire in the maintenance of prairies. Tharp's contribution is the more striking when contrasted with the failures of H. C. Sampson (431), B. Shimek (458), and others who have studied rights-of-way as relict "virgin" prairies. Regarding the "Composition of Prairies," Tharp wrote (p. 56):

> Railroad rights-of-way offer the best specimens of native climax vegetation. Such areas are not only protected from grazing, and usually from agriculture, but are also annually subjected to controlled burning in order to reduce fire hazard to railway property. Thus these bits of prairie are still subjected to approximately the same "natural" conditions as when white men first discovered them being burned by fires set by Indians, who presumably had had the practice for at least several thousands of year, having acquired it for the double purpose of providing better pasture for game and as an aid in the chase.

And on page 60:

> Secondary seres in pastures are not confined to herbaceous components. So numerous are the instances of invasion by *Conadlia, Zizyphus, Prosopis, Bumelia, Columbrina, Ilex decidua,* and *Ulmus alata* that they are almost the rule everywhere except in the extreme northeast (Collin, Hunt, and Delta Counties).
>
> While lay testimony is unanimous as to the present invasional activity of these species, not all instances of their presence can be charged to recent occurrence.

Tharp's exception is a thicket of mesquite observed on the prairie in 1844 and used by Tharp to illustrate "Prosopis-Quercus-Prairie Transition" in Robertson County. The invasion of all tall-grass, moist prairies of Texas by mesquite, oak, or other brush is confirmed beyond question, and the cessation of fire or its reduced effectiveness also appears to be the most important factor in that remarkably rapid change. It is not, however, only the moist grasslands where the invasion is taking place. "Short Grass Plains," in the drier regions of west Texas, are also being transferred into wooded savannas. The stand of trees and bushes remains scattered, but it will come as a surprise to many that there is any spread of woody vegetation onto grasslands that receive only 10 to 20 inches of rain annually (Tharp [506], pl. 2, p. 16) and have a precipitation-evaporation ratio, according to Transeau's formula, of as little as 20 and no more than 60 (Livingston and Shreve [327], fig. 15, p. 333).

It must be remembered that Transeau and his disciples believed that Iowa and Illinois prairies persisted because there was too little moisture available to plants where the precipitation-evaporation ratio was between

60 and 80. There is, furthermore, no grounds for postulating marked, general climatic change to account for this change in vegetation. The transformation has been much too rapid and the records of rainfall and temperature much too consistent to suggest that increased moisture has brought about the increase of woody vegetation on the grassland. Woody vegetation invaded grassland during the severe drought of the 1930s, which was supposed to have inhibited spread of trees on the prairies of the Middle West. Cottle (117) wrote in 1931 of what he called "probably the largest remaining area of native grassland in the United States," situated in west Texas, west of the Pecos River. The annual rainfall of the area averages 14.5 inches. On page 108, he wrote: "On the rougher lands and on porous soils, where grazing injury has been especially severe, other xeric types of vegetation occur. Among these are pinon-juniper woodland, yucca, mesquite and various other desert shrubs. The broken grass cover affords an excellent opportunity for these greatly to increase their territory."

Later in his article he reported the development of thickets of cat's claw (*Acacia* spp.) too dense for stock to enter (p. 138). He said that the shrub *Flourensis cernua* is spreading. On page 152 Cottle indicates his belief that Indians kept down the brush by fires and that mesquite has greatly increased in range since grass fires have been reduced to the minimum, while overgrazing is also important in the spread of woody plants onto grasslands.

A 1943 article in the USDA leaflet *Soil Conservation* by Bell and Dyksterhuis (36) produces a map of Texas showing large areas of short-grass plains and tall-grass prairies that have been invaded by mesquite and cedar. The authors say "cedar and mesquite [are] changing productive lands into a wilderness." They report the mesquite has invaded 51,000,000 acres of land that was once treeless grasslands.

Benson (37, p. 750) in 1941 indicated that mesquite, *Prosopis juliflora* var. *glandulosa*, occurs in far west Texas and confirms Bray's report of mesquite spreading across Oklahoma and into Kansas. Renner (414) in 1948 gives additional evidence of the reduction of Texas grasslands, and Fisher (173) in 1950 wrote of "The Mesquite Problem in the Southwest" in the *Journal of Range Management*. Fisher said (p. 60):

> In 1896 J. G. Smith, an agrostologist stationed at Abilene, Texas, called attention to the hardy, aggressive nature of mesquite and rather accurately predicted the mesquite problem we face today. In Texas alone recent surveys by the Soil Conservation Service . . . show that mesquite occurs on 55 million acres of grassland in 113 counties and that moderate or dense stands occupy approximately 30 million acres.

The invasion of mesquite on native grassland within the past forty years has taken place so rapidly that it is common knowledge among people of the southwest. The early introduction of key plants into open grasslands by roving herds of buffalo, and by the Spanish horse and cattle during trail drives . . . are often mentioned among the more probable causes of recent invasions. Other causes which have been suggested are: Lack of repeated burning of the grass, destruction of prairie dogs, floods, droughts, overgrazing.

Fisher gives the range of mesquite outside of Texas as southern New Mexico and Arizona and north into Kansas. He also defines it as a most hardy plant that has been grown from seeds stored for forty-four years in an herbarium. The August 18, 1952, issue of *Life* magazine reported that 75 million acres of grassland have become covered with mesquite during the last 100 years.

Before we leave Texas, some discussion of two other papers seems appropriate. The first is the one by Clements and Chaney (104) cited earlier, in which the authors in 1936 deny a primary role to fire in prairie formation and mention (p. 33) "the ability of most deciduous trees and shrubs to produce root sprouts is so striking that fire regularly favors them rather than the grasses, as demonstrated especially by the chaparral and mesquite in the West." The data I have presented are a direct refutation of the notion that fire favors mesquite rather than grass. The opposite is clearly established. As soon as fires were stopped or their destructiveness was reduced by grazing, mesquite rapidly invaded the most xerophytic grasslands.

Tharp's (506, p. 56) evidence that ungrazed but burned-over rights of way remained clear of mesquite while adjacent grassy areas were invaded establishes beyond question that fire favors grass rather than trees and shrubs. The second paper that might be discussed briefly at this point is A. W. Sampson's (430) report in 1948 to the Inter-American Conference on Conservation of Renewable Natural Resources. Although Sampson says, in effect, that range burning may be good or may be bad and that "fire in natural vegetation is ages old" (p. 552), he seems to ignore the effect of aboriginal use of fire to keep brush from invading grasslands. Had Sampson understood the record of the spread of mesquite onto Texas prairies, he could not have written, it seems to me, the following (p. 551):

Many former grasslands evidently became brush land [by severe overgrazing]. As the brush stand thickened and the understory herbaceous forage became sparse, a new factor, fire, was introduced by range men—often more or less in desperation. The practice of broadcast burning suddenly exposed the soil to erosion. It often resulted in regeneration of the brush over other forms of plant life and, in many instances, further lowered the quality of the site.

Brush invasion may also occasionally occur without the aid of fire.

The sequence of events is mixed up by Sampson, certainly for Texas, where the greatest area of grass has been invaded by brush, and probably for all grassy regions. Rather than fires being introduced by ranchers after brush had become a nuisance, grasslands were burned by Indians, and under the grazing of wild game such burning kept woody growth from becoming important. The early ranchers continued the Indian practice with the same results. With ever increasing herds of cattle and sheep, grasses were so reduced that the fires could no longer check the expansion of shrubs and trees. Without a thick stand of grass to carry the flames and produce sufficiently destructive heat, fires could no longer destroy brush. A very careful control of burning and grazing would be required to restore the grasslands to their presettlement condition and such control would have to be continued if fire were to serve the purpose it did for the Indians. To say that fire could not maintain grassy vegetation from invasion, or to imply that burning of grass aids brush to invade prairies, is simply unjustified.

In the summary of the effect of Indian fires on plains and prairies as a whole, the information regarding Texas grasslands is most significant. If woody vegetation has invaded thousands of square miles of Texas moist and dry grasslands, why could it not invade similar grasslands elsewhere? If destructive grass fires were the essential ecological force in maintaining Texas plains and prairies free from brush and trees, fire must be an important factor wherever it occurred.

OKLAHOMA

The early historic references to burning grasslands and forests in Oklahoma, although few in number, indicate that Indians in that area carried on the general "Plains Indian culture pattern" for use of fire for hunting and improving pasture. Eastern Oklahoma, designated by Shantz and Zon (454, fig. 2) as oak-pine and oak-hickory forest, was found by Nuttall (382) in 1819 to be very open woodland, as was the Ozark region. Nuttall wrote (p. 200):

> The soil, wherever there is the slightest depression, is of a superior quality, and thickly covered with vegetable earth. The trees appear scattered as if planted by art, affording an unobstructed range for the hunter, equal to that of a planted park.
>
> On the 29th, I took an agreeable walk into the adjoining prairie, which is about two miles wide and seven long. I found it equally undulated with

the surrounding woodland, and could perceive no reason for the absence of trees, except the annual conflagration. A ridge of considerable elevation divides it about the centre, from whence the hills of the Pottoe, the Cavaniol, and the Sugarloaf, at the distance of about 30 miles, appear partly enveloped in the mists of the horizon. Like an immense meadow, the expanse was now covered with a luxuriant herbage, and beautifully decorated with flowers, amongst which I was pleased to see the Painted Cup of the eastern states, accompanied by occasional clusters of a white flowered Dodecatheon or American primrose. The numerous rounded elevations which chequer this verdant plain, are so many partial attempts at shrubby and aborescent vegetation, which nature has repeatedly made, and which have only been subdued by the reiterated operation of annual burning, employed by the natives, for the purpose of hunting with more facility, and of affording a tender pasturage for the game.

Washington Irving's (270) "tour" across Oklahoma in October of 1832 is a basis for attributing prairie fires to the Osages, Kansas, and Pawnees. Irving went with soldiers up the Arkansas and Cimarron (which he called "Red Fork"), south to the North Canadian in the vicinity of what is now Oklahoma City, then southeast to the Canadian River and back to Fort Gibson. The party was exploring Pawnee hunting grounds, but Irving mentioned repeatedly that the area also was used by the Osages and Kansas. Of the vicinity of Oklahoma's "Cross Timbers," Irving wrote: "The fires made on the prairies by the Indian hunters, had frequently penetrated these forests, sweeping in light transient flames along the dry grass, scorching and calcining the lower twigs and branches of the trees, and leaving them black and hard" (p. 459); and "[t]his haziness was daily increasing, and was attributed to the burning of distant prairies by the Indian hunting parties" (p. 463).

Irving traveled on the eastern edge of the "Great Western Prairie," from which they returned east because "[t]he Indian fires on the prairies were approaching us from north, and south, and west; they might spread also from the east, and leave a scorched desert between us and the frontier, in which our horses might be famished" (p. 466).

Josiah Gregg (218) described traveling along the Santa Fe Trail in 1844. He was probably referring to western Oklahoma when he wrote:

The banks of the Canadian are equally naked; and, having fewer islands, the river appears still more barren. In fact, there is scarce anything else but cottonwood, and that very sparsely scattered along the streams, throughout most of the far western prairies.

It is unquestionably the prairie conflagrations that keep down the woody growth upon most of the western uplands. The occasional skirts and fringes which have escaped their rage, have been protected by the streams they border. Yet may not the time come when these vast plains will be covered with timber?

It would seem that the prairie region, long after the discovery of America, extended to the very banks of the Mississippi. Father Marquette, in a voyage down the river, in 1673, after passing below the mouth of the Ohio, remarks: "The banks of the river began to be covered with high trees, which hindered us from observing the country as we had done all along; but we judged from the bellowing of the oxen [bison] that the meadows are very near."—Indeed, there are parts of the southwest now thickly set with trees of good size, that, within the remembrance of the oldest inhabitants, were as naked as the prairie plains; and the appearance of the timber in many other sections indicates that it has grown up within less than a century. In fact, we are now witnessing the encroachment of the timber upon the prairies, where the devastating conflagrations have ceased their ravages.

Lt. Whipple (547a) a decade later explored for a railroad route from Fort Smith—then part of the Oklahoma Territory—to Los Angeles. His men (p. 21) "discovered two Indians setting fire to the prairie" on August 22, in the Cross Timbers country near what is now Purcell, Oklahoma. On August 26, near what is now Chickasha, he said (p. 24):

After traveling about five miles, our progress was suddenly arrested by a burning prairie. The grass was tall, thick, and dry. The wind had driven the widespread flames over the crest of a hill, directly towards us; and they now came leaping into the air, roaring in the distance, and crackling fearfully as they approached. There seemed to be no safety except in flight. The train, therefore, counter marched in double quick time, and took refuge behind a watery ravine, where grass was too green to burn freely. Taking advantage of a comparatively bare spot, the flames were fought, and a temporary opening made, through which the train passed to the black-burned prairie, which we traversed in safety. At last some ravines appeared which had interrupted the flames, and protected fine fields of grass having travelled sixteen miles.

In the most westerly section of Oklahoma, Whipple observed (p. 27): "Burnt prairies now surround us, accounting for the bright fires seen lately at night. This is probably the work of Indians to prepare fresh grass for the herds of buffalo that will be slaughtered on their return from the north."

Bray (58) in 1906, Gleason (207) in 1932, and Benson (37) in 1941 reported the spread of mesquite, *Prosopis glandulosa*, from Texas into the prairies of western Oklahoma. In 1950 Elwell and Cox (158a) expressed the view (p. 46) that overgrazing and fire were responsible for encroachment of brush in woodland and other pasture. They fell into the error, frequently repeated in recent literature, of combining overgrazing and present-day fires as a singular cause for the increase of brush on grazing land. The error is evident when it is remembered that during aboriginal times, during which burning was frequent but overgrazing absent, the prairies were tree-less and the Oklahoma woods were open "parks." Elwell and Cox showed (p. 42) that "after the brush was removed the grass developed rapidly" and recommended use of herbicides. Their experiments provided important data on the relative value of trees and grass for water conservation. They found that two to four times as much moisture is lost through transpiration from brush as is lost from grass and said (p. 46): "A cover of scrubby trees and brush on land does not provide as good protection cover for erosion control as does grass. During an 8-year period of measurement at Red Plains Conservation Experiment Station, Guthrie, Oklahoma runoff water was 44 percent less from good grass land than from areas covered with brush."

These data must be considered whenever complete fire protection is proposed as a means for flood and erosion control. They should also be remembered in connection with water conservation programs. In an earlier study Elwell, Daniel, and Fenton (158) found that the total yield of forage from an Oklahoma plot is less if it is annually burned for several years than from a similar unburned plot. Their experiment nonetheless confirmed the Indian perception that game preferred to graze new grass grown on burned-over places rather than to forage on unburned places. At least, Elwell and associates found that cattle favored grass grown on burned-over land to that grown on land not burned, as Indians said was true for deer and buffalo.

Two other studies conducted in Oklahoma are related to the question of the effect of fires on vegetation. Sears's (446) 1933 article "Climatic Change as a Factor in Forest Succession" is remarkable because it ignores fire as contributing to the distribution of vegetation in postglacial times. He does this while presenting a picture of "upland forest of oak and juniper, Caddo County, Oklahoma [which] occurs on sandy soil in a typical grassland climate" where it did not exist a few years before. The climatic fluctuations that Sears dates by peat bog analysis in northern Ohio are separated by two or three thousand years, yet he implies that the new tree growth on the Oklahoma prairies has taken place during the last few decades because of climatic change. The eradication of burning seems a far more plausible explanation in accounting for the recent growth of trees.

The second study also concerns vegetation in Caddo County. It appeared in 1939, written by E. L. Little (322), and attempted to account for a relict grove of sugar maple, *Acer saccharum*, surviving 175 miles west of forests containing this tree. Little also mentioned the presence of big tooth maple, *Acer granidentatum*, in the Wichita Mountains fifty miles farther west and quoted Palmer's (1934 [387a]) opinion that these indicate "a former invasion of Rocky Mountain plants into the region." Evidence was sought by Little at the time when climatic conditions were favorable for the continuous distribution of these trees from the east to those in which they are now small, isolated relict stands. He accepted Sears's (446) climatic time table and concluded that these maples reached their present locations from the two distant centers during the humid period of 4000 b.c. Big tooth maples survived in protected, moist, steep-sided canyons, although the connecting forests of the same type have succumbed, he maintained, to the drier climates during the last two or three millennia.

On the other hand, the grass and forest fires set by Indians could just as easily account for such isolated relics, even had climatic conditions remained relatively stable and able to support linked stands of forest. It is even possible that the removal of forests by fire accentuated the climatic change from the former humid to the present dry climate of western Oklahoma.

KANSAS

The vegetation of the eastern two-thirds of Kansas uplands is classified as tall-grass prairie; the western third as short-grass plains. In the vicinity of what is now Wichita, on the Arkansas River, Josiah Gregg (218) wrote in 1844: "The banks are very low and barren, with the exception of an occasional grove of stunted trees, hiding behind a swamp or sand hill, placed there as it were to protect it from the fire of the prairies, which in most parts keeps down every perennial growth."

Sternberg (481) in 1869 also concluded that the plains of Kansas were treeless as a result of fires. Dodge (139) in 1877 emphasized hot winds and deficient moisture as reasons for the absence of trees from the high plains yet described the fires there as follows:

> The Indians burn portions of the prairie every fall, setting the fires so as to burn as vast an extent of country as possible, and yet preserve unburned a good section in the vicinity where they purpose to make their fall hunt. The buffalo, finding nothing to eat on the burnt ground, collect on that

unburnt—reducing greatly the labour of the hunt. The prairie fires, which were formerly supposed to account for the treelessness of the plains, have really comparatively little to do with it. On the high prairie the grass is very short. When on fire, the blaze, from six to fifteen inches high, moves over the ground slower or faster, according to the wind, but not with vitality or heat enough to seriously injure a bush of a few inches in diameter. Yet the high prairie is bare.

Certainly, as Dodge says, short-grass fires would not remove trees, but they could just as certainly have burned off small seedlings. With more fuel supplied by the tall grass of east Kansas prairies, fires there could, Dodge said, kill trees and were largely responsible for the lack of woody vegetation. Plant scientists, writing of their observations and experiments in Kansas, have usually pointed to the climatic factors as wholly responsible for the distribution of vegetation of the state. Kellogg's (280) statement of 1905 is typical for western Kansas (p. 10): "The climate of nearly all this region is essentially semiarid. It is characterized by light and unevenly distributed precipitation, high winds, excessive evaporation, and great fluctuations of temperature. All these conditions . . . are clearly reflected in the character of the forest growth and the gradual disappearance of tree species."

Years with as little as ten inches of precipitation are not uncommon in western Kansas, whereas eastern Kansas has an average of twenty-seven to thirty-eight inches of rainfall annually. The uplands in all of Kansas are treeless. Although Kellogg did not suggest that the plains and prairies of Kansas lacked trees because of fire, some of his information strongly supports that view. He mentioned that "natural forest growth" of Kansas uplands is limited to pine and cedar. He said (p. 32) that many areas could be forests "at no greater cost than is entailed in keeping cattle and fire from the land." Red cedar (*Juniperus virginiana*) would be scrubby in western Kansas, Kellogg said, but it prefers "drier situations, and is quite indifferent to the kind of soil in which it makes its home." Hackberry (*Celtis occidentalis*) "is common in Kansas [and] isolated clumps of it are even found in the sand hills, far from any other timber."

Kellogg reported that mesquite was found in Barber and Comanche Counties, on the southern edge of Kansas, having spread "through Oklahoma during the past 25 years [1880–1905]." Bray (58), Gleason (207), and Benson (37) also reported the spread of mesquite into Kansas. In 1913 Bates and Pierce (29) combined Nebraska and Kansas in their work regarding *Forestation of the Sand Hills*. Since the sand hills of both states are in the western, driest sections, it is of interest to read the opinion of

Bates and Pierce (p. 7) that "with the prairie fire controlled, forest may easily be grown in the sand hills." Hensel (241, 242) reports on modern observations and experiments on burning of Kansas prairies that support the theories of the Indians regarding the value of grass fires. Both reports were published in 1923, and in the *Journal of Agricultural Research* (241) Hensel wrote (p. 631):

> No doubt the practice of grass burning is a relic of Indian days when it was customary for the different tribes to burn off certain, well-chosen areas in the spring. The main object apparently was to obtain fresh, green feed early in the year. Moreover, the areas made greener by burning would more likely attract game animals and hunting could be made easier. This practice was perhaps passed on to the earlier settlers and has been contained to the present day.

Hensel also found that burning produces a more rapid and heavier spring yield but that by the end of the growing season the unburned plot reached the same total yearly yield (p. 641). He reported (p. 642) that burning did not decrease the total number of grass plants but did reduce the proportion of weeds. His conclusion was that the experiment "failed to show that burning is injurious." In his article in *Ecology* (242), Hensel wrote (p. 183): "In Kansas, as well as in adjoining states, the custom of burning pastures in the spring is still practiced to a considerable extent. . . . The actual practice has its beginning perhaps in the Indian custom of burning to make available fresh feed early in the spring for use of game."

Ranchers, he reported, give three reasons for continuing the practice (pp. 184–85): the removal of "last year's residue"; assuring that "feed is made available sooner than on unburned areas"; and "burning keeps down weeds and brush." A four-year experiment, during which one section of prairie was burned and an adjacent section was left unburned, demonstrated that the burned section had more and better grass than the unburned section, in general confirming the practice of cattle ranchers.

Aldous (6) also conducted studies similar to those of Hensel, and in 1934 reported results differing from Hensel's in some respects. Aldous confirmed Hensel's research in finding that burning increased early growth but refined his observation to discover that weed and brush were reduced only if burning was done in late spring. Aldous also discovered that greater benefits resulted from burning the pasture every other year rather than every year. Perhaps of greater importance to the overall evaluation of fire as a factor in the formation and maintenance of prairies were Aldous's conclusions regarding the ability of woody vegetation to invade unburned sites. He wrote that "[b]uckbrush is one of the most common shrubs in Kansas bluestem pastures" and "is able to compete with the bluestem grasses and to increase on protected areas" and noted that "[b]urning in the late spring is effective in removing buckbrush" (pp. 19, 23).

Aldous reported that sumac invades prairie but is also markedly reduced by burning in May. On the unburned pasture buckbrush doubled itself in five years. The idea that prairie grasses are climax vegetation rests on the assumption that woody vegetation cannot invade them. Aldous's findings refute this idea. Hensel's statement that Kansas grasslands are still frequently burned must also be borne in mind, for many authors write as if grassland fires ended with the removal of the Indians.

Another conclusion from Aldous's report on Kansas is important in view of statements that maintain that all fires are bad because they remove organic matter from the soil, reducing its fertility. Aldous reported (p. 64) that burning did not cause any decrease in measurable organic matter in the soil or in the total nitrogen during the five-year period of study. Notwithstanding these results, Hopkins et al. (255) assert that burning is harmful, and they have been widely cited by Penfound and Kelting (394) among others.

Weaver and Albertson (541) and Weaver (543) recorded that severe drought in Kansas caused tall grasses to be replaced by short grasses or mixed grasses. Cornelius and Atkins (113), however, observed that sand sagebrush, *Artemisia filifolia*, in Morton County in far western Kansas, thrived during the drought but was reduced in vigor and size as grass increased following drought.

An extensive study, *Observations on the Grasslands of the Central United States*, by Schaffner (438) is based primarily on the author's intimate acquaintance "with the prairies of Kansas since 1871." The pamphlet was published in 1926 by Ohio State University, where Schaffner was professor of botany. As one might expect, Schaffner accepted Transeau's theory of climatic causation of prairies and spent much of his monograph recording the evidence of transition between tall-grass prairie and short-grass plains. Prairies occur where rainfall exceeds twenty-seven inches, plains where rainfall is less than twenty inches. In spite of Schaffner's firm belief that the grasslands were "correlated with certain ratios of rainfall to evaporation," he presented some data that support the thesis that fire is an essential factor in the existence of grasslands. On page 27 Schaffner wrote:

> Far more important than the buffalo or other animals on the prairie was the prevalence of prairie fires which occurred any time from early autumn to late spring. These fires destroyed the forests on the flood plains of rivers, creeks, and large ravines and on the more gentle slopes and bluffs

where there was enough moisture to support a forest. The fires are, however, not the cause of the prairie on the normal levels. In Eastern Kansas,
where fires have ceased for long periods, the steep bluffs are forested as
originally but this forest ends abruptly in prairie on the general level
above the bluff just as it did before the fire ceased.

If prairie fires were powerful enough to remove forests from river
floodplains, then certainly they were destructive enough to keep forest
growth from drier uplands where wind and topography made fire most
effective. In evaluating Schaffner's remarks, and similar views of others,
the question arises as to how much woody vegetation is required to
change the classification of a grassland to some other type. Is a "forest"
necessary? Or would the presence of brush or scrub suffice?

The report by Aldous (6) that buckbrush and sumac invade unburned
Kansas prairies allows one to question the dominance of grasses as being
unaffected by human agents in this region. Hensel (241, 242) reports that
grassland burning continues in Kansas; consequently, one may question
whether Schaffner ever observed prairie "when fire has ceased for long
periods." Other reports indicate that pastures were often mowed to remove
invading brush, if they were not burned. Another statement by Schaffner
(p. 9) is useful. He says that in Clay County he "collected a quite perfect,
petrified spruce cone and fragments of petrified wood, in sand deposits on
hillsides. . . . Geologically considered, therefore, this region has developed
from a conifer forest to a prairie within comparatively recent times."

This statement takes on greater meaning when placed beside the
following data presented in 1926 by Gates (193) regarding the county
immediately to the east of Clay County:

> In going through Riley County, Kansas, one is impressed with the number
> and thriftiness of the pine groves on certain of the hillsides . . . at the present
> time however conditions are not considered favorable for the growth of
> these trees on a natural scale. The position of the Rocky Mountains and
> the former prevalence of prairie fire are two factors concerned.
>
> In the prairie, pine seedlings are found in greatest numbers on the north
> side of the groves where shade cast throughout the year has thinned the
> prairie somewhat.
>
> Though the prairie cannot maintain itself against the pine grove, some
> of the deciduous forest associations normally can.
>
> While it is quite evident that there is a possibility of the extension of
> the pine groves, certain conditions made the matter very much less simple
> than it appears at first sight. Perhaps the most important factor has been
> that of fire. Although the prairie fires of former days do not take place,

nevertheless smaller fires are set occasionally in patches of plants, accidentally or otherwise which play havoc with pine seedlings in the vicinity
of the groves. Pine trees ten or more feet in height are not injured seriously
by such fires. The destruction of small pine has been well shown in a certain grove which four years ago had along its margin a large number of
pine seedlings from one to four or five years of age; these were entirely
eliminated by fire in the spring of 1922, except on the north side to which
the fire did not spread.

In Riley County, Kansas, pines can maintain themselves against the
prairie, as shown by several pine groves . . . there is evidence of the possibility of limited spread by natural means.

The most important limiting factors are fire, and severe dry winds,
especially in winter but also in summer.

There were no pines in Riley County when it was settled in 1850, and
plantings did not begin until about 1890; but if real forest conditions can
develop in planted groves, there is every reason to believe that pines either
would have survived from the early geological trees of Schaffner's sandhills
or would have spread from relicts in Nebraska, if there had not been present
over the millennia the very factor inimical to their present survival: fire.
Hatton in 1936 reported that groves planted in the driest section of Kansas,
near Dodge City and Goodland, had achieved good growth and approached
forest conditions, which suggests that the ameliorative effect of a grove of
trees on the climate of the grove would go far to compensate for the original deficiencies of the general climate of the driest part of Kansas. It was
on such assumptions that the Great Plains Shelterbelt project was based,
the success of which will be discussed later.

NEBRASKA

The earliest record found of Indian uses of prairie fires in Nebraska are
provided by Bradbury (56, pp. 71–74) who wrote in 1819, providing one of
the earliest references to its use in warfare:

> April 28th—We breakfasted on one of the islands formed by La Platte
> River, the largest river that falls into the Missouri. It empties itself into
> three channels, except in the time of its annual flood, when the intervening
> land is overflowed; it is then about a mile in breadth. We noticed this day
> the skeleton or frame of a skin canoe, in which the river had been crossed
> by Indians; we saw also other indications of war parties having been
> recently in the neighbourhood, and observed in the night the reflection
> of immense fires, occasioned by burning the prairies. At this late season,

the fires are not made by the hunters to facilitate their hunting but by war parties; and more particularly when returning unsuccessful, or after a defeat, to prevent their enemies from tracing their steps.

Two days later Bradbury described a "plain of about eight miles in length, and from two and a half to three in breadth." He noted further: "As the old grass had been burned in the autumn, it was now covered with the most beautiful verdure." The German scientific observer Maximilian Wied-Neuwied (556), who traveled on the Missouri from 1832 to 1834, reported on several occasions of seeing fires or their effects. Of what appears to have been Nebraska territory he wrote:

> In some places we saw smoke rising in the forest; in others, the trees and the ground were burnt quite black. Such fires are sometimes caused by the Indians, in order to escape the pursuit of their enemies, and sometimes, also, by the agents of the fur traders. (p. 259)

> The Omaha Indians hunt on both sides of this part of the river; they are said to be the most indolent, dull, unintellectual, and cowardly of the Missouri Indians. At two in the afternoon we landed on the prairie, which was covered with tall trees, and forty or fifty of our men immediately began to hew down wood for fuel; there was abundance of grass, but not a single flower, which was caused by the prairie having been set on fire; black burnt wood was scattered about, and the ground itself was discoloured in places by the effect of the fire.

> As soon as it was dark, the young men set fire to the dry grass of the prairie, to give us the pleasure of seeing how the fire spread, but the attempt did not fully succeed, because there was no wind. (p. 281)

> A little further up we witnessed a great prairie fire, on the left bank. The flames rose from the forest to the height of 100 feet—fiery smoke filled the air; it was a splendid sight. A whirlwind had formed a remarkable towering column of smoke, which rose, in a most singular manner, in graceful undulations, to the zenith. (p. 289)

Aughey (20) in his book *The Physical Geography and Geology of Nebraska*, published in 1880, said that Nebraska prairies were caused by Indian fires and the trampling of bison. Dr. C. E. Bessey, first professor of botany at the University of Nebraska, elected in 1884, stimulated and participated in the botanical survey of Nebraska. By 1900 Nebraska was one of the best studied areas in America, and Bessey's students were gaining fame for their individual contributions. Although his fame rests on rigorous collecting and systematic identification and publication, Bessey (38) reported on "a meeting-place for two floras," which was found "a few miles east of the 100 meridian" on Long Pine Creek, twenty to twenty-five miles south of the Niobrara River in north-central Nebraska. Black walnut (*Juglans nigra*) from the eastern woodlands and Rocky Mountain pine (*P. ponderosa*) from the Black Hills of South Dakota and the mountains of Wyoming mingled in Long Pine Creek canyon. Bessey reports numerous isolated stands of pine "found on hills and in canyons" between central Nebraska and the pine forests in the mountains. To me these relicts signify a former distribution which has been interrupted, probably by fire.

Bessey (39), after discovering in 1899 that oaks (*Quercus ellipsoidalis*) were invading the upland prairies of southeastern Nebraska, wrote an article titled "Are the Trees Advancing or Retreating upon the Nebraska Plains?" His interpretation was that forests were advancing wherever grass fires had stopped and wherever agriculture had not replaced fires as an inhibiting factor. Kellogg (280) in 1905 reported other examples of trees invading prairies. Concerning the region of the Dismal River in central Nebraska, he wrote (p. 30):

> Although most of the large [red cedar] have been cut, and cattle and fire are doing much injury to what is left, thousands of young cedar . . . are to be seen. . . . The cedar is mostly on the bluffs. . . . Where undisturbed by fire and cattle the young growth is thriving and tends to spread up to the tops of the bluffs. Above any of the large trees fine young cedars, from one to four feet in height, can be found growing isolated in the bunch grass.

And on p. 31:

> The smooth sumac (*Rhus glabra*), the woofberry (*Symphoricarpos occidentalis*), and the wild plum (*Prunus americana*) are among the species which grow in clumps and are able to win in the fight against grass. Favorable conditions for the germination of tree seeds are thus created, while the shrubbery protects the young seedlings until they are of considerable size.
>
> The one thing which, above all others, makes for improved conditions on the plains, and gives assured hopes for better tree growth . . . is the cessation of fires. Before the country was settled, fires were both frequent and extensive. Whether originating from some neglected campfire, a flash of lightning, or set by the Indians, they swept over vast areas unchecked and left nothing but a barren waste behind.

Kellogg published a picture (plate 6, figure 2) with the caption: "A Clump of Bur Oak Which Has Taken Possession of a Prairie within Twenty-five Years, Buffalo County, Neb." Kellogg (p. 20) argued that the "common enemies of young trees everywhere are fire and stock." He said

(p. 21) that "instances are not lacking in which abundant reproduction [of pine] is found in the sod at the beginning of the upland level" but that fires have restricted "pine to the rough situations." Since Kellogg's study concentrated on the driest, western section of Nebraska and Kansas, his conclusion is worth repeating. It is that "forests may be established at no greater cost than is entailed in keeping cattle and fire from the land" (p. 32). Condra (109), in his *Geography of Nebraska*, published in 1906, also placed heavy responsibility on fire as a factor in prairie formation.

Nebraska has been the early training ground and the site of experimentation of some of the country's leading botanists and ecologists; consequently, special attention must be paid to their work under the heading of the state as well as in the general prairie-plains analyses. Bessey, a noted teacher and early director of scientific botanical programs, has already been mentioned. The "giants" in the field of plant ecology, F. E. Clements and John E. Weaver, also conducted extensive research in Nebraska. An idea of the extent and comprehensives of the work of Clements, Weaver, and their collaborators is gained from the fact that Clements had twenty-five titles and Weaver had twenty-two titles in the bibliography of their jointly authored textbook, *Plant Ecology* (542), first published in 1929. Their exhaustive covering of the subject and the great detail of their experimentation are evident from even a hurried examination of Clements's (101) *Plant Indicators* (1920), with 383 pages, or Clements, Weaver, and Hanson's (102) *Plant Competition* (1929), with 340 pages, both published by the Carnegie Institution of Washington. I briefly mention the position in the field of plant ecology of these men to indicate that I am aware of the status of the authorities with whom I dare to differ. I have already expressed strong difference of opinion with the view of Clements and Chaney (104), and I find I must place a different interpretation on the results of careful experiments reported in *Plant Competition* (102) by Clements, Weaver, and Hanson. The experiment in question was carried out near Lincoln, Nebraska, for three years, 1924–26, and was designed to discover, analyze, and measure the reactions of numerous grassland plants in competition and also to determine the results of competition between trees and grasses. Their section of their study called "Competition in the Ecotone between Woodland and Prairie" bears directly on this report. They say (p. 154):

> The chief object of this group of studies was to throw light upon the relations between trees and shrubs on the one hand and grasses on the other, particularly with respect to the contact between the deciduous forest and the prairie, and the climatic processes involved. . . . The success of tree plantations in the prairie has led to the assumption that even the true

prairie owes its persistence to fire and that the climatic relations are not controlling.

The authors go on to say that because of the aid given trees by cultivation and by planting large seedlings the "competitive relations are profoundly modified to the advantage of the tree." Although I and others who recognize the controlling influence of fire point to the success of tree plantations as evidence supporting our ideas, it is only when natural reproduction starts spreading from such plantations, as was reported by Gates (193) in Kansas, that they are presented as irrefutable evidence. On the other hand, the unaided invasion of deciduous trees, as recorded by Kellogg (280) in Nebraska and mentioned above, which Clements et al. appear by the statement quoted to ignore but which they also recorded, is of greatest importance. The experiment of Clements, Weaver, and Hanson consisted in planting seeds and seedlings of maple, elm, locust, and other trees frequently planted in Nebraska wind-breaks and allowing prairie grass to compete with them under various conditions. The results indicated that seedlings grown in mulched soil had much better growth and that mulching aided growth more than watering. In fact, giving extra water did not increase size over the unaided plants (p. 156). Seedlings were also transplanted into the partial shade of the transition zone between prairie and scrub and in the dense shade of thick scrub (*Symphoricarpos* or coralberry). Seedlings of box elder (*Acer negundo*) and honey locust (*Gleditsia triacanthos*) were the only trees that survived competition with prairie and transition zone shade; none survived the dense shade. Sixty percent of the locust and fifty percent of the box elder seedlings successfully competed with prairie grass in partial shade and in the open. In addition to the experiments with seedlings, careful observations were made at areas of tension between forest and prairie where natural seedlings were invading prairie. Although their observations were limited to only three years, they interpreted them to be adequate to define a permanent condition. This attitude is expressed as follows (p. 201): "The slow advance of chaparral and forest will be hastened by the wet phase, retarded by the dry, or even converted into a retreat. It appears certain that there can be no final victory for either, only periods of varying duration in which one or the other holds the ground won by the favor of the changing [sunspot-caused climatic] cycle."

I feel that this conclusion is unwarranted, because of the effect of forest on climate, which was recorded by Clements et al. in the experiment. Measurements taken at noon during summer on the prairie and within an adjacent sumac thicket revealed remarkable differences (p. 179).

These data indicate that once the forest had succeeded in its slow initial invasion onto the dry high prairie against adverse conditions, the effect of the forest would be great enough to withstand any fluctuations in climate that have been discovered to have occurred during the last two thousand years. Clements et al. (p. 199) say: "In the high prairie, the average survival of the several species was 11% at the end of the third year. . . . In the more protected ecotone, as well as in the *Rhus* thicket, insulation was much less and survival correspondingly better, averaging 30%. . . ." The authors recognize (p. 201) that "[b]etween the true forest climate in which the shrubs and trees have only the competition of the grasses to overcome and the true prairie climate in which both climate and competition favor the grasses is a broad ecotone." They imply that the true prairie and true forest climates and the intervening ecotone, or intermediate tension zone, are fixed. Their data, however, would suggest that as the forest advances it changes the climate and would eventually engulf the prairie with forest and forest climate.

Finally, if the balance between forest and prairie in Nebraska is so fine, as Clements, Weaver, and Hanson (102, p. 201) indicate, it must follow that fire, if it occurred, would have a very decisive role. Fires have occurred for a long time in Nebraska grasslands. Weaver and Albertson (541) in 1936 and Weaver (543) in 1943 reported that the most severe drought ever recorded in Nebraska and neighboring states, that of 1934, caused tall-grass prairies to be replaced by short grass. There is no record of forests being removed by such a drought. Forests simply do not respond as sharply as the open prairie to every fluctuation of climate. Ecologists frequently indicate that they really accept prairie fires as a normal condition of prairies and, consequently, usually neglect to give fires any special prominence. Steiger (479) from Nebraska is an example of such an ecologist, who investigated, as he said, a "virgin prairie" near Lincoln. He called it an "undisturbed" tract (p. 170) except for "[t]he annual removal of the matured vegetation being comparable in some respects to its former removal by prairie fire."

Penfound and Kelting (394) reported on "Some Effects of Winter Burning on a Moderately Grazed Pasture." They discovered (p. 559) that "[b]urning resulted in earlier growth in the spring, a reduction of areal [*sic*] cover, and a much greater degree of utilization by grazing animals."

Unless you wish to ration the feed or put the cattle on a restricted diet, those effects listed do not seem to me to be entirely bad. Nevertheless, Penfound and Kelting quoted with apparent approval the following from Hopkins, Albertson, and Riegel (255): ". . . the detrimental effect of pasture burning, either accidentally or otherwise, cannot be overemphasized." Were the prairies such poor pasture when first settled that one must avoid the circumstances and change the conditions prevailing at that time? One would have to accept that conclusion if burning is as detrimental as Hopkins and associates declare, for Penfound and Kelting say (p. 554): "That the original prairie was subject to frequent and devastating fires is generally accepted by all grassland investigators."

The data so far presented for Nebraska are primarily from the tall-grass prairie eastern third of the state. They indicate that prairie fires were formerly common and still frequently occur. They also indicate that in spite of some fires forest vegetation can and does invade the tall-grass prairie. Since eastern Nebraska receives about thirty inches of precipitation annually, there should be adequate moisture for tree growth. The central half of Nebraska is defined as the sandhills formation by Pound and Clements (405). This area is characterized by Clements and Chaney (104) as follows (p. 43):

> Because of their numerous lakes and streams and tallgrass cover, the sand-hills received the most attention [from Bessey and his students for a decade starting in 1887], with the result that they were early designated as grazing range par excellence, in which crop production was possible only in the specially favored valleys. . . . Pound and Clements (1898) emphasized the serious effects of disturbance of the soil by man, directly and indirectly, and pointed out that breaking of sod and overgrazing were replacing the native perennial grasses by annual weeds. . . . It was insisted without qualification that much the greatest part of the sandhills and table-lands was wholly unsuited to cultivation and was serviceable to mankind only for purposes of grazing.

Thus Clements and Chaney reiterate in 1936 the views of Pound and Clements of 1898. Yet in the middle of Nebraska sandhills, near Halsey, Thomas County, an experiment of far-reaching theoretical importance was started in 1903 that Clements and Chaney overlooked: the Nebraska National Forest. In 1913 two papers appeared that discussed this project. Pool (402) mentioned it in his general "Study of the Vegetation of the Sand-hills of Nebraska," written as a doctoral dissertation under the direction of Dr. Bessey at the University of Nebraska.

In addition to the experimental planting near Halsey, which was to lead to the Nebraska National Forest, Pool presented other data suggesting that the sandhill climate, with its fifteen to twenty-five inches of rainfall annually (p. 207), could support woody vegetation. A few examples:

> The sumac exhibits the same extra-woodland aspect here that is so typical of its distribution over the bluffs of the Missouri where it is the almost ever-present forerunner of the forest. Extending from beneath the scanty

woodlands of the Dismal and Loup rivers numerous species of shrubs are to be found disposed in the form of dense marginal thickets. From such sites these species spread to a wide range of sites over the bluffs and far back into the hills. (p. 267)

The species that most commonly leave the neighboring fringe of woods are *Symphoricarpos occidentalis* and *Prunus americana*. . . . Frequently the floor of a dry valley is covered for many acres by this species alone or in mixture with *Rosa arkansana*, a regular member of the bunch-grass association. Smaller "pockets" or basins with a complete cover of this sort are especially conspicuous interruptions of the usual grassy tone of the uplands. Such stands of brush are often so dense as to exclude nearly every other species. The "buckbrush" has been carried into almost every part of the region and one may come suddenly upon such a "buckbrush pocket" in the bunch-grass association many miles from any woodland. The wild plum is also commonly seen in similar isolated situations. . . . A species with a decided tree-form that occasionally develops similar circum-scribed patches in the "pockets" among the driest hills is *Celtis occidentalis*. I have seen "hackberry pockets" with a clump of about a hundred trees. The peculiar distribution of all these species over the uplands away from woodlands is doubtless related to the influence of birds in seed carriage. (p. 268)

Out of the canyon proper there are very few spots where [pine] trees occur in sufficient density to shade out the grasses completely, and in general it appears that the invasion of the surrounding grassland by the pines is an extremely slow process, and it may be doubted if such invasion will ever progress far under the conditions existing at the present time. (p. 273)

There is evidence in some quarters of a slight displacement of grassy associations by woodland forms, but on the whole this tendency is so slight that it may be passed with mere notice (p. 304).

Pool passes over the woodland invasion of prairie with a "mere notice" while entirely ignoring fire as a factor that contributes to the distribution of grass and woods. Because he does not recognize fire as an ecological agent before settlement, he mistakenly combines fire and overgrazing as forces destroying the sod and thus allowing "blow-outs" to develop. Pool recognized the harm of overgrazing, as he shows on p. 306: "The degree of denudation produced by the stock is sometimes so great as to bring about a reversion to blow-out conditions." Not having observed the conditions brought about by numerous prairie fires before overgrazing, as in presettlement times, he added: "Prairie fires often initiate the same retrogressive cycle. Grazing and fire sometimes combine in bringing about the subjugation of the bunch grasses."

Pool did mention that fires continue, but he failed to see them as a force except to expose the sand to blowing. For example, on page 296: "A phase of wind action that must not be overlooked is related to prairie fires . . . if the wind is high . . . the fire frequently becomes of uncontrollable proportions . . . a fire may sweep for miles across the hills and may sometimes burn over thousands of acres."

Would not such fires have an influence on the distribution of various types of vegetation? It needs to be added to precipitation and competition (p. 218) as a factor determining the vegetation of Nebraska sandhills. Bates and Pierce (29), who also published their study in 1913, expressed such a view (p. 7): "[In Kansas and Nebraska sandhills] there is no real obstacle to forestation except fire. The damage through fire depends very largely on public sentiment; since sentiment has elsewhere been educated to consider fire a common enemy, it seems probable that the grass fires of the sandhills will cease to be treated as matters of no moment and will come to an end as they have in the prairies farther east. With the prairie fire controlled, forests may easily be grown in the sandhills."

On page 16, they say green ash, hackberry, cottonwood, and aspen will grow on the sandhills, yet "[a]ll of the trees so far found are less than 25 years old and have sprung from sprouts after the last general prairie fire." From the evidence of relicts of yellow pine and buried stumps, Bates and Pierce concluded (p. 17): "It seems likely that yellow pine was formerly common in all of the sandhill region of Nebraska. . . . [Pine was driven out by] repeated destructive fires in the past." And on p. 45: "Probably for centuries the prairie fire has been the expected, and sometimes the desired, thing in the sand-hill region. Prairie fires temporarily improve grazing conditions by destroying the old grass, which has no forage value, and making room for a more vigorous growth of the new grass."

Bates and Pierce estimated that 20,000 square miles of Nebraska sandhills could be forested and mentioned that the 1911 plantings in Nebraska National Forest appeared very successful, but they added (p. 45): "Of the enemies of the embryo forest, nothing can be considered of so great import as fire." Zon et al. (582) in 1935 reported the planting of jack pine a success. Figure 8 on page 37 has as caption: "Block plantations Nebraska National Forest, 1929. Such plantations, now extending over several thousand acres, demonstrate that under favorable local conditions [such as sandy soil] forest planting can be a success in a region occasionally beset by great droughts." And under figure 9 on the same page: "Part of a jack pine plantation about 25 years old in the Nebraska National Forest [sand-hill region], 1931. Forest conditions are evidenced by the good litter cover on the ground, the tall narrow crowns, and the dense stand."

Zon failed to mention one of the vital factors that make the Nebraska National Forest possible and that make knowledge of this forest of importance for this study. Davis (131) in 1951 so graphically supplies the data Zon neglected that I will quote him at length:

> The Nebraska National Forest, however, is keeping up a system of fire-breaks that has been maintained since 1910. Without such a system, it is doubtful if the forest could survive.
>
> This national forest is located in the vast sea of grass-covered dunes known as the Nebraska sand hills. Every tree on some 20,000 acres has been planted. It is a successful attempt to show that a forest can be grown under the somewhat adverse conditions in the sand prairie, and represents one of the largest single afforestation projects in the world.
>
> Lightning and man for centuries have caused vast prairie fires to sweep across the sand hills. The chemicals in the ashes gravitated into the major depressions and created potash deposits, which were recovered during World War I and used in the manufacture of explosives. The repeated fires that caused this potash accumulation probably prevented the build-up of surface litter for more than a few years at a time.
>
> When the plantation project was initiated, it was of course necessary to check periodic prairie fires in the afforested area. This soon caused an increase in the grass density between the trees and an accumulation of dry litter, which made it extremely difficult to check fires sweeping in from the outside. Consequently, a system of permanent firebreaks was devised.
>
> The major exterior firebreaks consist of three plowed and disked 20-foot sand strips separated by strips of grass at least 150 feet wide. The sand strips are disked annually, to prevent vegetation from creeping in, and one of the grass strips is burned annually; two years' growth of grass is required for a clean burn.
>
> Virtually all of the planted acreage of the Nebraska project was wiped out in the spring of 1910, when a disastrous prairie fire swept through the area.
>
> [The fire break system has protected] despite the fact that there have been a number of large "outside" fires. These advance with considerable rapidity; in one instance, a frontal spread of 6 miles in 40 minutes was clocked.
>
> Today, some of the older trees are approaching sawlog size, and natural reproduction is beginning to come in. Thanks to the protection system, of which the firebreak network is a vital part, an afforestation effort extending over nearly a half century is beginning to bear fruit.

What conclusions can we draw from the example of the Nebraska National Forest? First, trees in the sandhills survived the drought of the 1930s, the worst in history, and according to Weakley (532), who studied a 400-year tree-ring record in the area, as severe a drought as any in 400 years. The 1930 droughts pushed the tallgrass east but did not kill the young forest. Second, since relict pine groves are now growing in the hills of Pine Ridge and Lodge Pole, adjacent to the sandhills to the north and south (see Kellogg [280]), it can be assumed that without fire as a pro-hibiting factor the sandhills region would become forested naturally by the slow invasion of seedlings from those centers. Third, since the Nebraska National Forest has developed "forest conditions" and reproduces itself with natural seedlings, the general climate of the area is a "woodland climate." Fourth, since fire could destroy the forest that has developed under fire protection, and since fires have been known to sweep the grasslands of Nebraska for centuries, fire must be considered a controlling factor in determining the natural vegetation of Nebraska.

Before leaving Nebraska, a word should be added about the previously existing pine forests. Shantz and Zon (454, fig. 2) indicate a small area of pine in northwestern Nebraska but do not show the pine area of south-western Nebraska. Kellogg (280, p. 12) wrote of the areas in 1905 as follows: "The pine type forest . . . occupies two quite widely separated districts in Nebraska. These have no connection within the region here treated, though there is a junction farther west, in Wyoming. Pine Ridge proper is a ridge of low hills north and parallel with the Niobrara River. It extends some distance into South Dakota and contains a fair growth of pine." Kellogg's map (p. 8) indicates the southern area of Nebraska forest as located south of the North Platte River.

COLORADO

The evidence of Indians setting fire to grass in Colorado rests on the gen-eral statements regarding burning of the plains, such as that of Dodge (139), quoted for Kansas. Many of the data dealing with western Kansas and Nebraska would apply to Colorado. The presence of pines in south-western Nebraska, for example, is duplicated in northeastern Colorado. In the report of the 1906 "Scientific Expedition to Northeastern Colorado," Ramaley (407) discussed the woody vegetation discovered at Pawnee Buttes, "the driest part of the high plains," where limber pine (*Pinus flex-ilis*) and red cedar (*Juniperus scopulorum*) were found. In his general study of *Colorado Plant Life* in 1927 (409), he explained the relict forest as follows (p. 152):

Pawnee Buttes are seventy miles east of the foothills, with no intervening limber-pine country, although there are bluffs and ridges with cedars and occasional rock pines. . . . It is likely that [during the glacial period] limber pine grew down even into the lowest foothill districts, and also grew on ridges and bluffs perhaps far to the east . . . the little patch of limber pines now growing near Pawnee Buttes is but the remnant of what was continuous forest in the foothills, and which extended eastward in favorable situations many miles. . . . A similar colony of limber pines occurs in the Black Hills of South Dakota.

Ramaley says today's drier climate has caused the intervening forest to disappear. A relict of pines, which are typical of cooler, moister mountains and which exist on the "driest part of the high plains," suggests to me that something besides the general change in climate determined the distribution of vegetation on Colorado plains.

Colorado ecologists and botanists have left a number of careful studies of the vegetation along the "mountain-front area." They have recognized the scientific importance of this ecotone between grassland and forest and have described it in detail, beginning with Dodds et al. (138) in 1909 and continuing with Roach's (419) M.A. thesis of 1948. It is rather surprising that no scholars who have recorded the migration of trees down the front range of hills and out into the plains have mentioned that the reduction of grass fires may have been a factor in the changes they documented. In 1908 it was observed that the mesas extending out from the foothills were becoming forested with rock pine (*Pinus scopulorum*) and that the "outermost parts of the mesas have sparse growth of small trees of various size." Roach continued the study of the same mesas "by comparing a map made in 1948 with one made forty years ago." He found: "Pine has migrated rapidly and progressively down both rims of Long Mesa and has spread laterally and sporadically from these marginal areas into the middle of the mesa."

It is not necessary to map and count carefully the trees on a single mesa to learn that the distribution of trees in the vicinity of Boulder, Colorado, has greatly changed in the last half-century. A comparison of early photographs with what can be seen today indicates a marked increase of density of trees all along the foothills as well as upon the dry mesas extending eastward from the foothills. Without documenting any modification in intensity in grazing during the last forty years, the breaking of the sod or thinning of the grass by grazing is the only change in the environment suggested by Roach and others to account for the invasion of the grass by pines. There can be no doubt, however, that the settlement of the region and the cultivation of large areas of the adjacent plains have greatly reduced the number and intensity of grass fires. Could not the virtual cessation of grass fires burning from the plains into the foothills be the fundamental reason why the trees are moving out into the grass? Roach mentioned there was no evidence that fire had burned the mesa, but he failed to consider the absence of recent fires as a contributing factor in the remarkable change he documented. Why the pines were spreading faster on the mesa than on the plains he explained as follows: "The extension of the pines onto the plains is probably restricted solely because of their dependency upon the higher moisture supply found on rocky ground for germination. . . . It is a well known fact that plains are not too dry for ponderosa pine."

Roach did not, however, adequately explain why pines are now spreading on the mesa and were not doing so a century ago. Of course, since Ramaley, Vestal (518), and other famous students of Colorado grasslands neglected to consider fires an ecological factor worth mentioning, it is not unusual that a graduate student continuing their work should also neglect fire. Pines are not the only woody vegetation moving onto the plains. Schneider (442) wrote of the Pike's Peak region in 1909 as follows (quoting Shantz): "Along the ridges north and east of Colorado Springs there is certain evidence that the thicket formation is slowly pushing its way out into the grass formation. Of the shrubs, *Cercocarpus parvifolius* [*C. montanus*] [mountain mahogany] seems best adapted for this invasion, and is several miles in advance of any of the other dominant species."

Schneider, taking support from Shantz, believes grazing will remove the dominant brush and allow grass to remain in control, thus reversing the role of grazing suggested by Roach for pines. Although Schneider did not mention it, we know that burning can keep brush from spreading onto grassland if the grass is not too heavily grazed. A third study that has importance for an understanding of the role of fire in the competition between grass and woody vegetation was made by H. C. Hanson (227) and Hanson and Vorhies (229) in northern Colorado from 1927 to 1929. Under a photograph of the experimental area (229, p. 239) he wrote: "Due to overgrazing, sagebrush (*Artemisia tridentata*) has invaded much of the western edge of the grassland, greatly reducing the grasses, which however quickly return if seed plants are at hand and the sage is removed." The summary of the experiment (227, p. 11) is of sufficient importance to quote at length:

1. Experiments are being conducted on the improvement of sagebrush range in the Laramie River Valley in Northern Colorado. 2. The stand of highly palatable and nutritious grasses was greatly increased the first year

following the removal of the sagebrush by burning and grubbing. The stand increased even more the second year. Increases in the weights of the forage from clipped plots the second year after burning were 238 to 336 percent above the weights before burning. 3. Burning was more successful than grubbing in destroying the sagebrush. 4. Dense stands of sagebrush 3 or more feet tall can be readily burned with a suitable wind. The burning in this experiment was done in October. 5. Artificial reseeding was not necessary. Natural revegetation by the grasses on the ground was very satisfactory. 6. The experiments show that rodents greatly decreased the amount of forage. 7. Burned areas should be only lightly grazed before the seeds have matured the first two seasons after burning so as to give the grasses opportunity to grow. Cattle, horses and rabbits concentrate their grazing on burned areas. 8. It appears that the grasses can hold the sagebrush in check for a considerable time. Observations made on areas that were burned 5 to 10 years ago indicate that the stand of grasses is still very good, even when heavily grazed by livestock and rodents.

In recent times we find three types of woody vegetation invading the grassy plains region of Colorado. Experiments show that fire would greatly inhibit the spread of one type, and we can assume fires would do the same for the others. The question has frequently been asked of me, if Indian fires were the deciding causal factor, what has prevented woodlands from taking over grasslands once tribes were removed from the Colorado plains? One reason is that prairie fires have not been stopped and so remain a powerful determinant of the types of vegetation there. Whereas I have discovered no study of the extent and frequency of present-day grass fires, a cursory search has revealed that grass fires are still important. For example, during the two years of 1949 and 1950, the *Boulder Daily Camera* (53a) reported twenty-seven grass fires in the vicinity of the town. These varied from one acre to two hundred acres burned over. The *Sterling Advocate* (480), the daily newspaper of Sterling, Colorado, near the northeast corner of the state and surrounded by "short-grass plains," carried a number of items about grass fires in the spring of 1948. The first was published on March 26 and described a "Spectacular Prairie Blaze" that burned from 5,000 to 10,000 acres. The flames leaped roads and railroads, with shifting winds, rain, and snow eventually checking the fire. Part of the report read: "The fire was the second one of considerable size during the week in Logan county, several sections near Brook having been burned over on Tuesday." On April 5, under the lead "Prairie Fire Burns Pasture in Large Area," it was reported that "12,000 to 15,000 acres of sandhill pasture . . . was seared in a fast moving prairie fire." And near the end of the same item: "An estimated 30,000 acres of grassland were burned over Sunday . . . in Weld county." A week later, the *Sterling Advocate* headlined: "4 Perish, Others Menaced in Holyoke Prairie Fire," followed by "Flames Sweep Area Estimated at 50,000 Acres in Phillips and Yuma Counties." A road finally stopped the fire as it "bore down toward the Nebraska line." And further: "Sheriff Wilson at Wray estimated that a path five to six miles wide and 10 to 12 miles long was burned across the northeastern corner of Yuma county." Because of the deaths, this fire had wide publicity; but undoubtedly many less spectacular grass fires burn patches of grassland annually. One resident of Limon, Colorado, said there had been an average of at least one large grass fire a year in the vicinity of Limon during the last twenty-five years. *The Rocky Mountain News* (420) of Denver reported 400 acres of prairie burned south of Denver on March 7, 1951, although 150 men fought the flames.

With roads as barriers, hundreds of men with tractors and plows, and county fire trucks, it is obvious that prairie fires are not as extensive as formerly, but the few examples presented here leave no doubt that fire continues to be a powerful ecological force on the plains of Colorado, as elsewhere on the grasslands of America. That such fires would deter tree growth on the prairies and plains is indicated by a remark by Sheriff Clements reported in the *Sterling Advocate* of April 12, 1948, that "thousands of fence posts were charred or burned off."

Fire as a determining ecological factor was proposed by F. E. Clements (99) in 1910 in the case of the "so-called natural parks of Colorado." Clements (101) in 1920 summarized his earlier study as follows (p. 15): "The conclusion was reached that all such grassland areas in forested regions are but seral stages leading to a forest climax. The majority of them are due to repeated burns or the slow filling of lakes, with the result that they persist as apparent climaxes for several hundred years."

Although Ramaley (409, p. 81) in 1927, without mentioning Clements, argued against the theory of fire as an important factor in the existence of Colorado's large grass valleys in the higher mountains, the evidence presented by Clements appears convincing. On the other hand, it is strange that Clements would evaluate the role of fire so significantly in a region of mountain forests and deny fire a comparable role on the prairies and elsewhere.

WYOMING

For the purpose of this study, the research relating to Wyoming grasslands is important because of the evidence of the spread of sagebrush onto grasslands and because the area was used by F. E. Clements (105) as an example of the danger involved with using the vegetation present at one time as an indication of the general climate and as evidence of the real potentialities of an area. My purpose in this work is to warn against neglect of the role of fire as Clements warned against neglect of periodic climatic fluctuation and grazing when using plant cover as an indicator of the possible productivity of an area. In 1938 Clements (105, p. 194) explained how "two young botanists [probably meaning himself and Pound], just on the threshold of ecology, who explored the sandhills of Nebraska in 1892 and 1893" contributed to the idea that short grass or buffalo grasses "appeared to be indicators of arid climate." Since then Clements has discovered in many places on the high plains protected from over-grazing, relics of the original tall or mid-grasses. Small areas were fenced off and (p. 195):

> The desired evidence promptly appeared in the form of mixed prairie, so called because a layer of mid-grass developed above the short-grass sod and reduced both grama and buffalo grasses to a secondary role. . . . However, the most decisive testimony has come from photographs taken by the Hayden geological expedition in the Great Plains between 1867 and 1870. These pictures [one reproduced of eastern Wyoming] depict an undisturbed landscape with a luxuriant cover of tall wheat, spear and blue grasses, beneath which their shorter companions are completely hidden. The omnipresent sagebrush of later days, which has spread widely because of over-grazing and recurrent drought, is nowhere to be seen.

I have not found a report that clearly defines the area of Wyoming prairie that has been invaded by sagebrush. A suggestion is gained from a comparison of the map of the Prairie province published by Pound and Clements (405) in 1900 with figure 2 of Shantz and Zon (454) published in 1924. Most of the area in central Wyoming that Shantz and Zon designate as "sagebrush" is included with the foothill grassland by Pound and Clements. The Laramie River valley, in which Hanson and Vorhies (229) experimented on burning sage where it extends into Colorado, appears to be classified as prairie on the map of Pound and Clements and sagebrush on the map of Shantz and Zon. Including Wyoming in their generalization, Shantz and Zon (454, p. 22) wrote: "Overgrazing, and the resulting reduction of fire risk and the conservation of soil moisture in the subsoil, has greatly extended the sagebrush desert into the grassland area."

Thus Shantz and Zon confirm Hanson and Vorhies in the idea that fire inhibits the spread of sagebrush. Clements overlooked the fire factor in arguing that the plains could support mid-grasses, although he said (105, p. 195) that "the most wide-spread and extensive [relics of the original grassland] are the fenced right-of-ways of railroads." He knew that rights-of-ways are regularly burned and that all the grasslands were formerly set on fire by Indians but found it impossible to give much importance to the fires set by aborigines. In the paper by Clements and Chaney (104, p. 37), "grazing, fire and hay-making" are equated as forces modifying the prairie, but they deny in the same article that fire had a decisive role in the existence of prairies in presettlement times. In contrast to the statement of Shantz and Zon above, which appears to place overgrazing and fire in their correct relationship, Clements (101, p. 156) wrote in 1920: "The conversion of contiguous grassland into sagebrush has undoubtedly been caused by overgrazing during the past fifty years, aided in a large measure by repeated fires."

Had Clements remembered that "repeated fires" were active for centuries before the invasion of prairie by sagebrush, he would not have combined fire with overgrazing as a cause for the reduction of grassland by sage. This same error has been repeated many times and will be considered more fully later under the section on the Great Basin and Plateau. The only other information that I have found relating to Wyoming is contained in reports regarding the "Northern Great Plains" in which eastern Wyoming is included in discussions centered on North and South Dakota. One example is Cobb's (107) paper of 1929 regarding "The Possibilities of Growing Evergreens in the Northern Great Plains." He said (p. 301): "The many ridges in eastern and southeastern Montana and Wyoming and northwestern South Dakota are from scattered to heavily wooded with western yellow pine." All such relict woods must be included in the final analysis of the possibilities of tree growing on the plains and prairies.

South Dakota

In 1884 W. J. McGee (347) wrote the following statement concerning the Sioux Indians, traditional inhabitants of the Dakotas (p. 186): "Of all the great stocks south of the Arctic, the Siouan was perhaps least given to agriculture, most influenced by hunting, and most addicted to warfare; thus most of the tribes were but feebly attached to the soil, and freely followed the movements of the feral fauna as it shifted with climatic vicissitudes or was driven from place to place by excessive hunting or by fires set to destroy the undergrowth in the interests of the chase."

This and numerous other reports of Plains tribes indicate that Indians of the northern grasslands, like those of the southern plains, set fires that would have strongly influenced the vegetation of the region. One of the first botanical papers that I located deals with the South Dakota prairies and attests to the former frequency of fires and to the fact that trees are slowly invading the prairie. Nonetheless, in his paper of 1908, Harvey (236,

p. 86) attempted to refute the idea that fires were of primary importance. It reads:

> ... we must not disregard a secondary and artificial ... factor, which in recent times must have served ... to prevent tree establishment. I refer to prairie fires; yet even in the absence of prairie fires for half a century the prairie stands uninvaded ... prairie existed as a climatic formation long before these fires either of Indian or Caucasian origin, swept the prairies, it would appear that this fire factor has been overestimated by many and is in no sense to be regarded as the fundamental factor. That there is, nevertheless, an extremely slow advance of the forest ... is very evident.

Two of Harvey's assertions need questioning. The first, that prairies existed "long before" the fire of Indians, rests on the idea, which was general in 1908, that Indians are recent immigrants to the New World. Harvey believed that the prairie became established following the glaciers, which coincides with man's occupancy of the area, according to the dates assigned "Minnesota Man" as well as the Folsom culture. The second point to question is the declaration that prairie fires have been absent for fifty years. It is questionable that any large areas of prairie have escaped fire, or mowing, which would serve a similar purpose, based on records of the Nebraska National Forest in a similar climatic zone not far to the south of the region discussed by Harvey. An article by Cobb (107), written in 1929, reports the continuation of wild fires on the northern great plains while presenting evidence that pines will grow if planted, even if neglected thereafter. Regarding a 25-year-old planting of Scotch pine on an abandoned farm, Cobb wrote (p. 302) as follows: "Broome grass and prairie sod have grown about them; cattle graze and rub against them; and grass fires have many times gone through them, as evidenced by old charred places on the bark. In the spring of 1928 a prairie fire went throughout them which killed about a quarter of the trees."

With the information on the survival power of planted trees, Cobb tells of the scattered groves of yellow pine in the hills of South Dakota. McIntosh (349) in his "Botanical Survey of the Black Hills" in 1931 considered the presence of prairies in the forested sections of the Black Hills. He rejected the theory that burning was responsible for the prairies there, suggesting instead that they may have been due to local soil conditions. McIntosh also recorded (p. 208) that "yellow pines are invading [the bunchgrass] grassland" and admitted (p. 214) that "its worst enemy is fire." He added: "It seems not improbable that the tree is adapted to a wider range of conditions than is sometimes supposed," because it was invading the plains beyond the Black Hills. McIntosh thought that rainfall on plains, being as low as fifteen to nineteen inches annually, was insufficient to support trees.

In contrast to this is a 1942 study by Larson and Whitman (303) involving an ungrazed mesa in South Dakota that receives from fourteen to seventeen inches of rain annually. The authors compared the vegetation on Medicine Butte, a six-acre area inaccessible to grazing animals and, so far as was known, never burned, with the vegetation of a mesa nearby that had been grazed. The unburned isolated mesa would be an excellent example of an experiment in which grass and trees could compete without other factors weighting the balance in favor of either. The photograph of the ungrazed area shows that trees are scattered over the completely protected mesa.

In the spring of 1805 Lewis and Clark reported from Wyoming:

> March 29th. The weather clear and the wind from the N.W. The obstructions above gave way this morning, and the ice came down in great quantities the river having fallen 11 inches in the course of the last 24 hours. We have had few Indians at the fort for the last three or four days, as they are now busy in catching the floating buffalo. Every spring, as the river is breaking up, the surrounding plains are set on fire, and the buffalo are tempted to cross the river in search of the fresh grass which immediately succeeds the burning.

Beyond this statement, our knowledge of Indians setting fire to prairies is combined with that of other areas, such as McGee's (347) statement regarding the Sioux previously cited. The experience accumulated by the staff of the Northern Great Plains Field Station of the U.S. Forest Service at Mandan, North Dakota, is pertinent to our thesis. Climatic conditions at the station are thought to be representative of a large area west of the 100th meridian in North and South Dakota and the drier eastern parts of Montana and Wyoming. The annual precipitation is fifteen inches or less, with the evaporation at least twice the precipitation. High temperatures and almost constant winds further contribute to the northern Great Plains' being considered a true grassland because of the deficient moisture.

Based on twenty-five years of experience at the Field Station, George (195) wrote in 1939 that "[t]rees on the northern Great Plains are another farm crop, and any other concept usually will result in difficulty." This is undoubtedly true for deciduous trees of the eastern woodlands, which occur naturally on the plains only along streams. George (195, p. 697) suggests this may not be true for pine trees with this statement in the same article: "Coniferous species establish forest conditions very readily in reasonably full stand."

Once established, conifers reproduce and are able to survive severe droughts, such as that of 1934–39. Chokecherry and red cedar also grow from seed carried by birds into any grove that approaches forest conditions (p. 697). Although over 4,000 cooperative shelterbelts were successfully established on the northern great plains during the first quarter of the twentieth century (151, p. 593), these were not under forest conditions; consequently, they did not reproduce and seldom lived more than twenty-five years. Professor Selke (449, p. 545), geographer of Dickinson State Teachers College, in 1940 expressed his doubt that the northern plains were treeless because of climate.

> Many assume that grass is the plant life best adapted to the drier regions of the West, and that trees there are entirely out of their natural habitat.
>
> There are flaws, however, in this superficial reasoning. The fact is that there actually are wooded areas in certain favored places of both the Great Plains and the prairie regions. The Turtle Mountains, the James, Missouri, and other valleys, and many other rough areas in the prairies contain considerable timber. In the drier Great Plains to the west there are good tree growths in "breaks," in badlands, in valleys, on buttes, and sometimes even on relatively level land. Small areas, like the Custer National Forest of Montana, and South Dakota, are largely on or near buttes.
>
> The location of forests in the driest parts of the Dakotas, Nebraska, and other states shows that grasses are perhaps not such "natural" growths after all. Indians and white men alike cut down what timber there was. . . . Fires fatal to all taller vegetation became much more common when . . . the Indians and whites frequented the drier lands of the West. Many woodlands of the semi-arid regions were completely stripped of their trees within the memory of living men.

With the record that I present of more widespread occurrence of prairie fires over a greater period of time, Selke's doubt is supported. Stoeckeler and Dortignac (496) record evidence that the accumulation of snow in shelterbelts adds as much as ten inches of water to the vicinity. George (196) in 1943 confirmed the fact that shelterbelts receive additional water because of snowdrift formation in them. The ability of other planted trees to survive in North Dakota is recorded by Zon et al. (582, p. 53), who reported that at least 60 percent of the 8 million trees planted in North Dakota just prior to 1935 survived the drought.

MONTANA

Much of Montana was included in the region covered by reports of the Northern Great Plains Field Station. In 1948 Wright and Wright (576)

published a study on protected areas in south-central Montana in an attempt
to judge the ability of several species to compete. In protected prairie
spots, mostly cemeteries, the Wrights found typical tall grasses or mixed
grasses of the eastern prairies, such as *Festuca, Agropyron, Boutelova, Stipa,
Carex, and Koeleria*, dominant. *Artemisia tridentata* was also present in
unburned, unpastured sites. *Artemisia* dominated heavily pastured areas.
The Wrights were especially interested in Square Butte, an area of about
three acres, because it was inaccessible to livestock; consequently, it
allowed plants absolute equality in competition. They wrote (p. 453): "The
soil is Billings sandy loam and is firmly stabilized by a luxuriant cover of
native grasses . . . widely scattered bushes of *Chrysothamnus nauseosus*
and *Rhus trilobata* were present throughout the area. *Artemisia tridentata*
was of infrequent occurrence and confined to the edges of the butte, along
with several scraggly trees of *Pinus ponderosa*."

In the photograph that the Wrights reproduced of the top of the butte,
I counted fifteen pines. Of course, a grassland with scattered sumac and
rabbit brush and an open stand of pine would be quite different from the
plains covered for thousands of square miles with grass only. Yet this protected relict in a region of twelve to eighteen inches of rainfall annually
exhibited such a vegetation.

CANADIAN PRAIRIE PROVINCES

Finally, one of the most complete summaries of information on the prairies
is based on observations made of the northern plains in Canada as found
in the *Proceedings of the Royal Geographical Society and Monthly Record of
Geography* (London, 1892). After telling of his personal experience on the
prairies and briefly reviewing opposing theories, Christy (97) presented
his own views (p. 82):

> The number of theories that have been advanced at different times to
> account for the treelessness of the prairies is very great; but these theo-
> ries are, for the most part, more or less improbable. They all leave us face
> to face with the paradox that in spite of an abnormally fertile soil, a fairly
> heavy rainfall, a moderate elevation, and a favourable climate and geo-
> graphical situation generally, vast (and, perhaps, increasing) areas remain
> permanently treeless, although they produce a rich variety of grasses and
> other small herbaceous plants.
>
> To the solution of this point, then, let us now turn our attention. My
> unhesitating belief is that the treelessness of the prairies is due mainly to
> artificial causes; that the agency by which the prairies have been brought

to their present state is chiefly Fire—one of the best servants and worst masters man ever had.

To the prevalence of prairie fires in the past, I attribute, to a large extent at least, the very existence of the prairies themselves; the dreary treelessness; the extraordinary fertility of their soil, and its fine, black, soot-like texture, the alteration of the flora; and the extermination of certain organic creatures (which are usually abundant in similar situations, and would, I believe, exist now on the prairies had it not been for the fires). The idea that the treelessness of the prairies is due largely to the action of fire is not by any means new. It crops up continually, as an almost accepted fact, in the accounts of travel in the prairie region which the more observant travelers have given up.

Every one is familiar with the stirring tales of the huge fires which occur on the prairies, and of the way in which hunters and travelers are accustomed to "fight fire with fire," when placed in situations of danger. But not a few persons in this country have, I believe, a vague sort of idea that these fires are in some way due to natural agencies; but all the evidence goes to show that they are due to human agency, and there is little or none to the contrary.

Prairie fires, in the first case, originated among the Indians, who, when on their "great fall hunts," used to "put out fire" as a signal to their friends that they had found buffalo, or with the object of more effectually gathering the animals together, by limiting their feeding-ground.

In the present day, however, fires have probably a different origin from those of years past. They are caused in nearly every case by travelers who carelessly neglect to extinguish their camp fire; by persons who maliciously put out fire; or by settlers who do so for the purpose of improving the pasturage the following year, or with the mistaken idea that by burning the grass they lessen the number of mosquitoes.

Fires take place in the spring and autumn. When the buffalo existed, prairie fires mainly took place in autumn, before the winter snows had fallen, but the majority (or, at least, many more than formerly) now come in the spring. The reason for this is, that the settlers do not like fire in the fall, because they prefer to keep the pasturage for their cattle until as late a period in the year as possible, and also because there are at that season stacks of corn and hay standing about in every direction; but, in the spring-time, none of these reasons has any force, and the settlers then burn the prairie, as soon as the disappearance of the snow has left the dead grass dry enough to "carry fire."

Before visiting the prairies, I had no clear idea as to the great prevalence of the fires, regarding them as occasional occurrences only; but from what I have seen and heard, I imagine that by far the larger portion of the whole area of the prairies gets burned over annually. . . . This is not surprising when it is considered that the only conditions required for fire to run over hundreds of miles . . . are a more or less strong wind behind and a level stretch of dry grass in front. I myself saw a fire which I had reason to believe was 40 miles in length; while Professor H. Y. Hind [247] says: "From beyond the south branch of the Saskatchewan to the Red River, all the prairies were burned last autumn [1857]—a vast conflagration extending for 1000 miles in length and several hundred in breadth. The dry season had so withered the grass that the whole country of the Saskatchewan was in flames." The Rev. Henry Budd, a native missionary at the Nepowewin, on the north branch of the Saskatchewan, told me that, in whatever direction he . . . turned in September last, the country seemed to be in a blaze. We traced the fire from the 49th parallel to the 53rd, and from the 98th to the 108th degree of longitude. It extended, no doubt, to the Rocky Mountains.

It is certain, however, that the prairie fires now are not so extensive as formerly, although probably they are more numerous, on account of the very much greater number of persons there are to start them. That their courses should be shorter now than formerly is not due to any increase of the chief natural obstacle to their progress—namely, water, in lakes or streams—but to the amount of ploughed land which now, both in spring and autumn, largely checks their movements; for, on stubble, fire can "run" before very high wind only.

But, if I have been compelled to enlarge my ideas as to the ordinary frequency and extent of the fire, I have, on the other hand, found it necessary to contract my notions as to their average magnitude. It appears that everything depends on the length of the grass and the strength of the wind. Every settler with the slightest grain of forethought, provides his house and premises with what is known as a "fire-guard." This is done by the very simple process of turning a few furrows with a plough all round his premises. Many a settler through the neglect of this precaution, or when he has allowed his fireguard to become old and overgrown with grass, has suffered the loss of a stack of wheat, oats, or hay, his farm-buildings or a comfortable house or shanty, built with the labour of his own hands. Not a few persons, whose ideas of prairie fires have been gathered from what they have read, or from pictures in which men, horses, cattle, buffaloes, hares, deer, birds, and what not, are depicted as flying before the flames, may feel disinclined to believe that such a simple precaution could be sufficient to stay the onward progress of a fire; but in most cases it suffices.

On the drier portions of the prairies, the grass is short and scanty, and a fire will not "run" unless there be considerable wind to drive it. Even then it is but a very small affair—merely a narrow flickering line of advancing flame, which might almost be flicked out with a pocket-handkerchief; and indeed, as a matter of fact, is often brushed out for short distances with a wet sack or broom by settlers anxious to preserve their homes; for, if the fire be stopped along the windward side of a settler's premises, the wind carries the two wings of the fire on past the sides of the buildings; and although they may eventually join again to the leeward, they cannot then return to burn the premises, unless the wind shifts completely round.

Such small fires as those of which I now speak are often stopped for considerable distances by obstacles of much smaller importance than a settler's fire-guard; for instance, by numerous "trails," as the prairie roads are called in Canada. These though merely two narrow wheel-marks with an ox-path in the center and grass growing between, often stop fires for short distances; but, being able to cross the trail at other spots, the broken line of flame gradually joins again, leaving many triangular patches of unburnt grass on the leeward side of the trail, the apex of the triangle of course pointing in the direction in which the fire has gone.

I saw instances of this one bright moonlight night, when I was traveling over the dry, sandy prairie between Fort Ellis and Elkhorn. The short, scanty grass had been burned by a fire, the lurid glare of which I had plainly seen, miles away, after dark on the previous evening. The trail I traveled on, though but faintly worn, served nevertheless, to check the fire for 100 yards in some places, so that on one hand I had burned and on the other unburned prairie; but in places the flames had contrived to creep across, and had gone on their way rejoicing. On one occasion, too, I remember seeing a spot where a small fire had been checked, for several yards at least, by the wheels of a wagon having previously crossed its track, pressing down the short grass, though they had left almost no impression on the soil. Such trumpery fires as these are the rule in dry districts; but there are times when the wind is strong, and the waving grass grows long and rank in a moist soil, when fires occur of much more serious proportions. Then a great wall of flame, yards in height, rushes along, causing danger to travelers and destruction to all kinds of settlers' effects. I have been credibly informed that such fires find no difficulty in leaping such a river as the Assiniboine.

The spectacle presented by a large prairie fire at night is one of the most terrific sights imaginable. The lurid red glare from flames hidden below the horizon overspreads the entire sky, and gives to everything a most unearthly appearance; while, by day, the vast volumes of smoke, rising and blending with the clouds, are almost equally awe-inspiring. I have seen many such fires on my various visits to the prairies. As Prof. Hind

[247] says:— "The grandeur of the prairie on fire belongs to itself. It is like a volcano in full activity; you cannot imitate it, because it is impossible [elsewhere] to obtain these gigantic elements from which it derives its awful splendour." . . .

It being now understood how very prevalent these prairie fires are, the reader will, in a measure, be prepared for my statements as to the very powerful effect they have been able to exercise upon the face of the country in various ways.

First, let me take the matter of the blackness and fertility of the soil. That the soil is very black and very fertile has already been stated; and, with the knowledge already gained as to the prevalence of fire, it seems only like putting two and two together to make four, to conclude that these features are due to the fires. After a fire, the ash of the burnt grass is left as a black deposit upon the surface of the ground; and this is especially the case in the damp bottoms of "sleughs," where the willows make the grass long and rank by shading the soil and keeping it moist. Such spots, at a little distance, appear, when burned, much blacker than the rest of the prairie, and examination shows the deposit of ash to be sometimes as much as one-eighth of an inch in thickness. Now it is a matter of common observation that the black prairie loam is usually blackest in such situations, and I do not think it is at all difficult for any well-trained mind, capable of weighing the effect of a very small cause very often repeated, readily to comprehend that the blackness, fineness, and fertility of the soil of the prairies is the effect, in a very large measure at least, of the annual deposition, for many generations past, of a very small quantity of this grass ash, which must undoubtedly have great manurial value. In Minnesota and Manitoba, the thickness of the black loam varies from about-one to three feet; but, taking the average at about eighteen inches, and the average annual deposition of ash at only one-thirty-second of an inch, we find that it would have taken just 576 years to deposit eighteen inches of soil by this means alone. But the ash would certainly rot further and become consolidated after deposition; therefore let us double our figures, and we get 1152 years as the time required for the formation of eighteen inches of black loam. Of course, in moist districts, where the grass grows long, the rate would be higher, and in dry districts lower. I am perfectly aware that the foregoing is a very vague, and largely a speculative, calculation, but it will serve to illustrate my point.

The belief as to the black loam having originated thus is far from original, as I met and conversed with many settlers and others on the prairies who fully supported it. If the blackness and fertility of the soil are not due to the fires, to what are these features due? I have heard it maintained that the gradual decay of the grass for generations past was the cause; but dead grass and leaves have decayed in many other places for generations without leaving, so far as I have seen, a soil nearly so black as that of the prairies. The opinion of Prof. Sheldon, of the Agricultural College, Downton, Wiltshire, is only another piece of evidence in favour of the fires, though he does not allude to them. He writes: "The soil of Manitoba is a purely vegetable loam, black as ink and full of organic matter, in some places many feet thick resting on the alluvial drift of the Red and Assiniboine rivers."

Christy had found earthworms scarce in Manitoba, which he thought due to the small amount of organic material in the soil for worms to eat. He goes on to say (p. 89):

> We come now to the consideration of my assertion:—That the fires, by gradually killing and consuming the forests, have caused the treelessness of the prairies; or in other words, that the prairies themselves are, largely at least, due to fire. The evidence on this point is, I think, very clear. It can be shown, I think, on the clearest evidence, that, if the fires have not caused the prairies, they are at least now extending them in numberless places; that trees still grow on the prairies on spots that are to some extent protected from the fires; and that, over large portions of the prairies, young trees spring up annually, only to be at once burned; but, if protected from the fire, they would grow and in due time reproduce the banished forest-growth.

The fact that trees grew naturally in protected spots and that they flourished when planted was taken by Christy as proof that climate and soil were suited to tree growth. He said, for example (p. 90):

> If a portion of the prairie escapes the fire for one year, the growth of bushes has time to attain a height of (say) one or two feet; but, by keeping the ground moist, they encourage the growth of long grass, and thus bring about more surely their own destruction, for when the relentless fire comes, it catches the grass and burns the young shoots of the bushes along with it; but there is no reason whatever why the poplars, at least, should not grow into trees, if they were protected from the fire.
>
> One man, who had round his house several clusters of well-grown young poplars, told me that he had observed them springing up ten years before, and had preserved them solely by means of a fire-guard. In confirmation of what is here advanced, I might mention the case of a very intelligent Ontarian gentleman, now farming on the bare, treeless prairie, about five miles north of Brandon, Manitoba. On first taking up his land,

he was assured by his neighbours that it was unreasonable to suppose he would ever get trees to grow on his farm, for had the soil been suitable to them, they would certainly have been there. But he was too acute to believe this, and observing in the spring of 1883 a number of young seedling poplars springing up in a slight depression where the soil was more moist than on the level ground, he protected them by a fire-guard. The result of this was, that when I saw them in the following September, they were a flourishing lot of young trees some two feet high, which he hoped soon to be able to transplant. These trees must have originated from wind-blown seeds, as there were, I believe, no other trees whatever within three or four miles at least; and the gentlemen in question had to go eight or nine miles for his supply of winter firewood. . . .

My friend, Mr. Ernest E. Thompson, of Toronto, who is very familiar with the prairies of the Canadian Northwest, says, in an article on Prairie Fires: "If a piece of prairie, almost anywhere, be protected for two consecutive years, it will be found covered with a growth of poplars and willows; therefore I conclude that, but for the fires, the whole country would be covered with bush." . . .

In connection with my statement that almost everywhere upon the prairies—even many miles from any other trees—a growth of young poplars and willows is always endeavouring to spring up, it is interesting to consider whence come the seeds of these young trees. It seems not improbable (though I cannot adduce evidence) that the level lands which are now prairie were once covered with a coniferous forest-growth, but the nature and very slow growth of coniferous trees would render their extermination very speedy under the constant recurrence of fires. As a result, we now find that by far the commonest trees are the poplars, chiefly the aspen (*Populus tremuloides*), the balsam poplar (*P. balsamifera*), and the cottonwood (*P. monilifera*), and various species of willow. These trees have great vitality in their roots, and repeatedly send up fresh shoots after the annual fires, until death from exhaustion ensues. Their downy seeds, too, are readily carried for long distances by means of the wind, and may lie dormant in the soil for years. That these seeds are thus distributed over long distances by the wind may be readily seen by any one who happens to be on the prairies during the few days in the spring when they happen to ripen. . . .

May 27th, 1887, Winnipeg, Manitoba.—No one who has been here during the last few days, which have been bright and fine, need wonder any longer how it is that, wherever the fire is prevented from running, young poplars at once spring up upon the prairie, even in places far removed from any other trees. During the last day or two, the air has been full of poplardown, drifting slowly in the breeze, settling on one's clothes, tickling one's face, and catching in cobwebs wherever these are found. Probably the down comes from some considerable distance. From all this it is clear that the prairies would quickly become covered with timber trees, were it not for the frequent fires.

Evidence as to the past and present destruction of forests, and consequent extension of the prairie through fire, is not less conclusive. An old Halfbreed in Manitoba told an intimate friend of mine that when, as a boy, he used to hunt the buffalo on what is now known as the Big Plain, it was covered with bluffs of good timber, which have now almost entirely disappeared. Many settlers can point to some dead tree or small clump of bushes which forms the last remnant of a respectable sized "bluff" that has been destroyed by the fire within the last year or two. A settler always likes, where possible, to be able to shelter his house from the icy blasts of winter behind some small bluff; but if he wishes to preserve his shelter, it is imperatively necessary to surround it with a fire-guard. There is hardly a bluff that does not show signs of the fierce conflict it annually has to wage with the merciless fire.

A typical case is something of this kind:—A fire comes over the prairie, and, arriving at the edge of a "bluff" (as isolated clumps of trees are always called in Manitoba), or at the edge of the more extensive "bush," it attacks the outer trees, burning one side of their trunks just above the ground, also leaping up and consuming their smaller branches. Thus, perhaps, over an area of several acres, the fire has eaten into the bush as far as there was any grass to carry it, consuming the underwood, injuring (if not killing) the trees, but still leaving them standing. Next year the fire comes again from the same direction. If any young underwood has sprung up, it is again destroyed, and the fire enlarges the hollow in the trunks of the standing trees that it commenced the year before. This, if it does not prostrate them, effectually destroys their vitality; while the fire proceeds on still farther into the bush, destroying as it goes. The year after, the hungry fire comes again—nearly always from the same direction. Again the undergrowth is destroyed; again the hollows in the tree trunks just above the ground are enlarged; again some of the trees fall and lie charred and half-burned as the fire passes on, again adding a larger area to that over which it has already spread hideous disfigurement. Those trees which were first attacked, and which have not already fallen, have now great black hollows scooped out of their trunks, as if some animal had gnawed into their bases till nothing but a shell remained to support them. But the fire seldom forgets to return year by year. When it does come, it gnaws again at the same spot where it has already several times found food for its unappeasable appetite; the trees fall, and the fire, passing on in its haste to attack those it has as yet only partially overcome, leaves them as charred and blackened logs upon the ground. Year by year the fire comes; seizes on these logs; chars them more and more completely, and rushes on farther into the bluff, as the destruction of the trees on the margin allows the grass to grow further and further in; until, in a few years, it is all destroyed. Twenty or thirty acres of wood are often thus destroyed in, say, seven or eight years. Will any one imagine the trees will grow again in the same period? The bluff may have been destroyed in like manner many years before and have grown up again but, as growth is slow, and destruction by fire is swift, it is evident that, although some of the destroyed bluffs do grow again, on the whole the prairies would be extended. And with such havoc as I have described going on year by year, who can wonder it? I have sketched no fancy picture, but one which I have seen in all stages of completion in the bluffs around Carberry and elsewhere in Manitoba. It does not seem to me reasonable for any man who has seen the destructive effect of these fire to deny that sufficient time only is wanted for exactly the same means to have originated even the wide prairies themselves.

Over and over again Prof. Hind speaks of having observed the same thing—forests of large pines, spruces, or tamaracs, prostrated by the fire, to be partially succeeded by a less valuable growth of elm, poplar, or willow, which, in its turn, is at last destroyed. Here is what he says upon the subject:—"That forests once covered a vast area in Rupert's Land [an old name for the Hudson's Bay Company's territories], there is no reason to doubt. Not only do the traditions of the natives refer to former forests, but the remains of many still exist as detached groves in secluded valleys, or on the crests of hills, or in the form of blackened, prostrated trunks, covered with rich grass, and sometimes with vegetable mould or drifted sand. The agent which has caused the destruction of the forest which once covered many parts of the prairies is undoubtedly fire; and the same swift and effectual destroyer prevents the young growth from acquiring dimensions, which would enable it to check their annual progress. Nearly everywhere, with the exception of the treeless, arid prairie west of the Souris, and west of Long Lake on the north side of the Qu'Appelle [River], young willows and aspens were showing themselves in 1858, where fire had not been in the previous year. South of the Assiniboine and Qu'Appelle, few plains had escaped the conflagration of 1857, and the blackened shoots of willow were visible as bushes, clumps, or wide-spreading thickets, where the fire had passed."

Again, he says:—"The annual extension of the prairies from this cause [fire] is very remarkable. The limits of the wooded country are becoming less year by year; and, from the almost universal prevalence of small aspen woods, it appears that in former times the wooded country extended beyond the Qu'Appelle, for three or four degrees of latitude south of its present limit. . . . This lamentable destruction of forests is a great drawback to the country and a serious obstacle to its future progress." The same facts must strike every observant traveller on the prairies.

Prof. Macoun, of the Geological Survey of Canada, has frequently expressed his firm belief in the opinions I have here advanced, and many statements in support of these views may be found in his interesting work, "Manitoba and the Great North-West," where he states (pp. 27, 28) that between the Rocky Mountains and an imaginary straight line connecting Moose Mountain and the Touchwood Hills, the whole country is utterly devoid of wood as far north as lat. 52E, with the exception of Wood Mountain, the Cypress Hills, and certain narrow river-valleys. He also says (p. 104): "The real cause of the absence of wood on every part of the region under consideration is undoubtedly prairie fires, which sweep over every part of it year after year, destroying the seedling trees as long as there are any seeds left to germinate, and year by year killing the bushes, till the capacity of the root to send up shoots dies out, and then even willows cease to grow."

Elsewhere, in reference to Prof. Hind's journey of exploration, Prof. Macoun significantly adds that "where he in 1857 saw large forests, I passed over in 1880 and never saw a twig."

Dr. G. M. Dawson, of the Geological Survey of Canada, says of the prairies of the Peace River (which, however, are hardly true prairies) that "there can be no doubt that they have been produced and are maintained by fires. The country is naturally a wooded one, and, where fires have not run for a few years, young trees begin rapidly to spring up . . . and it is probable that, before the country was inhabited by Indians, it was everywhere densely forest-clad. . . ."

Prof. A. R. C. Selwyn, Director of the Geological Survey of Canada, writes:—"Whatever the effect may be of these destructive conflagrations, in reference to the water-supply of the region, there is no doubt that . . . hundreds of miles of forest have thus been converted into wide and almost treeless expanses of prairie." Dr. R. Bell, the Assistant Director, in forwarding a report to Prof. Selwyn shortly after says:—"Your remarks upon the destruction of forests by fire between Red River and the Rocky Mountains are corroborated by all that I could hear upon the subject. The rapidity with which some tracts between Prairie Portage and Fort Ellice were stated to have been converted from forest to prairie, is almost incredible."

Could anything show more conclusively than the foregoing statements of the destruction which these fires have wrought?

It may, however, be asked, What has become of the trunks and stumps of these destroyed trees? The former, lying upon the surface of the ground, would be annually attacked by the fire, and at last would be speedily disintegrated, when once well rotted, by a species of ants which drives tunnels through such soft logs in all directions. Dr. Bell, in speaking of the district south of Fort Ellice, writes:—"The aspens of that region burn much more readily than does the wood of the same tree in Ontario and Quebec, and the portions which escape total destruction by fire rot and disappear in the course of one or two years."

My friend, Mr. Ernest E. Thompson, of Toronto writes:—"Far out on the open plains, sticks may be picked up and charred wood unearthed, showing where once were trees."

I have also heard of charred logs being dug up from below the surface of the open prairie. They had probably been covered by the burrowings of gophers and badgers. The working of these animals will also, to some extent, account for the disappearance of the roots and stumps of the trees; but it certainly is surprising that these should have disappeared so completely as they have done.

In discussing the destruction of the forests, we must take into consideration the fact that the fires, in nearly all cases, travel eastwards with the prevailing winds. In Manitoba, the mean resultant direction of the wind for eleven years (1871 to 1881 inclusive) was N. 44EW. This will help us to understand why trees, in the majority of cases are upon the eastern side of a lake or river. Captain Butler remarks of the Red River:—"Its tributaries from the east flow through dense forests; those from the west, wind through the vast sandy wastes of the Dakota prairie, where trees are almost unknown."

Roughly speaking, the whole of the region for hundreds of miles, to the east and north of Red River and Lakes Manitoba, Winnipegoosis, Winnipeg, is one of dense forest, protected from the ravages of the prairie fires largely by those friendly pieces of water, while the whole region to the west is prairie, exposed to the fire.

Further, wherever there is an island in a lake that island, being protected from fire, is pretty certain to be covered with trees and bushes. Proofs of this may been seen everywhere on the prairies.

Another fact, familiar to every one that knows the prairies, which may, perhaps, be brought forward in controversion of the foregoing, is that nearly all the streams crossing the prairies are fringed with a narrow belt of trees on both sides, eastern and western or northern and southern alike. This is the case, even on absolutely treeless prairies, on which grass will scarcely grow, and is, I think, largely due to the fact that the wind is unable to drive the fire down the sloping sheltered banks of the stream, as it does on the level prairie.

But water is not the only obstacle to the progress of prairie fires. A range of sand-hills answers much the same purpose. These sand-hills, though composed of fine and almost absolutely-pure wind-blown sand, are usually sparsely covered with stunted timber trees, thus affording a paradox that, while vast tracts of abnormally fertile soil are treeless, smaller tracts of great sterility are fairly-well timbered. The explanation, as given by Prof. Macoun, seems to be that, whereas the fertile prairies produce an abundance of grass, which "carries" the fire to burn the trees, the sandhills, through their extreme poverty, do not grow sufficient grass to carry fire, and thus the few trees growing upon them are safe.

These, then, are the grounds on which I base my contentions—that fire is the agency which has destroyed the forest-growth which once covered the prairies, and that, were the fires stopped once for all, trees in plenty would soon grow up in all parts. Had these fires been stopped some fifty years ago, it is not, I believe, too much to say that the whole of the true prairie region would now have been more or less thickly covered with light forests of deciduous trees, while the province of Manitoba, instead of being known as the "Prairie Province," would better have merited the title of the "Sylvan Province."

I do not deny that there are subsidiary causes. For instance, were it not for the exceptional dryness of the North American climate, the grass would seldom be in a condition to burn over large areas; again, if the surface of the prairies was uneven and much broken, instead of fairly level, very few fires would travel for long distances; while, were it not for the high winds which are prevalent on the open prairies, the fires would find it equally difficult to travel far. All these causes have no doubt had their effect; but I contend that all of them conjointly would never have produced a prairie over an area which is naturally timbered were it not for the action of the fires.

The argument and evidence of Christy appear to me adequate to establish that prairie Canada is treeless because of fire, and the case he develops has importance for understanding other prairies as well. A few reports that have appeared since 1892 may be quoted to show that the process described by Christy continues. Stefansson (478) in 1913 saw fires along the Mackenzie River in the Northwest Territories, of which he wrote (p. 10):

Coming down the river we continually had before our eyes examples of how a new country, careless of its rich natural resources, allows them to go to waste. The value of the spruce forests of Canada is apparent to those who theorize about it but here day after day we traveled through a haze of forest fires, some of them burning at unknown distances from the river, others coming down to its very banks, with the flames licking the water.

Sometimes these fires start no one knows how; sometimes people know and do not tell and sometimes they are started intentionally by Indians, who consider that the hunting is made better by clearing the land so that they can see the game from greater distances. To do this is as short-sighted a policy for the Indian as it is for the government to allow its being done. True, there are forest rangers, but these I suppose exist to fulfill the letter of some law and to draw a salary. There is one who plies over two hundred and fifty miles from Athabasca Landing to Fort MacMurray, and another a somewhat shorter distance from Fort MacMurray to Smith Landing [all in northern Alberta]. But even he who has the shorter beat makes but three trips a year and these are perfunctory. One of these rangers was a fellow passenger with us and did exactly as we did—sat in his boat and lazily watched the flames as we drifted down the river. No doubt he reported the occurrence and presumably it was somewhere tabulated, to become a part of a useful body of statistics.

On my previous trip down the river, in 1906, there was in our company Mr. Elihu Stewart, Forestry Commissioner for the Dominion of Canada, and as he has made a report on the forest resources of the Mackenzie Valley, there is far less reason than otherwise for my dwelling on the extent of its natural wealth—vast even yet in spite of the periodic fires.

F. Harper (231, p. 28) wrote in 1931 of the areas of Athabaska and Great Slave Lakes in a similar vein as follows: "Unfortunately a considerable part of the country appears to have been swept time and again, and with disastrous effect, by forest fires, some of which are set purposely by the Indians in order to temporarily improve hunting."

Osgood (384, 385) was told by the Tanina and Kutchin Indians, who occupy the forests of the Alaska-Canada Boundary, that they did not set fire to drive game; yet Osgood added (384, p. 27) that "sometimes accidental fires burned over wide regions with the same result." McDonald (346) also reported extensive forest fires in Alaska. Shimek (458) wrote one paper on "The Persistence of the Prairie," published in 1925, in addition to his extensive work on Iowa vegetation.

Shimek, whose own ideas regarding the causes of the prairie differed markedly from those of Christy, mentioned Christy's explanation but refrained from comment. Shimek went to Manitoba expressly to compare the flora of 1920 with that reported by Christy for 1883. Shimek found (p. 26): "The best illustrations of the prairie flora were preserved in the unbroken strips along the railway right of way. . . ." He did not mention that the right-of-way was burned annually, as required by law. Leavitt (306) said the danger of fires being set by trains and spreading beyond the right-of-way was so great in the prairie provinces of Canada that the national railway acts from 1911 to 1922 specified that a fire guard be plowed at each side of the right-of-way.

Christy's observations and deductions are confirmed by Bird (44), who in 1930 documented the spread of trees into the Canadian prairie, much as Christy predicted would happen if prairie fire were reduced. Almost all the area in Canada designated prairie by Fernow (in 210, p. 56) is called "aspen parkland" by Bird. A comparison of Bird's map and Fernow's shows that the aspens have invaded all of the tall-grass prairie of Canada, except a small area just north of the Canadian–United States border where the Saskatchewan-Manitoba provincial boundary touches it. Trees have also invaded some short-grass plains, advancing in some sections over 200 miles. Of this advance Bird says (p. 363): "The aspen parkland thus forms an ecotone between the prairie and the coniferous forest. It is replacing the prairie over practically all of its southern front, and to the north in some localities, at least, is in turn being replaced by spruce. . . . Aspen groves are invading prairie." And on p. 370: "As far as was known it had not been burnt for many years or disturbed in any way. . . ."

And on p. 409:

The dead boughs, too, become as dry as kindling and enable prairie fires to sweep into groves and burn them out, killing many healthy trees. Even after severe burning, aspen quickly regenerates from the roots . . . .

It is by these two methods, cutting and fire, that man is chiefly detrimental to the aspen groves. Excessive trampling by grazing stock is also injurious . . . .

In years of abundance 90 to 100 per cent of the saplings are ringed and killed by rabbits.

Fire is a factor which has been present for a great many years. The Indians periodically burnt off large tracts of prairie to create fresh grazing grounds for the buffalo; then the fires would sweep on into the surrounding forests of aspen. Even before the time of the Indians, occasional fires were started by lightning. Following settlement the large fires were stopped, with the result that the aspen quickly encroached on the prairie.

Occasional fires do not particularly harm aspen. They kill the trees, but regeneration quickly takes place from the roots since they are unhurt. Continued burning, however, does seriously retard succession, for after a time, even the roots are killed. The shrubs are killed back, particularly *Symphoricarpoe*, which normally choked out the grass and tend to hold the moisture. By their removal drier conditions are created which enable grass to advance on the forest.

Fire is also well exemplified in the Spruce Woods Forest Reservation near Carberry, Manitoba, where former extensive tracts of prairie are now covered with aspen.

Halliday and Brown (226) also mapped the distribution of trees of the Prairie Provinces of Canada, and their account suggests further advance of the aspen between the time of Bird's article of 1930 and their own of 1943. Barnes, in the U.S. Department of Agriculture Yearbook (578) for 1948 (p. 45), also said: "In Manitoba and Saskatchewan . . . forest has advanced considerably into grassland during the past century." If we use the map of the prairies of Pound and Clements (404), published in 1898, as the indication of the northern extension of grasslands, the invasion of prairie by aspen would be over 500 miles.

Our review of some of the literature on Canadian prairies reveals conditions analogous to those in Texas, which is undisputed evidence that trees have invaded grassland since grass fires have been reduced although far from eliminated. Thus we come again to the conclusion that fires set by Indians were of primary importance for the maintenance of the dominance of grassy vegetation.

PRAIRIE PROVINCE

A number of authors have made general statements about American grasslands as a whole or about large sections of them that could not be identified with one state or one region. Some review of their publications is in order. The first such writer was Nutt (381), who wrote in 1833 that "prairies are formed and are now forming, by the operation of wind and fire" (p. 41). "As the fires are restrained, trees come forth, upon all the prairies that are formed of rolling land" (p. 43). G. P. Marsh (355), in 1867, also published a forthright support of fire as an essential factor in prairie continuance (p. 134):

> The origin of the great natural meadows, or prairies as they are called, of the valley of the Mississippi, is obscure. There is, of course, no historical evidence of the subject and I believe that remains of forest vegetation are seldom or never found beneath the surface, even in the sloughs, where the perpetual moisture would preserve such remains indefinitely. The want of trees upon them has been ascribed to the occasional long-continued droughts of summer, and the excessive humidity of the soil in winter; but

it is, in very many instances, certain that, by whatever means the growth of forests upon them was first prevented or destroyed the trees have been since kept out of them only by the annual burning of the grass, by grazing animals, or by cultivation. The groves and belts of trees which are found upon the prairies, though their seedlings are occasionally killed by drought, or by excess of moisture, extend themselves rapidly over them when the seeds and shoots are protected against fire, cattle, and the plough. The prairies, though of vast extent, must be considered as a local, and so far as our present knowledge extends, abnormal exception to the law which clothes all suitable surfaces with forest; for there are many parts of the United States—Ohio, for example—where the physical conditions appear to be nearly identical with those of the States lying farther west, but where there were comparatively few natural meadows. The prairies were the proper feeding grounds of the bison, and the vast number of those animals is connected, as cause or consequence, with the existence of these vast pastures. The bison, indeed, could not convert the forest into a pasture, but he would do much to prevent the pasture from becoming a forest.

From 1870 to 1910 the following authors wrote their belief that fire was of primary importance in prairie formation: Allen (8 and 9), Asa Gray (215), Meehan (359), Powell (406), Redway (413), Davis (132), Gaskill (192), and Hopkins (254). In 1913 Gleason (206) published his first paper presenting evidence in support of his conclusion (p. 181) that "it seems evident that prairie fires have been the deciding factor in determining the distribution of forests in the Middle West. With prairie fires, the forests have been driven back or destroyed, except in those areas where the favor of topography has enabled them to resist the encroachments of the prairie."

The career of F. E. Clements as a student of grassland vegetation extended for nearly a half-century, starting in 1892. Although in most of his writing he appears either to ignore fire as an ecological factor in prairie formation or to overtly deny its importance, in his monumental work entitled *Plant Succession* (100) of 1916 he gives full credit to fire. We read (p. 105): "Whatever the origin of prairie may have been, its extent and duration are largely due to the effect of fire upon woody communities, followed by a similar influence produced by clearing and cultivation." And on page 108: "Grassland areas are produced the world over as a result of burning and grazing combined, and they persist just as long as burning recurs."

In his book *Plant Indicators* (101) of 1920, Clements reviewed most previous works on the subject and then presented his own ideas. Several authorities cited by him recognized the importance of fire. An example

(101, p. 21): "Griffiths—Brush and timber are encroaching upon the grass-lands, due, it is believed, to protection from fire." Clements himself admitted the importance of fire on the eastern edge of the prairie, which he classified as "Subclimax." He wrote (101, p. 131): "All of these differences [between *Stipa-Koeleria* associations, 'True Prairie,' and *Andropogon* associations] are summed up in the fact that the *Andropogon* prairie over most of the region is subclimax in character, i. E., it will be replaced by scrub, wood-land, or forest wherever cultivation, fire, or grazing does not prevent."

Notwithstanding this evidence that Clements recognized that fire played a role in determining vegetation in some areas, for other grasslands where fires also frequently occurred he said in the same work (101, p. 116): "The plant must be taken as the best if not the only judge of climate." Elsewhere (101, p. 101) he revealed a complete disregard for the fires set by aboriginal American Indians, as shown by the following: "Practice indicators are naturally connected with the presence of man, and hence are restricted to the Pleistocene and recent periods. Grazing must have been the earliest of these. . . ."

Since North American Indians had no herds until after obtaining horses in post-Columbian times, the above would suggest they had no influence on the environment, except with their fields. For several thousands of years man probably used fire to alter the landscape before animals were domesticated and kept for grazing. Livingston and Shreve (327) published their important study *The Distribution of Vegetation in the United States, as Related to Climatic Conditions* in 1921. In their 525 pages, no word suggests that they recognized that fire may have influenced the distribution of vegetation. They stated (p. 37) without any explanation that "[t]he Grassland is locally invaded by plants of the types which are dominant in all of the surrounding regions. . . . In the vicinity of the mountains the Grassland is invaded by shrubs (*Cercocarpus, Quercus, Symphoricarpos*), and in some localities even by coniferous trees (*Pinus ponderosa*). . . ."

Livingston and Shreve, without mentioning fire, further support the thesis of this work. They classify almost the entire area designated "Tall-Grass Prairie" by other authors as "Grassland–Deciduous Forest Transi-tion." They say (p. 37):

> This is the broadest and most extensive of the transition areas, but is so purely transitional in its character that it does not merit recognition on any other basis. Its eastern limit has been fixed along the line at which the Deciduous Forest ceases to be an unbroken formation and begins to exhibit the islands of grasslands locally known as "oak openings." The western limit has been placed where timber ceases to occur on the upland.

It is to me a great surprise that Livingston and Shreve felt no need to account for the marked difference in vegetation within the climatic zone covered by their "transitional" area. Their whole idea of climatic determination of distribution of vegetation is laid open to question.

The publication in 1924 of the *Atlas of American Agriculture* was a milestone in American plant science. The section on "Natural Vegetation" by Shantz and Zon (454) is recognized by many as the best available summary on the subject. Without a special interest in the effects of fires set by Indians, they expressed a real appreciation of the fact that fires of aborigines were important in determining some types of vegetation discovered in America by European explorers and settlers. For example (p. 7): "Grasslands characterize areas in which trees have failed to develop, either because of unfavorable soil conditions, poor drainage and aeration, intense cold and wind, deficient moisture supply, or repeated fires." And on page 3: "The fact, however, that rainfall in the eastern portion of the prairie region is still sufficient to insure the growth of a heavy forest leads to the inference that it is not low precipitation which has prevented the growth of trees. . . . Repeated fires undoubtedly pushed the forest back and extended its boundaries farther eastward. Forests have begun to work westward since the settlement of the prairies has broken up the virgin sod and prevented to a great extent the occurrence of prairie fires."

Shantz and Zon (p. 16) question whether enough moisture is available for tree growth on the driest "Short Grass" plains, but of the tall-grass prairie they say:

> The soil moisture supply is great enough to support a tree vegetation, but on account of the drought of the autumn and late summer, grass fires have swept the area and destroyed the young trees as rapidly as they were produced. . . . During drought periods the [tall-grass] area has in the past been repeatedly burned by fires started either by Indians, travelers, or lightning. . . . In many places fires in the forests themselves have destroyed the trees and enabled the grasses to establish themselves. In the eastern portion of the area fires have in all probability protected the grassland from the encroachment of the forests. Aided by high winds, these fires swept with great rapidity across the grasslands of the prairies and plains, and early settlers and travelers could find safety only by starting back fires, since the broad band of burning grass, often 100 or 200 yards across, made it impossible to pass through the flames to the burnt areas of safety behind. Trees and shrubs are killed by fires, and as a consequence the grasses are able to maintain themselves on land which would support a good forest growth if the trees were adequately protected. Since the settlement of

these lands and the consequent checking of the prairie fires, tree growth has been gradually extended, either by planting or natural seeding, and trees now grow throughout the whole prairie region.

If big grass fires could kill fast-growing trees on moist prairies, then it is reasonable to conclude that small grass fires could stop the growth of slow-growing trees on dry plains.

In spite of the earlier statement of Clements and the view of Shantz and Zon quoted above, in 1929 in their book *Plant Competition*, Clements, Weaver, and Hanson (102) admitted that animals influenced plant competition (p. 153) but denied that fire was an important factor in prairie formation (p. 154), while recognizing its importance in forests (p. 329).

Gleason's (207) "Vegetational History of the Middle West" of 1932 contains many facts and arguments that the Middle West would have been forested except for the "arrival of the American Indian [and the] introduction of prairie fires." He states his history of the prairies as follows (p. 58): "We may believe, however, that the present climatic center of the Prairie Province in western Kansas and Nebraska and eastern Colorado has been occupied by this vegetation continually since its origin, and that amoeba-like arms have been pushed out many times in many directions and withdrawn again." Of the prairie peninsula, Gleason says (p. 70): "The eastern migration of the prairie proceeded as a wedge-shaped extension between the coniferous vegetation at the north and the deciduous forests at the south and reached limits considerably beyond the eastern margin of modern continuous prairies. Numerous relic colonies formerly occurred . . . in eastern Indiana, northwestern Ohio and southern Michigan." Concerning fires set by aborigines, he wrote (p. 80): "Prairie fires were set annually by the Indians in the autumn months to drive game from the open prairies into the forest, where it was more easily stalked. Sweeping eastward before the prevailingly westerly winds of that season, the fires destroyed seedling trees at the west margin of the forest, preventing further advance in that direction . . . they gradually reduced [some] forest to the open parklike condition known as oak openings."

The principal weaknesses in Gleason's report are, first, the too limited period of occupation assigned the Indians; and, second, the assumption that eastern Colorado, western Kansas, and Nebraska would be as dry as they are now while forests extended almost that far west. Regarding the first, Gleason assumed (p. 84) the "xerothermic climatic" following the retreat of the Wisconsin glacier brought about an extension of the prairie peninsula purely because of climatic conditions. However, if Indians were on the plains and prairies at that time, they may well have contributed the deciding factor then as well as later. Regarding the second weakness, Gleason based his argument on the ability of the eastern deciduous trees to extend west. It seems to me that if the eastern deciduous trees extended in forests on the uplands to eastern Colorado, certainly the pines from the mountains would have invaded the plains to join the two forests.

Pearson (392) in 1936 cites Dr. Heinrich Walter, "noted German authority on water relations and osmotics," who reached conclusions almost identical with those of Gleason, including the importance of fire. That same year Clements and Chaney (104), already quoted, admitted that fires were set by Indians but denied that they had a significant role in the origin or maintenance of prairies. They suggested that Indians were more important ecological factors as cultivators (p. 34). The fires of white settlers were accorded greater influence (p. 37).

Because of its very widespread adoption for university classes, the textbook *Plant Ecology* by Weaver and Clements (542), first published in 1929, with a second edition in 1938, must be considered in our review of ideas relating to prairies and plains. The authors appear to me to be somewhat inconsistent in their treatment of fire as an ecological factor. For example, in their section on "The Relict Method" of ecological study they say (p. 48) that "numerous are the relicts due to general disturbances due to man in the form of clearing, fire, overgrazing, draining, etc. . . . In grasslands, such areas are found. . . . Along fenced railways. . . . In spite of an increase in burning. . . ."

Weaver and Clements also admit that "[b]urns have a pronounced effect upon the composition and development of a forest" and that "when fire and logging can be eliminated" one can discover whether relicts belong to an existing climax. They believe "5 to 10 years" is sufficient time to determine which plants are dominant. In their chapter on "Plant Succession" they give additional recognition to the possible role of fire. Fire, they say, maintains the vegetation of an area in "subclimax." Their examples are primarily from forests, yet the principle would apply anywhere. Regarding grasslands, they say (p. 87): "Other grass disclimaxes are produced the world over as a result of grazing, or of burning and grazing combined, and they persist just as long as these disturbances recur." In spite of the statement above, when Weaver and Clements describe "The Grassland Climax" (pp. 516–29), the effects of overgrazing are enumerated several times, but no mention is made of the burning that the grasslands had been subjected to for millennia. Only as a subsidiary to overgrazing, to account for finding short grass where tall grass could grow, is fire given slight credit, as follows (p. 469): "The prairies, moreover, were repeatedly burned. Burning and trampling were distinctly more favorable to the short buffalo and grama grasses than to their taller competitors. The westward movement of the buffalo and their decrease in numbers coincided with the incoming of the settlers and the decrease in prairie fires. This resulted in renewed growth of the taller grasses."

The combining of fire with overgrazing by Weaver and Clements as a unitary force, as if both brought about the same results, is entirely unwarranted. Overgrazing, as one ecological force, will result in the deterioration of grasslands. Burning, an entirely separate ecological force, without overgrazing does not cause the grassland to deteriorate. Weaver and Clements, although employing historic documents (p. 49), seem to forget the historic evidence that all grasslands were regularly burned in presettlement times. The reports of the Hayden survey, cited by Weaver and Clements (p. 49), show that mid grasses dominated the short grasses in 1870 in Wyoming while Indians were still burning the prairies but overgrazing had not been introduced. The authors further ignore the fact that most grasslands are frequently subjected to fire up to the present. On pages 516–17 Weaver and Clements report that "[o]ver large areas of climatic grasslands, sagebrush, mesquite or similar shrubs are abundant and often appear to be controlling, but these are almost invariably responses to overgrazing."

Since numerous reports leave no doubt that the grasslands had been burned by Indians and early settlers, the authors appear to leave an important variable out of their consideration of the cause for invasion of grassland by sagebrush and other shrubs. The overgrazing so depletes the vegetation that fires will not burn over the grassland. Weaver and Clements, by leaving out this variable, leave room for doubt that a grassland invaded by shrubs is, as they say, a "climatic grassland." Maybe it is only a grassland while fires aid the grasses to maintain dominance. It may well be that the discontinuance of fire alone would have allowed the real climax vegetation to take over. In any event, in the plant history of grasslands the role of fire and that of overgrazing must be considered separately if sound conclusions are to be reached.

Clements and Chaney (104) in 1936 and Clements (105) in 1938 warn against the too ready acceptance of "man made cover" as true indicators of the climatic potentials of a region. Yet they fall into that same error by failing to evaluate the effects of thousands of years of Indian-made fires on the prairie. This is more incomprehensible after their review (104, p. 39) of "man and his animals upsetting the secular balance between climax and climate." Their denial (104, p. 33) that centuries of prairie fires could have any "significance" appears entirely inconsistent. Hanson and Vorhies (229) in 1938, after explaining (p. 231) that "[s]ixteen per cent of the total land area was tall grass or prairie; fourteen per cent short grass or plains," made a plea for more "research on grasslands." The tall-grass prairie, they said, "is unique in being the largest area in the world of this type of fairly moist grassland." An appreciation of the role of fire on the grasslands is essential to an understanding of their history and potentialities. Hanson (228) contributed another article in 1938 encouraging study of the effect of "Fire in Land Use Management," saying: "Fire has been used . . . for improving grazing conditions by destroying brushland trees, coarse grasses, dead vegetation, and to stimulate early spring growth."

Larson (302) in 1940 made a good case for considering grazing of bison and cattle as part of the natural environment, "the biome," and I would add fire, which Larson neglected to mention. If Larson is correct in his view that the grazing of thirty million bison had the same effect as that of modern cattle then change in amount of burning must be accorded an even greater part as a factor in the changes in plant cover over the past half-century that have been documented. It seems well established, however, that the most severe overgrazing has followed fencing.

Paleontology and Prairies

A theory that fires set by aborigines have had a profound influence on the origin and maintenance of grasslands should consider the evidence accumulated by paleontologists. Elias (156) in 1935 reported that "fossil grass husks are comparatively very common and are beautifully preserved" at many late Tertiary rock formation exposures on the high plains from South Dakota to Texas. During the Miocene and Pliocene at least two species of grasses flourished (p. 25), although, according to Elias (p. 29): "All collected grasses belong to the tribe Paniceae and to the subtribe Stipeae of the Agrostideae (there are 14 tribes of living grasses)."

Since the earliest appearance of man or evidence of his tools and fire anywhere on earth falls within the Pleistocene and since no evidence of man in the New World occurs before the late Pleistocene, man could not, of course, have had anything to do with the existence of these pre-Pleistocene grasslands. The progressive desiccation of interior North America during the Tertiary (Cenozoic) appears to have been brought about by the uplift of the Cascade, Sierra Nevada, and Rocky Mountains, which reached their present proportions and consequently their present influence on climate by the end of the Pliocene (104). Clements and Chaney (104, p. 29) estimated that the "climate of the Upper Pliocene was drier than the present" and consequently provided the climatic conditions for the greatest extension of grasslands. This would be, presumably, the absolute grassland; yet data from Elias allow one to question that such a condition existed.

Elias (156) reports (p. 25): "The only nonherbaceous plant, the remains of which is found in association with the grasses, is hackberry (*Celtis*), a typical xerophytic tree, sometimes dwarfed to a shrub, which is now infrequently found in ravines and valleys of the High Plains." The landscape of the Miocene and Pliocene was, of course, more eroded than at present; consequently, we must assume that the hackberry trees or shrubs were dispersed. Thus, during the driest period of plains history, drier than at any time after human occupation of the region, a woody vegetation was present. Clements and Chaney (104, p. 30) believed that "the widest extension of the prairie eastward took place at this time" of extreme aridity during the Upper Pliocene.

Sauer (435) in 1944 interpreted the paleobotanical evidence to indicate that both *Stipa* grasses and hackberry trees (*Celtis*) were abundant on the Tertiary Great Plains and denied that there were indications of extensive Tertiary prairies. He said further that since both *Stipa* and *Celtis* were good at invading new land they were probably not climax.

With the coming of the Pleistocene, roughly a million years ago, the extreme fluctuations of climate commenced, marked by the advance and retreat of great glacial ice sheets. Both mechanical and climatic forces thus wrought tremendous shifts in vegetation, which we may leave to others to explain and interpret.

We must consider, however, postglacial climates and vegetations and also the influence of fire during that entire period, for the data admit no other interpretation than that mankind had arrived in the New World before the final retreat of the Wisconsin Glacier. Clements and Chaney (104, p. 28) say that "[w]ithin the Great Plains proper, the relict pines (*Pinus ponderosa*) and the aspen are supposed to reflect the earlier cooler and moister period, and the present differentiation of the grassland climax, a succeeding warmer and drier climate, of which the Southwest exhibits the most marked effects." Numerous authorities cited by Clements and Chaney believe that there have been minor climatic shifts, as follows (p. 29): "A protracted dry period extended approximately from 3000 to 1000 b.c., followed by one of mostly higher rainfall from about 1000 b.c. to a.d. 300. To this succeeded a second dry interval lasting from a.d. 400 to 900; rainfall was generally higher from 1000 to 1400, followed by a sharp drop during the 16th century, and thus by a rise to approximately average rainfall from 1600 to 1800."

Clements and Chaney believe there was immediate and far-reaching reaction to these shifts: ". . . each warm dry phase caused the clisere of climaxes to push northward, but at the same time the grasslands moved farther east into the forest. . . . During the opposite phase. . . . The deciduous forest advanced. . . ." They go on to explain the backward and forward movement of grasses on the plains and prairies, until (p. 30) "[f]inally, the Andropogons came to maintain the position occupied at the time of settlement along the edge of the forests, the mid-grasses dominated the true prairie, were mixed with short-grass in the Great Plains. . . . This is the condition that prevails today, but it is much confused and obscured by the disturbances wrought by man through cultivation and grazing." It is really unfortunate that the neat summary of the history of postglacial vegetation presented by Clements and Chaney cannot be accepted without question. Their picture is "obscured by the disturbances wrought by man" during the 20,000 years preceding European settlement, which they neglected to take into account.

A history of postglacial climates is developed by Sears (446, 447), based on the variation of amounts of pollen in the different levels in peat bogs. His reconstructions can also be questioned, since he ignores the possible influence of early man in America upon the vegetation. Sears, like most botanists, interprets forest relics as survivors from earlier moister climates. They could also be explained as survivors from prairie fires.

The earliest generally accepted evidences of man in America are the stone tools of the Folsom complex. Of a peculiar and distinctive type, Folsom points have been found in connection with fossils of extinct bison, mammoth, camels, and horses, to establish their antiquity, and have been discovered from coast to coast, especially in the grassland area (see Fischel [172]). The excavations of Schultz (444), as well as the original Folsom site, suggest that great numbers of bison were killed by Folsom man during single hunts, with the implication that Folsom man used fire to drive game, as did later aboriginal inhabitants of the plains.

Even without the supporting data from the Late Pleistocene bone quarries, one must assume that primitive peoples used fires much as did the American Indians from the time they obtained fire. Sauer (436) in 1947 suggested it was use of fire that provided the space for sun-loving plants of early man, as Ames (14) classified the most useful vegetation of primitive man. Referring to paleolithic men of the Old World, Sauer said (p. 1) the use of fire was "a most potent aid to vegetative modification," and further: "Whenever it was used, it affected the reduction of plants and altered the composition of the vegetation."

In 1950 Sauer (437) wrote that the Pleistocene was a period of rapid and extreme climatic shifts that favored lower plant forms and heavy seeders and added (p. 17):

> [The] Pleistocene has been a major time in evolution and dispersal of many grassy and herbaceous forms. . . . The second great agent of disturbance

has been man, an aggressive animal of perilous habits, insufficiently appreciated as an ecological force and as modifier of the course of evolution. . . .
The earlier human economics collectively may be called fire economics.
Often, of course, fire escaped from control and roamed unrestrained until
stopped by barrier or rain. The fire-setting activities of man perforce brought
about deep and lasting modifications in what we call "natural vegetation,"
a term that may conceal long and steady pressure of human action on
plant assemblages. . . . Grasses have fared especially well in the late geological past and have expanded as dominants in many climates. The explanation does not lie as a rule in the unsuitability of such tracts for woody
growth. The normal history of vegetation is an accommodation into the
plant society of increasing diversity, of forming and filling of ecologic
niches by more and more diverse forms. In grasslands on the contrary
we have a simplification of plant structure and scale toward minimizing
differences in habit and size, simple and ephemeral stems, shallow and
fibrous roots. This is a most curious plant sociology, from which the
phylogenetically most varied woody plants are mainly or even wholly
excluded.

Grasslands and Climate

It will be evident to anyone who has read thus far that climate—usually
expressed in terms of available moisture or the precipitation evaporation
ratio—is frequently considered the absolute determining factor in origin
and maintenance of grassland vegetation. There can be no question, of
course, that climate either provides or withholds the means for growth of
all types of vegetation. If vegetation does not correspond to the type considered typical for any climate, soil is usually thought to be responsible.
Weaver and Flory (540) expressed this general attitude as follows (p. 337):
"The climax vegetation is the outcome of thousands of years of sorting out
of species and adaptation to the soil and the climate."

As early as 1935 Edgar N. Transeau, previously cited (513), devised
the precipitation-evaporation ratio and mapped eastern and midwestern
United States. The formula seemed to work and has been widely quoted
to account for the distribution of grasslands. Schaffner (438) summarized
it as follows (p. 5):

Transeau has shown that the typical grasslands of North America are correlated with certain ratios of rainfall to evaporation. The eastern boundary
of the prairie proper coincides quite closely with the 80 per cent ratio of
rainfall to evaporation from a free water surface while the western boundary
coincides closely with the 60 per cent ratio. The western boundary of the

short grass region of the great plains corresponds to a rainfall-evaporation ratio of about 20 per cent.

Schaffner (p. 6) adds:

The actual average annual rainfall in inches is from the eastern limits of the prairie to the Rocky Mountains of Central Colorado, about as follows:

1. Prairie, 38 to 27 inches.
2. Transition prairie, 27 to 20 inches.
3. Plains, 20 to 15 inches.
4. Xerophytic belt east of mountains, 15 to 10 inches.

One of the most ambitious studies applying the concept of ratio of different aspects of climate was that of Livingston and Shreve (327), already mentioned, in an exhaustive study made under the auspices of Carnegie Institution of Washington and published in 1921. Livingston and Shreve sought the correlation of many types of vegetation and many single species with numerous ratios, in addition to the Transeau ratio. A sample from their conclusion (p. 583):

The correlation of climate and vegetation has been carried out in three ways: The maximum and minimum values of each climatic condition have been determined for each vegetational area or for the distributional area of each species. . . . Comparisons have been made between positions of isoclimatic lines and the lines drawn to show the limits of botanical areas, for the purpose of discovering close correspondences. . . . With respect to the generalized vegetation areas of the United States, one of the most clear-cut evidences of a fundamental correlation exists in the correspondence between the position of the vegetational boundaries and the position of the isoclimatic lines expressing certain values of the moisture ratio for the average frostless season.

To one not familiar with the historic evidence of extensive prairies in Virginia or the irrefutable fact that the southeastern pine forests are absolutely dependant on fire for their existence, the tables, maps, and graphs of Livingston and Shreve would appear extremely impressive. Since they ignored, however, one ecological factor that can completely alter the vegetation without as greatly changing the climate, their conclusions must be accepted with reservation.

Koppen (290) in 1923 defined the climates of the earth in a similar yet less mathematical fashion. Koppen discovered the climate by a correlation of vegetation, temperature, precipitation, and season, and the climate type in turn characterized by vegetation, etc. For example, (p. 157), the climate of the southeastern United States "produces luxuriant forests of high trees, wherever tree growth is not restricted by excessive winds or adverse soil conditions."

Clements (101) rejected the idea put forth by Transeau with the statement (p. 118): "It will suffice to point out that no climatic chart, no matter how accurate, can hope to outline the vegetation of North America." Clements proposed that vegetation maps be based, first, on vegetation. He wrote (p. 116):

> Examples . . . can be multiplied almost indefinitely to prove that in the study of vegetation the plant must be taken as the best if not the only judge of climate. However sympathetic one may be with the use of physical factor instruments, he cannot afford to minimize the unique importance of the plant for the analysis of climates. To do otherwise is to substitute human judgment for plant judgment in the plant's own field. Hence, in the correlation of vegetation and climate, it has seemed imperative to determine at the outset and at first hand just where each formation or association is found. The next step is to accept the judgment of the formation as final, and to regard the climatic region as identical with the area of the formation. This done, it at once becomes possible to correlate climate and vegetation by means of phytometers and permanent quadrats, and to check the correlations in some degree by means of physical instruments.

A nonscientific statement of the same idea as Clements, which might be taken as the "popular notion," is found in *The Great Plains* by Webb (544), published in 1931:

> . . . attention has been devoted to grass because grass is the dominant feature of the Plains and is at the same time an index to their history. Grass is the visible feature that distinguishes the Plains from the desert. Grass grows, has its natural habitat, in the transition area between timber and desert. It grows where conditions are too hard for timber but not hard enough to destroy all vegetation. The history of the Plains is the history of the grasslands. Civilization develops on level ground. The fundamental problems that man faced when he crossed the line are not problems of the mountains but of the plains. In the United States these problems are found not only on the Plains proper but in the mountains wherever Plains conditions appear. So far as civilization is concerned the mountains are negligible. Unless they contain minerals they are of relatively little importance in the development of human society.

Carl O. Sauer (435, 437), one of America's most eminent geographers, has expressed doubt in the validity of a grassland climate, with which I concur. In 1944 he wrote (435, p. 546):

> The climatologic description of grasslands is not at all satisfactory. It proceeds from the existence of a grassland, for which a roughly limiting set of climatic values is sought. It thus happens characteristically that when rainfall and temperature values have been selected for a "savanna climate," they are found to apply to areas covered with shrub. The same thing is true in the case of "steppe climates." We confess thereby that the selected combination of climatic values is not reproduced everywhere by the same conditions of vegetation, and this places the causal relation in doubt. The premise of the climatic grasslands assumes that grasses have become dominant to the exclusion of nonherbaceous vegetation because of climatic factors that differ in different areas. This premise needs re-examination.

In 1950, in his article "Grassland Climax, Fire, and Man," Sauer (437) phrased his point of view more strongly (pp. 16–17):

> ... I have misgivings about equating climate and climax vegetation. . . .
>
> The usual classification of climates derives largely from the old premise that climate and vegetation are pretty much coincident. Actually, therefore, there has been a lot of fitting of isotherms and isohyets to generalized maps of dominant vegetation. . . . For the most part, critical climatic limits remain unknown as to physiologically limiting weather values for individual plant species. . . .
>
> One begins, for example, with the premise that grasslands have a climatic origin, sorts them into tropical and extratropical, semi-arid and humid, and high altitude grasslands, and selects the most closely agreeing climatologic values as their limits. . . .
>
> Any assertion that under a given climate there will form a stable self-perpetuating plant complex is likely to perpetuate an assumption that arose before there was modern biology and earth science.

After a review of the evidence for the evolution of grasses during the Pleistocene, Sauer says (p. 20):

> The more we learn of climatic data the less success is there in identifying climate with grassland. There are grasslands with as little as ten inches of rain a year, and with as much as a hundred a year, with long dry seasons, with short dry seasons, with high and low temperature ranges. In this country they occurred from the drier parts of the Great Plains to the

markedly mesophytic Pennyroyal of Kentucky and Black Belt of Alabama. Every climate that has been recognized in which there are grasslands has elsewhere dominance of forests, woodlands or brush, under the same weather conditions.

I must agree with Sauer when he adds: "I know of no basis for a climatic grassland climax, but only of a fire grass climax for soils permitting deep rooting."

Soil and Grassland

Grasslands of North America were said to result from peculiarities of soil in 1818, when Atwater (19) wrote "On the Prairies and Barrens of the West" in the first volume of the *American Journal of Science*. His opinion that prairie soils were of "lacustrine" origin, duplicated and refined by Winchell (561) in 1864, and Lesquereaux (313, 314) in 1865 and 1866, has had few if any supporters during the twentieth century. Although the idea that soil is the single cause of grassland vegetation is no longer popular, there persists, especially among soil scientists, the theory that soil shares with climate the power of determining what vegetation grows in any region. In other words, soil is viewed almost as a causative factor. Coffey (108) expressed such an idea in 1912 (p. 31): "The most important function of the soil is the support of plant life. The kind of plant life which is found is dependent more or less upon the character of the soil." Coffey (p. 41) says further: ". . . the origin of the Dark Prairie soils is due to a relation between lime, and possibly other soluble material, and moisture."

Marbut (353) in 1935, after mentioning (p. 63) that "[i]t is generally considered by botanists that the prairie region is potentially a forest region," gives his own opinion (p. 69) that "[i]t is a grassland region, the lack of forests being probably determined in part at least, by the high content of carbonates in the soils, which renders it toxic to most trees." Marbut was aware of burning, for he wrote (p. 63): "On account of prairie fires, prairie soil is rarely found with a layer of decaying vegetable matter overlying the mineral soil." Yet he chose to ignore the possible influence of fire in keeping trees off the prairies and also ignored the record of thousands of trees growing on prairie soil. In spite of the growing file of reports to the effect that it is the vegetation that determines the soil type, as much or more than it is the soil that influences the vegetation, soil scientists seem to experience difficulty in expressing themselves in accordance with this new emphasis. Kellogg (279), for example, writing in the U.S. Department of Agriculture Yearbook for 1948, entitled *Grass*, said on page 50: "In some landscapes tall, luxuriant grasses grow naturally and help make black soils that are naturally productive. . . . The invasion by forest degrades these soils and this may happen quickly in 200 years or so."

We need not dwell on the inconsistency of forests invading the natural grassland, but point out that here Kellogg first attributes the productivity of the black soil to the grass cover and then indicates that the forest changes the character of the soil. Nevertheless, on page 54 he wrote: "Grass is the natural cover of many soil types throughout the world. It is the natural cover of the Chernozem—the famous black soils of subhumid temperate regions."

This statement seems to emphasize the role of the soil in determining the cover, rather than the cover being decisive in producing soil type. The theory that the peculiarities of prairie soils have come from the vegetation, rather than vice versa, is not new, for Christy (97), as quoted earlier, proposed it in 1892 and Shaler (450) expressed it as follows in 1891 (p. 325):

> The extremely fertile nature of prairie soil when it is first tilled is easily explained. Owing to the generally level character of the district occupied by these open lands the soils were deep, for the reason that they did not have the chance to slide down to the streams in the manner which we have seen to be common in hilly districts. The frequent burning of the rank growth of vegetation constantly returned to the soil large amounts of potash, lime, soda, and phosphatic matter in the soluble form which is suited to the needs of grain giving plants. As the deposit lay on nearly flat surfaces and the rainfall was moderate in quantity, the ground water did not bear the soluble materials away to the streams as rapidly as they were formed. The result was that when these prairie regions were submitted to the plow they yielded in a few years the store of plant food which had been garnered during many centuries of preparation. . . .
>
> The effect of the vegetation which occupied the prairies for many centuries before the coming of white men was to draw the soluble portion of the fertilizing substances to the upper part of the soil, and to leave the subsoil unaffected by any of that peculiar work which is accomplished by the strong roots of forest trees. These, as we have seen, tend to draw mineral substances from the deeper portions of the subsoil and from the bed rocks, accumulating the material in the growing vegetation, whence it returns to the upper part of the soil by process of decay.

Hulbert (262), in his textbook *Soil*, printed in 1930, criticizes Shaler's explanation and presents his own (p. 66):

> As we enter the great Northwest in Section 5 we pass from the light-colored timbered soils and the area of light-colored prairie soils to the arid regions—

from the wooded portion of our East to the unforested Great Plains. Numerous explanations for this treeless empire have been offered, Professor Shaler's being most widely accepted: that the Indians burned the forests in order to start the fresh shoots which drew the game animals. This explanation, however, seems to the writer to take too little account of the age-long incompatibility of association between trees and grass. If such prairie burnings had been going on for centuries, as Shaler's theory supposes, would we have found an entirely different kind of native vegetation on the black soils of the Marshall series from that found on the light soils of the Miami series? In certain soils, grass and trees fight tremendous battles for supremacy, grass sometimes being victorious and sometimes vanquished. The map shows the western boundary of timber-growing soils. On these soils, fires do not destroy forests and no amount of burning would change the soil into "prairie sod." On the latter soil in its natural state, real forests are not found. The explanation of our treeless plains must, therefore, go back to the factors of rock, soil, and climate which determined vegetation.

As the quotations from Kellogg clearly indicate, soil scientists have not all accepted either Shaler's or Hulbert's opinion. There appears, however, to be an ever-growing weight of evidence on the side of Shaler and Christy. I have already mentioned the work of Heyward (243) in the southern pine region, which revealed that "[t]he greatest percentage of longleaf pine forest soils is morphologically more similar to grassland soils than to forest soils." Heyward also "found that ten years of protection from burning changes the character of the soil." Billings (43), also referred to previously, presented in 1941 many data from the literature as well as his own observations on the influence of vegetation on soil. Thorp (509), also in the 1948 Yearbook, supports Shaler's thesis in his article "How Soils Develop under Grass" and says that "dense stands of tall grasses in the United States have usually produced thick, darkcolored soils" (p. 55). A number of other authors have been cited who reported the "degradation" of prairie soil after invasion by trees (558, 115). There is, of course, the additional evidence of tree growth on prairie soil, already presented, which would support Shaler.

Sauer (437) in 1950 added his weight to the side of Shaler, as follows (p. 20): "For millennia, and tens of them, fires, for the most part set by man, have deformed the vegetation over the large plains of the world and their hill margins. The time of human disturbance is probably long enough, even in the New World, to allow also for the development of soils of characteristic profile and structure that are known as 'prairie soils,' a secondary product rather than cause of grassed surfaces."

From the material brought together in this section, I see no reason to doubt that for the major portion of the grassland the soil type resulted from the grass cover, thus could not determine the cover, and, furthermore, that the soil played no part in the tall-grass prairie in keeping trees from invading them.

Special consideration must be given, however, to the possible role of soil on the high, short-grass plains. The report published in 1922 by Weaver and Crist (537), entitled "Relation of Hardpan to Root Penetration in the Great Plains," at first reading seems to indicate that the soil might be a decisive factor on the driest grasslands. Weaver and Crist wrote (p. 237): "During the excavation of root systems of native and crop plants throughout the Great Plains region during the past five years. . . . Contact has been made in more than thirty fields with the so-called hardpan. Such a layer of soil underlies much of this area of low rainfall, at depths varying from 15 inches to 3 feet. It varies from 8 inches to over 1.5 feet in thickness . . . hardpan occurs at approximately the normal depth of water penetration."

A similar description of plains soil is given by Shantz and Zon (454, p. 16):

> By far the sharpest soil boundary line, that of the disappearance of the layer of carbonate accumulation in the subsoil, lies well within the area characterized as prairie grassland. This soil boundary corresponds in a general way with the eastern boundary of the needlegrass and slender wheat-grass association and the Bluestem bunch-grass association. East of this line the moisture penetrates below the reach of plant roots. Under these conditions there is no dry subsoil between the moist surface soil and the water table. The soil moisture supply is great enough to support a tree vegetation, but on account of the drought of the autumn and late summer, grass fires have swept the area and destroyed the young trees as rapidly as they were produced. Farther west, where the moisture penetration extends to a few feet only in depth, where the subsoil is permanently dry and there is a distinct accumulation of carbonates at a depth varying from 2 to 4 feet below the soil surface, the tall grasses still find sufficient moisture to maintain themselves. This is a true grassland, probably not dependent on prairie fire for its maintenance. To the west the depth of soil moisture becomes less than 2 feet and the tall grasses disappear because of insufficient moisture supply. This is due directly to decreased rainfall and indirectly to the competition of the short grasses. In general, the short grass grows on a shallow soil with a layer of carbonate accumulation at a depth of 1 to 2 feet. The vegetation boundary between the tall-grass and the short grass formation is of great agricultural importance, since it separates the

highly productive farm lands of the prairies from the less productive ranch lands of the plains, except where it swings west around the sand hills.

These two accounts of soil conditions on the Great Plains suggest that the coaction of water and soil has produced a hardpan that would inhibit deep-rooted plants, such as trees or shrubs. I know of no controlled experiments to refute this supposition, but I do believe enough evidence has been presented to justify saying, "It just isn't so." I refer to the record of invasion into the driest sections of the high plains by sagebrush in Wyoming and northern Colorado and by mesquite in Texas, Oklahoma, and Kansas. Furthermore, Weaver and Crist observed that roots penetrated and passed through the so-called hardpan while it was moist, indicating that the hardpan was not an absolute limit of moisture penetration. It is quite possible that the local climatic changes that forestation would bring about would markedly after the hardpan formation. Thus, even on the driest high plains, soil does not appear decisive.

Grasslands and the Shelterbelt

Whenever the question "Why are the grasslands treeless?" is asked, the answer usually received is simply: "Because trees won't grow on them." As long as no trees grow on the upland plains or prairies, it is difficult to convince people that their absence is due to fire or grazing or cultivation or any other man-made cause. It is for this reason that numerous references to trees growing on grasslands and to their invasion of grasslands have already been cited. I have reserved for special consideration, however, the most extensive experiment in forestation of the grasslands undertaken in our country. I refer to the Plains Shelterbelt Project, for which trees were first planted in 1935.

Although individuals, stimulated by federal "Tree Culture Acts" from 1873 to 1924, had successfully planted shelterbelts and woodlots on the plains, the majority of plant ecologists, botanists, and foresters expressed grave doubt as to the feasibility of the Shelterbelt Project when it was announced by President Franklin D. Roosevelt in June 1934. The research upon which the final decision was made and upon which the preliminary planting was based is summarized in a monograph by Zon, Silcox, Hayes, Stoeckeler, et al. (582), published in 1935. Unless otherwise identified, information in this sketch comes from that monograph (p. 5). "[The Shelterbelt Zone] is 100 miles wide and, roughly, 1,150 miles long and is confined to the transition zone between the tall-grass prairie and short-grass plains . . . the axis of this zone roughly follows the ninety-ninth meridian. . . . Its western limit is generally within the precipitation annually in the north and 22 inches, to allow for greater evaporation, in the south."

Study had convinced the sponsors of the project that trees could grow within that zone with a margin of safety; they believed shelterbelts would ameliorate the climate where this was most needed—through the center of the "Dust Bowl." Zon et al. (p. 5) admitted that "there are places in eastern Colorado, Wyoming and Montana where shelterbelts are growing well" on drier regions than that of the shelterbelt project, but large-scale planting there would be more hazardous.

A rapid survey in 1934 of groves of trees previously planted in the Shelterbelt Zone revealed (p. 40) 229,000 acres in tree lots. The overall average of survival in groves planted thirty years or more was 23.8 percent, ranging from 44 percent in North Dakota to 10 percent in Nebraska. Species of trees varied in percent of survival from 92 for eastern red cedar to 9.7 for catalpa. In addition to the past plantings within the Shelterbelt Zone, the report said (p. 40):

> The Northern Great Plains Field Station of the Bureau of Plant Industry, at Mandan, N. Dakota, affords an excellent example of what can be done in the planting of shelterbelts. From 1916 to 1933 it has been instrumental in establishing . . . in the western part of the Dakotas and in eastern Montana and Wyoming more than 2,700 demonstration shelterbelts. Despite the fact that this area lies west of the shelterbelt zone and has less favorable growing conditions, average survival for these plantings is over 70 per cent.

From a single government nursery in central Nebraska, 34,000 trees were sent to farmers in 1924; but in 1934 "the distribution was 1,125,000 trees" (p. 54). Mention has already been made of the 12,000-acre Nebraska National Forest and other old plantings. The advocates of the Shelterbelt Project drew support also from a number of successful similar projects carried out on the Russian steppes for a century. The Yearbook of Agriculture (579) for 1949 (p. 192) reports that 211 million trees have been planted in shelterbelts and windbreaks in the Prairie Provinces of Canada.

The best evaluation I found of the Great Plains Shelterbelt Project is by Munns and Stoeckeler (380), written in 1946 after the authors had made a spot check of about 4 percent of the project. Between 1935 and 1942, 18,600 miles of shelterbelts were planted in 30,000 separate belts; 220 million trees and 238,000 acres of land were required for the development of the shelterbelts. The belts varied from two to twenty-three rows of trees, with 56 percent having ten rows of trees and shrubs. Forest conditions developed only in belts of six or more rows. The average age of the shelterbelts was 6.7 years at the time of evaluation, which showed that 2 percent had been destroyed and almost 2 percent were in very poor condition; 58 percent of the belts were in excellent shape, having better than

80 percent survival of all trees planted. Trees varied in their ability to thrive. The best deciduous trees were green ash, American elm, hackberry, black locust, Siberian elm, honeylocust, and bur oak. For all seventeen deciduous species used, an average of 69 percent had grown. Conifer species most adaptable to the plains were eastern red cedar, Rocky Mountain juniper, and jack and ponderosa pines. Munns and Stoeckeler found "some possibility of [belts] reproducing naturally," for seedlings were discovered in some older belts. Their conclusion (p. 257) was that "the Shelterbelt Project has been a success."

The results of the project of pertinence to this work are that near, but not upon, the drier edge of the grasslands neither climate nor soil was an absolute barrier to tree growth. The project does not settle the question whether trees could invade the same area unaided, for the belts were planted with seedlings in prepared ground. Furthermore, the ground between the rows of trees was cultivated for one to five years, thereby reducing the competition with grass and weeds. My thesis is supported, however, by this statement regarding shelterbelts in the Yearbook (579, p. 199): "Two great enemies of trees are fire and livestock. When fire occurs, it is usually sudden and its destruction is complete. . . . The damage caused by livestock is as sure as fire. . . ."

If fire is today one of the greatest enemies of tree growth on the plains, there can be no question of its having also been an enemy in times past. Zon et al. (582, p. 47) said as much:

> Fire is still another factor which has a detrimental effect on tree growth in the shelterbelt zone. Residents of many communities recall destructive fires which swept over the Plains in earlier times, and these are generally conceded to be accountable in part for the sparsity of natural tree growth in the region. . . .
> Fire must be kept away from planted groves if they are to succeed.

Grasslands and Fire

In the record of Indian fires on the plains and prairies and in the eastern woodlands already presented with the similar data regarding the Mountain West to be set forth in sections to follow in this work, there is a substantial basis for the conclusion that every section of the continent having inflammable vegetation was periodically set on fire. Why did forests remain in control of some areas and extensive grasslands develop in others? Official documents indicate that woods of the southeastern states are at the present time regularly burned, whereas there are no detailed and continuing records of fires on the grasslands. If fire is as important as this study implies, why prairies in Nebraska and not in Georgia? The answer, of course, is that the ultimate influence of fire on vegetation depends upon the moisture, soil, temperature, wind, topography, and frequency of the fires, as well as upon the various types of vegetation natural to a region. Swamp grasses are usually too wet to burn, to give an extreme example; consequently, fire could influence them but slightly. If a prairie swamp dried up, there would be a "normal succession" from grasses to shrubs, to conifers, and finally to hardwood trees. Fires could arrest the succession, but whether it would be kept at the grass, the brush, or the conifer stage would depend upon the combination of all other environmental conditions and the amount and regularity of burning.

Fires on the plains and prairies maintained them as grassland, first, because of the topography and wind of the region. The great expanses of reactively flat land swept by almost constant wind made it possible for a single fire to sweep over many square miles of landscape. Were it not for this fact, the small aboriginal populations could not have burned off such large areas. Burning on flat topography and with high wind velocity probably would not have maintained the grasslands completely devoid of trees, however, if there had been much more moisture. Prairie fires were especially destructive because the vegetation became tinder dry for fairly long periods. Had there been an excess of moisture throughout the year, the fires would have been less destructive and the trees would have made a faster recovery, as in the eastern woodlands area.

Passing from the tall-grass prairies of Illinois to the dry, high, short-grass plains just east of the Rockies, the destructiveness of the fires would diminish in proportion to the thinning and shortening of the grasses, which in turn were dependent upon available moisture during the growing season. With sufficient moisture for fast tree growth in the east, very destructive and frequent fires would be required to keep the prairie treeless. With a bare minimum of precipitation available to support woody vegetation on the high western plains, small and infrequent fires would accomplish the same end. During droughts, which, according to Weakley (532, p. 816), have occurred with about equal intensity at intervals for over 400 years, the plains would produce too little vegetation for either extensive or intensely hot fires, but by the same token seedlings would have difficulty sprouting. During intervening moister periods bigger fires would destroy the bushes and trees that might otherwise have become established during those periods. Stumps recovered from hillsides and dry benches in Nebraska, where trees do not grow, showed Weakly in their tree-ring patterns that they survived the droughts.

It should be clear from the above analysis that I believe fire to be an essential ingredient in grassland formation but that fires can produce extensive grasslands only when other climatic and geographic factors are so adjusted as to allow fire to exert its maximum influence. Sauer (435, p. 551) said "the grasslands coincide in general with broad, smooth surfaces," confirming my view of the importance of topography. Sauer (437, p. 20) equated several geographic factors and fire, in 1950, as follows:

> Grasslands are found chiefly (a) where there are dry seasons or occasional short periods of dry weather during which the ground cover dries out, and (b) where the land surface is smooth to rolling. In other words, grasslands are found in plains, subject to periods of dry weather. They may also extend into broken terrain adjacent to such plains. Their occurrence all around the world points to the one known factor that operates effectively across such surfaces—fire. Recurrent fires, sweeping across surfaces of low relief, are competent to suppress woody vegetation. Suppression of fire results in gradual recolonization of woody species in every grassland known to me.

A number of plant scientists, although recognizing that fires have played a significant role in plant distribution, seem reluctant to accord primitive man a vital part in the process. Shantz (452, p. 43), for example, wrote in 1911: "The effect of fire must be regarded as having been always operative in the Great Plains region. Fires are started by lightning during almost every thunderstorm, and the advent of man, has, if anything, tended to check rather than to increase their ravages. The effects of fires on short-grass vegetation vary markedly. Grama grass seems to suffer but little, but in places that have been repeatedly burned the buffalo grass is completely killed out."

Weaver and Flory (540, p. 333) in 1934, although not entirely clear, give the impression of trying to minimize the role of fire: "The fires started by lightning or deliberately set by Indians to make travel easier and more secure, to furnish earlier grazing and better conditions for hunting, or for other purposes, have practically disappeared." This is borne out by their statement in the same article (p. 337) that "climax vegetation [of prairies] is the outcome of . . . adaptation to the soil and climate."

If prairie fires were frequently started by lightning, their effect would have been present before the advent of man, even in the Miocene and Pliocene. Were this true, the influence of man, especially the American Indian, in determining prairie vegetation would have to be judged less than suggested by the data amassed in this paper. Fire, however, as an ecological factor would not be diminished by having been started by lightning, if its frequency were beyond question. For the plains and prairies, there is room to doubt that lightning played a significant part in setting the grass afire, notwithstanding the two questions above. In contradiction, there is the statement by Gleason (206) of 1913, which says that "this writer has no record of a prairie fire produced by lightning." Sauer (435, p. 553) was more explicit in 1944, when he introduced his remarks with the admission that frequent fires were started by lightning in mountains. He went on to say: "Yet in these areas, peculiarly liable to such fires, lightning fires are not known to alter the ecology in any permanent direction. . . . Forest and brush dominate in the parts of the country that have the greatest number of natural fires. . . . For the plains I know of no documentation of lightning-set fires."

Nor have I documented any prairie fire having been started by lightning. After a search through many statistics on forest fires and through other literature on fires started by natural causes, I came to the unhappy conclusion that no one is interested in keeping records on the occurrences of grass fires, much less on the diverse ways in which they get started. The bulletin entitled *Lightning in Relation to Forest Fires* by Plummer (399), published in 1912, exhaustively reviews the information on the subject for the entire United States. Plummer's Region N (p. 20) corresponds closely to the plains and prairies. Of this area he wrote (p. 26): "Region N is naturally treeless, except for the moisture-loving species which fringe the watercourses, and a few upland species on isolated areas, the largest of these being the Wichita Mountains, Oklahoma. The fire hazard from lightning is very small, only 26 fires being attributed to it during 4 years."

Plummer presents a table of the actual number of "fires caused by lightning on the National Forests of the United States" (p. 30). There are few National Forests in the grassland states; consequently, these figures are not as indicative as for fully forested areas. Furthermore, there is no indication that unforested areas would attract as much lightning that would result in fires. The table covers the years 1907 to 1911. In Kansas, 14 fires were started by lightning during five years; in Nebraska, 15; in Oklahoma, 16; in South Dakota, 97. For contrast, during the same years Idaho had 312; Washington, 135; and Oregon, 464 lightning-caused fires.

Data are not available to warrant a final conclusion as to whether lightning may be or may not be considered of great importance in the history of grassland vegetation. The contradictory statements by the four authorities quoted, who constitute the total number I found who wrote explicitly regarding lightning on the grassland, leave the question open. Gleason and Sauer received my support, nevertheless, because of the virtual absence of references to grass fires caused by lightning in comparison to the dozens of accounts of Indian-made grass fires. Furthermore, Weaver and Flory, as well as Shantz, appear somewhat inconsistent in the statements they made. Why should lightning fires diminish with Indian fires, as Weaver and Flory imply? If lightning fires were as common and destructive of buffalo grass as Shantz suggests, there would have been no grass remaining for him to study.

To conclude this section on Grasslands and Fire, I reiterate that the final result of burning-over any landscape will be determined by the combination of climatic and geographic features and the frequency of burning. On the plains and prairies these variables combined to produce the treeless American grasslands over a vast region that would have been more or less densely covered with woody vegetation had it not been for the one factor—fire.

The Plains and Prairies without Fire

To clarify my position, a purely hypothetical reconstruction of the probable vegetation of the plains and prairie area of North America, were it not burned, is in order. What vegetation would the European settlers have found in the Middle West had not the American Indians been burning over the region for thousands of years? The tall-grass prairies, designated transitional forest-grassland by Livingston and Shreve (327), would have been a hardwood forest. The oak-hickory forest of Ohio and Indiana would have reached central Nebraska in rather a solid forest condition. In favored spots on the eastern edge of the prairies, chestnut in the south and maple in the north would replace the oaks. On some of the drier uplands, where lightning would be most likely to strike, infrequent natural fires would occur to thin the trees and brush and possibly produce open parklands. Grazing of buffalo and other large game would tend to perpetuate grassy places and openings but would not completely remove the trees and brush from large areas.

Toward the western edge of the forest the oaks and hickories would produce only an open forest of scattered trees that would be interspersed with conifer forest extending eastward from the Rocky Mountains. Because of the reduction in wind velocity and evaporation brought about by the forest, western Kansas, Nebraska, and the Dakotas could support some hardwoods but would also be able to maintain thick groves of ponderosa pine.

Westward where conifers meet and intermix with the hardwoods, the trees would be progressively more scattered until a very open forest, broken by numerous brush and grass parks, would occupy the highest, driest plains. On the driest plains the woody vegetation might not be considered a forest at all. The pines might be widely spaced and share the area with pinyon, juniper, and cedar. Hackberry trees and shrubs might reach the foothills from the prairie forest, and chokecherry would extend far onto the plains. Grass would, of course, occupy the spaces between trees and clumps of brush, and grazing of wild game would maintain a good proportion of the region free from woody growth. On the driest sections of the southern plains, mesquite would be the dominant tree and would mingle with juniper and pinyon in New Mexico and with pine in Oklahoma and Kansas. In Colorado and Wyoming sagebrush pines or juniper would dominate.

In eastern North Dakota hardwood forests, probably a birch-maple association, would intermix with the northern pines, which would in turn give way in Manitoba to spruce-fir forests. In the drier regions of western North Dakota and eastern Montana, or possibly in southern Saskatchewan and Alberta, open forests of ponderosa or yellow pine would give way to the jack, red, and white pines, except where aspen groves indicated that fires had been set by lightning.

This reconstruction is based firmly on the facts recorded of trees or other woody vegetation invading the grasslands from all directions during the last half-century. It receives support from the numerous relicts of pines far out on the plains, even joining hardwoods in Nebraska. Without the burning of the plains and prairies, there appears to me no doubt but that the forests of the Rocky Mountains would extend across the plains to meet the hardwood forest spreading from the Mississippi River. The forests would thin out and almost disappear where soil and moisture combined against the trees, but there brush and shrubs would hold part of the ground. Grass would be everywhere but would be secondary to trees and other woody vegetation.

THE MOUNTAIN WEST

Many difficulties are encountered in any attempt to give a history of the vegetation of the Mountain West, the area extending from the Rocky Mountains to the Pacific Coast, including parts of New Mexico, Colorado, Wyoming, and Montana and all of Idaho, Utah, Arizona, Nevada, Washington, Oregon, and California. The difficulties result from the differences in elevation, which produce different climates in short distances. I will consider this area under four general divisions: the Southwest, primarily New Mexico and Arizona; the Great Basin and Plateau, including western Colorado, western Wyoming, Idaho, eastern Oregon, eastern Washington, the mountains of Montana, and all of the states of Nevada and Utah; the Northwest: the moist western parts of Oregon and Washington; and finally, California. All four of these regions have varied climates, elevations, and, of course, extremely varied vegetation. For some areas, such as California, there is a wealth of ethnographic as well as ecologic data. For other areas the data are less numerous and also less explicit.

Another problem in much of the Mountain West is that of the desert terrain, on which so little vegetation grows that fires will not burn. Of the various vegetation types designated by Shantz and Zon (454, fig. 2) as falling within the Mountain West, the most extreme is "Greasewood" or "Salt desert shrub" and "Creosote bush" or "Southern desert shrub." Most of the Great Basin and Plateau is characterized as "Sagebrush" or "Northern desert shrub." Only in the favored sections of the country dominated by these vegetation types can fire once started run by itself; consequently, to burn them means to burn very small sections, carrying the fire by hand over country on which the vegetation will not carry fire. The whole region, however, is interspersed with mountains of various sizes and, of course, on these mountains and in favored valleys there are places where grass and forests were in sufficient quantity to be burned. The evidence we can find, although not representing the whole area, does suggest that fires were repeatedly set to the vegetations in the Mountain West wherever they could be lighted and could maintain themselves. In other words, the Indians of the West, like the Indians of the plains and prairies and of the eastern woodlands, set fire to all vegetation that would burn. The effects of such fires will be considered in detail in accordance with the evidence found in the literature.

THE SOUTHWEST

In this section I will consider Arizona and New Mexico, with slight extensions into southern California and southwestern Texas. This is the region of the ancient and modern Pueblo Indians, the Navajos and the Apaches, and the Pimas and the Papagos, with the addition of a number of smaller, less well-known tribes in the west along the Colorado River. The ethnographic literature is not explicit regarding every group of Indians within the area; however, there are enough references to suggest that burning of the natural vegetation was a general practice for the whole Southwest culture area. The earliest report we have by date is in 1897. In that year Hartmann (235) and Matthews (357) wrote concerning the Apaches and Navajos respectively. Hartmann wrote (p. 117):

> One of the most common methods of hunting amongst the Apaches in these regions, I was told by Mexicans who, when captives, had taken part in it, consisted in putting fire to the grass of large areas in these forests and driving the game against some narrow mountain-pass or abyss, where they could easily be killed. It was no doubt from similar fires that we found the ground and tree-trunks blackened in these territories, where no Mexican or other white man had entered since the campaign of 1884.

The information from Matthews is less explicit, for it consists of a Navajo legend concerning the activities of the mythical character Coyote. Were this the sole reference to this tribe it would only be an implication that we would assume that broadcast burning was also followed by modern Navajos. Its appearance in mythology, however, implies that it describes an ancient custom. The following quotation is from page 89 of Matthews's *Navajo Legends*:

> When breakfast was over she said: "Now the hunters are going out." He replied: "I will go with them." So he joined the party, and they travelled together till they got to the brow of a high hill which overlooked an extensive country. Here Coyote told his companions to remain concealed while he went into the plain and drove the game toward them. When he got out of sight, he tied to his tail a long fagot of shredded cedarbark, which he set on fire, and then he ran over the country in a wide circle as fast as he could go. Everywhere the fagot touched it set fire to the grass, and raised a long line of flame and smoke which drove the antelope up to where the hunters were concealed. A great quantity of game was killed; the hunters returned laden with meat, and their faith in Coyote was unbounded. Next morning they all went out once more to hunt. Again the hunters concealed themselves on the brow of a hill, and again Coyote tied the blazing fagot to his tail and ran. The people on the hilltop watched the line of fire advancing over the plain; but when it turned around as if to come back to the place from which it started, it suddenly ceased. Much game was driven toward the part in ambush; but Coyote did not return, and the hunters went to work cutting up the meat and cooking food for themselves.

Additional information regarding the practice of setting fire to vegetation by Navajos comes from Hough (259), Hill (246), Gifford (204), and Stewart (490). In 1926 Hough wrote the following (p. 61): "To this day the Navahos burn over large areas of the forests in the White Mountains of Arizona in their annual hunts. The fascination of fire by night is potent to the destruction of fish, bird, or beast, and thick smoke drives any unwilling animal whatever from his impregnable lair."

The fire drive described by Hill in 1938 indicates that driving game with fire in this area of sparse grass and widely separated brush was not easy. He wrote as follows on page 122:

> Two men with lighted torches ran in wide semicircles. They lit the grass, bushes, and anything combustible. They ran on until the two semicircles converged and formed a complete circle of fire. The rest of the runners started at intervals and fired the gaps left by those who went before.

Half of the remaining members of the party followed each of the runners. Their duty was to keep the fire from spreading and to make it burn toward the center of the circle from all sides.

In the *Culture Element Distribution* study of Gifford (204), published in 1940, we find that one of the two Navajo groups represented in that report indicated that they used fire in communal hunting. Stewart's (490) Navajo informant from a different group reported fire drives for rabbits and burning of wild seed plots. Of more importance for our study is the material Gifford obtained from his Apache informants. The western groups, represented by seven different bands, all reported use of fire either for driving game or for burning over seed-gathering areas to improve the yield of wild seeds. The eastern Apaches, the Lipans, of the plains denied to Gifford use of fire for hunting, but Hartmann (235) reported the practice as present in the same area. From the evidence of both accounts it appears that burning for driving game was general with the Apaches. Gifford also interviewed representatives of four different Pueblos. The Bunt said that fire was used to improve the yield of grass as well as to drive game. The Santa Ana Indians said that fire was used to drive game.

The other two Pueblo groups, Hopi and San Ildefonso, denied vegetation burning for any purpose. The denials of the Hopi informant of Gifford can be somewhat corrected from the report of Beaglehole (32), who wrote in 1936 that the Hopis did not set fire to brush to drive deer or antelope but that they did use the fire drive for hunting rabbits. He describes the hunt as follows (p. 12):

> On occasions when rabbits are numerous and doing marked damage to the crops, the procedure may vary slightly. Representatives from each kiva are expected to participate. The hunt leader remains beside the partially sand-covered fire throughout the day, taking no part in the actual hunting. The hunters set fire to the brush and grass as they advance toward the center of the circle. This variation was formerly also used in hunting coyotes by the communal method.

Gifford's Papago informants admitted the use of fire for hunting but denied the practice for improving pasturage. However, a personal communication, received in 1939 from the Papago Indian Juan Delores (133), establishes the fact that the Papagos also burned to improve grass yield and to maintain pastures clear of mesquite brush. I quote:

> There was just one area which was annually burned by the Papago. The region was along the northern slope of the mountain just south of the Sonora-Arizona boundary and extending from Paso Verde, Sonora, toward

the northwest for about 70 miles (i.e., a good day's ride on horse back). Formerly the area, 70 miles by 20 miles was a grassy pasture, with mesquite brush persisting only along a few streams or at the mouths of arroyas. Small mesquite bushes started to grow among the grass, but were destroyed before they became large. All of the Indians were notified when the fire was to be started at the western end, chosen because the prevailing wind was from that direction. Although some game were killed during the grass burning, the pronounced purpose of the fire was to keep down the mesquite and improve the feed for game.

Neither burning to drive game nor burning to improve wild seed crops were recognized as motives.

Since the Indians have ceased the annual burning of this area mesquite thickets have grown up and completely changed the appearance of the whole area.

The information above from Juan Delores can be interpreted to the effect that the Papagos burned all of the territory within their tribal area that could be usefully and successfully burned and is of special interest because it defines the very limited sections of the Papago country that could be profitably burned. The implication is that if larger areas would carry fire they would also probably have been set on fire. For the territory on the western edge of the Southwest, along the Colorado River, four anthropologists have reported that Indians set fire to the vegetation. The first was Hough (259), already mentioned, who said the following concerning the burning of grass to improve the yield of wild seeds (p. 67):

A similar process is observed among the Cocopa Indians on the Lower Colorado River. An important article of food of these Indians is grass seed. After harvest the Indians burn off the dry grass to clear the land of rubbish, so that when the new grass springs up the harvest may be facilitated. The Indians believe that the grass is benefited by burning, and their idea appears to be good. This is a case of unintentional fertilization. It also may be seen that a continuation of this process may work a change in the habits of the grass, leading in some respects to its domestication.

Spier (472) in 1928 reported that the Havasupais fired brush and grass as an aid in driving game, and Gifford (201) in 1936 reported that the northeastern and western Yavapais burned brush to drive rabbits. Drucker (146), in his *Culture Element Distribution* study of the Yuman-Piman Indians, published in 1941, included information on the use of fire for hunting by several tribes in Arizona and on both sides of the lower Colorado River. Drucker indicated that use of fire to drive antelope was "environmentally impossible" for the Mohaves and Cocopas but was employed by the Maricopas, Pimas, Papagos, Yavapais, and Walapais. The fire drive for rabbits was reported for Mohaves, Cocopas, Maricopas, Papagos, Yavapais, and Walapais. It thus appears clear from the anthropological literature that the Indians of the Southwest were in the habit of using fire to drive game, to increase the yield of wild seeds or grasses, and to improve the pasture for game. If we apply the culture area principle, we can assume that all of the Indians in this area from time to time set fire to the whole southwest country. Reports of scientists who have analyzed the vegetation in this region confirm this information from Indian informants.

The earliest scientific studies regarding the grasslands of Arizona and New Mexico were concerned with the desert grass and creosote bush area of the southern sections of both New Mexico and Arizona. The first I found is dated 1901 and was published by the U.S. Department of Agriculture, Division of Agrostology, in a bulletin by Shear (456). Writing of the Southwest in general— west Texas, New Mexico, Arizona, and southeastern California—Shear said (p. 42) that in times past there were frequently "prairie fires which the Indians are said to have set in order to improve the grazing.... As soon as the prairie fires became less frequent the shrubby vegetation spread rapidly, especially the mesquite bean ... [which] now forms a scattered growth over a great portion of central and western Texas as well as throughout the lower altitudes of this whole region."

The importance of fire in keeping down the woody vegetation is substantiated by Wooton (575). His observations are of special significance because they were made on an experimental area that for over ten years was protected as much as possible from grazing and from fire. While protected, neither grass or brush gained complete dominance. Nevertheless, Wooton said (p. 18):

> There is no doubt that the prediction made by Griffiths [219, dated 1904] that the mesquites and other shrubs would increase in size and number, is slowly coming true within the protected area. The only retardation they have received has been from the occasional fires, some of which have been severe enough to completely kill plants 10 to 12 feet high, though usually only the smaller bushes are killed back to the ground.

The ability of fire to control mesquite if the grass is allowed to accumulate was confirmed by Wooton in the same article (p. 33): "In June 1914, occurred one of the largest and hottest fires.... Along the arroyos where the grass was highest and thickest the mesquite bushes were killed completely in several places, and many were killed back to stumps."

Hensel (242) in 1923 recorded the belief of an early settler in southern Arizona, which shows that the power of fire to reduce mesquite was not unknown to the ranchers of the area. He wrote (p. 183): "While in Arizona a few years ago I was discussing the Santa Rita Range Reserve with an 'Old Timer' who was pointing out how mesquite had spread on areas under protection. . . . This man was making the point that regular burning at the right time of year would hold mesquite in check and not injure the grass."

A similar record of grasslands being covered by brush and trees was given by Leopold (311) in 1924. From a study of the vicinity of Prescott, Arizona, he found brush-oak, manzanita, and mountain mahogany invading former grasslands, to be followed by juniper and pinyon pine. He wrote (p. 2): "Previous to the settlement of the country, fires started by lightning and Indians kept the brush thin, kept the juniper and other woodland species decimated, and gave the grass the upper hand with respect to possession of the soil. . . . Overgrazing [automatically] checking the possibility of widespread fires."

That woody vegetation is continuing to increase at the expense of grass is recognized by Parker (389), who wrote as follows in a USDA leaflet in 1943:

Mesquites . . . are found in ever-increasing abundance on many grassland ranges of Arizona, New Mexico, Texas, and portions of adjoining States.

Mesquite constitutes a menace that in some sections has aroused determined effort to control the plant.

Two pictures published by Parker of a tract that appears to be New Mexico illustrate the marked change that has taken place in recent decades. A photo of the place taken in 1903 shows open prairie but no mesquite. The other picture of the same place taken in 1941 reveals mesquite in an "all too-firmly established stand." Inasmuch as the most severe drought since European occupation of America occurred during that period, there are no grounds for suggesting that the spread of mesquite was brought about by increased moisture.

The success of mesquite (*Prosopis*) over grass in the Southwest has been also documented by Campbell and Bomberger (73), Whitfield and Anderson (553), Whitfield and Brutner (554), and Olson (383) from 1934 to 1940, who mentioned overgrazing as the factor allowing for the change. The data from Wooton (575) and Hensel (242), given above, clearly demonstrate that reduction of grazing alone does not check the mesquite. Shrubs and brush now invading the grasslands were kept in check by fire, but there had to be present sufficient dry grass to make a hot fire and to carry it along. Certainly overgrazing is a factor in the process, yet its primary effect was in diminishing the effectiveness of fire or that of making impossible the unaided spread of fire.

In personal conversation with Indian Service employees, I was informed that during the last few decades juniper has increased on the Navajo Reservation enough to materially reduce feed for sheep. Means have been sought to remove and limit the growth of juniper. Lockett (328) presents 1939 photographs of places described by Beale in 1858. In general, the Navajo country seems drier and more desertlike in nearly all respects in 1938 than it was in 1858, partly because of overgrazing. In spite of this deterioration junipers have multiplied. Again it should be pointed out that the increase was recorded during a period of drought. Why more juniper trees than formerly? Not because of more moisture.

Since it is well known that junipers burn easily and completely (they are said to "explode"), the remarkable increase in the dominated area may very well have resulted from the cessation of grass fires. Overgrazing and government policy have virtually stopped grass and brush fires on the Navajo Reservation; consequently, junipers are becoming a serious problem. This invasion of grassland by juniper in an arid region with a wide range of temperature, hot in summer and below freezing in winter, suggests that this species might have had a much wider distribution were it not so extremely vulnerable to fire. Pearson (391) in 1920 and Howell (260) in 1941 present information regarding the ability of juniper and pinyon to thrive in places receiving as little as ten inches of rainfall annually. Juniper will grow where only two inches of soil covers bedrock. No section of the short-grass plains receives, on an average, less than twelve inches of moisture annually.

The evidence presented regarding the Southwest—Arizona, New Mexico, and portions of adjoining states—forces the following conclusions: (1) the Indians of the Southwest, both sedentary farmers and nomadic hunters, set fire to fields and forests in order to facilitate hunting and to improve wild seed growth and pasturage; (2) the vegetation burning done by Indians and early settlers had the effect of producing and maintaining grass against the encroachment of woody vegetation; (3) when fires were no longer common, brush and trees took possession of the grasslands; (4) the invasion of grasslands occurred whenever the fires were stopped either because of the lack of fuel caused by overgrazing or because of complete protection.

GREAT BASIN AND PLATEAU

Located between the Rocky Mountains and the Sierra-Cascades, the Great Basin and Plateau region is characterized by deserts and northern mesophytic evergreen forests. As characterized by Livingston and Shreve (327), the "Great Basin Microphyll Desert" is set off from the deserts of southern California, Arizona, and Texas. They have described the region as follows (p. 33): "This desert occupies the floor and low mountains of the Great Basin from southern Washington to southern Nevada and eastward to Colorado, lying at elevations of 1,000 to 5,000 feet. Throughout practically the whole of this area the vegetation is dominated by a single species, the sagebrush (*Artemisia tridentata*). . . ."

Following Transeau, Livingston and Shreve (327, p. 342) calculated the precipitation-evaporation ratios. All of the Great Basin-Plateau area has a P/E ratio of 20 or less for the average frostless season and most of the region has a P/E ratio of 20 or less for average annual precipitation. Shantz and Zon (454, fig. 2) designated the Great Basin natural vegetation as "Sagebrush (Northern Desert Shrub)," interspersed with "Pinon-Juniper (S. W. Coniferous Woodland)" on the small discontinuous mountain ranges; western pine forests occupy the Rocky Mountains and the high ranges surrounding the Great Basin-Plateau. A region called "Bunch Grass (Pacific Grassland)" is found in eastern Oregon and Washington. Shantz and Zon wrote (p. 21):

> The Great Basin region . . . may be characterized as sagebrush desert. . . . Although at high altitudes sagebrush extends to the Mexican boundary, it occurs only as small isolated patches south of latitude 34 degrees. From latitude 37 degrees north to the Canadian line most of the lower valley or basin land between the Cascade-Sierra on the west and Continental Divide on the east is occupied by this type of vegetation. . . . In a somewhat modified form it pushes far into grassland areas of the Great Plains, especially in Montana and Wyoming. . . . It also occurs in Colorado along the eastern base of the mountains; . . . pushes into the short grass; . . . bunch grass; . . . pinon-juniper; . . . and into the southern desert. . . . This great area of sagebrush desert is characterized by rainfall which is comparatively uniform throughout the year, being least during the months from July to September. Over much of the area the rainfall is less than 10 inches and in very little, if any, of the area does it exceed 15 inches.

And (on p. 223): "The sagebrush cover is usually a pure open stand, the plants being from 3 to several feet apart and varying in height from 2 to 7 feet. In general appearance this type represents a diminutive forest with silvery foliage and little undergrowth. . . . The sagebrush roots are well developed at the surface and extend also in good soil to a depth of 4 to 18 feet."

Since the areas burned by Indians were not always designated by vegetation type, a word regarding the woodlands of the Great Basin-Plateau is called for. Shantz and Zon (454, p. 8) wrote: "Over thousands of square miles pinon-juniper and sagebrush alternate, the former occupying rough broken country or shallow stony soil, while sagebrush occurs on the more level ground, which has a deep, uniform soil."

Juniper and pinyon trees are found particularly on the many small ranges rising above the floor of the Great Basin. High on the Rocky, Wasatch, and Uintah Mountains, because of altitude, grow spruce-fir forests. More typical of these mountains, however, are the forests of western yellow pine and Rocky Mountain Douglas fir. Territory capable of supporting Douglas fir and Engelmann spruce is covered with aspen (*Populus tremuloides*) and lodgepole pine (*Pinus contortus*) or even by grassland, as a result of fires (Shantz and Zon 454, pp. 8–9). Climate in the forests of the Great Basin and Plateau differs from those in the surrounding deserts or grasslands because of elevation. Rainfall reaches thirty-five inches annually in places and is accompanied by reduced evaporation and temperature.

Desert vegetation is usually so widely spaced that fire will not spread from one plant to another. For this reason it is surprising to find as many references to burning as we do. However, much of the area does not conform to the character of deserts. The many mountains in the Great Basin are exceptions, of course, but even valley and basin floors support enough vegetation on numerous large tracts to carry fire. After presentation of evidence showing that American Indians in the Great Basin and Plateau set fire to much of the vegetation in the region, the effects of that burning will be evaluated and considered in the context of contemporary ecological studies.

On September 23, 1776, Father Domínguez, Father Escalante, and their companions descended Spanish Fork Canyon and entered the valley of Utah Lake. In the diary of the expedition Escalante mentioned "meadows" along the river in the canyon and wrote of the valley as follows (160a, p. 179): "We went down to the plain, and entering the valley, crossed the river again. After traveling through the wide meadows on its north bank somewhat more than a league, we crossed to the other side, and camped in one of its southern meadows. . . . We found that the pasture of the meadows through which we were traveling had been recently burnt, and that others nearby were still burning." The Spanish priests "inferred" that the grass was burned to deprive their horses of pasture "so that the lack of grass might force us to leave the plain more quickly."

The second account of fire in the Great Basin is from the journal of Edwin Bryant (68), who describes Morgan Valley, Utah, on July 25, 1846:

> The valley in which our camp is situated is about fifteen miles in length, and varies from one to three miles in breadth. . . . The summits of this

range, on the west, exhibit snow. . . . The quiet, secluded valley, with its luxuriant grass waving in the breeze; the gentle streamlet winding through it, skirted with clumps of willows and the wild rose in bloom; the wild currant, laden with ripe fruit; the aspen poplar. . . . I noticed this morning, about ten o'clock, a column of smoke rising from the mountains to the west. The fire which produced it continued to increase with an almost frightful rapidity, and the wind, blowing from that quarter, was driving the smoke into the valley. . . .

And, near the site of the Salt Lake City, on July 30, 1846, Bryant wrote: "A fire was raging on the mountain-side all night, and spread down into the valley, consuming the brown vegetation. . . ."

On August 4, 1846, having crossed barren salty, mud flats west of Great Salt Lake, Bryant reported that a fire in the "canada" (canyon) on the side of Pilot Peak had burned all night. On August 8, on the Humboldt River, near the site of Halleck, Nevada, he wrote: "After dark, fires lighted by Indians were visible on the mountains through which we had passed, and in several places in the valley a few miles distant."

All of these fires mentioned by Bryant occurred before Europeans had settled in Utah and Nevada, the Bryant party being one of the first to enter the Great Basin in 1846. Egan (153), who worked among the Indians of Utah Territory from 1846 to 1878, described the rabbit-hunting fire-drive used by the Gosiutes, who lived along the central section of the Utah-Nevada state boundary. After noting that hunters with torches spread out in a circle about a mile in diameter, he then wrote:

Working all around the circle and towards the center was a continuous ring of fire and smoke, which was gradually closing in, and the rabbits were being crowded together thicker and thicker. Each Indian, squaw, and papoose had a stick about four feet long, the only weapon they carried. . . . [They made] as much noise as possible. The rabbits got so dazed by the fire, smoke, and tumult that they simply could not run. . . . I saw dozens of them stop within reach of the sticks, and many of them were picked up that had not been hit. When a rabbit was seen to pass out of the human ring, someone would follow him in the smoke and put his body in one of the piles of rabbits they had made as they proceeded towards the center. . . . When the drive was over, the field was a black, fire-swept, but still smoking, patch of ground. . . .

A number of early explorers noted that Indians set fire to vegetation in Idaho, along the Snake River. Bonneville (270a) and Townsend (511a) were in the vicinity of Boise in 1833, and both reported that the Indians set fire to the grassy plains in the fall. Townsend said that the Indians claimed it was "to improve the crops of next year." In 1839 Farnham (165, p. 75) saw where the prairie had been burned near Fort Hall, Idaho, but gave a different reason. He said: "These Indians had been gathering in their roots, etc., a few days previous to our arrival. I was informed, however, that the crop was barely sufficient to subsist them while harvesting it. But, in order to prevent their enemies from finding whatever might have escaped their own search, they had burned over large sections of the most productive part."

The use of fire to drive game was observed on the plateau of interior Washington by Cox (119, pp. 46–47), who wrote in 1831 as follows:

> In the great plains between Oakinagen and Spokane there are at particular seasons numbers of small deer. Towards the latter end of the summer they are in prime condition, and at that season we had excellent sport in hunting them. The Indians, however, are not satisfied with our method of taking them in detail. On ascertaining the direction the deer have chosen, part of the hunters take a circuit in order to arrive in front of the herd, while those behind set fire to the long grass, the flames of which spread with great rapidity. In their flight from the devouring element they are intercepted by the hunters, and, while they hesitate between these dangers, great numbers fall by the arrows of the Indians.

In 1854 Saint-Amant (426, pp. 264–66) wrote of the region of the Umatilla River, in northeastern Oregon, as follows:

> Destructeur par instinct, jamais le sauvage ne sera producteur. Combien de fois l'oeil n'est-il pas attristé, sur les bords des rivières ou dans l'in-térieure, par les traces des immenses incendies de forêts de plusieurs milles d'étendue; il les a détruites uniquement pour en faire sortir le gibier ou ses chevaux qu'il y supposait réfugiés, ou afin de s'y ouvrir un plus facile accès, quand il ira y cueillir ses graines. A la fin de l'été, il incendie avec encore plus de facilité les prairies entières; mais on sait qu'ici il y a un but d'utilité: quelques semaines après, une nouvelle herbe verte et savoureuse a repoussé, plus riche en qualités nutritives et préferée par le Betail. Il n'en est pas de même des forêts.
>
> [Destroyer by instinct, the savage will never be a producer. How many times has the eye not been saddened, along the riverbanks or in the interior, by the traces of immense forest fires stretching for several miles; he (the savage) has destroyed them (the forests) exclusively to drive out game or his horses that he believed took refuge there, or in order to open up access for himself, when he will go there to harvest his grain

(seeds). At summer's end, he sets fire with even greater ease to the entire prairies; but one knows that here he has a useful goal: several weeks afterward, a new, green, tasty grass has regrown, richer in nutritional value and preferred by the livestock. It is not the same for the forests.]

From the sources available to him, Bancroft (24) in 1875 wrote that the Flatheads, Nez Perces, Kootenais, and Spokanes used fire drives in hunting deer, elk, and mountain sheep. Darrah (125a), the biographer of Major Powell, wrote as follows (pp. 231–32):

In 1868 the Major had witnessed a fire in Colorado which destroyed more timber than all that used by the citizens of the territory from the time of its earliest settlement. Within the next few years he had seen a second fire of equal extent in Colorado and at least three in Utah, each of which destroyed more timber than had been taken by the people since the occupation of the territory. Every one of the government surveying parties that had traversed the western lands had met fires in progress or the charred remnants attesting to the former presence of this great destroyer. The younger forests were everywhere growing over fallen timber which had been burned during seasons of drought through the agency of the Indian. In every season of great drought the mountaineer saw the sky filled with clouds of smoke rising from great areas in the path of devastation.

Knowledge of one of the many fires came to Major Powell while he floated through Desolation Canyon, eastern Utah, in July 1867. Darrah wrote of this as follows (p. 132): "For two or three days the air was hazed with the acrid smoke of a distant forest fire. Great fires, which often were set by Indians driving game, ravaged thousands upon thousands of acres of timber."

W. L. Campbell (73a), a government surveyor, sent the following wire to Washington, D.C., in 1879: "Indians are keeping my surveyors out of North and Western Colorado burning forests, wantonly killing the game and threatening the settlers."

The historical references above have been confirmed and amplified by modern ethnographic studies among the Indians of the Great Basin and Plateau. Most helpful are the data recorded in the *Culture Element Distribution* (*CED*) studies carried on from 1933 to 1939 under the sponsorship of Professor A. L. Kroeber. Five monographs of the *CED* series are devoted entirely to the Great Basin and Plateau, and three others contain reports on three of the groups.

Gifford (204) reported the Southern Ute practice of driving game with fire on his Apache-Pueblo list cited earlier. O. Stewart (490) had three Ute informants who said their old people set fires to aid in hunting deer and six informants who said the Utes hunted rabbits by means of the fire circle. A similar statement regarding use of fire in rabbit drives was obtained by Lowie (337a, p. 199) from his Utah Ute informant in 1912. One Colorado Ute reported burning to increase yield of wild seeds and wild tobacco. Although some Ute informants denied knowledge of the practice of driving deer with fire and one did not know of the use of fire as an aid in taking rabbits, the modern ethnographic materials combined with the earlier historic data allow for the deduction that vegetation burning was very common among the Utes of Colorado and Utah.

Information for the Southern Paiutes of northern Arizona, southern Utah, and southern Nevada, who are linguistically and culturally similar to the Utes, is found in *CED* reports from three ethnographers. Drucker (146) recorded use of fire in antelope and rabbit drives by the Shivwits band of Southern Paiutes in his Yuman-Piman monograph. Stewart (490) obtained positive responses from one informant regarding fire drives for antelope and from three regarding the fire drive for rabbits. Southern Paiutes also told Stewart that they burned to increase yield of wild seeds and tobacco. J. Steward's (484) Southern Paiute informant from the western edge of that tribal area was uncertain as to whether his group had burned for deer hunting but was positive that they set fires to increase wild seeds. Thus the evidence for a Southern Paiute culture pattern of burning is strong in spite of their having lived in the driest and hottest part of the sagebrush desert.

North and west of the Utes and Southern Paiutes lived the Shoshonis. Their territory included the eastern half of Nevada, western and northern Utah, southern Idaho, and western Wyoming. Julian Steward (483, 484, and 485) studied most of the small Shoshoni groups scattered over this extended area and searched the published literature for information about them. Twenty-one informants from as many different localities were interviewed. Nine reported use of fire for hunting deer or antelope; seventeen reported burning to increase harvest of wild seeds. Another informant in central Nevada said that his "people continually burned over country," but he did not know the reason. A Lemhi Shoshoni in Idaho said they also "burned to get rid of cactus in good grass land." These modern studies added to the older ones of Egan (153), Bryant (68), Townsend (511a), and Bonneville (270a) of a century earlier concerning the same area indicate that the use of fire was a general practice among the Shoshonis. Northern Paiutes occupied the western edge of the Great Basin in an area shaped "like an isosceles triangle with its point at Owens Lake, California, and its 275-mile base at Blue Mountains in Oregon, about 600 miles to the north"

(Stewart 489). Before the *Culture Element Distribution* studies were undertaken, two ethnographies of two Northern Paiute bands had been published. The first was done by Isabel Kelly (281) on the Surprise Valley Paiutes who lived in extreme northeastern California and northwestern Nevada. She wrote (p. 82):

> The only means of taking a deer wholesale was by firing. This method was called *kupi tu* and was practiced in the late summer, about the middle of August. When deer were sighted on a hill, a group of hunters hastened there, some on either slope of the mountain. They started fires, working them around until the band was completely encircled. This accomplished, the fires were brought closer, constricting the circle until the animals were bunched on the crest of the hill where they could be shot conveniently. Deer firing was ordinarily executed without undue noise, but if a bear were accidentally caught in the fire, a great hue and cry was set up to warn the others and to inform them in which direction the animal was headed. Upon hearing the shouts, someone would sneak into the circle and conceal himself until he had opportunity to let fly. Deer were never driven into a corral "because they lived in the mountains and not in the open country."

The second ethnographic monograph of the Northern Paiute band was done by Julian H. Steward (482) on the Owens Valley group. He wrote (p. 253): "The deer drive was communal, directed by the district head man, whole families moving to the hunting country. Women and old men kept camp and cured the meat. Men, stationed 100 yards apart, hunted a large region, advancing with sage bark torches, 3 inches in diameter, 3 feet long, firing brush and closing in to drive deer into a great circle, then shooting them down."

Driver (142) included two Owens Valley groups in his *CED* report on Southern Sierra Indians. Both groups reported fire drives for hunting and "burning for better wild-food crops." Steward (484) also included in his *CED* monograph on Nevada Shoshonis two Northern Paiute lists from the vicinity of Owens Valley, and these agreed that fire was used to hunt deer and to increase the growth of wild seeds and wild tobacco. Stewart (489) had twelve Northern Paiute informants from different bands from Walker Lake, Nevada, to Burns, Oregon. Five knew of the ancient custom of setting fires to drive deer and antelope. Eleven of the twelve reported setting fires to increase the growth of wild tobacco, and half of them said wild seed-collecting areas were burned to increase yield. Thus, again the pattern for burning is established for another Great Basin tribe, which roamed over an extensive portion of the sagebrush desert that is broken up by juniper-pinyon–covered mountain ranges. Teit (504) in 1900 reported the following about the Thompson Indians of British Columbia: "They sometimes set fire to the woods in order to secure a greater abundance of roots on the burnt hillside."

A collection of ethnographic articles on the plateau area was edited by Spier (473) and published in 1938. In it appears the following (p. 19): "The Colville are reported to have set fire to the underbrush in the late fall to drive game through a defile as the Thompson did. This firing repeated over the same territory every three years would prevent the dead logs and underbrush from accumulating enough to permit a severe fire."

Only five of the sixteen informants used by Ray (412) for the *Culture Element Distribution* survey of the plateau gave affirmative answers to the question regarding brush burning "to drive game out." The tribes admitting use of fire in hunting were the Klikitats, Kalispels, Lower Carriers, Kutenaes, and Cour d'Alenes. Notwithstanding the denials of burning to drive game—the only item in Ray's report regarding the use of fire by some informants—fire may have been widely used for other purposes.

The foregoing published statements to the effect that Great Basin/ Plateau Indians burned the vegetation of the area may appear to be inconclusive evidence that fire was an important ecological force in the sagebrush desert region. A summary evaluation and the application of the culture area principle strengthen the assumption that Indians of the Great Basin and Plateau probably burned-over all places that could be burned with relative ease. It should be recalled that the *Culture Element Distribution* survey was based upon trait lists that recorded specific items about which to question. None of the ethnographers asked if Indians burned to clear the forests to facilitate travel, or to make game more easily discovered, or to improve the pasture for game. By applying the culture area principle, one might assume that burning for "good grass," as reported by the Lemhis, or continual burning without specifying the reasons, as mentioned by J. Steward's (484) Battle Mountain Shoshonis, would have been general throughout the Basin-Plateau region. In addition, the older documents already noted present positive evidence of the use of fire by the same tribes listed as negative on the CED lists. For example, Ray (412) recorded burning to drive game as denied by the Umatillas, whereas in 1854 Saint-Amant (426) had written that the Indians of the Umatilla river region burned "to drive out game," "to open the forest to make access easier," and to improve pasturage of the "entire prairie." These practices may well have been general. Bancroft (24) in 1875 wrote that the Flatheads burned to drive game, a practice unknown by Ray's Flathead informant. Furthermore, the Nez Perces and the Spokanes, important Plateau tribes not included in Ray's CED survey, were listed by Cox (119) and Bancroft (24) as having practiced hunting with fire.

The statements of burning by Indians presented above are sufficient to support the conclusion that fire was used by Indians of the Great Basin and Plateau regularly and for many purposes. Julian H. Steward, who wrote the most comprehensive work on the region, *Basin-Plateau Aboriginal Sociopolitical Groups* (483), apparently came to the same conclusion, for he said in 1948 (486, p. 278): "[Indians] changed the natural landscape by repeated firings, probably intentional as well as accidental, which burned off seedlings and created grasslands where climax vegetation would have been brush or forest."

With the direct evidence of burning by Indians in the Basin-Plateau region, we can turn to the indirect evidence for the evaluation of the role of fire in influencing "natural vegetation." The record of fire made in the trees themselves is clear and indicates that the forests of the Basin-Plateau have been frequently burned during the last several centuries. For example, Clements (99) determined in 1910 from tree-ring analysis that forest stands in the Estes Park region of Colorado were burned over in 1707, 1722, 1753, 1781, 1842, 1864, 1872, 1878, 1891, 1896, 1901, 1903, and 1905. Living trees in the Deschutes National Forest of interior Oregon were fire scarred in 1824, 1838, 1843, 1863, 1883, and 1888, according to Keen (277). Dates of known fires, before modern records, are found in the trees of Clearwater County, Idaho, as determined by Rapraeger (411), to be 1782, 1802, 1827, 1847, and 1852. These dates could not be ascertained, of course, if the fires of a century or half-century ago had completely destroyed the forests. They indicate that most fires in the past moved through the woodlands without killing many of the trees, and frequent burning undoubtedly reduced the numbers and effects of wildfires. Were the majority of the prehistoric forest fires, known by means of scar and tree-ring analysis, started by Indians?

Lightning as the cause of forest fires is so important in the Mountain West that it must be given full consideration before attributing ancient fires to Indians. In fact, were there no direct evidence that Indians set the mountain forests on fire, it could be argued that all fires in the territory under consideration in precontact times had resulted from lightning.

Plummer (399) in 1912 made a thorough study of *Lightning in Relation to Forest Fires*, which serves as a primary source for this evaluation. As shown on Plummer's map (p. 20), one can see that the Great Basin and Plateau are included in his regions B, C, D, F, G, H, K, L, and M. Regions B, D, K, L, and M extend beyond the Basin-Plateau.

Plummer's work illustrates the "lightning zone in mountainous country." It would appear that few trees were struck in Regions G and K because of the low elevation in comparison with surrounding mountains. Region B, although including the Palouse plains of eastern Oregon and Washington and a portion of the Great Basin in southeastern Oregon, probably has such a large number of lightning-struck trees because of the mountains included in the region. Plummer added (p. 22) that "only about 2 percent of the trees struck by lightning on the National Forests are ignited." Plummer presents another table (p. 30) giving the "Number and percentage of forest fires caused by lightning on the National Forests of the United States." For the five-year period 1907–11, lightning caused 8 fires or 6.7 percent of the total for Utah; 9 fires or 24 percent of the total for Nevada; 501 fires or 22.5 percent of the total for Idaho; and 78 fires or 7.4 percent of the total for Colorado. These figures, compared with those for "number of trees struck," indicate that lightning was not of great consequence in Utah and Nevada and could not have been responsible for the areas known to have been burned in Colorado and Idaho. More recent statistics, such as those in the report of the chief of the Forest Service in 1951, suggest an increase in forest fires resulting from lightning (p. 7): "Of a total of 12,393 forest fires in 1950 in the Rocky Mountain and Pacific Coast States, 5,709, or about 46 percent, were lightning caused."

Is the increase because of complete fire protection? This is implied by Plummer's (399, p. 30) statement: "A tree may be set on fire by lightning and burn for days without the flames spreading to other trees or to the ground, if the latter be free from litter, as is often the case in western yellow pine forests, the chances of the fire spreading are small. It is probable that the majority of forest fires caused by lightning striking trees is due to the presence of dry duff, humus, or litter at the base of the tree."

Frequent ground fires in forests would remove the litter, particularly on tracts where Indians regularly set fires to add to those started by lightning. It should be repeated that because of the nature of the terrain of the Great Basin and Plateau marked differences can occur in short distances. Lightning might repeatedly strike trees within a restricted area that the Indians never set on fire. The Indians could have repeatedly burned-over tracts never ignited by lightning. Both Indians and lightning may have started fires in other regions. The nature of the vegetation, the weather at the time, and the topography would greatly influence the area burned by any fire, whatever the cause. In other words, each locality must be considered separately if one is to obtain a correct understanding of the role of fire as an ecological factor in the Great Basin and Plateau. As early as 1891 the importance of fire in determining the vegetation in the Rocky Mountains was recognized by Brandegee (57, p. 118), who wrote:

The open forests of Colorado and Montana are composed of yellow pine (*Pinus ponderosa*) with a sprinkling of the Douglas fir, and are often endangered by fires which run through them, burning the grass, the underbrush, the fallen dead limbs and trunks but without injuring the trees themselves, excepting the thinbarked young ones. The Douglas fir, yellow pine, and a few others, will stand without injury a fire hot enough to blacken them many feet up their trunks, while the hemlocks and spruces (*Tsuga* and *Abies*) are killed by a slight fire at the surface of the ground about the base. Their inability to withstand heat arises from the fact that their bark is much thinner than that of the Douglas fir, yellow pine, Sequoia, etc. The trees of these forests, killed by a fire and becoming dry afford abundant material for a much hotter conflagration in succeeding years, when everything that may have escaped destruction at first is burned to the ground.

Blumer (50) expressed a similar view in 1910, as follows (pp. 42–43):

Fire is also important from the phytogeographer's viewpoint. It may have been a factor of far-reaching importance in the establishment of the prairie sod of the Mississippi Valley, the distribution of species, and composition of the societies of its grassy flora. Over the entire Rocky Mountain region it would probably be difficult to find a single square mile of forest that does not show signs of invasion by fire at some time in its history. Many areas can be found that have been razed repeatedly within the history of the passing forest generation. This is conclusively proven almost to the exact date, by counting the annual rings in old, fire-scarred trees. Unquestionably fire has been and is a most potent factor in disturbing the more or less well-established equilibrium among forest societies, and especially among the members of such societies. Invasion, succession, and re-establishment of equilibrium take place each time upon the virgin and sometimes practically sterile soil left by a very destructive fire. The character of these processes is determined by the severity of the fires, the degree of fire-resistance of the species, the productive, locomotive and propagative qualities of the surviving species on the ground, or in the vicinity, efficiency of wind and other carrying agencies, and the fighting qualities of the off-spring with, or fitness to, conditions of their immediate environment on the one hand, and the members of their own or associated species and generations on the other. This may be expected to apply not only to forest trees, but to shrubs, herbs, and all the lower orders of the plant kingdom, even down to the bacteria, both parasitic and of the soil. The new societies may thus be very different from their predecessors. In the case of the Douglas fir, a single characteristic, namely, its notably high fire-resistant powers, probably due to its thick, non-inflammable bark, in the course of ages may have had a far reaching influence in the determination of its enormous range and present prominent status in a large number of West American forest associations.

Clements (99), also in 1910, published the results of his two year investigation into *The Life History of Lodgepole Burn Forests*. He summarized his results as follows in Plant Indicators (101, p. 14):

> The investigation of the lodgepole-burn forests of northern Colorado in 1907–1908 was essentially a study of fire indicators, herbaceous as well as woody. Its real importance in this connection lay in the fact that it was the first study of forests made on the complete basis of instruments, quadrats, and succession. It was pointed out that lodgepole pine and aspen are practically universal indicators of fire and not of mineral soil or other conditions, at least for the Rocky Mountains. . . .
>
> A successional study was made of the so-called natural parks of Colorado in 1910 for the purpose of determining their indicator significance as to reforestation, both natural and artificial. The conclusion was reached that all such grassland areas in forested regions are but seral stages leading to a forest climax. The majority of them are due to repeated burns or the slow filling of lakes, with the result that they persist as apparent climaxes for several hundred years.

Clements (101, p. 92) lists other "fire indicators" of importance for the Great Basin and Plateau:

> The bush or scrub type is a characteristic fire indicator in forest climaxes the world over. . . .
>
> Fire has played a similar role in making certain genera and species of trees almost universal indicators of its action. The best known examples are found in *Populus* and *Betula*. *Populus tremuloides* [quaking aspen] and *Betula papyrifera* [paper birch] are the characteristic indicators of fire in forest communities throughout boreal North America, as well as in many mountain regions. . . . A second striking group of indicators is found among the conifers, and especially the pines. The latter are characterized by cones which may remain closed upon the branches for many years, but open readily after fire. . . . Three important species of this type occur in western North America, namely lodgepole pine, *Pinus contorta*, jack pine, *P. divaricata*, and knobcone pine, *P. attenuata*. These are all typical fire trees, and form sub-climaxes of great extent and duration in areas frequently swept by fire.

Plummer, the authority on the effect of lightning cited above, wrote a second pamphlet (400) in 1912 for the Forest Service on the "causes, extent and effects" of forest fires. He concurred with Clements's view that fire was responsible for the present extensive "parks" in the Rocky Mountain region. He equated the parts played by lightning and Indians in this quotation (p. 8): "At least two causes of fires operated in ancient times—lightning and Indians. The practice of Indians in firing forests, prairies, or swamps was to permit growth of berries, to drive game, and occasionally to impede an enemy."

Bruderlin (67) and Ramaley (409) also documented that fire has been important in determining vegetation types in the Colorado Rockies but did not mention Indians. Pearson (392, p. 408) published evidence that appears to indicate that the open grassy prairies in the drier, more pure stands of yellow pine may have been caused and maintained by fire. In 1936 he reported that "Government Prairie, several miles wide, on the Kaibab [Plateau, north of Grand Canyon, Arizona] is dotted with young trees." He went on to say that the "prairie" had been "controlled" (i.e., protected, from fire and from overgrazing) for a number of years.

Haig (225, p. 1045) in 1938 added his voice to those who documented occurrences of forest fires. He said that "everywhere [in America] occurred extensive areas of subclimax associations almost certainly of fire origin. . . . Indeed almost every forest climax of North America displays a fire subclimax, usually occurring over a considerable area." Haig said such subclimax are frequently of "prairie nature" but went on to say: "Sears calls attention to the fact that in analyzing the peat deposits in the Medicine Bow Mountains of Wyoming it is evident that fire has been a direct agent in causing an alternation between lodgepole pine and spruce-fir. Some of the peat deposits examined carry a story of fire going back more than 10 or 15 centuries, clear evidence of the work of fire long before the days of Columbus."

Haig could have added, but he did not, that the fires "long before the days of Columbus," even those of 10,000 to 15,000 years ago, might well have been set by the aborigines. Such an assumption regarding the Medicine Bow Mountains is supported by the statistics on fires for Wyoming published by Plummer (399, 400). From 1907 through 1911 for all of Wyoming only 63 lightning fire were noted. This was less than 20 percent of the total. For the five-year period 322 fires from all causes were known. Yet only 41,264 acres of timber land were burned. Since the Medicine Bow Mountains constitute less than one-tenth of Wyoming's forested highlands, it appears probable that man aided lightning to produce the dominant fire forests indicated by Sears's peat analysis. Braun-Blanquet (57a, p. 278) would probably agree, for he wrote: "While prairie and forest fires may occasionally be caused by lightning, that is the exception rather than the rule. In 90 out of 100 cases they are caused by man, either willfully or accidentally. Contrary to the opinion of some American investigators, therefore, fire is to be classed among the anthropogenous factors."

Information published by Stahelin (475) in 1943 supports this interpretation. From a study of burned areas in northern Colorado and southern Wyoming, the area of Medicine Bow range, Stahelin discovered that at elevations from nine to eleven thousand feet no fires had occurred during the last fifty years. There were extensive burns in 1860 and 1892, and Indians still controlled the area in 1860. Stahelin discovered that sod frequently became established after a fire unless aspen or brush grew. The lodgepole pine appeared to revegetate most easily. He found that the "sub-alpine" forests grew very slowly but did return if seeds were available. Stahlin's work suggests that lightning was not important in the area he studied; consequently, the fires may be attributed to Indians. Griggs's (221) study of "Timberlines in the Northern Rocky Mountains," published in 1938, is of interest in this regard. He found that great care must be exercised in the definition of the climatic limit of tree growth, called "timberline." In many places, treeless summits and alpine meadows that at first appeared to be above timberlines were discovered to have been forested in recent centuries. Charred stumps were found, which showed that many very high places had previously supported trees. Thus the honored concept of timberline as a climatic limit must be reexamined. If fire can modify high-elevation landscapes so that timberline cannot easily and certainly be recognized, there can be no doubt that fire is a powerful ecological factor.

Five publications from 1925 to 1938, concerning the forests of northern Idaho, appear to me to have some value for the thesis developed by this study. Larsen (299, 300), Huberman (261), Rapraeger (411), and Shames (451) indicate that fire has been the deciding factor in maintenance of the principal vegetation types in that area. Fire appears essential for white pine and Douglas fir reproduction. Only Rapraeger (411, p. 715), who determined from scar and tree-ring analysis that the same trees were repeatedly burned during their century and a half of existence, mentioned that Indians may have been responsible for much of the burning. Shames (451) emphasized lightning and said that "in the northern Rocky Mountains lightning causes 72 percent of the forest fires." Whether due to natural or human agency, fire was no doubt an important ecological factor in determining the vegetation types, past and present, of the northern Rockies.

Two authors provide significant data on the forest of the northwestern section of the Great Basin/Plateau region. Two articles by Keen (277, 278) and four by H. Weaver (533 to 536), appearing from 1937 to 1950, deal with the ponderosa pine area of interior Oregon and Washington. As mentioned earlier, Keen (277) ascertained that fires had swept the Watkins Butte section of the Deschutes National Forest six times from 1824 to 1888. This confirms the view that ancient fires, whether set by Indians or lightning, were not as harmful as modern attempts by "complete preventionists" would have us think. Keen (278) found many ponderosa pine were over 500 years old. He went on to say (p. 598): "Nor was their old age due to exceptional luck in escaping forest fires. One of the oldest trees, dating back to 1255 a.d., was cat-faced by a fire in 1481. Subsequently it weathered 25 fires occurring at approximately 18-year intervals (as shown by healing scars on the margins of the cat face) until the tree was cut in 1936."

The historic and ethnographic data for interior Oregon and Washington indicate that Indians intentionally set fire to fields and forests; consequently, it seems safe to assume that many, if not all, of the ancient fires recorded in the trees can be attributed to Indians. Since it is desirable that the forest lands of the Great Basin/Plateau be subjected to multiple exploitation—grazing, lumber, watershed—and since the Indians claimed that burning improved grazing, it is appropriate that the primitive tools of the natives should be tested. Travelers and early settlers discovered open forests and luxuriant grassy plains. Was there a connection between burning and the parklike forests and prairies? It is possible that the methods employed by the Indians to maintain good grazing for game in the forests of the Great Basin and Plateau can be as profitably copied as they were in the longleaf pine forests of the southern states. The work of Harold Weaver seems to support this idea. For over ten years Weaver studied the forests of the Colville Indian Reservation in northern interior Washington. In 1943 he wrote (533, p.7):

> Wherever man goes in the ponderosa-pine region of the Pacific Slope he sees evidence of past forest fires. The occasional charred remnants of old trunks and stumps, the partially burned snags and windfalls of trees killed by various causes in more recent times, and the charred bark and the basal fire scars or "cat faces" on the trunks of numerous standing live trees are everywhere in evidence.
>
> The writer believes that these facts indicate clearly that periodic fires . . . formerly operated to control the density, age classes, and composition of ponderosa-pine stands.

In 1946 Weaver (534) recommended controlled burning to clear slash and reduce the hazard of destructive wildfires. He noted:

The dry, ungrazed grass and brush were so dense that fires were able to creep about over a greater portion of the ground surface. An exceptionally good cleanup of the slash and other debris was obtained . . . with but little damage to the reserve stand and advanced reproduction. Such thinning appears distinctly beneficial because of the surviving seedlings, saplings, and poles of ponderosa pine still occupy the ground in sufficient numbers to comprise a fully stocked stand on all areas burned.

Areas thus treated now look "park-like" in contrast to other cutover areas.

Weaver (535) continued his writing in favor of controlled burning of ponderosa pine forest in 1947. He found a forty-year-old stand that had been completely protected during its growth to be worthless for lumber and of no use for grazing. It was a thick jungle of trees about 12.3 feet high with an average diameter of 1.7 inches a foot above ground. An adjacent tract had been accidentally burned-over seven years after the area had been logged clean. Twenty-five years after the tract had been thinned by a wildfire the trees averaged 32.2 feet in height and 7.4 inches in diameter at the one-foot level. To avoid the waste of forest resources and loss of grazing, Weaver proposed prescribed burning. Weaver's (536) 1950 contribution reported on the success of his experiments with careful use of fire in the management of the forest on the Colville Indian Reservations; he wrote (p. 22):

> Since attempted total fire suppression has been initiated and the dense reproduction stands have developed, the fire hazard has increased tremendously. The dense reproduction stands themselves are highly inflammable.
>
> It thus appears beyond question that fire can be used to advantage in silvaculture in the interior northwest forests as it is being used in the pine forests of New Jersey and of the southern states. But forests occupy a relatively small part of the Great Basin–Plateau region. Sagebrush is the typical plant cover for the greater portion of the Basin-Plateau and it will now receive our attention.

Were it not for the ethnographic evidence that Indians did burn sagebrush tracts, the arid floor of the Great Basin and Plateau where this drought-resistant shrub dominates could be passed over unnoticed in a study of burning. Deserts are usually thought of as having too little vegetation to sustain fires over more than the smallest areas. As stated by the ecologist Daubenmire (128a, p. 329), deserts like that of the Great Basin would be excluded from consideration: "Except in very cold or very dry regions, fire has always been an important factor in terrestrial environment." The Great Basin is "very dry," but apparently not dry enough to escape the influence of fire. Daubenmire has provided important information with which to evaluate the role of fire in the vegetation of the sagebrush desert. He found so much grass between the sage in the driest sections of eastern Washington that he proposed "semi-desert" as a more appropriate designation (128a, p. 62).

Whether the Great Basin floor and the driest sections of the Plateau should be called "desert," "semidesert," "steppe," or "grassland" depends, in many instances, upon whether the tract had been burned over or not and, furthermore, whether it had been overgrazed or not. This is so if the vegetation is used as the criterion for determining the designation. If only physical characteristics are used, such as amount of temperature, rainfall, evaporation, etc., the areas defined are not consistent with the vegetation. For example, Koppen (290, p. 20) and Russell (424) divided the Great Basin between "BWDesert" and "BS-Steppe," whereas Livingston and Shreve (327) and Shantz and Zon (454) found it to be "Sagebrush Desert," except for a few districts of "Salt Deserts."

The areas said by Shantz and Zon (454) to be covered by "Greasewood (Salt Desert Shrub)" are primarily ancient lake beds (such as the Great Salt Lake Desert) that are almost completely barren because of the amount of salt in the soil and need not be considered further. They do, however, illustrate the complexity of the problems encountered in the Great Basin, for there are tracts, in one case over a thousand square miles in extent, devoid of vegetation because of simple and obvious chemistry of the soil. The greater part of the Great Basin, characterized as "Sagebrush Desert" by the authorities cited, might be just as well called "Grassland." Although Clements (101) is not clear and consistent in his evaluation of the role of fire, the following passage from his book Plant Indicators illustrates the difficulty in determining what is the natural vegetation of the Great Basin (pp. 152–56):

> THE SAGEBRUSH CLIMAX. *Nature.* The sagebrush climax owes its character to the dominance of low shrubs or bushes, of which *Artemisia tridentata* is the most important. . . . The sagebrush dominants are not only well adapted to their habitat, but they are also particularly well fitted to invade other habitats, wherever fire or other disturbance has weakened the hold of the occupants. The result has been a widespread extension of sagebrush into all of the contiguous formations, the grassland, desert scrub, chaparral, and woodland, and even into the pine consociation of the montane forest.

Unity of the formation. The geographical unity is greater than that of most other climaxes in that the sagebrush occupies a natural physiographic unit, the Great Basin. While the most representative species, *Artemisia tridentata*, extends far beyond the limits of the latter, the formation proper does not. The Great Basin is likewise a climatic unit, and hence naturally corresponds to its climax. It is hemmed in by the high mountains, and contains by far the most extensive area with 5 to 10 inches of rainfall to be found on the continent. The general rainfall limits are from 5 to 15 inches in the interior, though to the eastward sagebrush mixes with or yields to grass as the rainfall rises above 12 inches.

Range. It is impossible to draw the limits of the sagebrush climax with accuracy, owing to the extent to which it mixes with contiguous formations. . . . As a matter of convenience, a formation is called dominant where it covers three-fourths of a particular area or region.

If the limits are set as indicated above, the sagebrush climax will include all of Nevada except the southeast, practically all of Utah, Colorado west of the Continental Divide, central and southwestern Wyoming, a part of southwestern Montana, all of south-central Idaho, Oregon south of the John Day Valley and east of the Cascades and California east of the Sierra Nevada. Disregarding the interruption due to isolated mountain ranges, this constitutes the largest central mass exhibited by any formation west of the prairies and plains. Tongues of sagebrush stretch out from this mass into eastern Montana, central Colorado, northern New Mexico, and Arizona, southern California and Mexico, while climax outposts are found in southeastern and eastern Washington, and even in southernmost British Columbia. These are practically all extra-regional, persisting because of peculiar local conditions or because the proper climax has not yet occupied all of its climatic region.

Subclimax sagebrush. . . . The longest contact of the sagebrush is with grassland. It meets the bunchgrass prairies in Washington, Oregon, Idaho, Montana, and Utah, the mixed prairies in Montana, Wyoming, and Colorado, and the short-grass plains in western Colorado, northern New Mexico and Arizona, and southeastern Utah. The ability of the sagebrush and grassland to live together is shown not only by the very broad transition between them all along the line of contact, but also by the fact that such dominants as *Agropyrum glaucum* and *Stipa comata* are found more or less abundantly throughout the climax area of the formation.

The actual relation between sagebrush and grasses is readily disclosed wherever sagebrush has been cleared and often also where it has been burned. . . . If the grasses do develop abundantly during the first few years and especially the first year, so that they dominate the root sprouts of the shrubs, the area is to be regarded as belonging to the grassland. . . . *Festuca ovina, Agropyrum glaucum*, and *A. spicatum* have frequently been found to replace cleared or burned sagebrush in Oregon. *Agropyrum glaucum* and *Stipa comata* have been seen in the same role in many parts of Idaho, northern Utah, and southwestern Wyoming. In addition, the grass dominants have been found killing out the sagebrush as a direct result of competition for water. This is not surprising along the eastern edge of Wyoming where the grasses have a definite climatic advantage, but it is unexpected in Utah and Nevada, where the advantage is reversed. . . . The evidence of the replacement of sagebrush by the grasses during the dry years of 1917 and 1918, either as a result of fire or clearing, or in consequence of competition, has been so abundant as to indicate that a broad marginal belt of the climax is really subclimax. . . . This subclimax belt is from 100 to 300 miles wide and extends all along the grassland contact from Oregon to Montana and from Wyoming to Arizona. If placed under proper treatment, it is felt that it can again be converted into the original grassland community.

The conversion of contiguous grassland into sagebrush has undoubtedly been caused by overgrazing during the past fifty years, aided in a large measure by repeated fires. This is confirmed not only by evidence of the controlling part formerly played by grasses in regions now covered by sagebrush, but also by the persistence of the grass covering in areas more or less protected.

Under the heading "The Bunch-Grass Prairie" Clements (101, p. 149) gave further data regarding the fact that fire was common in the area where sagebrush and grassland meet:

The bunch-grass prairies find their best expression today in the Palouse region of southeastern Washington and adjacent Idaho. Typical areas also occur in northern and eastern Oregon. . . . Cultivation, grazing, and fire have combined to destroy bunch-grass or to handicap it in competition with the invading sagebrush. In the form of outposts, this association is found eastward in Montana to Helena and Livingston, in western Wyoming from Yellowstone Park to the Green River region and southward through northwestern Colorado and northeastern and northern Utah. Over most of this region, it occurs on dry rocky hillsides surrounded by sagebrush, indicating that it formerly covered much larger areas. This is confirmed by the fact that burning or clearing the sagebrush from an area permits the development of typical bunch-grass prairie.

The views of Clements, as the outstanding plant ecologist in America for over a quarter of a century and, with Weaver, author of the most extensively used textbook in plant ecology, have very wide acceptance. Notwith-standing the tremendous volume of his writing and the recognition he holds in his field, the quotation presented above appears to me to contain serious errors of deduction. The mistakes occur, I believe, because Clements failed to properly assess the influence of fire on the grasslands as earlier demonstrated in the section of this work on Prairies and Plains. Failure to recognize that the grasslands and much of the sagebrush coun-try have been repeatedly and frequently burned-over by Indians in abori-ginal times caused Clements and a number of his colleagues to accept the vegetation described by the first Europeans as a truly climatic-determined plant cover.

Thus, they have reasoned that all changes, from the first vegetation known to the arrival of Europeans, have resulted from the combination of the influences exerted by recent users of the land. From this it followed that since overgrazing and burning have occurred in historic times, then, of course, overgrazing and burning were to be combined into a unitary cause for the changes recorded. If, however, Clements and his followers had accepted the fact that the vegetation first discovered was a result of repeat burning-over, they could not have attributed the changes in that vegeta-tion to burning. This is clear even in the data Clements himself presents. It is clearly the case that if removal of sagebrush by burning-over a tract allows grass to show its dominance, then burning-over a similar tract could not cause sagebrush to become dominant.

Pickford (398) in 1932, in an article entitled "The Influence of Continued Heavy Grazing and of Promiscuous Burning on Spring-Fall Ranges in Utah"; Weaver and Clements (542, p. 528) in 1938, in the textbook *Plant Ecology*; Enlow and Musgrave, in the 1938 USDA Yearbook (577); Stoddart (495) in 1941; Young (580) in 1943; Hull and Pechanec (263) in 1947; and A. W. Sampson (430) in 1948 all accept the fallacy expressed by Clements (101) in 1920 and unite "fire and overgrazing" as if they were together a single ecological factor.

Fortunately, a number of other ecologists have recognized the sepa-rateness of the two and have shown that fire produces one effect, whereas overgrazing produces an entirely different one. It is obvious that if there is overgrazing fire will not bring about the same result as will the use of fire without overgrazing. The data presented by Pickford (398, p. 165), in the article listed above, showed that sagebrush was eliminated by burning from plots that had not been grazed. On other plots that were protected from fire and grazing for many years the sagebrush and the grass both continued to grow. That fire greatly aids the dominance of grass over sage-brush was clearly demonstrated in 1929 by the experiment carried out by

H. C. Hanson (227) in Colorado, already described in the section on the Prairie and Plains. Hanson demonstrated that burning easily removed sagebrush, which allowed grasses to return and multiply. Larsen (301), writing of the northern Rocky Mountain area in 1930, also appeared to understand the way fire influenced the vegetation. Of the Palouse Region he said (p. 644):

> Between the semi-arid Columbia Basin and the western yellow pine forests is a billowy, treeless region . . . [that receives] yearly precipitation [of] 20.54 inches of which 2.49 inches occur during July, August and September. The air temperature, as well as the amount [of] precipitation which falls here, appear to be suitable for a forest of western yellow pine. Probably the principal reason why this area is not covered with timber is . . . due to extreme draught and high winds. It is not unlikely that recurring prairie fires . . . helped tip the scales to the disadvantage of the trees.

Larsen (p. 656) further considered fire of primary importance for formation and maintenance of prairies in the Flathead and Bitterroot Valleys as well as those in central Montana. Clements's (101) view that drought reduces sagebrush and allows grass to increase in competition for water appears to me to be refuted by Pechanec, Pickford, and G. Stewart (393) in an article printed in 1937. The authors had observed that on the upper Snake River plains of Idaho the drought of 1934 had reduced grass more than sagebrush. Furthermore, sagebrush recovered more quickly than grass as the moisture increased. This evidence heightens the importance of fire in all places where sagebrush and grass compete; and since sagebrush can, as Clements says, grow upon all the land of the short-grass plains, the role of fire in maintaining those grasslands is clear.

A number of other articles on the vegetation of the Great Basin can be interpreted as indicating the extensive and dominant effect of fires set by Native Americans. I believe that the increase of sagebrush and juniper during historic times, as recorded by numerous observers, has resulted primarily from the reduction of fire. Even when overgrazing is an obvious factor in vegetation changes, especially by allowing erosion to deepen washes and change the water table, fire was probably important in determining what vegetation had been present before. In other words, even where erosion has caused drying of meadows to reduce the water available for grass, it must be assumed that the reduction of burning has also been an important contributing factor in the increase of juniper and sagebrush.

A case in point is the study by Cottam and G. Stewart (116), published in 1940, entitled "Plant Succession as a Result of Grazing and of Meadow Desiccation by Erosion since Settlement in 1862." The locality studied is known as Mountain Meadow in southern Utah. In 1852 there were two types of meadow: a lower one near springs and an upper one including most of the valley three miles wide by four long. It was described (p. 614) as "a dry or grass meadow that covered the divide and the low foothills sloping gently upward both east and west." The entire section, which was formerly occupied exclusively by grass, is now completely covered by sagebrush, and juniper trees are rapidly invading the sagebrush. Using the detailed description of the vicinity of the Mountain Meadow of 1851 contained in the autobiography of Parley P. Pratt and other early travelers, in addition to interviews with surviving early settlers in the area, Cottam and Stewart believed that the juniper area had increased from 1,000 acres in 1864 to 6,000 acres by 1934. They wrote (p. 622): "Pratt's comment that the mountains surrounding the meadows were bordered only on their higher eminences with cedar and nut pine is confirmed by all who knew the locality fifty years ago. The thousands of junipers that now dot the entire landscape, and the hundreds of trees that now grow in the former wiregrass meadow, establish that vast changes have occurred in the plant cover since Pratt saw it in 1851."

The topography of the Mountain Meadow has been altered by a deep wash running nearly its entire length, which Cottam and G. Stewart believe resulted from overgrazing. They assert that the wash caused the desiccation of the meadow, which allowed sagebrush and juniper trees to invade it and completely dominate it. Knowing that the Southern Paiute Indians of the vicinity of Mountain Meadow set fire for rabbit drives and for improved yield from wild seed collecting tracts, as recorded by Stewart (490), in addition to knowing of the general Great Basin culture pattern for frequently burning-over meadows, causes me to doubt that Mountain Meadow as first seen by whites was without brush and trees solely because it did not have a deep wash cut into it. A dozen reports, from Clements's (101) of 1920 to Daubenmire's (128a) of 1947, firmly establish the fact that sagebrush and grasses will grow together on the same plot. Neither will dominate, as shown by Pickford (398), cited above, if the area is neither overgrazed nor burned. Cottam and G. Stewart report this fact in the study under discussion, for in places near the Mountain Meadow that have been protected from overgrazing for many years there is abundant grass among the sagebrush. That fire was the determining factor in the former treeless and brushless character of the Mountain Meadow is further supported by other data presented by Cottam and G. Stewart in the same article. In another plot not far from the meadow that had been protected from grazing and had been burned there was no sagebrush. They write (p. 626):

Removal of sagebrush by fire and protection against heavy grazing allowed in this case a rapid increase of grass. . . .

The increase of sagebrush has retarded the recovery of range grasses. Juniper invasion is even more detrimental to revegetation of valuable forage grasses.

In 1941 G. Stewart (487) wrote another article documenting the fact that sagebrush and juniper have invaded large areas in Utah that were meadows or prairies when the Mormons first settled the Great Basin during the decades following 1847. He should have been alerted against neglecting the fire factor, for he cites Escalante's (160a) account of Indian burning of meadows and grassy plains. Notwithstanding that G. Stewart attributes the change solely to overgrazing—without mentioning that Indians fired grasslands and forests—the U.S. Department of Agriculture finally took the chance of admitting in a popular, widely distributed pamphlet that growth of grass was encouraged at the expense of sagebrush by use of fire. Undoubtedly many top executive conferences were necessary before approval was received for the publication of facts that recognized the value of practices so long and so loudly condemned by the same department. Farmers' Bulletin No. 1948, entitled *Sagebrush Burning—Good and Bad*, written by Joseph F. Pechanec and George Stewart (393a), was issued in January 1954.

This study was based on carefully conducted experiments carried on by Hanson (227) in 1929 and by G. D. Pickford and associates from 1932 to 1936. On the flyleaf of the cover in extra large type is a warning against careless burning signed by Lyle F. Watts, chief, Forest Service. Notwithstanding the repeated warnings against carelessness, and the full account of the losses and damage resulting from one sagebrush fire in Utah that got out of control, the pamphlet describes a process that would bring about conditions similar to those prevailing in prewhite times. For burning to be effective, they wrote, the area should not be overgrazed before or after burning. If properly done, burning can change a Great Basin desert sagebrush–covered area into a grassland.

In spite of the recognition in 1944 of the role of fire in reducing sagebrush and juniper, Woodbury (572) in 1947 ignored fire as a possible factor in his study of the great increase of sagebrush he discovered in Utah and northeastern Arizona.

The European ecologist Braun-Blanquet (57a) had criticized his American colleagues in 1932 for neglecting fires set by man as an important biotic factor in plant sociology. It was not until 1947, with the appearance of *Plants and Environment* by R. F. Daubenmire (128a), that an American textbook on plant ecology made more than passing reference to fire. Daubenmire's book included a chapter titled "The Fire Factor," placing it on a level with soil, water, temperature, light, etc., as affecting plant life. I mention this because Daubenmire had, since 1940, been publishing the results of his study on the vegetation of southeastern Washington and adjacent Idaho. He devoted much of his energy to the understanding of the relationship between the *Agropyron* grasses and the *Artemisia* stage of the Palouse region of Washington. He wrote the following in 1940 (127, p. 63): "There also seem to be other factors (perhaps cultivation, fire, etc.) which promote dense stands of grass [at the expense of sagebrush]. . . ."

Daubenmire appears even more radical when he suggests, contrary to Clements, that "*Agropyron* and *Artemisia* seem to be complementary rather than competitive in central Washington. . . ." Although Daubenmire's detailed 1942 study (128) of the vegetation of the Palouse is a fairly typical ecological monograph, he devoted considerable space to the fire factor. He designated the driest part of Washington as the *Artemisia-Agropyron* zone, for undisturbed and protected sections—such as in rural cemeteries—in which both plants were in abundance. The description of sagebrush cover from Shantz and Zon (454, p. 22), quoted at the start of this section, as a "diminutive forest with silvery foliage and little undergrowth" does not correspond to the conditions of the relicts of undisturbed and protected sagebrush found on the Washington sagebrush desert. It does, however, correspond to Daubenmire's (128, p. 62) description of overgrazed sagebrush:

> The influence of heavy grazing upon the savanna-like Artemisietum tends to eliminate first the large forbs and grasses, and then the smaller plants, so that under extreme grazing the ground between the shrubs becomes almost barren of vegetation. . . . Under continued grazing and in the absence of fire there is a tendency toward the development of a biotic climax consisting of a nearly pure stand of *Artemisia tridentata*.

Under the subheading "The Fire Climax," Daubenmire (128, p. 62) established the paramount role of fire in determining the vegetation types that dominate both the sagebrush and bunchgrass zones, as defined by Daubenmire (p. 56) and by Shantz and Zon (454, fig. 2):

> Locally, the practice of burning the vegetation, which was started by the aborigines and is continued today, appears to have played a great part in eliminating *Artemisia* from the Artemisietum, especially in the northern and western parts of the zone. Apparent evidences of this influence are manifold. Often a remnant of the original vegetation on one side of a road (which acts as a fire barrier) contains none of the shrub while a remnant

on the other side does. Deeply charred fenceposts often accompany shrubless stands. Frequently there may be encountered stands in which *Artemisia* is regenerating after a light burn, with a cluster of straight sprouts emerging from a single charred crown. . . .

Another interesting example of the influence of fire is to be found in a cemetery about two kilometers south of Warden, Washington. Today the unused portion of this fenced enclosure supports a handsome stand of *Agropyron* together with other herbs of the Artemisietum, but sagebrush is absent. Furthermore, there is no trace of *Artemisia* along the fence rows adjacent to the cemetery. The farmer who lives across the road recalls a great fire which swept the country before the land was broken for cultivation. This fire, he stated, killed practically all the sagebrush so that a short while afterwards when the cemetery was established, there were very few shrubs (probably seedlings) to be grubbed out. In this region, which is considerably west of the Lamont area, *Artemisia* roots do not send up new shoots after a fire. The persistence of the herbs in the Warden cemetery, as well as in other locations, attests their relative immunity from fire in contrast with *Artemisia*. The fire climax differs from the Artemisietum chiefly in the absence of *Artemisia*.

The writer has found that studies of the unused portions of rural cemeteries in this zone are not as fruitful as in the prairie zones, for it is customary to grub out the sagebrush when the cemeteries are established, and often to burn them periodically as well. The only cases discovered where a cemetery in the Artemisietum seems to have escaped such disturbance are the stations near Lamont and Davenport.

The value of using relict vegetation preserved in cemeteries for ecological studies probably does not differ between Washington and the prairie states as much as Daubenmire suggests. The difference is rather in scholars' degree of awareness of the importance of fire. In the section on Prairies and Plains I have attempted to document the failure of ecologists and botanists working in the midwestern states to consider the role of fire, as when using railway rights-of-way as relicts, although the record of burning was general public knowledge. I suspect the same way to be true of cemeteries.

In his textbook, Daubenmire (128a) makes some general statements that may serve as summary for this section on the Great Basin and Plateau region. On page 341, he notes:

Originally the vegetation of the sagebrush-grass semidesert of western North America consisted of a dense cover of perennial grasses among which were scattered moderate-sized shrubs, chiefly *Artemisia tridentata*.

When this vegetation is subjected to heavy grazing the perennial grasses are reduced to a scattering of weakened plants, whereas the relatively unpalatable sagebrush increases in size and numbers to an extent that is highly objectionable from a grazier's standpoint. Fire, in contrast to grazing, kills the shrubs but does not injure the grasses when these are aestivating. On areas where the grasses have not been too severely depleted, it has been demonstrated that the forage production can be increased tremendously by burning to kill the shrub, then not allowing grazing for a few years until the grasses have multiplied to form a complete cover. Sagebrush eventually returns to such an area, but this is so slow a process that burning need be repeated only at intervals of many years. . . .

It is generally true that fire favors grass at the expense of woody vegetation. . . . Grass fires set by the aborigines were responsible for extending prairie eastward into the winter deciduous forest in the region centering about eastern Iowa.

Daubenmire could have said, but he did not, that without the fires set by aborigines there would have been no tall-grass prairies. The variety of topography, soil, elevation, rainfall, wind, evaporation, etc., of the Great Basin and Plateau precludes generalizing regarding the history of the vegetation of the whole area. About the only generalization I can make is that fire, used frequently by the Indians and employed widely since settlement, was extremely important, often the primary factor determining the so-called natural vegetation of the Great Basin and Plateau.

Northwest

Although Shantz and Zon (454, fig. 2) characterized the vegetation of Washington and Oregon between the summit of the Cascade Mountains and the Pacific Ocean as "Pacific Douglas Fir," they revealed in their text that this is not a climatically determined, dominant type of forest tree for the area. They wrote (p. 10):

This region is marked by a number of distinct forest types which also gravitate toward a western red cedar–hemlock forest. Thus on low, moderately humid slopes, from sea level to 3,000 feet, there are found large stretches of pure Douglas fir. On exactly similar areas there occur mixed stands of Douglas fir-hemlock-cedar which are a further stage in the development of the pure Douglas fir. If it were not for the periodical occurrences of fires, the pure Douglas fir stands would give way to a forest in which western red cedar and hemlock would be the principal species. . . .

The Pacific Douglas fir region includes the forests of western Oregon and Washington, and occupies 54,000 square miles. . . . The climate is generally mild and uniform, with frequent fogs and gradual and moderate changes in temperature.

The Pacific Northwest is one of America's forest regions par excellence. As of 1949, in Douglas fir forests of Washington and Oregon "stands one-third of the saw timber remaining in the United States" (579, p. 326). It was just such forests that John D. Guthrie (224), inspector, U.S. Forest Service, wished to protect by means of education aided by his pamphlet *Great Forest Fires of America*, published in 1936. In his enthusiasm to stop forest fires he was somewhat careless with facts; or perhaps he did not know that Indians intentionally set fire to fields and forests and that they, furthermore, had little concern with putting out campfires. The evidence presented so far in this paper indicates that Guthrie was clearly exaggerating when he wrote (224, p. 3):

> When Europeans first landed on these shores there were surely enough "forests to burn" and the white man began at once to burn them. It has long been the practice to lay the blame for forest fires of early days to the Indians, to prate, with little or no foundation in fact or records that the Indians willfully burned the forests off regularly. If the American Indian did all the forest burning he is credited with there would have been few forests left in America when the first settlers landed.

There were of course many districts of the climatic woodland region of the eastern and midwestern United States where there were "few forests left" or virtually none, as on the plains and prairies. But whether forests existed at the time of exploration appears to have been less a matter of presence or absence of fires and more a function of the response of the vegetation to fires. Again we learn from the history of the pine forests of the southeastern states that their existence depended upon fire. Universal burning practiced by the southeastern Indians has been continued to the present. The species of trees and the climate are not the same in the Pacific Northwest and the Atlantic Southeast, so that the forests are not the same. There can be little doubt, however, that the forests of both regions were primarily fire forests. And it is, furthermore, clear that fires set by Indians in both areas were important. The actual record of Indians setting fires to forests in both areas is not large, but the indirect evidence is overwhelming.

I suspect there are many statements about Indian uses of fire in the historical literature of the Pacific Northwest that I did not find. By the application of the culture area principle, nevertheless, it may be suspected that the references found are typical of the whole Douglas fir forest area. In the journals of A. Henry and D. Thompson (240), covering the years 1799–1814, the earliest statement found refers to the area of the lower Columbia, near Deer Island, Oregon (February 6, 1814): "Fire seems to have passed through the lower prairie last fall, and the green grass is already sprouted about four inches."

David Douglas (140) traveled in Oregon in the 1820s and reported that the Indians along the Columbia, near the site of Portland, set fire to "open places in the woods" to facilitate growth of tobacco. From Oregon City south through the Willamette Valley, Douglas saw many burned-over tracts that the settlers said had been set on fire by Indians.

In 1934 Boas (51) said that the Kwakiutl appeared to have burned woods often, and Lowie (338, p. 290) in 1938 gave additional details as follows:

> The attempt of man to control the wild growing food supply does not necessarily begin with actual sowing and planting. We find a number of cases in which man endeavors to make the conditions of growth more favorable. Thus all along the North Pacific coast of America woods are burned to improve the conditions of growth of berry-bearing bushes. On Vancouver Island this process is regulated in such a way that every social group claims the right to those berry patches which are burned over every third year and used in turn for picking berries.

Near the southern end of the Douglas fir zone, in southwestern Oregon, the Tolowa Indians and their neighbors reported to Drucker (144) that they used fire. In 1937 Drucker wrote (p. 233): "Informants maintain that nearby hills were kept clear of brush by annual burning; this also improved the grass, so that deer frequented such clearings and could be shot easily."

As part of the *Culture Element Distribution* survey, Barnett (25) questioned eight informants of Oregon coast tribes concerning the practice of brush burning to drive game. Only two remembered that their ancestors had such a custom. Five of the eight informants gave positive replies to the question about burning brush to stimulate growth of tobacco. Three informants from the Puget Sound area denied any knowledge of both practices when questioned by Gunther (222).

The direct ethnographic and historical data I have found regarding use of fire by indigenous people to influence the vegetation of the Pacific Northwest are not abundant, but they are sufficient to indicate that the Indians played a role in the formation of the fire forest that covers the Northwest. It may have been an equal role with lightning, as Isaac (271) seemed to imply in 1940 when he wrote of western Oregon and Washington: "This growing,

ever changing condition existed because the region had always been subjected to forest fire (set by lightning or by Indians). Fire therefore, always
has played an important part in the plant succession of this region."

Without mentioning Indians, Ingram (269) in 1928 reported that intentional burning of woods was an ancient practice in the Northwest. He
wrote (p. 998) that "large areas have been burned over for the purpose of
creating pasture; this still continues to some extent. . . .[There is] among
older residents . . . [the] belief that this practice was and still is justified."

Even the Yearbook of Agriculture for 1949 (579), entitled *Trees*, in its
article regarding the Douglas fir region appears to refute the statement
made by Guthrie (224) and published by the same federal government
department in 1936. About the Willamette National Forest we read (579,
p. 327):

> Fires here were endemic—a recurring phenomenon. Since the beginning of
> time, lightning had struck the high ridges and fires had burned unchecked
> until autumn rains put them out. In wet years, the fires were small. In dry
> years, the fires were catastrophic. In the high country, when fires did not
> occur naturally, the Indians set their own fires once in a while in the belief
> that old burns made the best grounds for hunting and huckleberry picking.
> Even the early miners and settlers considered it proper to touch off a few
> thousand acres of forest land if they thought any personal advantage
> would accrue.

Why say Indians fired only the high country? That hunting is best on
old burns is a well-attested fact. In 1912, according to the article above,
Plummer estimated that "10 percent of the area was covered by new burns
and that probably 90 percent of the entire [Willamette National Forest] at
some remote period had suffered from fires, of which traces still remained."

Hofmann (251), Munger (379), and Griggs (221) are three other writers
who have emphasized the importance of fire in the Northwest. The first
two demonstrated that without fire the Douglas fir area would be covered
by cedar and hemlock. Griggs studied the distribution of vegetation on
Mt. Rainier and concluded (p. 549): "In many places, timberline has been
injured by fire. . . . Many apparently anomalous features of timberline are
explained when evidence of an old fire is brought to light. . . . One suspects
that the abundant invasion of open ground by young trees in other parks
is a similar recovery from older fires, evidence of which is not so easily
detected."

Western mountains, more than other areas of America, receive lightning that causes forest fires, and the Pacific Northwest includes the Coast
Range and the western slopes of the Cascade Mountains of Washington

and Oregon. The region that Plummer (399, p. 20) designated as "A" corresponds closely with the Douglas fir forest area under consideration. In the national forests of this area, higher and more susceptible to lightning-caused fires than the rest of the region, 795 trees struck by lightning were counted during a three-year period. If the usual 2 percent of trees struck resulted in fires, that would be about 160 fires for three years or 53 lightning fires a year in the most susceptible section. In 1948, Morris (372, p. 1) made the following generalization: "In Oregon and Washington lightning causes 25 percent of the fires on state and private lands and 70 percent of those on national forests where more rugged topography favors lightning-storm development. Although many of these fires occur with rain and are quickly seen and easily suppressed, others cause great damage by smoldering unseen until dry, windy weather suddenly fans them to life in bad fuel types."

Bigelow (42) reported in 1949 that there had been an average of between 100 and 150 lightning-caused fires in Klamath National Forest from 1910 to 1930. Thus it is difficult to determine the relative importance of Indian-set forest fires in comparison with lightning-caused fires in an area where lightning is a frequent cause but varies from one part of the region to another. It is, however, hard to imagine that lightning could have caused the fires that burned over the full 555,000 square miles of the Northwest on which Douglas fir is dominant because of fire. That lightning has been a relatively minor factor is suggested by the fact that the zones where most of the lightning fires occur are a small part of the total area. Plummer's (399, p. 19) map of a portion of Santiam National Forest (now included in Willamette National Forest) in Oregon indicates that lightning zones cover less than one-tenth of the total area of about 200 square miles. Lightning repeatedly causes fires on those same spots. The concentration of lightning-struck trees is given by Plummer (399, p. 26) for a place in Arizona. A ranger reported: "I counted 100 trees on a small area close to Redrock that were struck within the last three or four years. Twenty trees were struck during one afternoon on 20 acres southeast of Redrock. Three spike tops almost dead, were struck one afternoon and all set on fire."

Since lightning-caused fires are so highly concentrated, the statistics on the relative numbers of fires started by lightning are meaningless by themselves. For example, the USDA 1949 Yearbook (579) reports on page 25 that "[i]n the Northwest, about half the fires start with lightning." However, on page 26, in answer to the question "Why are man-caused fires usually worse than lightning fires?" there is the following answer: "Lightning usually strikes on the tops of ridges and starts a small fire, which spreads slowly, especially if the lightning storm is accompanied by rain."

One other analysis indicates that lightning could not have been responsible for nearly all of the burning required to maintain the northwestern Douglas fir forest. The data came from Plummer (400) and Guthrie (224, 224a). First, remember that the northwestern Douglas fir area is about 55,000 square miles or 35,000,000 acres in extent. The Douglas fir area of Washington and Oregon constitutes about three-fourths of the total forest area of those two states, as I should judge from an inspection of the vegetation map of Shantz and Zon (454, fig. 2). Plummer (400, pp. 34–37) recorded the total area burned from the time of earliest records through 1911.

For Oregon, from 1846 to 1911 the total was 2,200,000 acres. For Washington, from 1868 to 1911 the total was 1,400,000 acres. If we say there were 4 million acres burned, the Douglas fir section could be allotted 3 million acres burned over in a half-century. If the ratio is correct there would be about 6 million acres of Douglas fir area to be burned over. Could lightning fire cause such conflagrations?

Lightning appears inadequate to account for the Douglas fir forest for several reasons. The first is the location of the great historic fires of the Northwest. The five great historic fires in Plummer's tabulation, accounting for half the area listed as burned for the states for the half-century, were all in the low Coast Range and valleys, not in the lightning zone of the higher elevations. As with the very destructive Tillamook fire of 1933, which burned over 267,000 acres of low-elevation Douglas fir, wherever the causes of these great fires were ascertained they were discovered to have been made by man.

Another reason for believing that the Indians of the Northwest set many fires is the age of the Douglas fir forest. Although some trees in humid valleys and canyons are nearly a thousand years old (579, p. 327), most of the Douglas fir forests are considered mature between one hundred and two hundred years old. As with the great historic fires, most of the burning in prehistoric times occurred during droughts such as that in 1910, when vast areas of Washington and Oregon were burned over and the great Idaho fire occurred. These were man-made fires. None of the great fires of the Northwest occurred during years of normal temperature and moisture.

From the evaluation of the available data for the Northwest, the conclusion that the Indian practice of setting fires to fields and forests was a necessary factor in the formation and maintenance of the Douglas fir forest appears fully supported. This conclusion rests primarily on the history deduced from the trees themselves but has some support from ethnographic references. Since burning provided improved grazing lands for the game they hunted and provided increased supplies of berries, the burning was fully justified from the point of view of the Indians.

CALIFORNIA

Although a great number of articles and several monographs have been written about the role of fire in the history of natural vegetation in California, much remains to be said. The central theme in the works of Show and Kotok (461) in 1923, Fritz (188) in 1932, A. W. Sampson (429) in 1944, Adams, Ewing, and Huberty (2) in 1947, Shantz (453a) in 1947, and Biswell, Taber, Hedrick, and Schultz (48a) in 1952, monographs of considerable length, has concerned the effect of fire. However, the absence of data on the extent of burning fields and forests in California by Indians is a serious deficiency in these otherwise major contributions. Of these, only Sampson's (429) brief summary "Burning by Indians in California" (pp. 18–20) refers to indigenous practices.

Sampson's inadequate evaluation is due in part, I believe, to the failure of ethnologists to properly document the full extent of Indian incendiarism and in part to Sampson's apparent desire to minimize burning by Indians as a factor in the plant ecology of California. The weighting of evidence and his choice of words in commenting on the evidence suggest that Sampson wished to refute the idea that Indians burned over extensive areas of California. He wrote:

> According to some advocates of broadcast burning, the Indians of California burned vegetation so frequently and extensively before white men settled in the region that the brush was kept down, and the timber and woodland kept open. Others claim that most of the fires were accidental, and not purposely set. Since the assertions of widespread burning by the Indians have not hitherto been studied closely, this phase of the present investigation was undertaken in an attempt to bring together the most reliable documentary evidence on the following questions: Why, where, how extensively, and under what conditions did the Indians burn grassland, chaparral, and forest? Answers to these questions are summarized here, according to the most reliable documentary evidence available.

After defining "broadcast burning" and "controlled burning," Sampson continued:

> Critical review of the mass of documents published from 1542 to about 1853 leads to the conclusion that California Indians burned vegetation, limitedly at least, to facilitate hunting, to secure native plant foods, and to clear small areas of woody vegetation for the growing of tobacco. But these documents indicate that the fires were seldom extensive. Kroeber, Barrett, and Barrett and Gifford incline to the belief that burning by Indians was

somewhat general in California, but that by far the most extensive and destructive fires have occurred since the coming of the white man. An indication that Indians probably did not burn extensively is suggested by the fact that only a small proportion of the more than five hundred narratives examined even mentioned fires in grassland, brushland, or forest.

Some Indians, notably those of the central Sierra Nevada, are reported to have cleared the underbrush with fire to facilitate travel, hunting, and planting. Gordon-Cumming, for example, stated in 1883 that the Indians in the Yosemite Valley burned some areas so frequently as to keep down the woody undergrowth. The Miwok Tribe, which inhabited the eastern edge of the grassland, and whose territory extended through the brush and into the lower part of the tree zone, burned grassland somewhat frequently, according to Barrett and Gifford. These Indians probably did little to prevent the spread of fire to the trees, and some of the fire-scarred older trees may have come about from such grass burning. Drucker, however, concluded that in Riverside, Orange, and San Diego counties the Indians did not set fire to the brush or trees. Nothing was found in the literature to refute this.

A few chroniclers reported Indian burning as locally destructive. Thus Costanso, who was on the Portola expedition to San Francisco Bay in 1769–1770, reported that at one point near the present Palo Alto, the progress of the expedition was halted because of the absence of pasture where the natives had burned. Palou, with the same expedition, reported several burns along the coast. Of one place in Monterey County, he stated that the soil is whitish and short of pasture on account of fires set by the heathen.

In a critical review of this manuscript, however, the late Dr. C. Hart Merriam, who devoted much of his life to the study of California Indians, stated in 1935 that he did not recall having heard of the use of fire in agriculture by the Indians except to clear the tiny spots used as seedbeds for tobacco. This conclusion is corroborated by Kroeber, who also points out that the Indians of the northwestern part of California practiced some degree of controlled burning in the preparation of seedbeds for small patches of tobacco.

The use of fires to drive rabbits, deer, and other game into the open, or into ambush, is reported by a number of writers. Before the valleys were settled by white men, the native tribes living in the grassland area burned small circular areas occasionally to collect grasshoppers and small game.

Fire was also used to some extent by the Indians as a means of obtaining plant food. Hinds and Belcher of H. M. S. Sulphur noticed in 1837 some trees and stands of small shrubs burning along the Sacramento River. They mentioned that the natives set fire to the bases of large oak trees, thereby destroying some of them while attempting to get acorns. Helper reported that the Digger Indians, when driven by extreme hunger, collected acorns by burning down oak trees the bark of which was used as a storage chamber of these fruits by birds. Kroeber reported some burning in oak groves for the purpose of clearing ground so that acorns (409) could be collected more easily. Baxley observed that Indians in Yosemite Valley burned small areas to facilitate gathering of their winter supply of acorns and wild sweet-potato roots. Gibbs reported that Indians burned grass spots along the Russian River so that aniseed might be collected with greater ease.

Kroeber concluded that the Indians burned "considerably" in both open country and forest for various reasons, but he expressed the opinion that "this burning was not indiscriminate, but tended to be limited to certain tracts in which they were interested." This worker furthermore concluded: "In general, the Indians nowhere burnt the chaparral with the idea of getting rid of it. A good stand of it is harder to get through after burning than before. If they fired the chaparral occasionally it was with the idea of driving the game out." Kroeber also affirmed that "the aggregate extent [of California lands] burned over occasionally or more or less regularly must have been considerable," but he expressed uncertainty as to whether burning in brushlands was extensive.

Various other references indicate that Indian burning of brushlands was on such a restricted scale that it could have influenced little, if at all, the present composition, or the distribution, of the chaparral over the state. This conclusion is supported by the fact that the major Indian population was along the coastal slopes and in the valleys, away from the present distribution of the chaparral lands.

Areas remote from the coastal and valley regions evidently were relatively little subject to directed or systematic burning. It is probable, therefore, that at least a fair (if not the major) proportion of the fires reported by the early explorers at the higher elevations were started by lightning, as they are today.

Review of historical documents indicates that the California Indians frequently used fire temporarily to clear various kinds of lands, including some chaparral areas, for different purposes. Since the few Indians who lived in the brush fields were apparently interested chiefly in local or "spot" burning to facilitate hunting of deer, it seems doubtful that they burned frequently or extensively enough in the chaparral association to keep much of the cover open, or that such burning resulted in either expansion or contraction of the brush cover as a whole. Evidently areas remote from the coastal and valley regions were little subject to Indian burning.

A large proportion of the fires reported by early explorers, particularly in the higher elevations, were presumably started by lightning. Accordingly, study of Indian burning in California is historically interesting, but of little application in the present-day effort of brush suppression.

Sampson's bias is beyond question. "Somewhat general burning" and "considerable" burning do not mean that "it could have influenced little, if at all, the present composition, or the distribution, of the chaparral over the state." That Sampson succeeded in giving the impression that fires set by Indians in California were unimportant is shown by the review of his monograph by Parker (390, p. 374), in the journal *Ecology*. Parker wrote: "The somewhat popular belief that prehistoric Indians carried on extensive burning either to facilitate travel or to improve their hunting grounds is discredited. Burning of brushlands in California by the Indians was undoubtedly so restricted (because of their sparse population and mode of life) as to have but little influence on the present distribution or floristic composition of chaparral."

I am not alone, however, in thinking that Sampson's review of the evidence is inadequate, as Major (352a) wrote in 1951: "We have, unfortunately, only limited data on the use of fire by American Indians."

My own compilation of sources, I believe, goes a long way toward supplying the data wished for by Major and should correct the false impression created by Sampson. My interpretation of the works cited by Sampson, plus a considerable body of evidence that he does not cite, leads to the conclusion that practically all but the most sparsely vegetated areas of California were frequently set on fire by Indians. Thus burning by Indians was extremely important. In areas outside the most arid deserts, fire was the major factor determining the type of vegetation discovered by the first Europeans on arriving in California. The following data are presented in four parts, corresponding roughly to geographic zones: Southern Coastal Range, Northern Coastal Range, Sierra Nevada, and Central Valley.

Because of the terrains involved, only the Central Valley is topographically uniform, yet this does not mean a uniform climate, according to Russell (423, 424). The other three regions have hills, mountains, canyons, and valleys so that elevation, fog, rainfall, evaporation, and temperature vary greatly and produce complex patterns of climates. The four regions nonetheless serve as convenient subdivisions of the state.

Southern Coastal Range

The earliest references come from the first Spanish explorations. Fray Crespi (122), who kept a diary while traveling with the Portola expedition from San Diego to San Francisco in 1769–70, described the territory through which they passed. After five days' march from San Diego, Crespi wrote of a place that editor and translator Bolton identifies as near the San Luis Rey River in San Diego County (p. 132): "We set out about seven in the morning, which dawned cloudy, and, taking the road straight north, we traveled by a valley about a league long, with good land, grassy, and full of alders. This passed, we ascended a little hill and entered upon some mesas covered with dry grass, in parts burned by the heathen for the purpose of hunting hares and rabbits, which live there in abundance. In some places there are clumps of wild prickly pear."

On July 24, 1769, near the site of Santa Ana, Orange County, Crespi said (p. 137): "We traveled through this valley for about two leagues; it is good land, but they had burned all the grass."

Of the San Gabriel Valley, just northeast of Los Angeles, Crespi wrote: "We then descended to a broad and spacious plain of fine black earth, with much grass, although we found it burned."

When the expedition members reached the mid Salinas Valley, between the outer and inner ridges of the Coast Range, near what is now King City, they traveled for five leagues (approximately thirteen miles) over burned-over country, of which Crespi wrote (p. 199): "We set out early in the morning, which was very cloudy, and followed the same valley and river by a level road, the grass all burned . . . [we] halted in the midst of a grove of live oaks, which had a little pasture that had not been burned."

Two days later, on September 30, 1769, Crespi recorded (p. 201) that the expedition was "short of pasture on account of fires set by the heathen." Two weeks later he wrote of the area near Santa Cruz (p. 214): ". . . near the beach, and the range of hills which follows, which has good pasture, although it has just been burned by the heathen."

The whole region was so completely burned that Crespi remarked (p. 215) that near the San Lorenzo River, at what is now Santa Cruz, "we found a good patch of ground that is not burned." Further north along the coast, however, he observed (p. 216): "We traveled . . . two leagues [over five miles], during which we descended and ascended four deep water courses carrying running water which empties into the sea. Only in the water courses are any trees to be seen; elsewhere we saw nothing but grass, and that was burned."

On October 27, 1769, of the vicinity of San Gregorio, midway between Santa Cruz and San Francisco, Crespi wrote (p. 222) that the explorers took "the road to the north over high hills all burned." The next day he made a similar entry (p. 223), noting that "we set out about ten in the morning, traveling near the beach and over low mesas of good land, although all the grass had been burned." And for October 30 he entered (p. 225): "We started about nine in a northwesterly direction along the beach, near which there are mesas and low hills with good grass although burned."

It is strange that A. W. Sampson could have examined Crespi's diary and found only the one reference to burning, which he lists as one of eight he reported for driving game by using fire. Although he quotes Costanso (114) and Palou (388), two other chroniclers of the same expedition, Sampson minimizes their contributions by the prefaced remark that "a few chroniclers reported Indian burning as locally destructive." By applying the culture area principle, Crespi alone provides enough evidence to assume that setting fire to grassy vegetation was practiced generally by Indians from San Diego to San Francisco. But there are other direct statements about burning as well.

Fray Pedro Font (179, p. 188) on January 8, 1776, wrote this of the coastal section of Orange County: "It is also called La Quema [the burning], because of a somewhat dangerous fire which occurred in the grass patches, caused in part by accident and in part by the heathen."

A proclamation (17) published at the Santa Barbara Mission, May 31, 1793, provides strong evidence that grass burning was a common practice. The report suggests that setting fires may have been so common as to cause them to be taken as a matter of course and that special instructions were needed to encourage subjects to fight the fires. The report reads, in part:

> That in virtue of repeated complaints about the losses resulting from the fires the Christian and heathen Indians set to the grazing lands every year, he has issued a proclamation of which he remits a copy. And he requests him to advise the priests to give the Indians and particularly the old women, to understand to refrain from committing such offense, severely punishing anyone who commits such.
>
> And that in case of fires the captains and their guards will help them to check them, for which purpose he communicates with the Commandants so that they may so inform them.

A report dated July 2, 1800 (415), from the San Juan Bautista Mission, inland from Monterey Bay, suggests that Indians may have used fire as a weapon: "Father . . . Pedro Martinez advises me in his letter of the 27 of the same month, about the unfortunate murders and the threats of the Ausayames, and that they have threatened to burn the Indian farmer's house. They carried out this threat by setting fire to the Pajano field and had it not been for the quick action of the captain of the guard they would have burned all the fields, for a part of a wheat field was burned."

Kotzebue (291), having visited the San Francisco Mission in 1818, wrote (vol. 3, p. 48) that the Indians "neither sow nor reap, but burn their meadows from time to time to increase their fertility." Of the vicinity of San Jose, Ryan (425, vol. 1, p. 208) wrote in 1850: ". . . we found ourselves between lofty hills, those to the right [east] being covered with wild oats, whilst on the left everything looked black and dreary, all traces of the vegetation being burned up by the Indians. . . ."

Modern ethnographic accounts add some support to the picture supplied by the early explorers and travelers. Inasmuch as the region of the Coast Range, from San Diego to San Francisco, California, was where the Indians were first Europeanized or exterminated, it is not surprising that ancient practices are forgotten. It is, nevertheless, odd that Sampson (429, p. 19) should have said that Drucker (145) reported that "in Riverside, Orange and San Diego counties Indians did not set fire to the brush or trees." In his 1934–35 study, now published as *Culture Element Distribution: V, Southern California*, Drucker said nothing concerning setting fire specifically to "brush or trees." There are, however, positive statements (p. 9) from seven informants located in the three counties, saying that chia (*Salvia*) patches were "burned over to improve" them. Two informants in the same counties remembered that fire had been used in communal game drives. Related peoples living just below the border in Lower California, as represented by two informants, said that fire drives were used for hunting rabbits and quail, as Drucker (146) recorded in his Yuman-Piman list. Spier (471, p. 337) in 1923 wrote of the Southern Diegueno of interior San Diego County as follows: ". . . for rabbit hunting . . . a group . . . surround and set fire to a patch of brush to drive the animals out, hallooing the while."

The reference cited indicates beyond any doubt that the aborigines set fire to vegetation in the Coastal Mountain region of California, south of San Francisco. The sufficiency of the above record might be questioned if that were the only evidence that Indians burned over the region. The vegetation provides further proof that can be considered; again the reports of the early Spanish travelers are vital.

The point emphasized is that Indian fires were responsible for the absence or sparseness of woody vegetation wherever climatic and geographic conditions would allow trees or shrubs to grow. It can be demonstrated that extensive regions that can support woods were maintained as grasslands by Native Californians. In addition to the eleven references cited from Crespi (122) that Indians burned the grass-covered hills and valleys, his descriptions of other treeless plains and hills are also significant. After repeatedly stating that the grassy hills and valleys of southern California had been burned, Crespi wrote as follows about the Canada del Coja north of Santa Barbara (p. 174): "This place is short of firewood, but the land is good and has much grass"; and of the vicinity of San Luis Obispo (p. 186): ". . . we set out to the northwest over mesas of good land covered with grass and well supplied with water but without trees."

After drawing attention to the forests on the high mountain on their trail between San Luis Obispo and the Salinas River, Crespi again described the burned areas and the unburned grass of the entire Salinas Valley, from the site of King City north to Monterey Bay. The account was the same for the section traveled up the coast from Monterey Bay to Half Moon Bay. Forests were found in the canyons and observed on the tops of some of the mountains; but of the site of San Francisco, Crespi recorded (p. 228):

> [We] pitched camp in the middle of a small valley, some six hundred varas long and about a hundred wide, which has plenty of water in two small arroyos which unite to enter the sea. The valley has a great deal of reed grass and many blackberries and roses, there are a few trees in the beds of the arroyos, and some moderate sized willows, but on the hills there was not a single tree to be seen except some on a mountain range which encircles this bay.

As quoted earlier, Sampson (429) cited Costanso (114) of the same expedition to the effect that burned pasture halted the expedition near Palo Alto. Crespi also noted (p. 234) a scarcity of pasture from Palo Alto to San Francisco.

Fray Font (179), diarist for the Anza expedition of 1775–76, did not record as many instances of seeing burned areas as did Crespi (122), possibly because he traveled in winter and early summer before the grass was completely dry. He did, however, make numerous observations concerning the landscape, which confirm the impression given by Crespi of the almost total absence of woody growth on the hills and valleys of coastal southern California. Regarding the country from the present site of Riverside to that of Los Angeles, Font said (pp. 169–71):

> The Santa Ana River is a stream with plentiful water. Some cottonwoods grow upon its banks, but they are the only trees in all these plains, for only in the Sierra Nevada are some pines seen. . . .
>
> The road is all very level except on leaving the Santa Ana River, where we crossed some long and low hills which, like all the rest on the way, were covered with good pasturage, both dry and green—a country very well suited for sheep and goats because it is very clean, without anything which might injure the wool.

On the trip from San Gabriel Mission (now in greater Los Angeles) to San Diego in January 1776, Font complained several times of the cold nights because of the absence of wood for fire. Near Capistrano he recorded (179, p. 190): "During the night we were very cold for want of firewood, which is the thing most lacked in all these lands and hills." And again (p. 191): "Afterward the road enters hills covered with a scrubby growth composed of rosemary, small live oaks, cactus and similar growths. . . . The road is broken, the same as yesterday, all hills and valleys, ups and downs, without trees and lacking in firewood; but the country is green like the rest, with a great deal of grass." Of San Diego, Font wrote (p. 194): "On the land is plenty of grass, although not so good or so abundant as in other places; and the site is very short of firewood and very much shorter of timber."

Dana (124b) in 1840 also complained of scarcity of wood, yet his description suggests there was more in the vicinity than seen by Font sixty years earlier. Dana said (p. 177):

> Wood is very scarce in the vicinity of San Diego, there being no trees of any size for miles. In the town, the inhabitants burn the small wood which grows in thickets. . . . With us, the getting of wood was a great trouble; for all that in the vicinity of the houses had been cut down, and we were obliged to go off a mile or two, and to carry it some distance on our backs. . . . These trees are seldom more than five or six feet high, and the highest that I ever saw on these expeditions could not have been more than twelve, so that with lopping off the branches and clearing away the underwood, we had a good deal of cutting to do for a very little wood.

The comparison of the vegetation picture of the early Spanish settlers in San Diego with that of Dana suggests that a half-century of grazing and suppression of fire had allowed the chaparral to invade the grasslands of that region. Font (179) also described the landscape of the central Coast Range, especially that from Monterey to San Francisco. He spoke of the country between Monterey and Salinas as follows (p. 318): "All the road is very level, through pasture covered lands for the most part, but without trees except the cotton woods on the banks of the river." Concerning the trail along the hill near Gilroy Valley, Font wrote (p. 320): "During the whole distance there are few trees, but in the sierra many spruce and other trees are seen." Santa Clara Valley was described as an oak plain, with scattered trees surrounded by abundant grass. Font said of the vicinity of San Jose (p. 327): "We continued through a very beautiful plain full of oaks, which we saw all the way yesterday and today, and which are likewise seen at a distance."

Font accompanied Anza on his exploration of the hills east of San Francisco Bay and repeatedly mentioned the extensive grasslands and the scarcity of wood, except along streams. The question at issue is whether the grasslands observed by the early Spaniards were the results of climatic and geographic conditions or whether the burning-over done by Indians was an essential factor in their formation and survival. The final conclusion is complicated by three circumstances. The first is the large proportion of the area that is still subjected to fire. The second is the amount of the territory now under cultivation. The third is overgrazing. Notwithstanding these new elements, the data appear to leave little doubt that the Spanish would have found nearly all of the grassland areas of the region of the Coast Range, south of San Francisco, covered with either woodland or forest if the Indians had not regularly and frequently set the whole area afire. This study presents abundant proof that Indian fires could reduce forest and brush areas to grassy plains and prairies. That was recognized by A. W. Sampson (428, p. 429) in 1911, when he wrote:

> Historically considered, the Indians took the initiative in manipulating forest fires. It is well known that the Indians, before the advent of the white men, set fires on grass and wood lands. Their object in doing this was apparently to bring about a fresh growth of grass in the autumn upon which numerous game animals and wild fowl would accumulate and thus make it possible for them to secure their supply of meat, and also for the purpose of killing and roasting for food the great quantities of grasshoppers that nearly every season fed on the tender growth of grass. The aborigines in various parts of the West are recorded to have kept vast tracts of forest lands denuded of timber for a similar purpose. Upon the cessation of these fires, through the Government, timber of remarkable uniformity and symmetry has encroached upon these areas through natural seeding without the aid of the forester.

Clements (101, p. 21) in 1920 paid tribute to the earlier work of Griffiths and quoted with evident approval the following: "Brush and timber are encroaching upon the grasslands, due, it is believed, to protection from fires." On page 190, Clements (101) explained the effect of overgrazing as follows: "The size and continuity and the height of the shrubs reflect the water relations. . . . This relation is naturally disturbed or obscured by fires and grazing, though it is not hidden by them. Repeated fires confine or destroy the shrubs, while grazing reduces the water requirements of the grasses and correspondingly increases the growth and spread of chaparral." That chaparral has increased in the San Diego area is suggested by Clements's statement on page 192: "Practically the same grouping [of species] occurs through the Laguna and Cuyamaca Mountains to the coast about San Diego."

Although it is common knowledge that many areas of south and central
California are now brush covered, careful documentation is not found for
the whole region. I have observed great brushy sections along the road
from Salinas to Monterey, for example, which were described as treeless
pastures by the Spaniards. And I know from experience that brush would
invade the Berkeley hills if they were not annually burned off. Nevertheless, more explicit documentation is desirable. Brandegee (57, p. 119) in 1891
wrote as follows regarding the continuation of burning in the general area
under consideration:

> The Coast Range of California, south from San Francisco, excepting the
> redwood forests and occasional groups of other conifers, is not distinc-
> tively a forest region, but its hills and mountains are covered by a thick,
> almost impenetrable growth of *Adenostoma fasciculata*, commonly called
> "greasewood" or "chamis," manzanita, Garrya, oak, *Ceanothus* (California
> lilac), etc., which seems to be periodically destroyed by fire. Indeed, it is
> almost impossible to find a hill or mountain covered with bushes, even of
> great age, where some old charred ends of roots may not be seen, showing
> that at some previous time they had suffered from fire.

The vegetation maps of California are not entirely satisfactory for our
purpose because they vary greatly in details. Shantz and Zon (454, fig. 2),
from whom I have copied, show "Bunch Grass" covering large areas of Los
Angeles, Ventura, and Santa Barbara Counties, which are indicated as "Brush
and Woodlands" on the much larger-scale map of the Gianini Foundation
(198). Both differ somewhat from the maps of distribution of chaparral
published by A. W. Sampson (429) and Shantz (453). A different type map,
which would appear to support my thesis, accompanies the exhaustive and
very widely quoted study by W. S. Cooper (112) published in 1922, entitled
The Broad-Sclerophyll Vegetation of California. His plate 1, showing species-
density of broad-sclerophylls, indicates that the Coast Range has the area
of greatest concentration with the San Francisco Bay section and that a
tract from the coast near Ventura across Los Angeles County has the greatest density. Cooper's map implies that all the southern Coast Range is
chaparral country. To justify placing the hills and valleys of the Coast
Range completely in the chaparral zone, Cooper said (p. 26): "I believe
that there are certain extensive areas now inhabited by grasses and by
half-shrubs that climatically and potentially are chaparral regions."

Cooper then listed forty-two plants of importance in the chaparral and
went on to say: "With so large a list of species there is naturally great diversity in the composition of the association. Anyone given to splitting of hairs
would easily separate many communities of lower rank. This is in part due

to slight habitat differences, but also in an important degree to the great number of species with restricted range and to the frequent occurrence of fires. . . ."

Cooper (p. 76) later expressed a conviction that southern California is a true climatic chaparral area and said:

> The foothills and low mountains of southern California are the most certain. . . . In these places *Adenostoma* is usually the dominant species, or if cultivation has largely destroyed the native vegetation, remnants show it to have been so at former time. Such is the case in portions of the Los Angeles and San Bernardino Valleys and on the broad mesas east of San Diego. As we ascend the higher mountain ranges of southern California, the evidences of climactic character in chaparral become less and less convincing.

The strongest support for the view that Indian burning was the factor determining the types of plant cover observed by the first Europeans in California is found in Cooper's discussion of Santa Clara Valley (pp. 78–81). One should recall that both Crespi (122) and Costanso (114) of the 1769 Portola expedition and Font (179) of the 1776 Anza expedition were explicit about the open grassy nature of Santa Clara Valley. Also, one should remember that Ryan (425), who visited it in 1848, described it as very open grassland. Of this same area Cooper wrote:

> For example, the floor of the Santa Clara Valley southeast of Palo Alto, which is today one of the great orchard regions of the State, was less than half a century ago solid chaparral. The bare grassy hills nearby, with their thin growth of oaks, were similar. . . .
>
> Mr. G. F. Beardsley, a retired mining engineer . . . spent several years of his boyhood in this vicinity and is able to recall with considerable accuracy the general character of the vegetation at the time. About 1870, according to Mr. Beardsley, the present orchard land between Palo Alto and San Jose was solid chaparral, and patches of the scrub occurred on the floor of the valley between San Jose and Gilroy. . . . Those cleared areas which are not under cultivation are today typical California grassland, sometimes with young oaks scattered through them. . . .
>
> It remains to account for the absence of the chaparral in those areas of grassland, where it is hypothetically the climax. . . . Clearing for firewood has been locally effective; clearing for cultivation much more so. By far the most important cause of destruction has been fire. It has been stated that fire favors the extension of the chaparral. A single burning of chaparral will result merely in a crop of stump sprouts and greater density than

before, but yearly burning will inevitably destroy the brush completely or prevent invasion by it. Cattlemen and sheepmen in the early days, according to unpublished Forest Service reports, were accustomed to fire the brush annually in the foothills to destroy it and thereby improve the grazing conditions. This resulted in a great increase of grassland at the expense of the chaparral. Such recent events, however, are of small importance compared with the effects produced by the aboriginal population. . . .

It is certain, therefore, that extensive areas which are now dominated by grasses or thin forest of xerophytic trees were formerly controlled by chaparral or would come to support chaparral if destructive agencies were eliminated; and the principal causes of the destruction of the chaparral or prevention of its establishment have been clearing or repeated fires.

Comparing the vegetational picture of the Santa Clara Valley of Cooper and that of the early travelers, the conclusion must be drawn that the burning of the valley by Indians was abruptly reduced by settlement following the Gold Rush of 1849. As happened with the Shenandoah Valley of Virginia, as reported in the first section of this work, Santa Clara Valley must have rapidly changed between 1848 and 1870, so that the grassland changed into a chaparral thicket and had to be cleared again to make way for orchards. A knowledge of the vegetation changes that occurred in the Shenandoah Valley helps one to understand those of Santa Clara Valley, although the two are separated by the continent.

Bauer (30), who published the results of his study of the "Vegetation of the Tehachapi Mountains, California" in 1930, explicitly agrees with Cooper's views concerning the importance of fire. He stated his conviction that neither grassland nor chaparral, both widespread on the Tehachapis, was climax for the region. Both resulted from the Indian practice of burning over the area, a practice continued to the present by ranchers. In 1932 Storer (498, p. 317) expressed a similar opinion, as follows: "The restriction of burning in forests, and especially in chaparral areas, is leading in some instances to replacement of grassland by chaparral and possibly also leading to alteration of soil mineral relations."

A. W. Sampson (429) summarized his attitude as follows (p. 129):

Contrary to the claims of some persons, burning of brushlands by the Indians evidently was restricted both because of their sparse population in chaparral regions, and because of their mode of life. Fire, when used, was primarily to facilitate hunting and to aid in gathering food plants. Burning for such purposes apparently was not extensive enough measurably to enlarge or to decrease the present chaparral areas, or to keep extensive stands open by repeated burning.

Yet in spite of such views Sampson collected conclusive evidence that repeated burning could convert chaparral into grassland and if continued could maintain the dominance of grass over brush. The relative effectiveness of fire to clear chaparral depended upon the site and the plant species. He said, for example (p. 119): "Heavy broadcast burning, although entailing fire risk, is the least expensive in temporarily opening up dense stands of sprouting forms of brush; but the benefits derived seldom exceeded a duration of about three or four years. . . . On nonsprouting brush areas a two-year burning plan . . . is usually effective in converting the brush cover to grassland."

Inasmuch as extensive areas like Los Angeles and Santa Clara Valleys, to cite only two of many, were kept clean of chaparral by Indians, the Indians did exert a great influence on California vegetation. They appear to have discovered the same practices for the control of chaparral that Sampson found during a fifteen-year research project (429, p. 4).

Sampson's views have been presented and discussed at some length in connection with the southern Coast Range, primarily because he was so clearly wrong regarding Indian use of fire in that region, although he considered all the chaparral areas of the state and did most of his research in the northern Coast Range. The arguments appear to be valid for both areas; consequently, I will not repeat the analysis but will allow the record to speak for itself.

Northern Coastal Range

The complexity of the geography and climate of the region of the northern California Coast Range has been recognized by many. Clark (98, p. 10) summarized some expressions regarding that complexity in saying that "these ranges form a broad strip of rugged mountain terrain whose climatic, vegetational, and faunal features are exceedingly diversified and extremely difficult to interpret."

Harshberger (1911 [234a, p. 271]), in speaking of the coast mountains of California, says that "nowhere in the range is there greater variety than in the area comprised within Mendocino and Lake counties." He comments on the irregularity of the temperature and states that the rainfall is "even more capricious than the temperature."

Clark described in detail four climates and then numerous ecotones, associations, and subtypes of the grassland, chaparral, woodland, and forest formations. The difficulty encountered in understanding and describing the tremendous variety of vegetation and its complex, spotty distribution is in part due to the very slight attention given to the effects of fire in ecological studies on this region. In a master's thesis that appears to weigh and evaluate carefully all ecological factors bearing upon each of the reasons for different types of vegetation being where they were, Clark dismissed an ecological consideration of fire with this statement: "*Changes in vegetable cover.*—Fires and cutting have produced, and are producing, profound changes in the vegetable cover. The general effect is to cause the forest to be replaced by woodland and chaparral, and chaparral by grassland, at least temporarily."

There is considerable direct evidence that the Indians of the northern Coast Range set fire to the vegetation regularly and widely. Again, Spanish sources provide the earliest references. The fact that an agreement not to burn the fields was written into a treaty with the "Guapo" (Wappo) Indians, who occupied some of the interior valleys just north of San Francisco Bay, suggests that the practice had been general. Vallejo's (516) treaty of 1836 with the Wappo was "said to have been typical of those made with other Indians." Article 4 reads: "The fields shall not be burned in time of drought on any pretext whatever, but if this is done by other tribes the contracting parties shall not be held responsible, but they shall do all in their power to prevent it."

In a report of a trip through the county to the west of the Wappo at Christmas time in 1850, Marryat (354, p. 135) wrote as follows concerning Sonoma County:

> The rainy season was now approaching, and the heat became occasionally intense. At times the Indians would fire the surrounding plains, the long oat-straw of which would ignite for miles. The flames would advance with great rapidity, leaving everything behind them black and charred. At these times dense smoke would hang over the atmosphere for two or three days, increasing the heat until it became insupportable.
>
> The Digger Indians burn the grass to enable them to get at roots and wasps' nests; young wasps being a luxury with them. These fires have the good effect of destroying immense quantities of snakes and vermin; and one can scarcely imagine the extent to which these might multiply were they not occasionally "burnt out."

That fires have continued to be a recurring phenomenon in the Coast Range is common knowledge. That burning may have been responsible for the region just north of Golden Gate being designated grassland on the most widely quoted map of California, *Natural Cover and Agricultural Land Use* (198), is suggested by this statement published in 1891 by Brandegee (57):

> This year, on Mt. Tamalpais, near San Francisco, an extensive fire destroyed again the vegetation of part of the mountain slope, from which

everything green had been burned several years ago, and today, in the burned district, not a single bush or plant can be found, excepting along the edge of the wagon road; in the damp gulches and on the northern slopes. Last year similar fire swept through the vegetation upon that part of the mountain known as Bolinas Ridge, destroying everything green, leaving the ground black and with only upright remnants of charred manzanita and oak to show where the larger bushes had grown. This year, during the early part of the season, this ground was green with a rank annual vegetation, composed mostly of species common in the neighborhood of San Francisco, all growing much larger and ranker than usual. The perennial plants and bushes are reappearing, and in a few years, doubtless, the mountain side will be clothed with its former vegetation, and the annuals now so abundant will be found only along trails and in openings under the shade of bushes.

It is interesting to note how differently Marin County, in which Mt. Tamalpais is a dominant feature, is classified on various vegetation maps. Livingston and Shreve (327, pl. 1) in 1921 and Crawford and Hurd for the Gianini Foundation (198, pl. 1) in 1934 designated the area "Pacific Semi-Desert" and "Grass," in both cases bracketing it with the Sacramento Valley. Shantz and Zon (454, fig. 1) in 1924 placed Marin County in their "Yellow Pine–Sugar Pine" zone. Cooper (112, pl. 1) in 1922 placed it completely in chaparral, with much of the county and Mt. Tamalpais covered with the symbol for extreme species-density of broad-sclerophylls. A. W. Sampson (429, fig. 4, p. 12) in 1944 and Shantz (453a, cover) in 1947 covered different areas of the county with their symbols for chaparral. The above indicates that authorities are not in agreement as to whether the region is by nature an area of grassland, chaparral, or forest. The difficulty is compounded by aboriginal and historic burning over much of the county.

The vegetational picture of coastal northern California is further complicated by the forests of tremendous redwood trees that are scattered throughout the region. Since redwoods in the area are known to have attained over 1,000 years of age, it is significant that one of our very early records mentions Indian burning of redwood forests. Massey (356, p. 63) wrote the following in his journal in 1848:

Here were pines [redwoods] growing one hundred meters high that measured twelve to fifteen meters in diameter [*sic*, surely circumference] and capable of making planks six meters or more wide. Many of them were hollow and could easily shelter six or seven persons for the night. Others were half-burned, maybe by lightning, by the Indians, or by some careless trapper.

The Indians, particularly in the spring and autumn, set the stubble in the pastures on fire to destroy the insects and reptiles, and to make hunting easier.

In 1851 Gibbs (199) traveled the length of the northern California Coast Range and recorded many details regarding the types and distributions of vegetation. A. W. Sampson (429) mentioned that Gibbs said Indians burned grass "spots . . . for the purpose of collecting aniseed." Sampson did not mention that the "spots" burned extended for four miles near the site of Willits, in Pomo Indian territory. Gibbs's journal contains much more direct and indirect evidence of Indian burning in the region under consideration. For example, the day after seeing the burned-off Willits valley, he wrote as follows concerning Long Valley, in Yuki territory (p. 118):

> It is apparently twelve or fifteen miles in length, by four or five wide, the general course conforming to the bend of the Coast range, being from south-east to north-west. That part lying on the easterly side of the stream consisted entirely of open prairie, fertile and producing an abundance of fine grass, while the westerly side is mostly wooded. The timber, as on the hills around, was of mixed oak and fir. A few Indians visited us, and were directed to call in the adjacent tribes.

Did the climate and soil differ so markedly on the two sides of the stream? A couple of days later, Gibbs reported traveling down a ridge "covered with chemisal and other shrubs, and exceedingly rough," but wrote this about their evening camp (p. 121): "Water was in sufficient quantity near camp, but the grass was poor, and we were compelled to tie up the animals, as well to prevent their straying, as from fear of Indians. The frequent occurrence of showers in those mountains during the summer months, seems probable, as we found new grass sprouting where it had been burnt over."

Of what was probably Mattole Indian territory on the lower South Fork of the Eel River, Gibbs wrote (p. 123): "The last part of our march let us into a thick redwood forest, upon a mountain, through which we were obliged to cut our trail, the ground being covered with underbrush and fallen timber. A fatiguing climb and an excessively bad descent brought us again to the South Fork. On the other side was a small prairie of about eighty acres, from which, however, the grass was mostly burnt, a bare sufficiency only remaining."

That this prairie in the midst of a forest owed its existence to repeated broadcast burning is suggested by the following from Gibbs concerning the same vicinity (p. 124):

Our camp was a very pretty one, the little prairie being level and rich, and encircled by a magnificent redwood forest. One tree near the tents I measured, and found it to be fifty-two feet in circumference, at four or five feet from the ground, and this although the bark and a portion of the wood were burned away. It was still erect and alive at the top, notwithstanding the interior had been hollowed out to the height of probably eighty feet, and the smoke was even yet escaping from a hole in the side. The diameter, measured through a chasm at the bottom, was eighteen feet. Another, likewise much burnt, measured forty-nine feet in circumference, at five feet from the ground.

Gibbs reached the coast in the territory of the "Weeyat" Indians, of whom he wrote (p. 127): "Their food consists principally of fish, eels, shellfish, and various seeds, which, like those in the southern valleys, they collect after burning the grass."

After returning inland to the Trinity River drainage into what was probably Chilula Indian territory, Gibbs wrote some generalizations regarding the whole north end of the Coast Range in California (p. 133):

Leaving the river, we ascended a long spur of mountain to the top of the dividing ridge between it and Redwood creek, through alternate forest and prairie land. The character of the mountains, from this to the Klamath, differs widely from those we have before passed over. Their summits are broader, and the declivities less steep and broken. Prairies of rich grass lie on their southern slopes, and especially on their tops, from whence their name of Bald Hills is derived. This grass was now yellow with ripeness, and the wind, sweeping over its long slender stems, gave it a beautiful appearance. The Indians used the stalks in their finer basket work; and, when split, in the braids with which they tie up their hair and other ornamental fabrics. The timber here becomes much more open, and fir, white and yellow, predominates over the redwood. This last is now chiefly confined to the immediate neighborhood of the coast. Springs of good water occur near almost all these prairies, and camps are therefore selected on their skirts. Late in the season, however, the grass is often burned, and dependence cannot always be placed upon the usual grounds.

Although over a half-century later than the account of Crespi (122), Gibbs's document is comparable because in 1851 northern California was virtually unexplored.

The famous California botanist W. L. Jepson (273) may best be quoted here, for he claimed (273, p. 80) to have gathered evidence "from members of the Nyah, Hupa, Pomo and other tribes; also from verbal relations of early Californians" upon which to base his statement regarding periodic burning by Indians. Thus, although his generalization encompassed other areas and he emphasized specifically "annual fires" on the South Coast Range, it is appropriate here because the Hupas and Pomos are from the North Coast Range. In 1910 Jepson published the following statement in his book *The Silva of California* (pp. 11–12):

> Clays do not crack so much in the dry season as adobe, and loams still lesser but the drying out of the soil accounts in part for the absence of trees on these soils, as also scanty rainfall or intermittent dry years, the effects of hot north winds at critical periods, or the attacks of browsing animals. All of the above reasons are not, however, sufficient to account for complete absence of trees over wide areas, especially on the alluvial soils where the conditions are as perfect for the maintenance of trees as in similar areas where there are fine stands of Valley Oaks or the Interior Live Oak. Why are the plains treeless, is a question repeatedly asked. An understanding of the problem can only be had historically, by a considera-tion of the former annual vegetation and the habits of the California Indians. The herbaceous vegetation in aboriginal days grew with the utmost rank-ness, so rank as to excite the wonderment of the first whites, who repeatedly tell of tying wild oats or grasses over the backs of their riding horses. This dense growth was usually burned each year by the native tribes, making a quick hot fire sufficiently destructive to kill seedlings, although doing little injury to established or even quite young trees. It was, therefore, only in certain years as a result of a combination of local conditions or indirect influences now only to be guessed, such as the character of sea-sonal rainfall, winds, fire, flood or pestilence, that germinating seedlings were enabled to persist in particular areas. The presence, therefore, of groves of oaks is rather to be explained than their absence. It is note-worthy, then, that on the plains proper the groves or scattered trees were always of two species, the Valley Oak and Interior Live Oak. These species when once established are well adapted by their thick bark to withstand grass fires, while their scattered method of growth, so characteristic everywhere in the Great Valley, is undoubtedly the result of repeated annual fires.

Modern ethnographic studies of the Indians of the northern California Coast Range began with Goddard (208), who published his classic report on the Hupa in 1903. He wrote the following significant sentence regarding vegetation burning (p. 22): "Late in summer the grass on Bald Hills and perhaps in other places was fired and the fleeing deer taken in snares or killed with weapons while frantic from fear."

Goldschmidt (209) received similar information from the Hupas in 1939: "Hupa burned out whole Hupa valley and other small flats, occasionally the forests. Burnt to increase grass supply and to drive game. Burned yearly."

The next reference is found in Loud's report on the Wiyots (335, p. 230), who lived on the coast a little south and west of the Hupas, in the vicinity of Humboldt Bay. Loud cited Gibbs (199), Wood (570), and Jepson (273) in his statement that follows:

> Within the forests, at all elevations from sea level to the top of the ridges, there were small open patches, known locally as prairies, producing grass, ferns, and various small plants. These prairies are too numerous to mention in detail. A few of the more important are located on the map. Most of theses patches if left to themselves would doubtless soon have produced forests, but the Indians were accustomed to burn them annually so as to gather various seeds, especially a species of sunflower, probably *Wyethia longicaulis*. The statement of Professor Jepson that "there is today more wooded area in Humboldt County than when the white man came over a half century since," was confirmed by reports made to the writer that some of the old prairies had come up to young growth of forest.
>
> These prairies were of incalculable value to the Indians, not alone for their vegetable products, but also for the game found upon them. A sharp contrast is drawn between the animal life in the forests and on these prairies, in the accounts of the exploration party previously mentioned. At one time the party fasted three days and lost two pack mules by hunger and exhaustion, before they came to a prairie stocked with game and grass. From there they went on for ten days without "the sight of any living thing that could be made available or useful for food." Then ascending a rocky eminence they reached another prairie where they saw "on one side . . . little knots of deer, on another and nearer . . . a large herd of elk, and still in another direction both." Before reaching any of this game they met and shot five grizzly bears.

The following account from Harrington (233, pp. 63–65) appears to be a direct recording of a Karok informant's account:

HOW THEY USED TO SET FIRE TO THE BRUSH

Our kind of people never used to plow, they never used to grub up the ground, they never used to sow anything, except tobacco. All that they used to do was to burn the brush at various places, so that some good things will grow up.

That way the huckleberry bushes grow up good, the young huckleberry bushes, they call them "iramxit." And the hazel bushes, when they burn them off for hazel sticks they pick them two years, then they are good, good hazel sticks, they get so hard. And the bear lilies also they burn off, they pick them the next summer, in July; that they pick the bear lily.

And the wild rice plants also they burn, so that the wild rice will grow up good. They burn it far up on the mountains.

And sometimes they also burn where the tan oak trees are, lest it be brushy where they pick up acorns. They do not want it to burn too hard, they fear that the oak trees might burn.

And sometimes they used to set fire there long ago where they saw lots of acorns on the ground, in a tanbark oak groves they made roasted unshelled acorns. They do not set the fire for nothing, it is for something that they set the fire for.

And where they are going to sow tobacco, too, they burn it, too. It is the best place if there are lots of logs there, for there are lots of ashes; where lots of logs burned there are lots of ashes. Ashes are good on the ground, where fir logs have burned, where pitchy stuff has burned.

It is in summer when they set fire to the brush, at the time when everything is dry, that is the time that is good to set fire, in the fall before it starts in to rain. At different places up back of the people's rancherias they set the fires.

Tobacco was all that one used to sow. First they set fire upslope, in the summertime, in the summertime they set fire there; they set fire to logs. They do not go by the moon when they burn it. They burn it any time, in the summer. When walking around upslope first they see a good place to plant a tobacco garden; when they see a good place, they burn the logs.

Then too the rattlesnakes go upslope; they say that that also is what they set fire for, to kill snakes that way.

Some kinds of trees are better when it is burned off; they come up better ones again. But some kinds of trees when it is burned off disappear, another never comes up again. The manzanita, another one does not come up, when it is burned off. An old tree bears way better too. And the tan oak is not good when it is burned off, the tree dies. When they are burning, they are careful lest the trees burn.

In 1939 Gifford (203) allowed me to copy the following from his Karok field notes:

Burning The Countryside—The Karok habitually burned the brush with the idea that better growth resulted the following year. Hazel, iris and *Xerophyllum* were burned off regularly to produce better growth. July and August were best months for burning off country. Firing of hazels was done after nuts gathered.

When setting a fire, the fire setters said formula (made incantations?) for a big fire, yet one which would do no harm. . . . Then the formulist blows in all four directions to keep fire from spreading. The formulist is a fire setter who knows the proper medicine. All formulas begin with "hukenvapaho." "You are a long snake. Let's see you run water in." The snake referred to is Water snake (absumxarak). The reference to "run water in" refers to fire going out.

A statement regarding burning by the Yuroks, who occupied the region near the mouth of the Klamath River to the west of the Karoks, was obtained in 1939 from Kroeber's field notes (296):

BURNING—The Yurok used to burn regularly prairies where there were grass seeds; also places where the white squaw-grass (*Xerophyllum*) grows, and also hazel, both used for baskets. They would take turns, burning one piece of ground over and the next year another one and only in the second year would they come back to where they had burned first. The hazel would be fired in fall and would burn to the roots, and then along about the second year after, the shoots for baskets would be ready. Men did the firing but women gathered the shoots. They did not gather hazel sticks for basketry just anywhere; but the hazel burning-places were not owned.

The *Xerophyllum* was also burned in fall, and was ready for picking again the next season.

They would burn in the forest, too, to protect the trees and to help the deer. Especially the small prairies in the forest would be burnt out, and from those the fires would spread into the forest around. This would give the deer and elk better grass. This burning would be done in summer after the grass was dry. Burning near villages was done after the first good rain, so as not to endanger the redwoods and trees near the village which were used for house lumber and boats.

In the forest the fire would be controlled by clearing out fire trails the way the white people do. In the prairie, people would stand some little distance apart, men and women, carrying branches of fir or something green, and when the fire started to spread into the timber, they would beat the fire out. . . . If the fire got away into the timber, they would start one from the opposite side and let the two fires meet. Brush is called "wehipserik." In burning a prairie in the timber they would first start small fires all around the edge and then set fire to the main prairie. Doing this is called "wiohpeloil."

The hazel that grew after burning the prairies is called "ohegolilko." Hazel also grows along the river and this could be used for baskets but such baskets do not last. The same is true of *Xerophyllum*. This grows in all kinds of places, but they only use what grows in certain spots which they burn over.

Burning to give the elk feed was done as far back from the river as Helkerayetca, which the whites call Red Mountain and which in Indian means "long ridge." . . . Up there they burned to make the elk grass peyup, grow for the elk. This stretch would be burned every fourth or fifth year, in fall, and allowed to burn until the rains put it out.

In the redwoods they would wait until the brush and windfalls were thick and then burn it out. This might be three or four or five years. Where there were pine nuts they would mostly burn every three years.

They would also burn out under the tan oaks whenever the brush grew thick and this was done with the same sort of control as wiohpeloil for the hazel. This was about every third year, because the ground had to be pretty clean for gathering the acorns.

Around Johnsons, they used to burn behind the houses, up the hill; partly to keep rattlesnakes away. Since they stopped this, the brush has grown close to the houses and there are more snakes about the villages.

In 1928 Kroeber (294) published an account of a Kato war (pp. 396–97):

Black Rock (Se'k'ang) is a fighting ground. It is a dark, rocky ridge about six miles east of here (the present "reservation" near Laytonville). They dug obsidian from the ground there. The Yuki quarreled about this: they were stingy and did not like to see the Laytonville Kato burn over the ground at White Rock (Se'katikat). That is how the war began. . . .

Two men were sent northeast to notify the Yuki that they would be ready to fight tomorrow. They came back and reported: "They will burn the grass. When the smoke rises they will fight."

Then the people here also burned the ground, and were ready.

Loeb (330, p. 46) mentioned the same war but said it was fought because the Katos killed grasshoppers "by burning grass (as among Pomo)." Evidence that the Pomo Indians set fire to fields and forests is very strong. That they frequently burned over their territory has been implied by data from Gibbs (199) and Jepson (273), already cited. Additional statements will be presented, however, because the Pomos occupied the part of the northern Coast Range where extensive tracts were covered by chaparral and by grass. Most of Mendocino, Lake, and Sonoma Counties were in ancient Pomo Indian territory.

Loeb (329, p. 163) in 1926 published the following regarding Pomo use of fire to collect insects: "A circle of fire was made around a group of grasshoppers, and as the fire advanced the insects were forced to make their way to the center. After the grasshoppers had been caught and burned they were gathered up and reparched if of sufficient size."

Although the Lake Pomos, according to Kniffen (288, p. 335), "disclaim all knowledge of former deliberate burning over of tracts of land," contrary to Gifford and Kroeber (202), he wrote the following regarding the Redwood Valley "Kacha" Pomos (p. 373):

> The vegetational covering has experienced great changes. Certainly the chaparral thickets of manzanita, madrona, scrub oak, and buckbrush which now characterize many sections of the valley were formerly restricted to the higher slopes and ridges of the mountains. A beautiful park landscape, largely of oaks, was maintained by annual burnings, done "when the straw was dry." In this manner the brush was held down; the larger trees were uninjured. The tanbark oak, the acorns of which were very much prized by the Indians, and which was found quite abundantly far up the mountain to the west of the valley, has almost disappeared through commercial exploitation.

Of the Southwest Pomos, who lived along the coast from Stewart's Point to the mouth of Russian River, Kniffen wrote (p. 388): "To assure the permanency of the natural openings and to maintain the quality of the oat crop, the dry straw was burned off every few years, generally after the first good rain fall."

During a two-month field trip in the summer of 1935, I studied the ethnogeography of the Pomos (see 491). Burning of vegetation for one reason or another was reported for nearly every group. Although some informants denied knowledge of the practice, the testimony I received seems to me to warrant the conclusion that the whole Pomo area was periodically burned over. The various bands or tribes were so close together that if one set fire, as reported, it might very well have spread to the territory of a neighboring group. The following quotations and names of informants are from my field notes (488):

> *John Smith*, an old Indian from Potter Valley, 15 miles north of Ukiah. "Every year the land was burnt-off to make the grass grow better; mountains burned. There was little or no brush any place because of this practice of burning the dry stubble."
>
> *Lucy Lewis*, 80, Ukiah. "The grass was burned each year. This burned the brush, but the trees were just scorched. The fires were started, and they were just allowed to burn every place. Special spots were prepared to serve as safe spots. Big trees were not hurt, small ones covered with

moss were killed sometimes. Burning was to make the wild oats and tar-weed grow better, and to keep down the brush. Special type of burning to get grasshoppers."

Charlie Bowes, about 75, Calpella. "In old days the valley was rather open, less brush. Every year the grass was burned in the fall. All the valleys and hills were burned to keep down the young brush. This caused more grass to grow." (Several of the Indians as well as two of the old, early white settlers made statements to the effect that much of the area now covered with manzanita was formerly open grassland, and they attributed this to the Indian firing. This was true especially for the country near Ukiah.)

John Stewart, 70, Sherwood Valley, northwest of Willits. "Once in a while they would set fire to the grass. It didn't burn the whole country, although no one stopped it; it just went out by itself. They didn't burn it every year, just once in awhile. They never watched it; they just set the fire and let it go. It looks like they didn't give a damn. It just burned the grass and brush, and the grass, especially the tar weed, was better after."

Dan Scott, 65, Annapolis. "My mother said that they used to set fire to the grass and brush each year; they just set the fire and let burn." (This tribe lived in the Redwood Belt, just about 20 miles from the coast.)

Steve Knight, 50, Ukiah. "Old Chief Lewis said that they burned one side of the river one year, and the other side the next. This was to keep down the brush and fertilize the grass. Fires wouldn't burn the trees."

Rosa Sherd, 72, Stewart Point. "In the old times the coast people burned the grass. The fire was started and allowed to burn wherever it wished; it went out by itself. The brush was burned even in the redwood forest."

Steve Perrish, 65, Point Arena. "I never heard of burning grass or brush."

Martin Smith, 75, Point Arena. "Fires were made in the fall to catch grasshoppers and to improve the crop of wild oats."

Jeff Joaquin, 80, Hopland. "We never heard of general burning of the grass. Only the burning for grasshoppers was told." (This is very near the Ukiah where land was undoubtedly purposely cleared by fire.)

Pete Mariano, 85, Cloverdale. "Fire was used only to get grasshoppers."

Henry Maxmillian, 73, Santa Rosa. "I never heard of the people eating grasshoppers. My mother didn't tell me that the people burned the grass."

Sally Ross, 88, Annapolis. "All around Makaushe (Annapolis) the fields were numerous, and the field grasses grew very thick. The openings were in the forests, and they were kept clean by constant burning which made the grass grow better. The fires were allowed to burn any place. Large trees were not harmed, but the brush and grass was cleaned out. Grasshoppers were caught by fire also. Five different grass seeds were used to make penole (flour)."

Billy Gilbert, 60, Upper Lake. "The land was burned every year to make the clover and wild oats grow, and to keep down the brush."

Three aged Wappo Indians were also questioned. Their testimony concerning ancient burning practices provides a reason for the clause in the Vallejo Treaty (516) quoted earlier in this section. The following is also from my own field notes (488):

Mary Ely, age 80, Geyserville. "Each year the people set fire to the whole country to burn off the grass. This improved the next year's crop."

Jim Tripp, age 65, Geyserville. "Grass was burned to get grasshoppers and to make the next year's grass grow better."

Martha McCloud, age 64, Healdsberg. "People always burned the grass in the old days."

Two references in Kroeber's (295, pp. 301–2) ethnography of the Patwins, who occupied the eastern slopes of the northern Coast Range, mention setting grass on fire:

About fifteen men from Pone went down to the plains (river territory) to hunt elk. Their wildcat skin quivers were loaded with arrows and they carried net sacks on their backs hung from straps over the forehead. They ran down some elk, but the mosquitoes troubled them until they set the grass on fire. The river Indians, seeing the smoke, came to drive them away.

Another time when the Pone people had been hunting in the plains and had set fire to the grass to protect themselves from the mosquitoes, the river people from about Waitere saw the smoke, gathered their men, and came up to the hills.

Although the ethnographic data regarding the Indian inhabitants of the northern Coast Range leave no room for doubt that fire was a primary factor in the vegetational history of the area, there remains to be considered the *Culture Element Distribution* surveys carried out from 1934 to 1939 for the region. Gifford and Kroeber (202) asked sixteen Pomo informants whether or not they knew of the practices of "brush burning to drive game" or "burning for better wild crop." Ten of the sixteen, representing all of the Pomo subdivisions, gave affirmative answers to either one or the other of the mentions. One Hill Patwin said his people burned brush to drive game.

Essene (161) did the *CED* survey of Indians in and near Round Valley. His Northern Pomo informant agreed that burning to improve yield of wild seeds was practiced. His Kato informant affirmed the same, and Essene added the note that "Kato did burn in area of Long Valley and top of ridge west of Laytonville; thus burned all of valley. This was mostly to improve wild seed." The informant from the Lassiks, who claimed as aboriginal territory the region from Eel River near Alder Point to the headwaters of the South Fork of Trinity River, gave positive replies when asked about the use of fire to drive large game, to improve yield of wild seed, and to stimulate growth of wild tobacco. I wrote the following statement from Essene's dictation shortly after he returned from the field:

> Lassik burned a *hell-of-a-lot*. Informant said country was kept burned off completely—almost a prairie. First, to keep down rattlesnakes and to make it impossible for rattlesnakes to strike from hidden places. Second, to improve wild seed. Did not harm oak trees. Kept brush from getting too thick or higher. Third, to drive game with fire and improved hunting. Indians complain about modern restrictions. Fishing in small streams possible formerly; now completely choked by brush.

Essene's Yuki informant denied setting fire to vegetation, but Foster (183a, p. 167), who worked with the Yukis in 1937 in Round Valley, recorded: "Grasshoppers were taken in fire drives. A large group of people assembled on an open hillside in a circle, and fired the grass in a ring. The advancing flames drove the insects toward a common center, where they were finally burned to death, and in the process, parched sufficiently for eating."

Furthermore, Driver (143, p. 314) recorded that the Coast Yukis burned "for better wild-seed crop." Driver's CED monograph (143) for Northwest California contains information from fifteen informants from eleven different tribes, in addition to the Coast Yukis. Those tribes said to have used fire to drive game were the Chimarikos, Wiyots, Hupas, Chilulas, Nongatus, Mattoles, Sinkyones, and Katos. Driver's notes (p. 374) on fire drives give the following additional information:

> *Yurok* and *Tolowa*: "Hunting tracts burned to facilitate pursuit of game."
>   *Mattole*: "Annual burning in September. One side of river burned one year, other following year. Animal tracks visible in ashes."

"Burning for better wild-seed crops" was affirmed by Chimarikos, Yuroks, Wiyots, Hupas, Chilulas, Nongatus, Mattoles, Sinkyones, and Katos. About the Wiyots, Driver wrote in the notes to the element list (p. 381): "Burning every two or three years, to get better berry and seed crops, and to increase feed for deer."

All of the tribes in Driver's Northwest California survey, except the Mattoles, Katos, and Coast Yukis, burned to increase growth of wild tobacco. The Tolowas and Yuroks reported burning leaves to aid in the recovery of acorns, and the Karoks and Wiyots asserted that burning produced better hazel willows for manufacturing baskets. A personal communication from Bill Gianella (197a), advocate of "burning to make the springs flow," contains information on two other reasons the Indians had for setting fire to the vegetation on Trinity River. He received his data from an old Indian in 1933. Gianella wrote: "He told me that they were sure that the burning made the springs run better, the clover grow better and the quail more plentiful and that the smoke kept the bugs down and kept the country healthy. He also added a good bit of information to the effect that in those days the Indians had no pants and that anyone who tried to go through brush without pants would appreciate the advantages of open country."

Foresters have paid special attention to the effects of burning in the northern Coast Range because in this area are found the most extensive stands of redwood trees in the world. According to Shantz and Zon (454, fig. 2), the only extensive redwood forest in America extends from Point Reyes (just north of San Francisco) to a little beyond the Oregon-California state boundary. Nearly all of the tribes listed in this section probably set fires that spread through the stands of redwoods in their territories, although this is not always specified. Massey (356) and Gibbs (199), quoted above, were explicit about Indians in 1848 and 1851 burning the redwoods.

The reports of foresters, based primarily on the record preserved in the trees themselves, confirm and support the direct statements and observations concerning the fact that Indians set fires within redwood groves. Emanuel Fritz published a pamphlet (188) entitled *The Role of Fire in the Redwood Region* and two articles (187, 189) with similar titles. Fritz asserted that Indian fires had been a very important factor in the history of the redwoods. In 1937 Fritz (189, p. 757) presented the different points of view of aborigines and modern lumbermen and confirmed the idea that there was a relationship between distribution of grass and fire: ". . . we are trying to raise trees, whereas the Indians sought to raise forage; because of over grazing, many of the best ranges have become unable to cope with the encroachment of brush."

More extensive quotations from Fritz's pamphlet (188) are warranted:

In the redwood region of California there is a very common apathy toward the prevention of fires on forest and cut-over lands. Many local residents believe that fires do no harm in the forest; some go so far as to claim that periodic burning of the forest is good for the trees and that it stimulates their growth. Some believe that exclusion of fires invites the growth of "undergrowth" or shrubs which "sap the vitality" of the trees and cause "spike-tops" and eventually death. "Old-timers" believe that in the early days fires were not so destructive as they are today because the more frequent burning kept the woods open. They claim that all of the forest was burned deliberately in those days every few years. . . . The virgin redwood forest has been irreparably damaged by past fires; current fires aggravate the damage and on cut-over land they materially reduce its ability to produce new tree growth.

Fires ran through redwood forests long before the white man arrived. On one experimental plot individual fires have been dated back by wound tissues on stumps to over 1,200 years ago. They have become more prevalent and on the whole more severe since the arrival of the white man. The stories of old residents of the redwood region concerning the acts of the Indians are conflicting. Some believe that the Indians set the woods afire every season that there was a sufficient accumulation of litter to support a fire—every four or five years, according to them—and that the course of an Indian traveling through the woods could be charted from a distance by the succession of smokes as he set fires. Others say that the Indian was afraid of fire and set it only to drive game or to burn out his enemies, or that his prairie fires escaped into the woods. Others argue that Indians set fires deliberately to make travel easier. Many white men ascribe to the Indian superior powers of intelligence and a forestry knowledge not equaled by present-day students of the forest. This group believes that "Indian forestry," or frequent burning, is a type of fire-proofing *by the use of fire* and that it is the only type of forestry that should be practiced in the standing timber today. The early Indian of the redwood region was of a lethargic type. No doubt he did occasionally set wood fires for a period of many centuries but it is extremely doubtful that he did it with any thought in mind of improving or safe-guarding the forest for the trees themselves. He was not a malicious or willful destroyer, yet his fires were doubtless set for his own convenience or needs rather than for the welfare of the forest. The Redwood forest has survived in spite of many pre-white-man fires, the causes of which can only be surmised. Were it not for the remarkable fire resistance of the redwood species and its great vitality it would have succumbed to such treatment long ago. The many fires of the past are responsible for the very ragged appearance of the present-day forest, the many hollow-butted trees, and most of the heart rot.

Unless Indians set them, it is difficult to explain the causes of fires of centuries ago except by spontaneous combustion or lightning. The region is too moist for us to give credence to the spontaneous combustion theory, likewise it is one of very infrequent lightning storms during the dry season. Normally it is difficult to start a fire in the virgin redwood forests except with some preparation. Occasionally, however, there come times, such as the disastrous September of 1923, of very low humidity accompanied by high temperature during which fires start very readily. When they occur during seasons of exceptional drought such as 1923, 1924, 1929, and 1931, there is great danger of small fires reaching catastrophic proportions. Lightning-struck trees are extremely rare. There are only a few authentic reports of fires started by lightning.

Fire history was studied by the author in 1928 on over 100 stumps on an area of 30 acres in Humboldt County, and the conclusion drawn that during the past 1,100 years there were at least 45 severe fires in that particular locality or at least 4 each century. The data, obtained from ring counts, indicate many more fires, but the exact dates of past fires cannot be determined very accurately because redwood appears to produce only partially continuous rings, or possibly none at all, at the stump height during some years, although in the same years it may produce fairly wide ones in the top logs. There is danger, therefore, of counting some fires more than once. The figure given above has all possible duplicates eliminated and is considered to be very conservative.

Fires are probably responsible for the admixture of Douglas fir and white fir which reproduce from seed more readily than the redwood and which gain entrance in openings left by the falling of burned-off veterans. Without fire there would be fewer openings and fewer opportunities for the other conifers to enter. Only the redwood (and spruce in the northern sections of the region) can exist in the dense shade and bide its time for a falling veteran to make way for it. White fir and particularly Douglas fir are less able to endure shade and have less longevity than the redwood. They, therefore, should have difficulty in maintaining themselves on sites suited to good growth for the redwood. This is well proven on the "flats" on which there apparently have been fewer fires and where there are larger trees and more of them. The redwood here occurs in pure stands and the crown canopy is too dense to permit the entry of Douglas fir and white fir. These species do not grow so tall as redwood and consequently are eventually eliminated, but where fires cause openings they readily enter and attain large dimensions.

This authoritative statement by Fritz should clinch the argument that Indians have for centuries burned over the northern Coast Range and that fires set by Indians have had a very great influence on the diverse flora of the whole area. His information regarding the extremely slight role played by lightning supports my similar conclusion for the coastal area of Washington and Oregon.

The separation of the coast ranges, both northern and southern, from the interior mountains is arbitrary and for convenience only. The coastal mountains are joined to the Sierra Nevada of eastern California by the Tehachapi Mountains in the south and by the Klamath Mountains and Mt. Shasta in the north. The vegetation of the Coast Range extends across to the Sierra Nevadas. Shantz and Zon (454, fig. 2) indicate that the yellow pine–sugar pine type of forest vegetation dominates both the Sierras and the mountains of north coastal California. Chaparral occupies the foothills of the interior mountains, as well as the Coast Ranges. Having considered chaparral at some length, we will touch upon it but lightly in our review of the evidence for forest burning by Indians of the Sierra Nevada.

Sierra Nevada

The Indian groups who lived in the Sierra Nevada frequently had linguistic and cultural relatives living in the great Central Valley of California. For this reason it is often difficult to know whether references apply to valley, foothills, or high mountains if only a linguistic or tribal name is used to designate the Indians concerned. Furthermore, there were a number of subgroups of various tribes whose territory extended from the valley to the high Sierras, and various sections might be used by the same people at different seasons of the year. Notwithstanding these difficulties, careful reading of the source material makes it possible to determine with some accuracy whether the fires set were in the valley or in the hills and mountains. I will consider in this section the evidence that Indians set fire to the plant cover of the Sierra Nevada and its foothills extending toward the west.

Although A. W. Sampson (429) listed about a dozen references to Indian burning of hill and mountain vegetation in eastern California, he gave the impression that fire was an unimportant factor in the history of the plant cover of that region. My own conclusion is to the contrary, arguing that fire was extremely important in the Sierra Nevada as it was in the Coast Range. I have discovered a few sources not cited by Sampson, but our difference of opinion stems mostly from a different weighting of the evidence. I take strength from an article published in 1949 by Emil F. Ernst, park forester in Yosemite National Park (160). Ernst quoted a number of unpublished and published reports, some also cited by Sampson, and documented the vegetational changes that have occurred in Yosemite by publishing copies of photographs of the area taken in the 1890s and in the 1940s. The pictures show beyond question that Yosemite Valley has changed from an area of extensive meadows and open stands of trees to small meadows and dense forests choked by underbrush. Ernst's interpretations and extended list of quotations is presented in detail (160, pp. 34–39):

Until March 1851, the Indians of Yosemite had managed the Valley in a primitive but, to them, effective way.

The management of the lands of the Valley . . . involved processes of plant control for several objectives including: (1) Clearings for the hunting of game; (2) Clearings to aid the procurement of roots, rhizomes and tubers at the end of the growing season; and (3) Clearings to eliminate lurking places for their enemies. These clearings were accomplished mainly through the use of fire and through the imposed clearing activities of children in the vicinities of their camping places which are now called "rancherias."

By 1937, when the last estimate was made, the aggregate area of the meadows of Yosemite Valley had declined to a total of 327 acres. In 1866, or 15 years after the coming of the white man, the total area of meadow land in the Valley was computed by State Geologist J. D. Whitney to be 750 acres. In the intervening years—1866 to 1937—the forests had encroached upon and taken over more than 56% of the meadow area in existence at the time of Whitney's survey. And, in the same years, the open, park-like, land commented upon many times in old writings and reports has become more densely tenanted with trees, brush and debris due to this white man's protection. . . .

Dr. L. H. Bunnell, a member of the 1851 discovery party, many years later in an article apparently prepared for but not published by the *Century Magazine*, states,

> The Valley at the time of discovery presented the appearance of a well kept park . . . there was little undergrowth in the park-like valley, and a half day's work in lopping off branches along the course enabled us to speed our horses uninterrupted through the groves.

Galen Clark was for many years the Guardian of the Valley during the period of trusteeship by the State of California. In 1894 he wrote to the Board of Commissioners of Yosemite Valley and the Mariposa Big Tree Grove:

> My first visit to Yosemite was in the summer of 1855. At that time there was no undergrowth of young trees to obstruct clear, open views in any part of the Valley from one side of the Merced River across to the base of the opposite wall. The area of clear open ground, with abundance of luxuriant native grasses and flowering plants, was at least four times as large as at the present time.

William H. Stoy, Rector of St. Paul's Episcopal Church at San Rafael, has stated in a letter to the Secretary of the Interior dated December 10, 1890:

> I visited the valley again . . . a lapse of twenty-four years since I had first seen it. The contrast between things then and now is something

remarkable . . . another thing that struck me forcibly in the contrast with 1866 was the immense increase of trees and small undergrowth everywhere visible in the valley . . . while the majestic Giant Trees of primeval growth seemed to be as numerous as in former days. The valley, as I saw it in 1866, was more in the condition that the aborigines had left it. . . . In consequence, also, of the openness then existing, much better views existed of the waterfalls and cliffs, from the floor of the valley, in any direction.

H. J. Ostrander was a cattleman who, in his day, ran herds of cattle on lands now in the park. In one of the October, 1897, issues of the *San Francisco Call* he is quoted as saying of the Yosemite which he had first seen a third of a century before:

And the windings of the beautiful clear Merced River could be traced for miles up the valley until lost sight of at the base of "Cathedral Rocks." At that time in the graceful bends nestled beautiful meadows. Outside of the meadows noble pines, Douglas firs, and cedar dotted the valley. No underbrush, cottonwood nor second growth pines and fir to obstruct the view of the marvelous walls of the valley.

Another of the well known State Guardians, James M. Hutchings, as early as 1881 in a report to the State Commission complains:

A dense growth of underbrush, almost from one end of the valley to the other, not only offends the eye and shuts out its magnificent views, but monopolizes and appropriates its best land, to the exclusion of valuable forage plants and wild flowers.

Hutchings was a confirmed nature lover and the unwarranted destruction of a tree or a flower was a disgraceful thing in his eyes. The situation must have been serious and its potentialities apparent to Hutchings who had settled in the Valley as early as 1861.

Reference has previously been made that the Indians of Yosemite Valley practiced clearing of the meadows and the adjacent forests. The Indians did not have any labor saving mechanical devices. It was natural for them to use fire.

At least in one instance the Indian inhabitants of Yosemite Valley were observed to be using fire to clear the ground. H. Willis Baxley [31], recorded this observation in the fall of 1861:

A fire-glow in the distance, and then the wavy line of burning grass, gave notice that the Indians were in the Valley clearing ground, the more readily to obtain their winter supply of acorns and wild sweet potato root (huckhau).

Speaking of the Miwoks, of which the Indians of Yosemite were a branch, Barrett and Gifford [28] state,

The only other control of vegetation which they attempted was burning off of dry brush about August. This was said to have been done
to get a better growth the following year. Underbrush was less abundant anciently than now, so informants said, and perhaps was due to
this periodic burning.

When in 1928 Carl P. Russell talked to Maria Lebrado, a member of the
Yosemite band taken into custody by Captain Boling's party of 1851, she
expressed a good deal of concern because the Valley is now "too brushy."

The Miwoks also used fire for hunting. Fires were set around meadows
which deer frequented. New fires were built from time to time and the
deer approached out of curiosity and were noiselessly shot with arrows by
the Indians from their places of ambush.

Dr. Bunnell, in the unpublished *Century Magazine* article, further
says of the discovery expedition:

There was a great variety of evergreen and deciduous trees, planted
by Nature's landscape gardeners and, as the undergrowth was kept
down by annual fires while the ground was yet moist, to facilitate the
search for game, the Valley at the time of discovery presented the
appearance of a well kept park.

Galen Clark in 1894 also wrote:

The Valley had then been exclusively under the care and the management of the Indians, probably for many centuries. Their policy of management for their own protection and self-interests, as told by some
of the survivors who were boys when the Valley was first visited by
Whites in 1851, was to annually start fires in the dry season of the
year and let them spread over the whole Valley to kill young trees just
sprouted and keep the forest groves open and clear of all underbrush,
so as to have no obscure thickets for a hiding place, or an ambush for
any invading hostile foes, and to have clear grounds for hunting and
gathering acorns. When the forest did not thoroughly burn over the
moist meadows, all the young willows and cottonwoods were pulled
up by hand.

M. C. Briggs, December 18, 1882, complains rather bitterly of the underbrush:

While the Indians held possession, the annual fires kept the whole
floor of the valley free from underbrush, leaving only the majestic
oaks and pines to adorn the most beautiful of parks.

To this could be added the citation given by A. W. Sampson (429) for
1883 from Gordon-Cumming, to the effect that "some areas" were frequently
burned. This is typical of Sampson's minimizing, whereas Ernst leaves no
doubt but that the entire valley was burned over.

Recent ethnographic studies suggest that the extensive burning done in Yosemite Valley was in no way unique or limited to that valley. Not only must we assume that setting fire to vegetation was a culture pattern of the Miwoks as a whole but that it was also typical of other Sierran tribes, according to information at hand. For example, Aginsky (3) interviewed nine Miwok informants in 1936, who lived in the area from Ahwahnee, near the south edge of Yosemite National Park, to Pine Grove, at the northern end of Miwok territory, and was told by all that the Miwoks burned over the country for one reason or another. Five said fire was used to drive game; five said the Miwoks burned to collect grasshoppers; eight said land was burned over to improve yield of wild crops; two reported use of fire to clear off the brush. There is no reason to believe other Miwoks used fire less than those in Yosemite, nor is there any basis for assuming that the fire outside of Yosemite Valley had less pronounced influence on the plant cover than did those in Yosemite.

The Miwoks, however, do not seem to have differed from their neighbors with regard to use of fire. Aginsky (3) recorded in the same *CED* report cited above that two Yokuts and one Mono, living in the hills south of the Miwoks, said their people used fire in game drives. One Yokuts informant reported that his people "just burned." Two Yokuts and two Mono inform-ants, that is, all who were interviewed, affirmed "burning land for better wild crops."

Driver (142) carried out the *CED* survey among the other southern Sierran tribes. All five Mono informants, who lived in the mountains between Yosemite and Sequoia National Parks east of Fresno, said that their ancestors set fire to vegetation to drive game, to improve wild seed crops, and to increase growth of wild tobacco. Of five Yokuts informants from hill dwelling groups, four knew of burning for one or more of the above reasons.

The Tubatulabal and Kern River Indians, southern neighbors of the Monos, told Driver that fire was used for the three reasons listed above for the Monos. In addition, Voegelin (523, p. 13) published in 1938 the fol-lowing concerning the Tubatulabals: "Rabbits obtained on valley floors by firing dry brush; 20 or more men stood in circle outside burning brush; as rabbits fled men shot them with bow and arrows."

The data provided above establish beyond reasonable doubt that the Indians of the southern Sierra Nevada and foothills, that is, from east of Sacramento and south beyond the Kern River, where the Sierras end and the Tehachapi Mountains begin, regularly and frequently fired the country-side. To the north of the Miwoks lived the Maidus, whose territory extended along the Sierras and in the valley north from Sacramento to Lassen Peak, a distance of about a hundred miles. References dealing with the mountains and hills are fairly recent. Arranging them geographically from south to north, I would list first one by lumberman J. A. Kitts (286, p. 36) who wrote in 1920 that Indians in the vicinity of Grass Valley fired the forests to "keep down the young growth and underbrush, to permit the growth of berries, to drive game and to impede an enemy." Kitts claimed he had been told by an Indian that they had the belief that frequent light burning prevented destructive crown fires.

Faye (167, p. 40), an ethnologist, wrote of the Southern Maidus in 1923 as follows:

Deer were hunted by means of a fire built in a circle so that they would be caught in an ever narrowing corral. The men kept close behind the fire as it ate its way inward and shot the deer when they were finally marooned in an area so small that they had no opportunity to flee.

It was a general practice of these Indians to clear the forest of undergrowth by setting fire to it. They seem to have been able to keep the fire under control. They claim that it prepared the ground to receive seeds.

In 1933 Beals (33, pp. 347, 363) published this statement regarding the same group, which he called Nisenan:

In fall brush burned toward center of large circle where frequently several hunters stationed in clearing who shot animals as driven in.

The land was apparently burned over with considerable regularity, primarily for the purpose of driving game. As a result there were few young trees and all informants were agreed that in the area of permanent settlement, even so far up in the mountains as Placerville, the timber stand was much lighter than at present. That region, for example, is almost completely timbered except where clearings have been made for orchards. The Indians insist that before the practice of burning was stopped by the whites, it was often a mile or more between trees on the ridges, although the canyons and damp spots held thickets of timber.

That such a considerable change in the flora of a region may take place in a relatively short time is illustrated near Nevada City. The major portion of the ridge on which Wokodot is situated (north of Nevada City) was an open grain field about forty years ago. Today it is largely covered by Timber fifty or sixty feet high. There is also a thick underbrush, largely of ceanothus and manzanita, that is said to have all grown in the last ten years.

For the Northern Maidus we have the classical study by Dixon (135), published in 1905, in which he wrote (pp. 190, 193):

Grasshoppers and locusts were eaten eagerly when they were to be had. The usual method of gathering them was to dig a large, shallow pit in some meadow or flat, and then, by setting fire to the grass on all sides, to drive the insects into the pit. Their wings being burned off by the flames, they were helpless and were thus collected by the bushel. They were then dried as they were. Thus prepared, they were kept for winter food, and were eaten either dry and uncooked or slightly roasted.

Often fires were set to drive deer.

Kroeber (293, p. 396) wrote in 1925 concerning the Maidus as a whole:

Like most of the Californians who inhabited timbered tracts, the Maidu frequently burned over the country, often annually. It appears that forest fires have been far more destructive since American occupancy, owing to the accumulated underbrush ignited the large trees. Of course the Indian was not attempting to protect the stand of large timber: he merely preferred an open country. This is shown by the fact that he also burned over unforested tracts. Travel was better, view farther, ambuscades more difficult, certain kinds of hunting more remunerative, and a crop of grasses and herbs was of more food value than most brush.

The latest report on the Maidu is Voegelin's CED report (524). Five informants were from the hill and mountain section of Maidu territory, four of whom reported use of fire to surround game. The one who denied knowledge of burning connected with hunting affirmed the practice of "burning for better wild seed crops," as did three others. A Wintun Indian from the foothills to the west of the valley also agreed that fire drives were used by his people. In the mountains at the northern end of Sacramento Valley lived the Yanas. One of two informants from the group reported to Gifford and Klimek (200) the practice of burning to increase wild seeds and to collect grasshoppers. The tribes occupying the high valleys and plateaus of the northeastern section of California also set fires to the plant cover, according to several authorities. Dixon (137, p. 212) in 1908, Kniffen (287, p. 311) in 1928, O. Stewart (489) in 1941, and Voegelin (524) in 1942 reported that the Achomawis ignited vegetation to drive game. O. Stewart and Voegelin reported burning to improve wild seed crops and growth of wild tobacco, and Stewart learned they used fire to catch grasshoppers (p. 427, note 356). Of their linguistic and cultural kin and neighbors, the Atsugewis, Garth (191) reported:

Hunters lit fires all around a mountain, leaving gaps at intervals where bowmen could hide in shallow holes. The entrapped deer were shot as they tried to escape through the gaps. J. L. stated that the Atsugewi burned 5 or 6 mountains in a year.

Informants stated that the higher slopes were burned over every 3 years or so. The wooded land was kept open and free of underbrush by these periodic burnings.

Voeglin's Atsugewi informant confirmed this view. Three ethnographers, Dixon, Voegelin, and Holt, learned that the Shasta Indians set fire to their country. Dixon wrote in 1907 (136, p. 431): "The other method could not be used until the oak-leaves began to fall. Men then went out and set fires in circles on the hills. The ends of the curved lines forming the circles of fire did not meet, and in this opening women stood rattling deer-bones, while men concealed in the brush were ready to shoot the deer as they rushed out."

Holt (253, pp. 309–10) published a similar account in 1946:

The Shasta Valley and Rogue River groups ate one kind of grasshopper, a very large form. They set fire to the grass, thus cooking the grasshoppers which were then dried, pounded, and mixed with grass seed for eating.

The second [for hunting] was used on the more open hills of the north side of the river, where oak trees grew. When the oak leaves began to fall fires were set on the hills.

Two Shasta informants told Voegelin (524) of fire drives and of burning for better wild seed crops. Of the Modocs, who lived east of the Shastas and north of the Achomawis, Bill Gianella (197a) wrote: "Dennis Kane of Canby told me . . . that when he came to Modoc about 1873 the Indians burned the bunch-grass country every few years and sage brush was hardly in evidence. But the stockmen made the Indians stop burning the land. Then the sage brush took over."

Voegelin (524) recorded that the Modocs, as well as the neighboring Klamaths in Oregon, set fires for driving game and for improving yields of wild seeds. My search of the literature, which is certainly incomplete, has revealed positive data on the vegetation burning of all Indian tribes of northeastern California, except the Washos, who lived around Lake Tahoe in summer and near Carson City, Nevada, in winter. This direct testimony appears to me conclusive that fires set by aborigines were both frequent and extensive. In fact, these data, if interpreted according to the concept of the culture area, leave no room to doubt that the grass and forest fires periodically set by Indians burned over the whole of mountainous region of northeastern California.

Again, however, there are the records of the trees themselves, which show that the Sierras were frequently burned over. Inasmuch as the zones of the different types of vegetation extend over the full length of the Sierra Nevada, a number of the statements that follow apply to the whole range.

Before presenting the indirect evidence for extensive fires in the woody vegetation of the Sierra Nevada, however, it may be well to recall the types of vegetation in the region. Shantz and Zon (454, fig. 2) show a strip of chaparral extending roughly ten to twenty miles into the foothills along the margin of the full length of the Central Valley. Higher on the western slopes, with greater variation in width, from five to sixty miles, occurs the yellow pine–sugar pine forest association. It starts at the east end of the Teha-chapis and reaches into south central Oregon. The high Sierra summits are assigned to the spruce-fir (northern coniferous forest) type. The high area of extreme northeastern California was covered by the symbol for yellow pine–douglas fir.

According to Daubenmire (128a, p. 332), three conifers common in western forests have "serotinous cones," which means the cones do not open except under exceptional circumstances. Fire is one of these circum-stances; consequently, seeding from these species is greatly increased by fire. These species are knobcone pine (*Pinus attenuata*), jack pine (*P. banksiana*), and lodgepole pine (*P. contorta* var. *latifolia*). The wide distribu-tion of these trees suggests frequent burning. The ability of redwood to survive fires has already been described. Daubenmire (p. 332) states further that ponderosa pines, the yellow pines of California, are excep-tionally well equipped to escape injury during forest fires.

Information from the USDA Yearbook (579) entitled *Trees* confirms the importance of the fire resistant species in California. The article on "Pine Forests of California" by B. O. Hughes and D. Dunning (pp. 352–48) con-tained the following:

> Five conifers make up more than 95 percent of the volume of the standing timber. Of these, ponderosa pine is the most generally useful and of widest occurrence. The fine textured sugar pine. . . . Constitutes only one-tenth of the volume. Both pines reach their best development along the western slope of the Sierra Nevada.
>
> Douglas fir and white fir each make up about one-third of the timber volume and are important components of the mixed forests of both the Sierra Nevada and Coast Range, sometimes forming almost pure stands.
>
> California incense cedar occurs intermingled with the other species, forming only one twenty-fifth of the volume.

The facts presented in this introduction seem to give added signifi-cance to statements such as the following published in 1894 by John Muir (377, p. 199):

> The entire forest belt is thus swept and devastated from one extremity of the range to the other, and, with the exception of the resinous *Pinus contorta*,

Sequoia suffers most of all. Indians burn off the underbrush in certain localities to facilitate deer hunting, mountaineers and lumbermen carelessly allow their campfires to run; but the fires of the sheepmen or muttoneers, form more than ninety percent of all destructive fires that range the Sierra Forests.

A similar view was published in 1921 by Jepson (274, p. 243):

The Sierran forest is typically a fire forest, that is to say, all the tree species have shown reaction in structure of life history to long continued fires which have undoubtedly run over California woodlands for many thousands of years and perhaps for a longer period. The trunks of the pines, firs, and cedars have become encased in exceedingly thickened bark which is undoubtedly a very effective protection to the vital cambium layer which lays between the bark and the wood and provides for the tree's increase in thickness. The bark of these trees, on the other hand, contains more or less resin which increases the fire hazard.

In the case of the Big Tree [sequoia], however, there is practically no resin in the whole trunk. Resin is found not at all in the trees except in microscopic quantities in the first annual layer of wood, in the leaves, and in the staminate catkins. The bark is quite free from resin except for its possible occurrence in case of mutilation, and by its peculiar fibrous nature forms an almost asbestos-like covering to the trunk. . . . Nearly all mature trees or trees past maturity show signs of fire ravage, although in many cases the attack has been negligible.

Two publications by Show support the opinion that California forests were regularly subjected to fire in aboriginal times. He wrote in 1920 (460a, p. 37) that foresters can show by analysis of trees that California forests were burned over on an average of "every eight years" up to 1900. He said many trees survived twenty or more fires. When the national forests were created in 1897, forest burning was reduced, he said, but added: "The virgin forests we take over are badly fire-scarred as a result of past fires." On the cause of past fires, Show and Kotok (462, p. 5) wrote in 1924:

The forests were long inhabited by the Indian, a user of fire, and he also has been a cause of forest fires. A persistent tradition, much discussed in the last quarter century, holds that it was the regular practice of the Indian to fire the forests as frequently as fire would run through them. On this hypothesis much has been said and written extolling this primitive race as the original foresters and guardians of our forest resources. Without reciting in detail the conflicting statements of fact and surmise on the Indian as an agency responsible for forest fires, it may be said that in some parts of the pine region he undoubtedly fired the forests or at least regarded forest fires with equanimity, which in other parts of the region the evidence is just as conclusive that he regarded forest fires with fear and did not deliberately set them. In any event, his motive had nothing to do with the forest as a growing timber crop. It was to his interest to prevent the growth of brush and reproduction which would hinder him in hunting, and this purpose was admirably served by the use of fire.

Incidentally, I have found no evidence that Indians "regarded forest fires with fear and did not deliberately set them." In 1941 William Gianella (197a) sent me two of his statements that bear out the theory that Indian burning produced open stands of timber.

Well, in the Modoc forest there is a patch of some ten acres (a few miles north of Lookout on the road that goes to Klamath Falls) that accidentally burned at the right time of the year to kill the under growth without injuring the timber. Then I saw it four years ago every tree in this patch had a heavy green top and was making healthy growth. For thirty miles in any direction the timber that was protected from fire had dying tops, scanty foliage and many trees were dying.

In some places, I know of, the "natives" have done quite a bit of burning as early in the spring as the surface needles would burn. This singed off the underbrush, thinned out the saplings, and if done early enough leaves plenty of young trees. Government men looking these places over have figured 904 of the trees killed. To the average man this sounds terrible until he considers that 90% mortality leaves from 200 to 500 trees to the acre on land that can only support 40 to 80 to the acre. The fact is that a 90% killing does not kill out half enough of the saplings, and before the timber crop matures it will be reseeded many times and will need many 90% killings to prevent the useful trees from dying from lack of water. After the needles are fairly well burnt out, this mortality is confined to the young stuff that is too thick and to the infirm of the older trees. I have been in districts where the old stumps were some two and a half rods apart. To survive to the age of 240 years, which the largest did (and it had a diameter of 90 inches), and to be spaced this far apart, these trees had gone through many a fire. The Indians burnt when the burning was good, not looking out for the benefit of the timber. If these trees made such magnificent timber in spite of struggle, should not we be able to conserve and grow equally fine timber if we use fire as a tool to be guided by our intelligence?

Clements (101, p. 180) and Weaver and Clements (542, pp. 81, 533) and others say that forest fires have been responsible for extension of chaparral into forest zones; consequently, they may have contributed to its extension to its present distribution. On the other hand, much of the increase of chaparral in the foothills of the Sierra Nevadas may reflect the reduction of regular burning of the thick grass that formerly grew among the shrubs. Frequent burning with adequate herbaceous fuel might have produced results very unlike those of infrequent burning of tracts that have been thoroughly grazed.

Thus, extension of chaparral in the foothills does not by itself indicate increased burning of forests or replacement of forests by chaparral because of fire. Open forests that are removed for timber could be replaced by pure stands of grass if the burnings that produced the open forests were continued. On the other hand, open forest tracts may be invaded by chaparral in spite of continued burning if the tracts are overgrazed. The extension of chaparral in the foothills cannot be attributed simply to increased burning.

There remains one more important factor to evaluate in order to understand the true importance of fires set by Indians in the plant history of the Sierra Nevada. It is the role of lightning. The statistics are not available to me to give a completely satisfactory answer to the question of the relative influence of forest fires started by lightning and those started by Indians in the Sierran forests before white settlement. The problem is comparable in some respects to that considered in relation to the Northwest and can be attacked in the same way. The data that I have found on lightning fires are too general to be very useful. Nevertheless, something can be gained from their analysis.

I must start again with Plummer's reports (399 and 400), published in 1912. Most of the Sierra is included in his region J. (399, p. 20), but that region also includes the Coast Range south of San Francisco. During three years ending with 1911, 3,912 trees were struck by lightning in national forests in region J. Sections of the Sierra Nevada certainly come within Plummer's mountain zone of greatest hazard from lightning as shown on his figure 5. Plummer's (399, p. 30) table 4, "Number and Percentage of Forest Fires Caused by Lightning in the National Forests of the United States," shows that from 1907 through 1911 a total of 683 fires were started by lightning in California National Forests. That is an average of about 133 per year, although the range is from 42 in 1907 to 282 in 1911. Table 4 reveals that lightning-caused forest fires were an average of 23.1 percent of total fires during that five-year period, the range being from 13.8 percent to 35.4 percent per year.

Plummer (400, pp. 26–27) records that there were slightly more than 2 million acres of forest lands burned-over from 1906 through 1910. If we accept that lightning-caused fires produced one-fourth of the damage it would mean 500,000 acres for the five-year period or about 100,000 acres per year burned-over as a result of lightning. Hughes and Dunning (579, p. 352) state that there are nearly 8 million acres of forest in California. By lumping all together and assuming that lightning fires would be randomly scattered, lightning caused fires could burn through the forest once every eighty years.

Lightning, however, does not strike with equal frequency throughout all of California's forests. One need only recall the statement of Fritz (188, p. 3), quoted above, to the effect that for the entire northern Coast Range "there are only a few authentic reports of fires started by lightning." That lightning is inadequate to account for the very widespread, almost universal, evidence of prehistoric burns on trees is implied by another statement by Ernst (160, p. 40):

> If the statements recorded here have any truth in them, then evidence supporting them should be available in the forests of the valley and elsewhere. Study of those trees on the floor of the Yosemite Valley which are obviously over one hundred years old, reveals that large numbers of them have signs of severe or repeated fires. Those trees less than 100 years old are remarkably free of signs of fire. The evidence on the ground indicates that fires were, whether deliberately set or not, common enough to leave clear indications on trees existing before the coming of the white man. Although many more trees invaded the Valley since the coming of the white man, there is little or no evidence of fire on them.
>
> On lands in the adjoining Stanislaus National Forest, E. I. Kotok, formerly of the California Region Forest and Range Experiment Station, made a study of fire scars on trees which showed that fires that had swept the 74 acres investigated 221 times between 1454 and 1912. This averaged one fire every two years. It is doubted that Nature could be so regular with fire for such a long period of time.

Lightning in the valley would not have changed with settlement. If a single tract in Stanislaus National Forest were set on fire by lightning on an average of every two years, it would indicate that certain small areas received the greater proportion of all lightning strikes, so that it could be assumed that other anciently burned areas were set on fire by Indians. A statement from the USDA Bulletin by Show and Kotok (462, p. 5) appears pertinent in this regard:

> Huntingston's investigations of big trees (*Sequoia washingtoniana*) enable us to carry the fire history even further into the past than the study of the

relatively short-lived pines, firs, and cedars. Although the fire history depicted by the big trees is fragmentary indeed, it is shown that back as far as 245 a.d. fires occurred in the pine region in restricted localities in which the big tree is found.

Whether these early fires were light or heavy there is no way of determining, the records on surviving trees merely indicating that fires occurred. The fact that a forest of a sort was able to survive these frequently recurring fires would indicate that most of them were in all probability light surface fires.

The causes of the fires of the past are, in most cases, not known.

Fire records for 10 years in the California pine region show an average of 350 lightning fires every year, and show also that even under systematic fire protection some have attained enormous size. For the 10 year period ended 1920 an area of 415,000 acres was burned over by fires from that cause. The zone in which lightning fires are known to occur embraces an area of nearly 11,000,000 acres, and coincides in general with the commercially important portions of the California pine region.

If only 415,000 acres of forest under protection are burned off in ten years from fire caused by lightning, it might be reasonable to suppose that twice as many acres suffered before fire fighting was organized. Such a figure approaches the average of 100,000 acres per year mentioned above. If we take Show's figure of 11 million acres for the size of the area to be burned, it would take over a hundred years to burn it over starting at one end and going to the other. Repeat fires on the same area would slow up the process. With some areas receiving fires every two years, as Show and Kotok reported (462, p. 40), then other areas would have been neglected by the lightning. Yet it should be remembered that Show (460a, p. 37) found that individual trees throughout the Sierran forests indicated that forest fires had occurred before 1900 on an average of "every eight years" and that many trees survived twenty or more fires. The averages do not justify emphasizing lightning as the source for prehistoric fires and minimizing Indians, as did A. W. Sampson (429, p. 20).

Notwithstanding the importance of lightning as a fire starter in the Sierra Nevada forests, the facts from Yosemite and elsewhere indicate that man, either aboriginal or modern, is needed to accomplish all of the burning that was indisputably done. In 1923 Show and Kotok (461) reported that lightning caused 41.5 percent of the forest fires yet was responsible for only 30 percent of the area burned. Two fires in the same area a month or a year apart would be counted twice. Show and Kotok imply that this is the case by their evidence that lightning-caused fires are very concentrated in place and time. In the 1945 report of the chief of the Forest Service (p. 29) is this statement regarding concentration of fires: "Almost one-third of all fire-fighting expense on the national forests during 1944 was incurred in California during a three-week period of extreme fire danger."

The report of the same department head for 1951 has this statement (p. 8): "Forest fires started by lightning are usually tough to handle; they often occur in rugged, high-country areas difficult to reach and difficult to work in."

The 1949 USDA Yearbook (579, p. 25) reported that lightning caused 23 percent of the forest fires in California, reducing the percentage to about that for 1906–10. The drastic reduction in fires on national forests, also mentioned by Show (460a, p. 37), when the policy of complete protection was initiated, further reduces the role of lightning in igniting forest fires. Greeley (216, p. 39) substantiated this view by proclaiming in 1920 the great changes that fifteen years of protection had wrought.

To conclude descriptions on California Indian uses of fire in the Sierra Nevada, I reiterate the points so far established: (1) Indians of the Sierra Nevada almost annually set fire to grass, brush, and forest lands, primarily to aid hunting and to improve the yield of wild seed; (2) since these fires were so general and were set without thought of preventing their ignition of woods and forests, it can be assumed that virtually all of the vegetation of the Sierra Nevada was frequently burned over by fires set by Indians; (3) the trees themselves confirm the ethnographic record of fires passing periodically throughout the Sierra Nevada; (4) although lightning has contributed to the burning-over of the Sierras, especially in the higher, rougher regions, lightning is entirely inadequate as a cause for the very extensive, almost universal, fire-scarred or fire-influenced vegetation.

Central Valley

Between the Coast Range and the Sierra Nevada, and occupied by the San Joaquin and Sacramento river systems, is the great interior valley of California. The floodplain of the two rivers, but especially that of the San Joaquin, was an extensive tule swamp, called the "tulares," when first seen by Spanish explorers. Shantz and Zon (454, fig. 2) in 1924 designated the floodplain "Greasewood Desert" on their map of "Natural Vegetation," but Crawford and Hurd in 1934 on their map of California *Natural Cover and Agricultural Land Use* (198, pl. 1) place the same area under the symbol for "Irrigated Agriculture." Surrounding the floodplain on all sides is a zone called "Bunch Grass" by Shantz and Zon and called simply "Grass" on the Gianini Foundation map prepared by Crawford and Hurd. Beyond the grassland, Shantz and Zon indicate chaparral encircling the valley, presumably in the foothills. The Gianini Foundation map (198) shows just a couple of spots of chaparral on the eastern edge of the valley and thus indicates grasslands passing directly into forests. The two maps differ considerably as to space assigned various vegetation types in the western hills and mountains also, with one (198) showing more grassland in the south and more chaparral in the north, the other having the relative-sized areas reversed.

The grasslands of the Central Valley were originally of great interest and hold most attention because of the problem of whether they result entirely from botanical, geographic, or climatological forces. In other words, one may question whether the Central Valley grasslands were in any way dependent for their origin and continuation upon the aborigines who inhabited them in prehistoric and historic times. Has fire been an important ecological factor in the history of vegetation in the Central Valley?

The problem is complex, in spite of the fact that the Central Valley is fairly level over its entire length of four hundred and fifty miles and its width of forty to eighty miles. Notwithstanding its uniformity of elevation and topography, Koppen (290, p. 20) and Russell (423, 424) divide the valley into two different general climates. The northern half, the Sacramento Valley, is Mesothermal. The southern half, the San Joaquin, is Arid, with the valley floor characterized as Desert, and surrounded by a zone of Steppe. Koppen and Russell thus unite the northern part of the Central Valley with the moist coast range and place the southern valley in the same climatic types as the Great Basin. The floor of the San Joaquin Valley is shown as having the same climate as that of the Mojave Desert.

Although Livingston and Shreve (327, pl. 1) classify the Central Valley as "Semi-Desert," they combine the Sacramento with the San Joaquin, except for a small area around Tulare Lake called "Grassland." Their "Semi-Desert" also includes the northern Coast Range for about fifty miles north of Golden Gate and most of the southern Coast Range from San Francisco to San Diego. Livingston and Shreve distinguish the area of the southern interior of the state as "California Microphyll Desert."

That differences exist between the Sacramento and San Joaquin parts of the Central Valley is evident to all who know the area, but the question arises whether the differences should be emphasized to separate the two halves or whether the similarities warrant combining the two parts into an ecological unit. Clements (101, p. 40) would insist upon the unity of the Central Valley:

> Progressive changes of rainfall, temperature, and evaporation occur with increasing altitude, latitude, and longitude. Further, each climate shades imperceptibly into the next, often through wide stretches. These are all

elementary facts and the climatologist might well say that they are taken account of in the ordinary way of determining means or normals. As a matter of climatology this is true, but from the standpoint of indicator vegetation it is not. It is a simple matter to trace the line of 20 inches of rainfall, or of the 60 percent ratio of rainfall to evaporation and to assume that it marks the line between prairies and plains. Such an assumption reverses the proper procedure, in which the associations themselves must be permitted to indicate their respective climates.

On page 116, and in a similar vein, he adds: "However sympathetic one may be with the use of physical factor instruments, he can not afford to minimize the unique importance of the plant for the analysis of climates. To do otherwise is to substitute human judgment for plant judgment in the plant's on field."

In spite of his great faith in plants as the sure indicators of climate and soil of any given area, Clements also stated that non-natural factors could so influence the vegetation that it was not a simple matter of studying the vegetation to ascertain the true climatic potentialities of a region. In 1920 he expressed this principle as follows (101, p. 31):

> . . . plants may indicate conditions, processes, or uses. . . . The plant may indicate a particular soil or climate, or some limiting or controlling factor of either. This would seem to be axiomatic, but it is well known that grassland, which is typically a climatic indicator, often occupies extensive areas in forest climates. Thus the presence of a plant, even when dominant, is only suggestive of its meaning. It is necessary to correlate it with the existing factors and, better still, to check this correlation by experimental planting, or an actual tracing of the successional development.
>
> Indicators of processes usually require a double correlation, namely, that of the plant with the controlling factor, and that of the factor with the causal process, such as erosion, disturbance, fire, etc.

Clements, unfortunately, did not follow his own advice in many of his studies of grasslands and appears to have neglected fire entirely in his discussion of the Central Valley. By emphasizing the role of fire in this area, as indeed throughout the country, I am bringing Clements's "process" of fire into proper perspective. The data I have collected suggest that fire was a powerful, even determining factor in the formation and preservation of the dominance of grass in California's Central Valley.

Additional evidence that Indians regularly and widely set fires in the Central Valley begins with Font (179, p. 407), who recorded observations made on a visit to the northwestern edge of San Joaquin Valley in April

1776: "And so we traveled more than three leagues, which in general may be estimated as to the southeast, going with some difficulty in the midst of the tulares, which for a good stretch were dry, soft, mellow ground, covered with dry slime and with a dust which the wind raised from the ashes of the burned tule. . . ."

A note in Driver's (142) CED report on the use of fire for hunting is the only other account of deliberate burning of tules. It is significant that confirmation of Font's observation should be obtained from a living informant over a hundred and fifty years later. Driver recorded (p. 110) the following from a Tachi Yokuts living near Lemore: "No particular species of small game hunted [with fire] separately. Rabbits, squirrels, rats, etc., lived among tules, which were set afire and all species burned to death, clubbed or shot."

It may well have been the burning of the tules that kept them in pure stands and inhibited the growth of willows and other water-tolerant trees on the swampy floodplain of the San Joaquin.

To support the thesis that valley grasses were burned, I call attention first to the five references cited by A. W. Sampson (429). Between 1844 and 1860, Beckwith (35), Hastings (237), Hinds (248), Kern (284), and Taylor (502) published accounts of Central Valley Indians setting grass fires for one purpose or another. In addition, six other early references not cited by Sampson are worth quoting. The first is Moerenhout (364), who traveled in the Central Valley during July 1848. He wrote (pp. 73–74):

> However, I obtained some watermelons and cantalopes there and some Indians who have a rancheria or village nearby sold us a quarter of venison. With these provisions we went to make our camp on the bank of the Arroyo de las Calaveras, under a group of oaks, one of which I measured and found to be twenty-one feet in circumference with a perfectly healthy trunk and an even spread of at least forty-five feet.
>
> One remarkable thing that I have observed in all parts of Upper California in which I have traveled is that one never finds any of the large oaks broken down, fallen into decay or partly consumed by age and weather. All are sound and vigorous, all seem of the same stage of growth, and to see this great number of enormous trees, strong and full of life, one would say that they had all sprung up at the same time, and that they were the first of their kind to appear on this earth. These handsome trees, with the willows and the laurels, lent the greatest beauty to the place where we were camped.
>
> July 15. During the whole night we had seen a fire in the plain to the east of us, in the direction toward which we were going. There was a line

of it three or four leagues long, rapidly approaching. Hardly had we
started this morning when we were suffocated by a thick smoke which
made it impossible to see anything at the least distance. For more than
an hour we suffered from this discomfort, which at times was very great,
until we reached the very place where all was aflame. While this fire was
very lively, it was only consuming the grass and wild oats which, being
very thick and dry, threw up a bright flame and were burning so fast that
it would have been impossible to stop or to extinguish the fire. Moreover,
several trees were afire and some, partly burned, had fallen across our
way. This was but a slight obstacle to our progress, however, and the only
one, for since the road was quite wide and free of grass and trees, the fire
had stopped at its edges. We noticed even several places where this slight
break had cut the line of the fire and had sufficed to save some considerable areas from destruction. In less than half an hour we had passed the
fire. That is to say, that as we approached the Moquelames (Mokelumne)
River the fire was burned out, but everything was black and dismal. No
more pasturage, no more grass, no more verdure—even the leaves of the
trees had either been burned or withered by the fire. It was no longer the
same country. This desolation extended for about a quarter of a league
from the river—as far as the lowlands which are overflowed in the season
of high water, for there the grass and all the plants were still green, and
the fire could not touch them. The contrast was the greater in that the
surroundings of this river are very pretty—groups of superb trees, meadows
covered with verdure. . . .

Having traveled across the valley from east to west, Moerenhout wrote
(pp. 268–69):

On coming into the valley I was struck by its desolate state. Since leaving
the Moquelumne River I had almost constantly been going through
burned districts, still smouldering or partly ruined by fire, but nowhere
had I seen such complete and general destruction—the valley, the mountains, all were black and frightful in appearance. Nothing had been spared.
The wheat, the crops, had been burned; the trees were leafless; and over
a space of more than eight leagues there was not a blade of grass to be
seen, not an animal, not a living being. It was a dreary desert from which
all had fled and where neither men nor animals could find the slightest
nourishment.
    Upper California has always been exposed to these fires, for its plains
and its mountains are covered with grass and wild oats which toward July
are quite dry and will catch fire from the slightest spark. The least thing—
a cigar tossed into the fields, the discharge of a rifle—is enough to set all

aflame and to cause the most terrible fires. To this it must be added that the Indians, after they have made their harvest of wild grain, frequently set fire to the grass either intending to improve the next year's crop or to kill the rabbits, the hares, and other animals that they eat.

Formerly, when one of these fires approached a Mission, a farm, or some inhabited place, both whites and Indians joined and tried to stop the progress of the flames by uprooting shrubbery and clearing a certain space from grass, etc., or by any other means, so that these fires were then never so extensive or so destructive. This year, however, the roads are constantly filled with travelers who camp in the middle of the woods and the fields and, without taking the slightest precautions, light fires there that they fail to put out when they leave. In consequence, during the past two months fires have been almost general in the whole country and the ruin that they have caused is the more complete since the abandoned and deserted farms and those tended only by women have no means of stopping the progress of the fire, and in many places it has not only destroyed the pastures but also, as in this valley the grain and all the products of the fields.

Ryan (425, pp. 302, 307) wrote as follows concerning a trip through the San Joaquin Valley in 1848 and 1849:

We started off again early next morning, and, in the course of that day's march, came upon a large prairie fire, which burned with extraordinary rapidity and fierceness. . . . The flames devoured every blade of grass in their way, roaring, and crackling, and leaping from side to side according to the varying direction of every fitful gust that blew. . . .

Fires of this kind, amongst the long grass and wild oats, are not unfrequent in California; and, in the midst of the summer . . . often burn furiously during many days. . . .

We passed the fire, and soon reached the Stanislaus river. . . . The further we advanced, the scarcer was the herbage, the oats and grass having been burned by the Indians so that the face of the entire country appeared black and gloomy in the extreme. . . . Every now and then we came up with trees, around whose huge trunks heaps of acorns lay strewed.

Mooney (366, p. 260) obtained the following information from Col. L. A. Rice, concerning the Cosumnes tribes of 1850:

The grasshopper hunt was a great event in Digger society, and was conducted in a very systematic manner. A whole settlement would turn out and begin operations by starting a number of small fires at regular intervals in a circle through the woods, guiding the flame by raking up the pine needles, and stamping out the fire when it spread too far. When the fires burned out there was left a narrow strip of bare ground enclosing a circular area of several acres, within which the game was confined. A large fire was then kindled at a point inside of the circle, taking advantage of the direction of the wind, and allowed to spread unchecked. The men, armed with bows and arrows and accompanied by their dogs, kept to the windward in front of the fire and shot down the rabbits and other small animals as the heat drove them from cover, while the women, with their conical baskets on their backs, followed up the fire to gather up the grasshoppers, which merely had their wings singed by the fire, but were not killed. As a squaw picked up a hopper she crushed its head between her thumb and finger to kill it, and then tossed it over her shoulder in the basket.

Farnham (166, pp. 330–31) visited the Sacramento Valley before 1848 and wrote of the area as follows:

These grains [wild oats and rye], resowing themselves from year to year, produce perpetual food for the wild animals and Indians. The plains are burned over every year by the Indians; and the consequence is, that the young trees, which would otherwise have grown into forests, are destroyed, and the large trees often killed. Nevertheless, the oak, the plane tree, of immense size, the ash . . . fringe the stream everywhere, and divide the country into beautiful glades and savannas.

. . . within the verge of the valley, grows a belt of oak trees, about three hundred yards wide . . . beyond this belt, on either side of the river, stand clumps of forests over the endless seas of grass that reach away to the distant mountains. . . .

Bryant (68) in 1848 also described the Indian custom of burning over the Central Valley. My final historical statement regarding vegetation burning in the Central Valley is from Bancroft (24, p. 374): "Grasshoppers are taken in pits, into which they are driven by setting on fire, or by beating the grass in a gradually lessening circle, of which pit is the centre."

Kroeber's ethnographic map (293, pl. 1) showing the locations of California Indians by linguistic stocks and tribes indicates that the Central Valley was shared by at least five tribes, all of which also possessed some foothill and mountain territory. The tribes were the Yokuts, Miwoks, Maidus, Wintuns, and Yanas. I have already presented conclusive evidence that all five of these tribes started grass, brush, and forest fires. Had we no additional information, we would have to assume that the members of these tribes living on the valley floor had customs similar to those of their hill-dwelling kin. The historical material already presented concerning the valley supports that assumption.

There are, in addition, a few statements from informants whose ancestors claimed the valley as home. The *Culture Element Distribution* (*CED*) surveys carried on during the 1930s and published in the 1940s by Aginsky (3), Driver (142), and Voegelin (524) record information from nine valley-dwelling informants. Five Yokuts from the southern end of San Joaquin Valley were placed by Driver in the valley proper. Four of these believed their ancestors drove game by means of fire. Two said their people burned to increase yield of wild seeds. (Driver questioned the accuracy of the denials of either of these practices.) One who denied grass burning gives the account of tule burning mentioned above. One of Aginsky's Miwok informants claimed to be of the Plains (i.e., Valley) subdivision of that tribe. He told Aginsky that his people had burned the valley grass during hunting to collect grasshoppers and to get better wild crops. The Wintuns and Maidus of Sacramento Valley gave Voegelin negative responses when questioned regarding use of fire to surround game, and only one of the three had positive knowledge of burning for better wild seed crops. However, they all agreed brush was burned to increase wild tobacco.

This review of the literature that specifies burning the Central Valley by aborigines allows for no doubt that frequent and widespread firing of the grasslands was a culture pattern of the Indians of the Central Valley. There remains to be considered the indirect evidence, that is, the interpretation of the vegetation itself. Such evidence for grasslands is less exact than for forests where fire scars on living trees have been analyzed to furnish actual dates when the trees were subjected to fire. Nevertheless, here as on the plains and prairies of central United States, there are indications that fire was an essential force in the existence of the grassland. It is well to recall that the "Bunch-Grass" association, as it is designated by Clements (101, p. 149) and by Shantz and Zon (454, fig. 2), includes with the Central Valley the valleys of the southern Coast Range and the Palouse of interior Washington and Oregon. If burning was essential to produce pure grasslands in these areas, as I believe has been established, one can logically suggest that fire was essential for the maintenance of the Central Valley grassland. Furthermore, the data from the plains and prairies give cause to doubt that grass is ever a true climatic climax vegetation on good, deep soil. A generalization from Shantz (453a, p. 13) dated 1947 supports this view and applies particularly to grasslands like those of California, having a Mediterranean climate: "Much of the earth's surface now in grassland would without fire surely pass to forests, many coniferous forests would pass to hardwoods, and much of the higher and better parts of the Mediterranean type would pass to forest. . . . The Mediterranean types the world over with a long hot dry period which means recurrent fires, would become woodlands and forests."

On page 125 of the same publication Shantz further suggests that fire may be a factor in determining the grassy nature of the Central Valley:

> There is every reason to believe that the valleys and hills where only an annual grass is found, were once covered with bunch grass. Under natural conditions, bunch grass can compete with and replace brush and annual grasses in many areas. When fire passes over an area burning off the brush, both bunch grass and sprouting chaparral begin to grow. The bunch grass will grow at once. . . . Experiments in many places emphasize the necessity of protection from grazing after the burning. . . . Perennial or bunch grasses . . . when not subjected to the handicap of grazing often are completely successful with shrubs.

It is not clear from the statement above what are "natural conditions" for bunchgrass. Clements (101, pp. 149–50) said: "The *Stipa* consociations seem formerly to have dominated the interior valley from Bakersfield to Mount Shasta and from the foothills of the Sierra Nevada and Cascade Mountains, through and over much of the Coast Range."

Clements seemed unconcerned that he extended his grassland into the brush- and forest-covered Coast Range, for it seems the bunchgrass dominants in California, as in the Great Basin/Plateau region, could share the same territory with shrubs. In fact Clements says just that on page 152: "The Societies of such grassland areas at present are essentially the same as for chaparral."

Since both bunchgrass and chaparral flourish in California in areas receiving as little as ten inches of rainfall annually and are frequently found together, it appears to me necessary to find some nonclimatic condition or "process," as Clements called it, to tip the scales in favor of one or the other. Cooper (112, p. 82) reasoned in a similar fashion and in 1922 stated:

> He [Clements] admits the unlikeness of the climate, especially in seasonal distribution of precipitation, to that of other regions of grassland climax, but rightly affirms that the climax plant community is itself the best available indicator of climate. The decision rests, therefore, upon correct identification of the climax community. Clements' evidence of grassland dominance is based upon assumed relicts, and my evidence of chaparral dominance is of the same nature. In an area where individuals and patches of both types occur today, the weight of probability would, in my opinion, favor the chaparral plants as being the survivors of the true regional climax. It has already been stated that most of the species of the climax chaparral, notably *Adenostoma*, reestablished themselves with the utmost difficulty once their mass control has been destroyed, and that therefore

thoroughly isolated individuals or patches of such plants are almost certainly relicts of former dominance rather than centers of recent colonization. The same is not true in the case of grasses, even the perennial species which make the grasslands climaxes. . . .

The acceptance of my conclusions as to former control of certain regions (the main mass of the Coast Ranges with its minor valleys, the foothills of the southern Sierras, and perhaps the northern end of Sacramento Valley) by chaparral does not necessarily preclude the possibility of climatic grassland over much of the Great Valley.

. . . the climax chaparral has transgressed its normal climatic limits along its mesophytic border through its invasion of the forest, fire being the causative agent; on its xerophytic border it has been pushed back a considerable distance by the grasses. . . .

Cooper had said (p. 31) that "the principal causes of the destruction of the chaparral or prevention of its establishment [in the Central Valley] have been clearing and repeated fires."

Bauer (30, p. 270), in 1930, went beyond Cooper in stating that:

Cooper argues that the Great Valley of California, or a large portion of it, was first chaparral and that this was supplanted later by grassland, placing much weight on the influence of fires, particularly in aboriginal days. He states that the southern end of the Great Valley (southern part of San Joaquin Valley) may not come under this category, because of its near desert aspect. The writer does not believe it necessary to make this exception, since chaparral remnants do occur here; grasses grow abundantly in normal seasons, and grass fires are still frequent.

There is some evidence that students of California grasslands are simply prejudiced against fire. Shantz (453a), for example, after several times stating many prairies were created by fire, asserted (p. 126): "Repeated burnings alone are usually effective in eliminating the better bunch grass."

Clements (101, p. 150) revealed a similar objection to accepting fire as a responsible agent in producing bunchgrass. It would appear impossible to deny that fire aided the production and maintenance of bunchgrass prairies in the face of the overwhelming evidence for Indian use of fire. Bunchgrass prairies were in their best "natural" state where Indians regularly burned them. Overgrazing, as Shantz and Zon (454, p. 17) said in 1924, has reduced the bunchgrass and allowed foreign herbaceous vegetation to gain control. Both Clements and Shantz and Zon presented photographic proof that frequently burned but ungrazed bunchgrass would develop pure stands. Neither reported that the relicts of bunchgrass prairies they photographed had been burned, and because of that oversight both failed to give fire its just due as the causative agent. Clements (101, p. 151) wrote: "The best expression of bunch-grass prairies today occurs in that part of the Palouse with 15 to 25 inches rainfall (plate 31)." Plate 31, however, has pictures of relicts in California. Photograph A is identified as "*Stipa setigera* consociation in trackway, Fresno, California."

Shantz and Zon (454, p. 18) gave the following legend under their photograph (fig. 33): "California needle grass on land protected from grazing. (Bunch-grass.) This open stand of perennial bunch grasses probably represents the original grassland of the central valleys of California . . . Perris, California." In the background of the photo are railway tracks, a water tank, and a railway station. Since railroad rights-of-way in California grasslands, as on the plains and prairies of the Middle West, are regularly burned off, these two photographs establish beyond reasonable doubt that fire aided the development and survival of bunchgrass and that fire would restore the bunchgrass if it were not overgrazed.

Careful experiments by Love and Jones (336) reported in 1952 also supported this conclusion. The most rank chaparral can be removed, and a prairie grassland can be maintained by fire, if the tract is properly managed. As summarized by the two authors, the procedure is as follows:

> 1st year. Burn clean and allow no grazing so that grass can get started.
> 2nd year. Graze lightly after the seeds are set.
> 3rd year. Graze normally early in season.
> 4th year. Do not graze and reburn in late summer.
> Burning should be repeated every third or fourth year, with normal grazing on intervening years.

The key to the process is to avoid overgrazing and to allow an accumulation of grass to serve as fuel to burn off brush sprouts periodically. The Indians burned under such conditions and kept the Central Valley as a bunchgrass prairie.

Summary for All California

After citing twenty-five sources that described the California Indian practice of setting fire to vegetation, A. W. Sampson (429, p. 20), as quoted above, concluded in 1944 that "study of Indian burning in California is historically interesting, but of little application in the present-day effort of brush suppression."

I have presented material from seventy-six references that stated that Indians set fire to California vegetation. With one or two exceptions, all of the major tribes and subdivisions are represented, a number by several authors. If the culture pattern concept has any validity, these data leave room for only one conclusion: burning-over was not, as Kroeber reported, "considerable" but was absolutely universal, wherever vegetation was sufficient to carry fire. The evidence presented leaves no room to minimize the role of the Indians in the complete burning to which California fields and forests were subjected by saying that lightning was the major cause. Lightning was very concentrated in area and time; consequently, it could not have been responsible for the very general extent of the known effects of fire.

A. W. Sampson also tried to use the relatively small population of aboriginal California to justify his view that Indian fires were unimportant. Although there were only about 133,000 Indian inhabitants of the state, our knowledge indicates that the entire area of California was regularly exploited to the fullest, according to the various ways of life of the people. There is no reason to believe that a single canyon or mountain top escaped the attention of the aboriginal hunters. Every acre of land that would produce food was known and utilized. In fact, the population density was probably a fairly accurate indication of the total productivity of the state as it could be developed by the methods employed by the Indians.

The difference in number of inhabitants of the mountains and of the valley reflected the differences in amount of food that could be obtained from the two areas, not the degree to which the two areas were used. Both were subjected to complete exploitation. It should be obvious that a very small number of Indians who believed it advantageous frequently to burn-over their territory could have kept it well burned. Since all groups of California Indians believed it was good to set fire periodically to the vegetation and let the fire spread as it would, one must conclude that the whole state was frequently burned-over.

Indians burned for a number of reasons, most frequently as an aid in hunting. Other expressed reasons were to improve pasture for game, to improve visibility, to collect insects, to increase yield of seeds, to increase yield of berries, to increase wild foods other than seeds and berries, to make wild vegetable foods more available, to remove or thin forests to allow growth of other vegetation, to stimulate growth of wild tobacco, to aid in warfare, to facilitate travel, and to protect from snakes and insects. Not all of the above reasons were recorded for every group, and possibly some tribes did not use some of the reasons to justify the burning-over they did. Furthermore, burning vegetation for any reason would accomplish several of the other results expressed as desirable by some Indians.

That recent fires in forests are more destructive than formerly, as Kroeber and Sampson stated, has been attested to by many others, including

Indian informants. It is incorrect to accept this as evidence that the Indians did not frequently set vegetation on fire in aboriginal times. Instead, the opposite is a better interpretation. Annual burning would keep inflammable material at a minimum and would insure that such regular fires would not individually be as destructive as modern fires, which feed on the debris and brush accumulation of a number of years. Worden's (575a) article in the October 4, 1952, issue of the *Saturday Evening Post* contains the proof of this idea. The evidence presented strongly supports the idea that fire can be a useful tool in silviculture as in range and game management, in California as in other areas of the United States. Controlled light burning would help to reduce the very harmful wildfires. It is very possible that grass-covered hills or open woodlands would be better for watersheds, as they would be better for grazing than would be complete jungles of chaparral. Certainly the disastrous floods following the denuding wild fires would be avoided. Also, the danger to homes that are built in chaparral jungles would be reduced.

I do not, of course, advocate the precise practices of burning employed by Indians. Rather, I strongly urge careful study, such as that done by Love and Jones (336) and many others, to discover the best way to use fire. Complete fire prevention does not appear to be the proper ideal in California forests any more than it is for those in Washington, New Jersey, or Louisiana.

Abbreviations

❖

AA *American Anthropologist*

AF *American Forests*

AJS *American Journal of Science*

AMNH-AP American Museum of Natural History Anthropological Papers

AMNH-B American Museum of Natural History Bulletin

AMNH-M American Museum of Natural History Memoir

AN *American Naturalist*

BAE-B Bureau of American Ethnology Bulletin

BAE-*R* Bureau of American Ethnology (Annual) *Report*

BG *Botanical Gazette*

CED *Culture Element Distribution* Studies of the University of California

CI-P Carnegie Institution of Washington Publications

JF *Journal of Forestry*

KGS Kentucky Geological Survey

UC-AES University of California Agriculture Experiment Station

UC-AR University of California Anthropological Records

UC-PAAE University of California Publications in American Archaeology and Ethnology

UC-PG University of California Publications in Geography

UCS *University of Colorado Studies*

USDA-*AAA* United States Department of Agriculture, *Atlas of American Agriculture*

USDA-BPI United States Department of Agriculture, Bureau of Plant Industry

USDA-FS-B United States Department of Agriculture, Forest Service, Bulletin

YU-PA Yale University Publication in Anthropology

Bibliography

Omer C. Stewart

1. Adams, Arthur. 1870. *Travels of a Naturalist in Japan and Manchuria*. London.
2. Adams, Frank, Paul A. Ewing, and Martin R. Huberty. 1947. *Hydrologic Aspects of Burning Brush and Woodland-Grass Ranges in California*. California Division of Forestry.
3. Aginsky, B. 1943. *CED: XXIV, Central Sierra*. UC-AR 8.
4. Aikman, J. M. 1930. "Secondary Plant Succession on Muscatine Islands, Iowa." *Ecology* 11:577–88.
5. Aikman, J. M., and A. W. Smelser. 1938. "The Structure and Environment of Forest Communities in Central Iowa." *Ecology* 19:141–50.
6. Aldous, A. E. 1934. *Effect of Burning on Kansas Bluestem Pastures*. Kansas Agricultural Experimental Station Technological Bulletin 38.
7. Allen, H. H. 1937. "Origin and Distribution of the Naturalized Plants of New Zealand." In *Proceedings of the Linnean Society of London*.
8. Allen, J. A. 1870. "The Flora of the Plains." *AN* 4. Cited by Shimek (457), p. 218.
9. Allen, J. A. 1871. "The Fauna of the Prairies." *AN* 5. Cited by Shimek (457), p. 218.
10. Allen, J. A. 1874–76. *The American Bisons, Living and Extinct*. Memoirs of the Museum of Comparative Zoology, Harvard 4.
11. Alvord, C. W., and Lee Bidgood. 1912. *The First Exploration of the Trans-Allegheny Region by the Virginians, 1650–1674*. Cleveland.
12. Ameghino, F. 1909. "Dos documentos testimoniales a proposito de las escorias producidas por la combustion de los cortaderales." *Anales des Museo Nacional de Buenos Aires* 12:71–80. Cited by Schmieder (441), p. 268.
13. *American State Papers*. 1830. "Public Lands." Vol. 6. Cited by Sauer (433), p. 53.
14. Ames, Oakes. 1939. Economic Annuals and Human Cultures. Cambridge, Mass.: Botanical Museum, Harvard University.
15. Anonymous. 1942. "Record Survival Made by Shelterbelt Trees." *JF* 40:456.
16. Arend, John L. 1941. "Infiltration Rates of Forest Soils in the Missouri Ozarks as Affected by Woods-Burning and Litter Removal." *JF* 39:726–28.
17. "Arrillaga a . . . Francisco De Laseun." 1793. MS (proclamation concerning fires at Santa Barbara Mission, May 31, 1793). Archives of California, Provincial State Papers, vols. 21–22, Bancroft Library, A. 14.
18. Ashe, W. W. 1915. *Loblolly or North Carolina Pine*. North Carolina Geological and Economic Survey Bulletin 24.

315

19. Atwater, Caleb. 1818. "On the Prairies and Barrens of the West." *AJS* 1:116–25.
20. Aughey, Samuel. 1880. *The Physical Geography and Geology of Nebraska.* Cited by Shimek (457), p. 218.
21. Azara, Felix de. 1847. *Descripcion e historia del Paraguay y del rio de la Platta.* Madrid. Cited by Schmieder (441), p. 269.
22. Baker, H. P. 1908. *Native and Planted Timber in Iowa.* USDA-FS-B 154. Cited in Shimek (457), p. 218.
23. Baker, Sir Samuel. 1874. *Ismailia.* London.
24. Bancroft, H. H. 1875. *The Native Races of the Pacific States of North America.* New York.
25. Barnett, H. G. 1937. *CED: VII, Oregon Coast.* UC-AR 1.
26. Barnett, H. G. 1939. *CED: IX, Gulf of Geogia Salish.* UC-AR 1.
27. Barrett, L. A. 1924. "California Indians Not 'Light Burners.'" *Sierra Club Bulletin.*
28. Barrett, S. A., and E. W. Gifford. 1933. *Miwok Material Culture.* Public Museum of the City of Milwaukee Bulletin 2.
29. Bates, Carlos G., and R. A. Pierce. 1913. *Forestation of the Sand Hills of Nebraska and Kansas.* USDA-FS-B 121.
30. Bauer, H. L. 1930. "Vegetation of the Tehachapi Mountains, California." *Ecology* 11:263–80.
31. Baxley, H. Willis. 1865. *What I Saw on the West Coast of South and North America and in the Hawaiian Islands.* New York: D. Appleton. Cited by Ernst (160).
32. Beaglehole, Ernest. 1936. *Hopi Hunting and Hunting Ritual.* YU-PA 4.
33. Beals, Ralph A. 1933. *Ethnology of the Nisenau.* UC-PAAE 31.
34. Beals, Ralph. 1940. "Cahita Ethnology: I. Aboriginal Culture." MS.
35. Beckwith, E. G. 1855. Report of Explorations for a Route for the Pacific Railroad of the Line of the Forty-first Parallel of North Latitude. In *Reports of Explorations and Surveys to Ascertain the Most Practical and Economical Route for a Railroad from the Mississippi River to the Pacific Ocean.* House of Representatives Executive Document No. 91, 33rd Cong., 2nd Sess., vol. 2. Cited by Sampson, p. 19.
35a. Belknap, J. 1792. *History of New Hampshire.* Vol. 3.
36. Bell, H. W., and E. J. Dyksterhuis. 1943. "Fighting the Mesquito and Cedar Invasion on Texas Ranges." *Soil Conservation* 9(5):111–14.
37. Benson, Lyman. 1941. "The Mesquites and Screw-Beans of the United States." *American Journal of Botany* 28:748–54.
38. Bessey, Charles E. 1887. "A Meeting-Place for Two Floras." *Bulletin of the Torrey Botany Club* 14:189–90.
39. Bessey, Charles E. 1899. "Are the Trees Advancing or Retreating upon the Nebraska Plains?" *Science* 2(10):768–70. Cited by Gleason (207).
40. Beverley, R. 1722. *The History of Virginia.* 2nd ed. London. Cited by Maxwell (358), p. 89.
41. Bews, J. W. 1929. *The World's Grasses.* New York.
42. Bigelow, T. A. 1949. "Fighting Lightning Fires on the Klamath National Forest." *Fire Control Notes USDA-FS* 10(4):7–9.
43. Billings, W. D. 1941. "Quantitative Correlations between Vegetational Changes and Soil Development." *Ecology* 22:448–56.
44. Bird, Ralph D. 1930. "Biotic Communities of the Aspen Parkland of Central Canada." *Ecology* 11:356–442.

45. Birket-Smith, K. 1918. "A Geographic Study of the Early History of the Algonquian Indians." *International Archiv für Ethnographie* 24:213.

46. Birket-Smith, K. 1929. *The Caribou Eskimos: Report of the Fifth Thule Expedition, 1921–1924.* Vol. 5.

47. Biswell, H. H., and Paul C. Lemon. 1943. "Effect of Fire upon Seed Stalk Production of Range Grasses." *JF* 41:844.

48. Biswell, H. H., J. E. Foster, and B. L. Southwell. 1944. "Grazing in Cutover Pine Forests of the Southeast." *JF* 42:195–98.

48a. Biswell, H. H., R. D. Taber, D. W. Hedrick, and A. M. Schultz. 1952. "Management of Chamise Brushlands for Game in the North Coast Region of California." *California Fish and Game* 38(4):453–85.

49. Blizzard, Alpheus W. 1931. "Plant Sociology and Vegetational Change on High Hill, Long Island, New York." *Ecology* 11:208–31.

50. Blumer, J. C. 1910. "Fire as a Biological Factor." *Plant World* 13:42–44.

51. Boas, Franz. 1934. *Geographical Names of the Kwakiutl Indians.* Columbia University Contributions to Anthropology 20.

52. Bodrov, V. 1936. "The Influence of Shelterbelts over the Microclimate of Adjacent Territories." *JF* 34:696–97.

53. Botha, C. Graham. 1924. "Notes on Early Veld Burning in the Cape Colony." *South African Journal of Science* 21:351–52. Cited by Shantz (453a), p. 23.

53a. *Boulder Daily Camera.* 1949–50. File.

54. Bourne, A. 1819. "On the Prairies and Barrens of the West." *AJS* 2:30–34.

55. Brackenridge, H. M. 1819. *Views of Louisiana.*

56. Bradbury, J. 1819. *Travels in the Interior of North America, 1809–1811.* Early Western Travels, ed. Reuben Gold Thwaites, vol. 5. Cleveland, 1904.

57. Brandegee, T. S. 1891. "The Vegetation of Burns." *Zoe* 2:118–20.

57a. Braun-Blanquet, J. 1932. *Plant Sociology.* New York: McGraw-Hill.

58. Bray, William L. 1906. *Distribution and Adaptation of the Vegetation of Texas.* University of Texas Bulletin 82. Cited by Gleason (207), p. 46.

59. Bray, William L. 1901. "The Ecological Relations of the Vegetation of Western Texas." *BG* 32:262–91.

60. Brickell, John. 1737. *The Natural History of North Carolina.* Dublin (rpt. Trustees of Public Libraries, N.C., 1911).

61. Bridges, Thomas. 1948. "The Canoe Indians of Tierra del Fuego." In *A Reader in General Anthropology*, ed. Carleton S. Coon. New York: Henry Holt, 1948.

62. "Brief Relations of New England, 1607–1622." In *Purchas, His Pilgrames*, vol. 19. 1906.

63. Bruce, David. 1947. "Thirty-two Years of Annual Burning in Longleaf Pine." *JF* 45:809.

64. Bruce, David, and C. Allen Bickford. 1950. "Use of Fire in Natural Regeneration of Longleaf Pine." *JF* 48:114–17.

65. Bruce, David. 1951. "Fire, Site, and Longleaf Height Growth." *JF* 49:25–28.

66. Bruce, Philip Alexander. 1895. *Economic History of Virginia.* Cited by Maxwell (358), p. 87.

67. Bruderlin, Katherine. 1911. "A Study of the Lodgepole Pine Forests of Boulder Park (Tolland, Colorado)." *UCS* 8:265–76.

68. Bryant, E. 1848. *What I Saw in California (1846).* Rpt. in part (pp. 142–93) as "The Journal of Edwin Bryant." *Utah Historical Quarterly* 19 (1951): 50–107.

69. Bullock, William. 1649. *Virginia Impartially Examined.* London. 3. Cited by Maxwell (358), pp. 89–90.

70. Burnaby, Andrew. 1798. 3rd ed. "Travels through the Middle Settlements in North America . . . 1759–1760." In *Voyages and Travels,* ed. John Pinkerton, vol. 13. London, 1812.

71. Byrd, Wm. 1841. *Histories.* Ed. Boyd. Raleigh, N.C., 1929.

72. Cabeza de Vaca, A. N. 1555. *The Journey of Alvar Nunez Cabeza de Vaca 1528–1536.* Trans. Fanny Bandelier. New York, 1905.

73. Campbell, R. S., and E. H. Bomberger. 1934. "The Occurrence of *Gutierresia sarothrae* on *Bouteloua eriopoda* Ranges in Southern New Mexico." *Ecology* 15:49–61.

73a. Campbell, W. L. 1879. Telegram to J. A. Williamson, General Land Office, Washington, D.C., from Denver, Colorado. In National Archives, Office of Indian Affairs, Letters Received, Colorado, L614.

74. Carver, J. 1778. *Travels through the Interior Parts of North America, in the Years 1766, 1767 and 1768.* London.

75. Cary, Austin. 1936. "White Pine and Fire." *JF* 34:62–65.

76. Case, Robert Ormond. 1944. "Big Timber Gets Religion." *Saturday Evening Post* 217 (December 30): 14–15, 46–47.

76a. Catesby, M. 1731. *Natural History of the Carolinas.* London. Cited by Watson (531), p. 44.

77. Catlin, George. 1842. *Manners, Customs, and Conditions of the North American Indians.* New York.

78. Caton, J. D. 1880. *Miscellanies.* Boston.

79. Chapman, A. G. 1937. "An Ecological Basis for Reforestation of Submarginal Lands in the Central Hardwood Region." *Ecology* 18:93–105.

80. Chapman, Frank M. 1891. In AMNH-B 3:316. Cited by Christy (97), p. 95.

81. Chapman, H. H. 1932. "Some Further Relations of Fire to Longleaf Pine." *JF* 30:602–3.

82. Chapman, H. H. 1932. "Is the Longleaf Type a Climax?" *Ecology* 13:328–34.

83. Chapman, H.H. 1940. "Forest Fires in 1938." *JF* 38:64–65.

84. Chapman, H. H., and H. N. Wheeler. 1941. "Controlled Burning." *JF* 39:886–91.

85. Chapman, H. H. 1942. *Management of Loblolly Pine in the Pine-Hardwood Region in Arkansas and Louisiana West of the Mississippi River.* Yale University School of Forestry Bulletin 49.

86. Chapman, H. H. 1943. "A 27-Year Record of Annual Burning versus Protection of Longleaf-Pine Reproduction." *JF* 41:71–72.

87. Chapman, H. H. 1944. "Fire and Pines." *AF* 50:62–63, 91–93.

88. Chapman, H. H. 1947. "Prescribed Burning versus Public Forest Fire Service." *JF* 45:804–8.

89. Chapman, H. H. 1947. "Prescribed Burning in the Loblolly Pine Type." *JF* 45:209–12.

90. Chapman, H. H. 1947. "Results of a Prescribed Fire at Urania, La., on Longleaf Pine Land." *JF* 45:121–23.

91. Chapman, H. H. 1947. "Natural Areas." *Ecology* 28:193–94.

92. Chapman, H. H. 1948. "The Initiation of Early Stages of Research on Natural Reforestation of Longleaf Pine." *JF* 46:505–10.

93. Chapman, H. H. 1950. "Lightning in the Longleaf." *AF* 56(1):10–12.

94. Chapman, H. H. 1950. "An Unknown Pioneer in Prescribed Burning in Burma." *JF* 48:131–32.

95. Charlevoix. 1763. *Letters*. R. Goadby's English ed. Cited by Allen (10), p. 202.

96. Chavennes, Elizabeth. 1941. "Written Records of Forest Succession." *Scientific Monthly* 53:76–77.

96a.   Chevalier, A. 1925. "Essai d'une classification géographique des principaux systèmes de culture pratiques à la surface du globe." *Rev. Intern. Rens. Agrools.* 3. Cited by Braun-Blanquet (57a) p. 282.

97. Christy, Miller. 1892. "Why Are the Prairies Treeless?" *Proceedings of the Royal Geographical Society and Monthly Record of Geography* (London): 78–100.

98. Clark, Harold Willard. 1933. "Biotic Associations in the North Coast Ranges of California." University of California master's thesis.

99. Clements, F. E. 1910. *The Life History of Lodgepole Burn Forests*. USDA-FS Bulletin 79.

100. Clements, Frederic E. 1916. *Plant Succession*. CI-P 242.

101. Clements, Frederic E. 1920. *Plant Indicators*. CI-P 290.

102. Clements, Frederic E., John E. Weaver, and Herbert C. Hanson. 1929. *Plant Competition*. CI-P 398.

103. Clements, F. E. 1934. "The Relict Method in Dynamic Ecology." *Journal of Ecology* 22:39–68.

104. Clements, Frederic E., and Ralph W. Chaney. 1936. *Environment and Life in the Great Plains*. Carnegie Institution of Washington Supplementary Publications 24.

105. Clements, Frederic E. 1938. "Climatic Cycles and Human Populations in the Great Plains." *Scientific Monthly* 47(3):193–210.

106. Cline, A. C., and S. H. Spurr. 1942. *The Virgin Upland Forest of Central New England*. Harvard Forest Bulletin 21.

107. Cobb, F. E. 1929. "The Possibilities of Growing Evergreens in the Northern Great Plains." JF 27:301–3.

107a. Cockayne, A. H. 1910. "The Effect of Burning on Tussock Country." *Journal of the New Zealand Department of Agriculture* 1:7–15. Cited by Shantz (453a), p. 25.

107b. Cockayne, L. 1928. "The Vegetation of New Zealand." In Engler and Drude, *Die Vegetation der Erde XIV*. Cited by Shantz (453a), p. 16.

108. Coffey, G. N. 1912. *A Study of the Soils of the United States*. U.S. Department of Agriculture, Bureau of Soils, Bulletin 85.

109. Condra, George E. 1906. *Geography of Nebraska*. Cited by Shimek (457), p. 218.

110. Cook, O. F. 1908. *Change of Vegetation on the South Texas Prairies*. USDA-BPI Circular 14.

111. Cook, O. F. 1921. *Milpa Agriculture*. Smithsonian Institution Annual Report 1919.

112. Cooper, W. S. 1922. *The Broad-Sclerophyll Vegetation of California*. CI-P 319.

113. Cornelius, Donald R., and M. Donald Atkins. 1946. "Grass Establishment and Development Studies in Morton County, Kansas." *Ecology* 27:342–53.

114. Costanso, M. 1911 [1770]. *The Portola Expedition of 1769–1770*. Diary of Miguel Costanso, ed. Frederick Teggart. Academy of the Pacific Coast Historical Publication 2(4). Cited by Sampson (429), p. 52.

115. Cottam, Grant. 1949. "The Phytosociology of an Oak Woods in Southwestern Wisconsin." *Ecology* 30:271–87.

116. Cottam, W. P., and George Stewart. 1940. "Plant Succession as a Result of Grazing and of Meadow Desiccation by Erosion since Settlement in 1862." *JF* 38:613–26.

117. Cottle, H. J. 1931. "Studies in the Vegetation of Southwestern Texas." *Ecology* 11.

118. Cowles, Henry C. 1928. "Persistence of Prairies." *Ecology* 9:380–82.

119. Cox, Ross. 1831. *Adventures on the Columbia River.* Vol. 2. London.

120. Cox, William T. 1936. "Do Droughts Explain the Prairies?" *AF* 42:556–57.

121. Craddock, George Washington, Jr. 1929. "The Successional Influence of Fire on the Chaparral Type." University of California master's thesis.

122. Crespi, Juan. 1769–70. *Fray Juan Crespi: Missionary Explorer on the Pacific Coast, 1769–1774.* Trans. and ed. H. E. Bolton. Berkeley, 1927.

122a. Culbertson, Thaddeus A. 1952. *Journal of an Expedition to the Mauvaises Terres and the Upper Missouri in 1850.* BAE-B 147.

123. Curtis, John T., and Max L. Partch. 1948. "Effect of Fire on Competition between Blue Grass and Certain Prairie Plants." *American Midland Naturalist* 39(2): 437–43.

124. Dana, James D. 1862. *Manual of Geology.* New York: American Book Co.

124a. Dana, James D. 1865. "On the Origin of Prairies." *AJS* 89–90:293–304.

124b. Dana, Richard H., Jr. 1868 [1840]. *Two Years before the Mast: A Personal Narrative of Life at Sea.* New York: Houghton, Mifflin and Co.

125. Darby and Dwight. 1833. *Gazetteer.* Cited by Sauer (434), p. 129.

125a. Darrah, William Culp. 1951. *Powell of the Colorado.* Princeton: Princeton University Press.

126. Darwin, Charles. 1852. *Journal of Researches into the Natural History and Geology of the Countries Visited during the Voyage of H.M.S. Beagle around the World.*

127. Daubenmire, Rexford F. 1940. "Plant Succession Due to Overgrazing in *Agropyron* Bunchgrass Prairie of Southeastern Washington." *Ecology.* 21:55–64.

128. Daubenmire, R. F. 1942. "An Ecological Study of the Vegetation of Southeastern Washington and Adjacent Idaho." *Ecological Monographs* 12:53–79.

128a. Daubenmire, R. F. 1947. *Plants and Environment.* New York: John Wiley and Sons.

129. Davenport. 1830. *Gazetteer.* Cited by Sauer (434), p. 129.

130. Davila, Pedrarias. 1514. "Relacion de . . . las provincias de Tierra firma o Castilla del oro (Darien)." In *Coleccion de los viajes y descubrimientos* by Martin Navarrete, vol. 3. Madrid, 1829.

131. Davis, Wilfred S. 1951. "Nebraska Firebreaks." *Fire Control Notes* (USDA-FS: January) 12(1):40–43.

132. Davis, William N. 1900. In Mill's *International Geography.* Cited in Shimek (457), p. 218.

133. Delores, Juan. 1939. Personal communication on Papago burning.

134. De Vries, David Pieterz. 1655. *Korte historiael.* T'Hoorn.

135. Dixon, Roland B. 1905. *The Northern Maidu.* AMNH-B 18.

136. Dixon, Roland B. 1907. *The Shasta.* AMNH-B 17.

137. Dixon, Roland B. 1908. "Notes on the Achomawi and Atsugewi Indians of Northern California." *AA* n.s. 10:212.

138. Dodds, Gidion S., et al. 1909. "Studies in Mesa and Foothill Vegetation, I." *UCS* 6:11–50.

139. Dodge, Col. R. I. 1877. *Plains of the Great West.* New York.

140. Douglas, David. 1914. *Journal Kept by David Douglas during His Travels in North America, 1823–27.* London: Royal Horticultural Society.

141. Drew, William B. 1947. "Floristic Composition of Grazed and Ungrazed Prairie Vegetation in North-Central Missouri." *Ecology* 28:26–41.

142. Driver, H. E. 1937. *CED: VI, Southern Sierra Nevada*. UC-AR 1.

143. Driver, H. E. 1939. *CED: X, Northwest California*. UC-AR 1.

144. Drucker, Philip. 1937. *The Tolowa and Their Southwest Oregon Kin*. UC-PAAE 36.

145. Drucker, P. 1937. *CED: V, Southern California*. UC-AR 1.

146. Drucker, P. 1941. *CED: XVII, Yuman-Piman*. UC-AR 6.

147. Drucker, P. 1938. "CED: Northwest Coast." MS.

148. Duben. 1824. *Der Ansiedler im Staat Missouri*. Cited by Sauer (433), p. 53.

149. Du Bois, Cora. 1940. Personal communication. "Burning on Alor, Dutch E. Indies." MS.

150. Dwight, T. 1822. *Travels in New-England and New-York*. Vol. 4. New Haven.

151. Editorial. 1939. "A Silver Anniversary on the Golden Plains." *JF* 37:593–94.

152. Edwards, Everett, E. 1948. "The Settlement of Grasslands." In *Grass*. Yearbook of USDA, Washington, D.C.: Government Printing Office.

153. Egan, Major Howard, and Howard R. Egan. 1917. *Pioneering the West, 1846 to 1878*. Ed. William M. Egan. Salt Lake City. Cited by Steward (483), pp. 38–39.

154. Egler, Frank E. 1950. Review of McDougall's Plant Ecology, "Throughly Revised." *Ecology* 31:312.

155. Eiseley, Loren C. 1946. "The Fire-Drive and the Extinction of the Terminal Pleistocene Fauna." *AA* 48:54–60.

156. Elias, M. R. 1935. "Tertiary Grasses and Other Prairie Vegetation from the High Plains of North America." *AJS* (5th series) 29:24–33.

157. Ellsworth, H. L. 1837. *Illinois in 1837*. Cited by Shimek (457), p. 218.

158. Elwell, Harry M., Harley A. Daniel, and F. A. Fenton. 1941. *The Effects of Burning Pasture and Woodland Vegetation*. Oklahoma Agricultural Experimental Station Bulletin B-247.

158a. Elwell, Harry M., and Maurice B. Cox. 1950. "New Methods of Brush Control for Mare Grass." *Journal of Range Management* 3:46–51.

159. Englemann, Henry. 1863. "Remarks upon . . . Prairies, Flats, and Barrens in Southern Illinois." *AJS* 36:384–96.

160. Ernst, Emil F. 1949. "Vanishing Meadows in Yosemite Valley." *Yosemite Nature Notes* 28:34–40.

160a. Escalante. 1776. In *Pageant in the Wilderness* by H. E. Bolton. Utah Historical Quarterly, vol. 18, 1950.

161. Essene, Frank. 1942. *CED: XXI, Round Valley*. UC-AR 8.

162. Evans, Charles F. 1932. "Flaming Florida." *AF* 38:344, 376.

163. Evans, C. R. 1944. "Can the South Conquer the Fire Scourge?" *AF* 50:227–29, 265–66.

164. Eyre, F. H. 1938. "Can Jack Pine Be Regenerated without Fire?" *JF* 36:1067–72.

165. Farnham, T. J. 1843. *Travels in the Great Western Prairie, the Anahuac, and Rocky Mountains, and in the Oregon Territory, May 21–October 16, 1839*. Early Western Travels, 1748–1846, ed. Reuben Gold Thwaites, vol. 28. Cleveland: Arthur H. Clark Co., 1904.

166. Farnham, T. J. 1850. *Life, Adventures, and Travels in California*. New York.

167. Faye, Paul Louis. 1923. *Notes on the Southern Maidu*. UC-PAAE 20.

168. Featherstonhaugh, G. W. 1844. *Excursion through the Slave States*. Vol. 1. London.

169. Fendler, A. 1866. "On Prairies." *AJS* (2nd series) 41:154–58.

170. Fewkes, Jesse Walter. 1907. "The Aborigines of Porto Rico and Neighboring Islands." In BAE-*R* 25 (1903–4): 48–49.

171. Finley, J. B. 1857. *Life among the Indians.* Ed. Clark. Cincinnati.

172. Fischel, Hans E. 1939. "Folsom and Yuma Culture Finds." *American Antiquity* 3:232–64.

172a. Fischer, C. E. C. 1912. "The Need of Fire Protection in the Tropics." *Indian Forester* 38(5):191–221. Cited by Shantz (453a), pp. 15, 84.

173. Fisher, C. E. 1950. "The Mesquite Problem in the Southwest." *Journal of Range Management* 3:60–70.

173a. Fisher, R. S. 1853. *Gazetteer.* Cited by Sauer (434), p. 130.

174. Flannery, Regina. 1939. *An Analysis of Coastal Algonquian Culture.* Catholic University of America Anthropological Series 7.

175. Fleming, Guy L. 1932. "So This Is Florida." *AF* 38:345.

176. Flint, James. 1822. *Letters from America, 1818–1820.* Early Western Travels, ed. Reuben Gold Thwaites, vol. 9. Cleveland, 1904.

177. Flint, Timothy. 1826. *Recollections of the Last Ten Years.* Boston.

178. Flint, Timothy. 1832. *History and Geography of the Mississippi Valley.*

179. Font, Fray Pedro. 1775–76. "Diary of an Expedition to Monterey by Way of the Colorado River." In *Anza's California Expeditions,* trans. and ed. H. E. Bolton. Berkeley, 1930.

180. Fontaine, Rev. James. 1716. *Journal of a Huguenot Family.* Ed. Ann Maury. Cited by Maxwell (358), p. 94.

181. Foote, W. H. 1855. *Sketch of Virginia.* Cited by Maxwell (358), p. 96.

182. Fordham, E. P. 1817–18. *Personal Narrative of Travels in Virginia and of a Residence in the Illinois Territory.* Ed. F. A. Ogg. Cleveland, 1906.

183. Fortune, Reo. 1940. Personal communication. "Burning in New Guinea." MS.

183a. Foster, George M. 1944. *A Summary of Yuki Culture.* UC-AR 5.

184. Fowke, Gerard. 1894. *Archaeologic Investigations in James and Potomac Valleys.* BAE-B 23.

185. Friederici, G. 1925. *Der Charakter der Entdeckung und Eroberung Amerikas durch die Europaer.* 3 vols. Stuttgart-Gotha.

186. Friederici, G. 1930. "Der Grad der Durchdringbarkeit Nordamerikas im Zeitalter der Entdeckungen und ersten Durchforschung des Kontinents durch die Europaer." *Petermann's Mitteilungen* 209:223–26.

187. Fritz, Emanuel. 1931. "The Role of Fire in the Redwood Region." *JF* 29:939–50.

188. Fritz, Emanuel. 1932. *The Role of Fire in the Redwood Region.* UC-AES Circular 323.

189. Fritz, Emanuel. 1937. "Redwood Forestry Program Jeopardized by Public Apathy toward Fire." *JF* 35:755–58.

190. Fuller, George D. 1935. "Postglacial Vegetation of the Lake Michigan Region." *Ecology* 16:473–87.

191. Garth, T. 1939. "Atsugewi Ethnography." MS.

192. Gaskill, Alfred. 1905. "Why Prairies Are Treeless." *Science* n.s. 22:55–56. Cited in Shimek (457), p. 218.

193. Gates, Frank C. 1926. "Pines in the Prairie." *Ecology* 7:96–98.

194. Gemmer, Eugene W., T. E. Make, and R. A. Chapman. 1940. "Ecological Aspects of Longleaf Pine Regeneration in South Mississippi." *Ecology* 21:75–86.

195. George, Ernest J. 1939. "Tree Planting on the Drier Sections of the Northern Great Plains." *JF* 37:695–98.

196. George, Ernest J. 1943. "Effects of Cultivation and Number of Rows on Survival and Growth of Trees in Farm Windbreaks on the Northern Great Plains." *JF* 41:820–28.

197. Gerhard, Frederic, 1857. *Illinois as It Is.* Cited by Sampson (431), p. 557.

197a Gianella, Bill. n.d. Personal communication. Notes on "Burning to Make the Springs Flow." MS.

198. Gianini Foundation. 1934. *Map of California Natural Cover and Agricultural Land Use.* University of California Forest and Range Experiment Station.

199. Gibbs, George. 1851. "Journal of the Expedition of Colonel Redich . . . through Northwestern California . . . 1851." In *Archives of Aboriginal Knowledge,* collected by H. R. Schoolcraft. Vol. 3. 1860.

200. Gifford, E. W., and S. Klimek. 1936. *CED: II, Yana.* UC-PAAE 37.

201. Gifford, E. W. 1936. *Northeastern and Western Yavapai.* UC-PAAE 34.

202. Gifford, E. W., and A. L. Kroeber. 1937. *CED: IV, Pomo Area.* UC-PAAE 37.

203. Gifford, E. W. 1939. "Karok Field Notes." MS.

204. Gifford, E. W. 1940. *CED: XII, Apache-Pueblo.* UC-AR 4.

205. Gleason, Henry Allen. 1912. "An Isolated Prairie Grove and Its Phylo-geographical Significance." *BG* 53:38–48.

206. Gleason, Henry Allen. 1913. "The Relation of Forest Distribution and Prairie Fires in the Middle West." *Torreya* 13:173–81.

207. Gleason, H. A. 1932. "The Vegetational History of the Middle West." *Annals of the Association of American Geographers* 12:39–85.

208. Goddard, Pliny Earl. 1903. *Life and Culture of the Hupa.* UC-PAAE 1.

209. Goldschmidt, W. 1939. "Hupa Field Notes." MS.

210. Goode, J. P. 1932. *School Atlas.* New York.

211. Gordon-Cumming, F.C. 1883. "Wild Tribes of the Sierras." *National Review* 2(8):412–21. Cited by Sampson (429), p. 19.

212. Gorrie, R. Maclagan, D. Sc. 1935. "Protective Burning in Himalayan Pine." *JF* 33:807–11.

213. Gow, James E. 1899. "Forest Trees of Adair County (Iowa)." *Proceeding of the Iowa Academy Science* 6:56–63.

214. Graves, H. S. 1920. "Graves Terms Light Burning 'Piute Firestry.' " *Timberman* 21:35.

215. Gray, Asa. 1884. "Characteristics of the North American Flora." *AJS* (3rd series) 28:322–40.

216. Greeley, W. B. 1920. " 'Piute Forestry,' or the Fallacy of Light Burning." *Timberman* 21:38–39.

217. Greene, S. W. 1931. "The Forest That Fire Made." *AF* 37:583–84, 618.

218. Gregg, Josiah. 1844. *Commerce of the Prairies.* Early Western Travels, 1748–1846, ed. Reuben Gold Thwaites, vols. 19 and 20. Cleveland, 1905.

219. Griffiths, David. 1904. *Range Investigations in Arizona.* USDA-BPI Bulletin 67.

220. Griggs, Robert F. 1934. "The Edge of the Forest in Alaska and the Reasons for Its Position." *Ecology* 15:80–96.

221. Griggs, Robert F. 1938. "Timberlines in the Northern Rocky Mountains." *Ecology* 19:549–64.

222. Gunther, E. 1939. "CED: Puget Sound." MS.

223. Gustafson, R. O. 1946. *Forest Fires, Basal Wounds, and Resulting Damage to Timber in an Eastern Kentucky Area.* Kentucky Agricultural Experiment Station Bulletin 493.

224. Guthrie, John D. 1936. *Great Forest Fires of America.* U.S. Forest Service pamphlet. Washington, D.C.: USDA.

224a. Guthrie, John D. 1943. "Historic Forest Fires of America." *AF* 49:290–94, 316–17.

225. Haig, Irvin T. 1938. "Fire in Modern Firest Management." *JF* 36:1045–47.

226. Halliday, W. E. D., and A. W. A. Brown. 1943. "Re Distribution of Some Important Forest Trees in Canada." *Ecology* 24:353–73.

226a. Hanno. 500 b.c. "Periplus." Cited by Werner (547), p. 7.

227. Hanson, H. C. 1929. *Improvement of Sagebrush Range in Colorado*. Colorado Agricultural Experiment Station Bulletin 356.

228. Hanson, Herbert C. 1938. "Fire in Land Use Management." *JF* 36:1054.

229. Hanson, Herbert C., and C. T. Vorhies. 1938. "Need for Research on Grasslands." *Scientific Monthly* (March) 46:230–41.

230. Hardtner, Henry E. 1935. "A Tale of a Root. . . ." *JF* 33:351–56.

231. Harper, Francis. 1931. "Physiographic and Faunal Areas in Athabasca and Great Slave Lakes Region." *Ecology* 12:18–32.

232. Harper, R. M. 1912. "The Hempstead Plains of Long Island." *Torreya* 12:277–87.

232a. Harper, Roland M. 1943. *Forests of Alabama*. Geological Survey of Alabama Monograph 10.

232b. Harper, Roland M. 1952. Personal communication.

233. Harrington, John P. 1932. *Tobacco among the Karuk Indians of California*. BAE-B 94.

234. Harrington, J. P. 1942. *CED: XIX, Central California Coast*. UC-AR 7.

234a. Harshberger, John W. 1911. *Phytogeographic Survey of North America*. Weinheim: H. R. Engelmann.

235. Hartmann, C. W. 1942 [1897]. "The Indians of Northwestern Mexico." *Congrès International des Américanistes* 10:117–19.

236. Harvey, LeRoy Harris. 1908. "Floral Succession in Prairie-Grass Formation of Southeastern South Dakota." *BG* 46:81–108, 277.

237. Hastings, L. W. 1845. *The Emigrants Guide to Oregon and California, Containing a Description of California*. Cincinnati: George Conclin Co. Cited by Sampson (429), p. 19.

238. Henkel, J. S. 1943. "Preservation of Mountain Vegetation of the Southwest Districts of the Cape Provence (South Africa)." MS read before the Royal Society of South Africa.

239. Hennepin, Father Louis. 1683. *A New Discovery of a Vast Country in America. 1675–1680*, ed. R. G. Thwaites, vol. 1. Chicago, 1903.

240. Henry, Alexander, and David Thompson. 1799–1814. "Journals." In Elliott Coues, *New Light on the Early History of the Greater Northwest*, vol. 2. New York, 1897.

241. Hensel, R. L. 1923. "Effect of Burning on Vegetation in Kansas Pastures." *Journal of Agricultural Research* 23:631–47.

242. Hensel, R. L. 1923. "Recent Studies on the Effect of Burning on Grassland Vegetation." *Ecology* 4:183–88.

243. Heyward, Frank. 1937. "The Effect of Frequent Fires on Profile Development of Longleaf Pine Forest Soil." *JF* 35:23–27.

244. Heyward, Frank. 1939. "The Relation of Fire to Stand Composition of Longleaf Pine Forests." *Ecology* 20:287–304.

245. Hilgard, E. W. 1906. *Soils*. New York.

246. Hill, W. W. 1938. *Navaho Agricultural and Hunting Methods*. YU-PA 18.

247. Hind, H. Y. [1969.] *Narrative of the Canadian Red River Exploring Expedition of 1857, and of the Assiniboine and Saskatchewan Exploring Expedition of 1858*. Vols. 1 and 2. New York: Greenwood Press. Cited by Christy (97), pp. 84–94.

248. Hinds, R. B. 1844. *The Botany of the Voyage of the H.M.S. "Sulphur," under Command of Captain Sir Edward Belcher during 1836–1842.* London: Smith, Elder, and Co. Cited by Sampson (429), p. 19.

249. Hodge, F. W. (ed.). 1907. *Handbook of American Indians.* BAE-B 30 (vol. 1).

250. Hoffman, C. F. 1835. *A Winter in the Far West.* London.

251. Hofmann, J. V. 1920. "The Establishment of a Douglas Fir Forest." *Ecology* 1:49–53.

252. Holbrook, Stewart H. 1943. *Burning an Empire.* Macmillan.

252a. Holmes. 1839. *Exploration.*

253. Holt, Catharine. 1946. *Shasta Ethnography.* UC-AR 3.

254. Hopkins, Cyril I. *Soil Fertility and Permanent Agriculture.* Cited in Shimek (457), p. 218.

255. Hopkins, Harold, F. W. Albertson, and Andrew Riegel. 1948. "Some Effects of Burning upon a Prairie in West-Central Kansas." *Transactions of the Kansas Academy of Science.* 51:131–41.

256. Houck, Louis. 1908. *A History of Missouri.* Chicago.

257. Hough, A. F. 1936. "A Climax Forest Community on East Tionesta Creek in Northwestern Pennsylvania." *Ecology 17* 17:9–28.

258. Hough, A. F., and R. D. Forbes. 1943. "The Ecology and Silvics of Forests in the High Plateaus of Pennsylvania." *Ecological Monographs* 13:299–320.

259. Hough, Walter. 1926. *Fire as an Agent in Human Culture.* U.S. National Museum Bulletin 139.

260. Howell, Joseph, Jr. 1941. "Pinon and Juniper Woodlands of the Southwest." *JF* 39:542–45.

261. Huberman, M. A. 1935. "The Role of Western White Pine in Forest Succession in Northern Idaho." *Ecology* 16:137–51.

262. Hulbert, Archer B. 1930. *Soil.* New Haven.

263. Hull, A. C., Jr., and J. F. Pechanec. 1947. "Cheatgrass—A Challenge to Range Research." *JF* 45:555–66.

263a. Humbert, H. 1923. *Les composés de Madagascar.* Caen. Cited by Braun-Blanquet (57a), p. 282.

264. Hursh, C. R., and C. A. Connaughton. 1938. "Effects of Forests upon Local Climate." *JF* 36:864–66.

265. Hussey, John. 1884. *Botany of Barren and Edmonson Counties.* KGS—Timber and Botany, part B, pp. 8–11.

266. Hutchings, J. M. 1888. *In the Heart of the Sierras.* Oakland, Calif.: Pacific Press and Pub. House. Cited by Sampson (429), p. 19.

267. Ihering, H. V. 1907." A distribuição de campos e mattas no Brazil." *Revista do Museu Paulista* 7:129–31.

268. Imlay, Gilbert. 1797. *Topographical Description* (of Kentucky). London.

269. Ingram, Douglas C. 1928. "Grazing as a Fire Prevention Mesure." *JF* 26:998–1005.

270. Irving, Washington. 1897. "A Tour on the Prairies." In *The Works of Washington Irving.* New York: P. F. Collier.

270a. Irving, Washington. 1898. *The Adventures of Captain Bonneville.* Pawnee ed. Vol. 2. New York. Cited by Steward (483), p. 206.

271. Isaac, Leo A. 1940. "Vegetative Succession following Logging in the Douglas Fir Region with Special Reference to Fire." *JF* 38:716–21.

272. Jacobs, M. 1939. "CED: Kalapuya." MS.

273. Jepson, Willis Linn. 1910. *The Silva of California*. University of California Memoirs 2.
274. Jepson, Willis Linn. 1921. "The Giant Sequoia." In *Handbook of Yosemite National Park*, ed. Ansel F. Hall. New York.
275. Kalm, Peter. 1772. "Travels in North America." In John Pinkerton, *Voyages and Travels*, vol. 13. London, 1812.
275a. Johnson, Conrad J., Jr. 1952. Personal communication. "Guadalcanal." MS.
276. Jones, A. D. 1838. *Illinois and the West*. Boston. Cited by Gleason (206), p. 175.
277. Keen, F. P. 1937. "Climatic Cycles in Eastern Oregon as indicated by Tree Rings." *Monthly Weather Review* 65:175–88. Cited by Weaver (533), p. 7.
278. Keen, F. P. 1940. "Longevity of Ponderosa Pine." *JF* 38:597–98.
279. Kellogg, Charles E. 1948. "Grass and the Soil." In *Grass*. Yearbook of the USDA.
280. Kellogg, R. S. 1905. *Forest Belts of Western Kansas and Nebraska*. USDA-FS-B 66.
281. Kelly, Isabel T. 1932. *Ethnography of the Surprise Valley Paiute*. UC-PAAE 31.
282. Kelly, William. 1851. *An Excursion to California*. London.
283. Kercheval, Samuel. 1833. *History of the (Shenandoah) Valley of Virginia*. 3rd ed. Woodstock, Va. Cited by Maxwell (358), p. 95.
284. Kern, E. M. 1850. "Indian Customs of California." In Henry R. Schoolcraft, ed., *Information Respecting the History, Condition, and Prospects of the Indian Tribes of the United States*. Archives of Aboriginal Knowledge, vol. 5. Philadelphia: J. B. Lippincott and Co. Cited by Sampson (429), p. 19.
285. Kittredge, Joseph, Jr. 1934. "Evidence of the Rate of Forest Succession on Star Island, Minnesota." *Ecology* 125:24–35.
285a. Kittredge, Joseph, Jr. 1948. *Forest Influences*. New York: McGraw-Hill.
286. Kitts, J. A. 1920. "California Divided on Light Burning." *Timberman* 21(3):36, 81–86.
287. Kniffen, Fred B. 1928. *Achomawi Geography*. UC-PAAE 23.
288. Kniffen, Fred B. 1939. *Pomo Geography*. UC-PAAE 36.
289. Koen, Henry R. 1948. "What Intensive Management of the Forests Will Mean to the Ozark Region of Oklahoma, Missouri, and Arkansas." *JF* 46:165–67.
290. Koppen, W. 1923. *Die Klimate der Erde*. Leipzig.
291. Kotzebue, Otto von. 1821. *Voyage of Discovery . . . 1815–1818*. 3 vols. London.
292. Kraus, P. S. 1940. Personal communication. "Burning in Sumatra." MS.
293. Kroeber, A. L. 1925. *Handbook of the Indians of California*. BAE-B 78.
294. Kroeber, A. L. 1928. "A Kato War." In *Festschrift: Publication d'Hommage Offerte au P. W. Schmidt*.
295. Kroeber, A. L. 1932. *The Patwin and Their Neighbors*. UC-PAAE 29.
296. Kroeber, A. L. 1939. "Yurok Field Notes." MS.
297. Kroeber, A. L. 1939. *Cultural and Natural Areas of Native North America*. UC-PAAE 38.
298. Kroodsma, R. F. 1937. "The Permanent Fixation of Sand Dunes in Michigan." *JF* 35:365–72.
299. Larsen, J. A. 1925. "Natural Reproduction after Forest Fires in Northern Idaho." *Journal of Agricultural Research* 30:1196–97.
300. Larsen, J. A. 1929. "Fires and Forest Succession in the Bitterroot Mountains of Northern Idaho." *Ecology* 10:67–76.
301. Larsen, J. A. 1930. "Forest Types of the Northern Rocky Mountains and Their Climatic Controls." *Ecology* 11:631–72.
302. Larson, Floyd. 1940. "The Role of the Bison in Maintaining the Short Grass Plains." *Ecology* 21:113–21.

303. Larson, Floyd, and Warren Whitman. 1942. "A Comparison of Used and Unused Grassland Mesas in the Badlands of South Dakota." *Ecology* 23:438–45.

304. Las Casas, Bartolome de (1542). 1875–76. *Historia de las Indias*. Vols. 1 and 5. Madrid.

305. Lawson, J. 1718. *History of Carolina*. London. Cited by Flannery (174), p. 14; and Birket-Smith (46), pp. 330–31.

306. Leavitt, Clyde. 1928. "Railway Fire Protection in Canada." *JF* 26:871–77.

307. Lederer, John. 1670. *Discoveries*. Charleston, S.C., 1891. Cited by Maxwell (358), p. 92.

308. Legge, J. 1871. *Shi-King, or Book of Poetry*. Vol. 4, parts 1 and 2. Cited by Birket-Smith (46), p. 160.

309. Lemon, Paul C. 1946. "Prescribed Burning in Relation to Grazing in the Longleaf-Slash Pine Type." *JF* 44:115–17.

310. Lemon, Paul C. 1949. "Successional Responses of Herbs in the Longleaf-Slash Pine Forest after Fire." *Ecology* 30:135–45.

311. Leopold, Aldo. 1924. "Grass, Brush, Timber and Fire in Southern Arizona." *JF* 22(6):1–10.

312. Le Page du Pratz, Antoine Simone. 1758. *Histoire de la Louisiane*. Vol. 1. Paris.

313. Lesquereaux, Leo. 1865. "On the Origin and Formation of Prairies." *AJS* 39:317–27; 40:23–31.

314. Lesquereaux, Leo. 1866. *On the Origin and the Formation of the Prairies*. Geological Survey of Illinois 1.

315. Levichine, A. 1840. *Description des hordes et des steppes des Kirghiz-Kazaks*. Trans. from the Russian. Paris. Cited by Birket-Smith (46), p. 160.

315a. Levy, E. B. 1937. "The Conversation of Rainforest to Grassland in New Zealand." *International Grassland Congress Report* 4:71–77. Cited by Daubenmire (128a), p. 342.

316. Lewis, Albert B. 1932. *Ethnology of Melanesia*. Field Museum of Natural History-Department of Anthropology Guide. Part 5.

317. Lewis, Meriwether, and Wm. Clark. 1814. *Lewis and Clark Expedition*. Ed. Elliott Coues. Vol. 1. New York, 1893.

317a. *Life*. 1952. "Man vs. Mesquite." August 18, pp. 69–72.

318. Liming, Franklin G. and John P. Johnston. 1944. "Reproduction in Oak-Hickory Forest Stands of the Missouri Ozarks." *JF* 42:175–80.

319. Lindblom, G. 1925. *Och fangstime toder bland afrikanska folk*. Vols. 1 and 2. Stockholm. Cited by Birket-Smith (46), pp. 160–61.

320. Lindenmuth, A. W., Jr. 1949. "Fires and Trends of Fire Occurrence in the Northeast." *Fire Control Notes of USDA-FS* 12(1) (January 1951): 1–5.

321. Lindstrom, P. 1691. *Geographia Americae*. Trans. Johnson. Philadelphia, 1925.

322. Little, Elbert L. 1939. "The Vegetation of the Caddo County Canyons, Oklahoma." *Ecology* 20:1–10.

323. Little, S. 1946. *The Effects of Forest Fires on the Stand History of New Jersey's Pine Region*. Northeastern Forest Experiment Station Forest Management Paper 2.

324. Little, S., and E. B. Moore. 1945. "Controlled Burning in South Jersey's Oak Pine Stands." *JF* 43:499–505.

325. Little, S., and E. B. Moore. 1949. "The Ecological Role of Prescribed Burns in the Pine-Oak Forests of Southern New Jersey." *Ecology* 30:223–33.

326. Little, S., J. P. Allen, and E. B. Moore. 1948. "Controlled Burning as a Dual-Purpose Tool of Forest Management in New Jersey's Pine Region." *JF* 46:810–19.

327. Livingston, Burton E., and Forest Shreve. 1921. *The Distribution of Vegetation in the United States, as Related to Climatic Conditions.* CI-P 284.

328. Lockett, H. C. 1939. *Along the Beale Trail.* U.S. Office of Indian Affairs.

329. Loeb, Edwin M. 1926. *Pomo Folkways.* UC-PAAE 19.

330. Loeb, Edwin M. 1932. *The Western Kuksu Cult.* UC-PAAE 33.

331. Lofgren, A. 1906. "Ensaio para uma distribuição dos vegetaes grupos floristicos no Estado do São Paulo." *Boletim da Commissão Geographica e Geologica de São Paulo* 11:28. Cited by Ihering (267), p. 130.

332. Loomis, Chester. 1825. *Notes of Journey to the Great West in 1825.* Pamphlet. Cited by Gleason (206), p. 175.

333. Lorenz, Ralph W., and J. Nelson Spaeth. 1947. "The Growth of Conifers on Prairie Soil." *JF* 45:253–56.

334. Loskiel, G. H. 1794. *History of Mission (Livonia, 1788).* London. Cited by Flannery (174), p. 14.

335. Loud, L. L. 1918. *Ethnogeography and Archaeology of the Wiyot Territory.* UC-PAAE 14.

336. Love, R. M., and Burle J. Jones. 1952. *Improving California Brush Ranges.* California Agricultural Experiment Station Circular 371.

337. Loven, Sven. 1924. *Über die Wurzeln der Tainischen Kultur.* Göteborg (Gotesberg).

337a. Lowie, Robert H. 1924. *Notes on Shoshonean Ethnography.* AMNH-AP 20.

338. Lowie, Robert H. 1938. "Subsistence." In *General Anthropology,* ed. Franz Boas. New York.

338a. Lucretius. 55 b.c. *On the Nature of the Universe.* Trans. H. A. J. Munro. London: George Bell and Sons, 1908.

339. Lund, R. W. 1835. "Bemaerkinger over Vegetationen paa de indre Hoisletter af Brasilien isaer i plantehistorik Henseede." In *Det Kgl. Danske Vidensk. Selsk. Skrifter.* Cited by Ihering (267), p. 130.

340. Lundell, Cyrus Longwarth. 1934. *Preliminary Sketch of the Phytogeography of the Yucatan Peninsula.* CI-P 436.

341. Lutz, H. J. 1930. "The Vegetation of Heart's Content, a Virgin Forest in Northwestern Pennsylvania." *Ecology* 11:1–29.

342. Lutz, H. J. 1934. *Ecological Relations in the Pitch Pine Plains of Southern New Jersey.* Yale University School of Forestry Bulletin 38.

343. Lyell, Sir Charles. 1849. *A Second Visit to the United States of America.* New York: Harper and Brothers.

344. Macbride, Thomas N. 1894–1900. *Iowa Geological Survey* 4:115–16; 9:148–49; 10:228–39.

345. McClure, David. 1899. *Diary, 1748–1820.* Ed. Dexter. New York.

346. McDonald, W.J. 1939. "Fire under the Midnight Sun." *AF* 65:168–69, 231.

347. McGee, W. J. 1884. "The Siouan Indians: A Preliminary Sketch." *BAE-R* 15:113–204.

348. McGuire, W. W. 1834. "On the Prairies of Alabama." *AJS* 26:93–98.

349. McIntosh, Arthur C. 1931. "A Botanical Survey of the Black Hills of South Dakota." *Black Hills Engineer* 19:157–286.

350. Macoun, John. 1882. *Manitoba and the Great North-West.* Cited by Christy (97), p. 95.

351. Maissurow, D. K. 1935. "Fire as a Necessary Factor in the Perpetuation of White Pine." *JF* 33:373.

352. Maissurow, D. K. 1941. "The Role of Fire in the Perpetuation of Virgin Forests of Northern Wisconsin." *JF* 39:201–7.

352a. Major, Jack. 1951. "Functional Factorial Approach to Plant Ecology." *Ecology* 32:392–412.

353. Marbut, Curtis Fletcher. 1935. "Soils of the United States." In USDA-*AAA*, part 3.

354. Marryat, Frank. 1955 [1850]. *Mountains and Molehills*. London.

355. Marsh, G. P. 1867. *Man and Nature*. New York.

356. Massey, Ernest de. 1927 [1848]. *A Frenchman in the Gold Rush*. Trans. Marguerite Eyer Wilbur from the journal of Ernest de Massey. San Francisco: California Historical Society.

357. Matthews, Washington. 1897. *Navajo Legends*. Memoirs, American Folk-Lore Society 5.

358. Maxwell, H. 1910. "The Use and Abuse of Forests by the Virginia Indians." *William and Mary College Historical Magazine* 19.

359. Meehan, T. 1886. "Warum die Prairen ohne Bäume Sind?" *Humboldt* 5:158. Summarized in *Just's Bot. Jahres-bericht* 14 (pt. 2, 1886): 240.

360. Melchert, Major. 1876. In R. Napp, *Die Argentinische Republic*. Buenos Aires. Cited by Schmieder (441), p. 268.

361. Michaux, F. A. 1802. "Travels in America, 1802." English translation in *Early Western Trails*. Cleveland: A. H. Clark Co., 1904.

362. Michel, F. L. 1701–2. "Report of Journey . . . to Virginia." *Virginia Magazine of History and Biography* 24 (1916): 41–42.

363. Mirov, N. T. 1935. "Two Centuries of Afforestation and Shelterbelt Planting on the Russian Steppes." *JF* 33:971–73.

364. Moerenhout, Jacques Antoine. 1843–56. "The French Consulate in California." Ed. Abraham Nasatir. *California Historical Society Quarterly* 13 (1934).

365. Monks. 1844. *History of Southern Missouri and Northern Arkansas*. Cited by Sauer (433), p. 56.

366. Mooney, James. 1890. "Notes on the Cosumnes Tribes of California" (obtained from Colonel Rice, 1850). *AA* 3.

367. Mooney, James. 1894. *The Siouan Tribes of the East*. BAE-B 22.

368. Mooney, James. 1900. *Myths of the Cherokee*. BAE-R 19 (1897–98).

369. Moore, E. B. 1939. *Forest Management in New Jersey*. New Jersey Dept. Conservation and Development. Cited by Little and Moore (325).

370. Morey, H. F. 1936. "A Comparison of Two Virgin Forests in Northwestern Pennsylvania." *Ecology* 17:43–55.

371. Morgan, L. H. 1851. *League of the Iroquois*. New York: Dodd, Mead.

372. Morris, Wm. G. 1948. "Lightning Fire Discovery Time on National Forests in Oregon and Washington." *Fire Control Notes of USDA-FS* 9(4) (October): 1–5.

373. Morriss, Donald J., and H. O. Mills. 1948. "The Conecuh Longleaf Pine Seed Burn." *JF* 46:646–52.

374. Morse, Jedediah. 1797. *American Gazetteer*. Cited by Sauer (434), p. 124.

375. Morton, Thomas. 1632. "New English Canaan." In Force's *Collections* 2, no. 5, pp. 36–37.

376. Muir, John. 1867. "A Thousand-Mile Walk to the Gulf." In *The Writings of John Muir*, vol. 1. 1916.

377. Muir, John. 1894. *The Mountains of California*. New York.

378. Muir, John. 1913. *The Story of My Boyhood and Youth*. New York: Houghton Mifflin Co. Cited by Cottam (115), p. 272.

379. Munger, T. T. 1940. "The Cycle from Douglas Fir to Hemlock." *Ecology* 21:451–59.
380. Munns, E. N., and Joseph H. Stoeckeler. 1946. "How Are the Great Plains Shelterbelts?" *JF* 44:237–57.
381. Nutt, Rush. 1833. "On the Origin, Extension and Continuance of Prairies." *AJS* 23:40–45.
382. Nuttall, Thomas. 1821. *A Journal of Travels into the Arkansas Territory, 1819.* Early Western Travels, 1748–1846, ed. Reuben Gold Thwaites, vol. 12. Cleveland, 1905.
383. Olson, Clarence E. 1940. "Forests in the Arizona Desert." *JF* 38:956–59.
384. Osgood, Cornelius. 1936. *Contributions to the Ethnography of the Kutchin.* YU-PA 14.
385. Osgood, Cornelius. 1937. *The Ethnography of the Tanaina.* YU-PA 16.
386. Oviedo y Valdez, Gonzalo Fernandez de. 1534. *Sumario de la natural historia.* In Col. Vedia, 1:490. Cited by Friederici (185), 1:91–96.
387. Owen, David Dale. 1854–55. (Kentucky "Barrens.") KGS 1:83–84.
387a. Palmer, E. J. 1934. "Notes on Some Plants of Oklahoma." *Journal of the Arnold Arboretum* 15:127–34.
388. Palou, F. F. 1926. (Portolo Expedition, 1769–70, to San Francisco). In *Historical Memoirs of New California,* vol. 4. University of California. Cited by Sampson (429), p. 19.
389. Parker, K. W. 1943. *Control of Mesquite on Southwestern Ranges.* USDA Leaflet 234.
390. Parker, Kenneth W. 1944. Review of Sampson's "Plant Succession on Burned Chaparral Lands." *Ecology* 25:374–75.
391. Pearson, G. A. 1920. "Factors Controlling the Distribution of Forest Types." *Ecology* 1:139–59.
392. Pearson, G. A. 1936. "Why the Prairies Are Treeless." *JF* 34:405–8.
393. Pechanec, J. F., G. D. Pickford, and G. Stewart. 1937. "Effects of the 1934 Drought on Native Vegetation of the Upper Snake River Plains, Idaho." *Ecology* 18:490–505.
393a. Pechanec, J. F., and G. Stewart. 1944. *Sagebrush Burning—Good and Bad.* USDA Farmers' Bulletin 1948.
394. Penfound, Wm. T., and R. W. Kelting. 1950. "Some Effects of Winter Burning on a Moderately Grazed Pasture." *Ecology* 31:554–66.
394a. Perrier de la Bathie, H. 1921. "La végétation malgache." In *Ann. Musée Coloniale Marseille.* Cited by Braun-Blanquet (57a), p. 282.
394b. Perrot, Nicolas. 1911. *The Indian Tribes of the Upper Mississippi Valley and Region of the Great Lakes.* Trans. Emma Helen Blair. 2 vols. Cleveland.
395. Pessin, L. J., and R. A. Chapman. 1944. "The Effect of Living Grass on the Growth of Longleaf Pine Seedlings in Pots." *Ecology* 25:85–90.
396. Phillips, J. F. V. 1930. "Fire: Its Influence on Biotic Communities and Physical Factors in South and East Africa." *South African Journal of Science* 27:352–67.
397. Phillips, J. F. V. 1931. "Vegetational Regions of Tanganyika Territory." *Transactions of the Royal Society of South Africa* 19:363–72.
397a. Phillips, J. F. V. 1936. "Fire in Vegetation: A Bad Master, a Good Servant, and a National Problem." *Journal of South African Botany* 2:35–45. Cited by Daubenmire (128a), p. 340.
398. Pickford, G. D. 1932. "The Influence of Continued Heavy Grazing and of Promiscuous Burning on Spring-Fall Ranges in Utah." *Ecology* 13:159–71.
399. Plummer, Fred G. 1912. *Lightning in Relation to Forest Fires.* USDA-FS-B 111.
400. Plummer, F. G. 1912. *Forest Fires.* USDA-FS-B 117.

401. Pomeroy, Kenneth B., and N. T. Barron. 1950. "Hardwood vs. Loblolly Pine." *JF* 48:112–13.
402. Pool, Raymond John. 1913. "A Study of the Vegetation of the Sandhills of Nebraska." *Minnesota Botanical Studies* 4:189–312.
403. Poppig, Eduard F. 1835–1836. *Reise in Chile, Peru.* Vol. 1. Leipzig.
404. Pound, Roscoe, and Frederic E. Clements. 1898. "The Vegetation Regions of the Prairie Province." *BG* 25:381–94.
405. Pound, Roscoe, and Frederic E. Clements. 1900. 2nd ed. *The Phytogeography of Nebraska.* University of Nebraska Botanical Seminar.
406. Powell, J. W. 1896. *The Physiography of the United States.* Cited by Shimek (457), p. 218.
407. Ramaley, Francis. 1907. "Scientific Expedition to Northeastern Colorado." *UCS* 4:145–66.
408. Ramaley, Francis. 1908. "Botany of Northeastern Larimer County, Colorado." *UCS* 5:119–31.
409. Ramaley, Francis. 1927. *Colorado Plant Life.* Boulder: University of Colorado.
410. Ramsey, Guy R. 1936. "Drouth Susceptibility of Evergreen Trees in Iowa." *JF* 34:424–29.
411. Rapraeger, E. F. 1936. "Effect of Repeated Ground Fires upon Stumpage Returns in Western White Pine." *JF* 34:715–18.
412. Ray, Verne. 1942. *CED: XXII, Plateau.* UC-AR 8.
413. Redway, T. S. 1894. "The Treeless Plains of the United States." *Geographical Journal* 3. Cited by Shimek (457), p. 218.
413a. Reed, Franklin W. 1905. *A Working Plan for Forest Lands in Central Alabama.* USDA-FS-B 68.
414. Renner, F. G. 1948. "Range Condition: A New Approach to the Management of Natural Grazing Lands." In *Proceedings, Inter-American Conference on Conservation of Renewable Natural Resources.* Washington, D.C.: Department of State.
415. Report from Monterey. 1800. (On fires started by Indians, San Juan Bautista Mission.)
416. Reveal, Jack L. 1944. "Single-Leaf Pinon and Utah Juniper Woodlands of Western Nevada." *JF* 42:276–78.
417. Rhodes, J. W. 1933. "An Ecological Comparison of Two Wisconsin Peat Bogs." In Public Museum of the City of Milwaukee, *Bulletin* 7:311–58.
418. Rice, Lucile A. 1932. "The Effect of Fire on the Prairie Animal Communities." *Ecology* 13:392–401.
418a. Riley, R.M. 1932. "Ancient Mayas Burned Their Forests." *AF* 38(8):442–43, 450.
419. Roach, Archibald W. 1948. "The Ecology of Vegetational Change in the Foothills Ecotone near Boulder, Colorado." M.A. thesis, Department of Biology, University of Colorado.
420. *Rocky Mountain News.* 1951. Article, "150 Check Fire Racing to Edge of Black Forest." March 8. Denver, Colorado.
421. Rogers, David H. 1942. "Measuring the Efficiency of Fire Control in California Chaparral." *JF* 40.
422. Roth, Filibert (dean, Michigan School of Forestry). 1920. "Another Word on Light Burning." *AF* 26:548, 572.
423. Russell, R. J. 1926. *Climates of California.* UC-PG 2.
424. Russell, R. J. 1931. *Dry Climates of the United States.* UC-PG 5.

425. Ryan, William Redmond. 1850. *Personal Adventures in Upper and Lower Califor-nia in 1848–1849*. London.

426. Saint-Amant, Pierre-Charles de. 1854. *Voyages en California et dans l'Oregon, par M. de Saint-Amant en 1851–1852*. Paris.

427. Saint-Ange et Renaubière. 1724. Journal. In Pierre Margry, *Mémoires et documents pour servir à l'histoire des origines françaises des pays d'Outre-Mer*, vol. 4. Paris, 1879–81.

428. Sampson, A. W. 1911. "Concerning Forest Fires." *Breeder's Gazette* 59:429–30.

429. Sampson, A. W. 1944. *Plant Succession on Burned Chaparral Lands in Northern California*. UC-AES Bulletin 685.

430. Sampson, A. W. 1948. "The Use of Fire in Range Forage Production." In *Proceed-ings, Inter-American Conference on Conservation of Renewable Natural Resources*. Washington, D.C.: Department of State.

431. Sampson, H. C. 1921. "An Ecological Survey of the Prairie Vegetation of Illinois." *Illinois Natural History Survey Bulletin* 13:523–77.

432. Sargent, C. S. 1897. In "Hartmann's Indians of Northwestern Mexico." *Congrès International des Américanistes* 10:117–19.

433. Sauer, Carl O. 1920. *Geography of the Ozark Highland of Missouri*. Geographical Society of Chicago 7.

434. Sauer, Carl O. 1927. *Geography of the Pennyroyal*. KGS series 6(25).

435. Sauer, Carl O. 1944. "A Geographic Sketch of Early Man in America." *Geographic Review* 34:529–73.

436. Sauer, Carl O. 1947. "Early Relations of Man to Plants." *Geographic Review* 37: 1–25.

437. Sauer, Carl O. 1950. "Grassland Climax, Fire, and Man." *Journal of Range Manage-ment* 3:16–22.

438. Schaffner, John H. 1926. *Observations on the Grasslands of the Central United States*. Contributions in Botany No. 178. Columbus: Ohio State University.

439. Schmidels, Ulrich. 1889. *Reise nach Sud-Amerika in den Jahren 1534–1554*. Tübin-gen. Cited by Schmieder (441), p. 268.

440. Schmidt, Karl P. 1938. "Herpetological Evidence for the Postglacial Eastward Extension of the Steppe in North America." *Ecology* 19:396–407.

441. Schmieder, O. 1927. *The Pampa*. UC-PG 2.

442. Schneider, E. C. 1909. "The Distribution of Woody Plants in the Pike's Peak Region." *Colorado College Publications, Science Series* 12:137–70.

443. Schoolcraft, H. R. 1821. *Narrative Journal of Travels . . . Great . . . Lakes . . . Mis-sissippi River, 1820*. Albany, N.Y.: E & E Hosford. Cited by Wissler (567), p. 50.

444. Schultz, C. B. 1943. "Some Artifacts of Early Man in the Great Plains and Adjacent Areas." *American Antiquity* 8:244–48.

445. Scribner's. 1883. *Statistical Atlas of the United States*. Cited by Christy (97), pp. 91–92.

446. Sears, Paul B. 1933. "Climatic Change as a Factor in Forest Succession." *JF* 31: 934–42.

447. Sears, P. B. 1948. "Forest Sequence and Climatic Change in Northeastern North America since Early Wisconsin Times." *Ecology* 29:326–33.

448. Seifriz, William. 1934. "The Plant Life of Russian Lapland." *Ecology* 15:306–18.

449. Selke, Arthur C. 1940. "Prairie Forestry from a Prairie Dweller's Viewpoint." *JF* 38:545–46.

449a. Semple, Ellen Churchill. 1922. "The Influence of Geographic Conditions upon Ancient Mediterranean Stockraising." *Annals of the Association of American Geographers* 12:3–38. Cited by Shantz (453a), p. 14.

450. Shaler, N. S. 1891. *Origin and Nature of Soils.* U.S. Geological Survey-Annual Report 12 (part 1).

451. Shames, Leo. 1938. "Measurements of Forest Fire Danger." *Science* 88: 401–2.

452. Shantz, H. L. 1911. *Natural Vegetation as an Indicator of the Capabilities of Land for Crop Production in the Great Plains Area.* USDA-BPI Bulletin 201.

453. Shantz, H. L. 1922. "Urundi Territory and People." *Geographical Review* 12(3): 329–57. Cited by Shantz (453a), p. 15.

453a. Shantz, H. L. 1947. *The Use of Fire as a Tool in the Management of the Brush Ranges of California.* Sacramento: California State Board of Forestry.

453b. Shantz, H. L., and C. F. Maarbut. 1923. *The Vegetation and Soils of Africa.* American Geographical Society Research Series No. 13. New York. Cited by Shantz (453a), p. 15.

454. Shantz, H. L., and Raphael Zon. 1924. "Natural Vegetation." In *Atlas of American Agriculture, Part I, Section E.* USDA Bureau of Agricultural Economics. Washington, D.C.: U.S. Government Printing Office.

455. Shea, John P. (psychologist, U.S. Forest Service). 1940. "Our Pappies Burned the Woods." *AF* 46:159–62, 174.

456. Shear, Cornelius L. 1901. *Field Work of the Division of Agrostology.* USDA, Division of Agrostology, Bulletin 25.

457. Shimek, B. 1911. "The Prairies." State University of Iowa (Bulletin 35). *Contributions from the Laboratories of Natural History* 6(2):169–224.

458. Shimek, B. 1925. "The Persistence of the Prairie." *University of Iowa Studies in Natural History* 11:3–24.

459. Shimek, B. 1948. "The Plant Geography of Iowa." *University of Iowa Studies in Natural History* 18:1–178.

460. Shostakovitch, V. B. 1925. "Forest Conflagrations in Siberia." *JF* 23:365–71.

460a. Show, S. B. 1920. "Forest Fire Protection in California." *Timberman* 21(3):37, 88–90.

461. Show, S. B., and E. I. Kotok. 1923. *Forest Fires in California 1911–1920.* Washington, D.C.: USDA-FS-B.

462. Show, S. B., and E. I. Kotok. 1924. *The Role of Forest Fire in California Pine Forests.* USDA Dept. Bulletin.

463. Siggers, Paul V. 1944. *The Brown Spot Needle Blight of Pine Seedlings.* USDA Technical Bulletin 870.

464. Simerly, N. G. T. 1936. "Controlled Burning in Longleaf Pine Second-Growth Timber." *JF* 34:671–73.

465. Simón, Fray Pedro. 1981 [1625]. *Noticias historiales de las conquistas de tierra firme en las Indias Occidentales.* Bogotá: Biblioteca Banco Popular.

466. Smith, Jared G. 1899. *Grazing Problems in the Southwest.* USDA, Division of Agrostology Bulletin 16.

467. Smith, John. 1624. "The Generall Historie of Virginia, New England, and the Summer Isles, Third Book." In Edward Arber, *Travels and Works of Captain John Smith, 1580–1631.* New edition by A. G. Bradley. Vols. 1 and 2. Edinburgh, 1910.

468. Soergel, W. 1922. *Die Jagd der Vorzeil.* Jena. Cited by Birket-Smith (46), pp. 160–61.

468a. Speck, F. G. 1909. *Ethnology of the Yuchi.* University of Pennsylvania, Anthropological Publication 1.

469. Speight, R., L. Cockayne, and R. M. Laing. 1910. "The Mount Arrowsmith District: A Study in Physiography and Plant Ecology." *Trans. New Zealand* 43:315–78. Cited by Shantz (453a), pp. 16, 25.

470. Spelman, H. 1609. "Relation of Virginia." In Edward Arber, *Travels and Works of Captain John Smith 1580–1631.* New edition by A. G. Bradley. Vol. 1. Edinburgh, 1910.

471. Spier, Leslie. 1923. *Southern Diegueno Customs.* UC-PAAE 20.

472. Spier, Leslie. 1928. *Havasupai Ethnography.* AMNH-AP 29.

473. Spier, Leslie. 1938. *The Sinkaietk or Southern Okanagon of Washington.* General Series in Anthropology No. 6.

474. Squires, John W. 1947. "Prescribed Burning in Florida." *JF* 45:815–19.

475. Stahelin, R. 1943. "Factors Influencing the Natural Restocking of High Altitude Burns by Coniferous Trees in the Central Rocky Mountains." *Ecology* 24:19–30.

476. Stallard, Harvey. 1929. "Secondary Successions in the Climax Forest Formations of Northern Minnesota." *Ecology* 10:476–547.

477. Staples, R. R. 1926. *Experiments in Veldt Management.* Union of South Africa Department of Agriculture, Science Bulletin 49. Cited by Craddock (121); and Shantz (453a), p. 23.

478. Stefansson, Vilhjalmer. 1913. *My Life with the Eskimo.* New York.

479. Steiger, T. L. 1930. "Structure of Prairie Vegetation." *Ecology* 11:170–217.

480. *Sterling Advocate.* 1948. Articles regarding prairie fires. March 26 and April 3, 5, and 12. Sterling, Colorado.

481. Sternberg, G. M. 1869. "The Plains of Kansas." *AN* 3:162. Cited by Shimek (457), p. 218.

482. Steward, Julian H. 1933. *Ethnography of Owens Valley Paiute.* UC-PAAE 33.

483. Steward, Julian H. 1938. *Basin-Plateau Aboriginal Sociopolitical Groups.* BAE-B 120.

484. Steward, Julian H. 1941. *CED: XIII, Nevada Shoshoni.* UC-AR 4.

485. Steward, Julian H. 1943. *CED: XXIII, Northern and Gosiute Shoshoni.* UC-AR 8.

486. Steward, Julian H. 1948. "Anthropology and Renewable Resources." In *Proceedings of the Inter-American Conference on Conservation of Renewable Natural Resources.* Washington, D.C.: Department of State.

487. Stewart, George. 1941. "Historic Records Bearing on Agricultural and Grazing Ecology in Utah." *JF* 39:362–75.

488. Stewart, O. C. 1935. "Pomo Field Notes." MS.

489. Stewart, O. C. 1941. *CED: XIV, Northern Paiute.* UC-AR 4.

490. Stewart, O. C. 1942. *CED: XVIII, Ute-Southern Paiute.* UC-AR 6:231–360.

491. Stewart, O. C. 1943. *Notes on Pomo Ethnogeography.* UC-PAAE 40.

491a. Stewart, O. C. 1951. "Burning and Natural Vegetation in the United States." *Geographical Review* 41:317–20.

492. Steyermark, J. A. 1940. *Studies of the Vegetation of Missouri—I: Natural Plant Associations and Successions in the Ozarks of Missouri.* Field Museum of Natural History Botanical Series 9(5).

493. Stoddard, Amos. 1812. *Sketches, Historical and Descriptive, of Louisiana.* Philadelphia.

493a. Stoddard, Herbert L. 1932. *The Bobwhite Quail: Its Habits, Preservation and Increase.* New York.

494. Stoddard, Herbert L. 1935. "Use of Controlled Fire in Southeastern Upland Game Management." *JF* 33:346–50.

495. Stoddart, L. A. 1941. "The Palouse Grassland Association in Northern Utah." *Ecology* 22:158–63.

496. Stoeckeler, J. H., and E. J. Dortignac. 1941. "Snowdrifts as a Factor in Growth and Longevity of Shelterbelts in the Great Plains." *Ecology* 22:117–24.

497. Stoeckeler, Joseph H. 1945. "Narrow Shelterbelts for the Southern Great Plains." *Soil Conservation* (USDA) 11: 16–20.

498. Storer, T. I. 1932. "Factors influencing Wild Life in California, Past and Present." *Ecology* 13:315–34.

499. Strachey, Wm. 1612. *Historie of Travell into Virginia Britania*. London: Printed for the Hakluyt Society, 1953.

500. Swallow, G. C. 1879. "Prairie and Timber." In *History of Missouri*, pp. 528–29. Cited by Shimek (457), p. 218.

501. Swanton, J. R. 1928. "Aboriginal Culture of the Southeast." BAE-*R* 42, 1924–25. Washington, D.C.

502. Taylor, A. S. 1860–63. "The Indianology of California." In California Notes, column in the *California Farmer* (weekly). San Francisco.

503. Taylor, Walter P. 1934. "Significance of Extreme or Intermittent Conditions in Distribution of Species and Management of Natural Resources, with a Restatement of Liebig's Law of Minimum." *Ecology* 15:374–79.

504. Teit, James. 1900. *The Thompson Indians of British Columbia*. AMNH-M 2 (part 4).

505. Terry, Elwood I. 1941. "The Future of Forestry and Grazing in the Southern Pine Belt." *Scientific Monthly* 52: 245–56.

506. Tharp, B. C. 1925. *Structure of Texas Vegetation East of the 98th Meridian*. University of Texas Bulletin 2606.

507. Thomas, N. W. 1906. *Natives of Australia*. London: Constable & Co.

508. Thompson, E. E. 1883. *Report*. Manitoba Department of Agriculture. Cited by Christy (97), p. 91.

509. Thorp, James. 1948. "How Soils Develop under Grass." In *Grass*. Yearbook of the USDA.

510. Tisdale, E. W. 1947. "The Grassland of the Southern Interior of British Columbia." *Ecology* 28:346–82.

511. Tolstead, W. L. 1941. "Plant Communities and Secondary Succession in South-Central South Dakota." *Ecology* 22:322–28.

511a. Townsend, John K. 1839. *Narrative of a Journey across the Rocky Mountains to the Columbia River*. Philadelphia. Cited by Steward (485).

512. Tracy, S. M. 1898. *Forage Plants and Forage Resources of the Gulf States*. USDA, Division of Agrostology Bulletin 15.

513. Transeau, Edgar Nelson. 1935. "The Prairie Peninsula." *Ecology* 16:423–37.

513a. Trimble, Robert E. 1928. *The Climate of Colorado*. Colorado Agricultural College Experiment Station Bulletin 340.

513b. Troup, R. S. 1919. Problems of Forest Ecology in India. In A. G. Tanseley and T. F. Chipp, *Aims and Methods of the Study of Vegetation*. London. 1926. Cited by Shantz (453a), pp. 15, 84.

514. Tschudi, J. J. von. 1868. *Reisen durch Sudamerika*. Vol. 4. Leipzig. Cited by Schmeider (441), p. 268.

515. Upham, Warren. 1895. *The Glacial Lake Agassiz*. Monographs of the U.S. Geological Survey No. 25. Cited by Shimek (457), p. 218.

516. Vallejo, Mariano Guadalupe. 1836. MS (treaty with Wappo Indians). In University of California Ph.D. thesis of Marian L. Lothrop, 1927.

517. Van der Donck, Adrian. 1656. *A Description of the New Netherlands*. 2nd ed. Trans. from Dutch by Jeremiah Johnson. Rpt. in Collections of the New York Historical Society, 2nd Series, 1841, vol. 1.

517a.   Vergil. 70–19 b.c. *Georgics* and *Aeneid*. Trans. Mrs. Elmer T. Merrill, Santa Barbara. Cited by Shantz (453a), pp. 14, 51.

518. Vestal, Arthur G. 1914. "Prairie Vegetation of a Mountain-Front Area in Colorado." *BG* 53:377–400.

519. Vestal, A. G. 1918. "Invasion of Forest Land by Prairie along Railroads." *Transactions of the Illinois State Academy of Science* 11:126–28.

520. Vestal, Arthur G. 1918. "Local Inclusions of Prairie within Forests." *Transactions of the Illinois State Academy of Science* 11:122–26.

521. Vestal, Arthur G. 1931. Review of *Plant Ecology* by John E. Weaver and Frederic E. Clements. *Ecology* 12:232–39.

522. Vivier, F. 1750. In *Jesuit Relations*. Cited by Houck (256), pp. 26–27.

523. Voegelin, Erminie W. 1938. *Tubatulabal Ethnography*. UC-AR 2.

524. Voegelin, E. W. 1942. *CED: XX, Northeast California*. UC-AR 7.

525. Vyssotsky, G. N. 1935. "Shelterbelts in the Steppes of Russia." *JF* 33:781–88.

526. Wackerman, A. E. 1929. "Why Prairies in Arkansas and Louisiana?" *JF* 27:726–34.

527. Wackerman, A. E. 1939. "Fire: The Greatest Threat to Southern Forests." *JF* 37:63–65.

528. Wahlenberg, W. G., S. W. Greene, and H. R. Reed. 1939. *Effects of Fire and Cattle Grazing on Longleaf Pine Lands, as Studied at McNeill, Mississippi*. USDA Technical Bulletin 683.

529. Wakeley, Philip C., and H. H. Muntz. 1947. "Effect of Prescribed Burning on Height Growth of Longleaf Pine." *JF* 45:503–8.

529a. Walder, H.C. 1912. "Fire-Protection in the Tropics." *Indian Forester* 39(9):436–52. Cited by Shantz (453a), pp. 15, 84.

530. Waller, Adolph E. 1921. *The Relation of Plant Succession to Crop Production*. Ohio State University Bulletin 25, No. 9, Contributions in Botany No. 117.

530a. Watson, John F. 1830. *Annals of Philadelphia, being a Collection of Memoirs, Anecdotes, & Incidents of the City and Its Inhabitants, from the Days of the Pilgrim Founders*. Philadelphia: E.L. Carey & A. Hart.

531. Watson, Le Roy, Jr. 1940. "Controlled Burning and the Management of Longleaf Pine." *JF* 38:44–47.

532. Weakley, Harry E. 1943. "A Tree-Ring Record of Precipitation in Western Nebraska." *JF* 41:816–19.

533. Weaver, Harold. 1943. "Fire as an Ecological and Silvicultural Factor in the Ponderosa-Pine Region of the Pacific Slope." *JF* 41:7–15.

534. Weaver, Harold. 1946. "Slash Disposal on the Colville Indian Reservation." *JF* 44:81–88.

535. Weaver, Harold, 1947. "Fire—Nature's Thinning Agent in Ponderosa Pine Stands." *JF* 45:437–44.

536. Weaver, Harold. 1950. "Shoals and Reefs in Ponderosa Pine Silviculture." *JF* 48:21–22.

537. Weaver, J. E., and John W. Crist. 1922. "Relation of Hardpan to Root Penetration in the Great Plains." *Ecology* 3:237–49.

538. Weaver, J. E. 1927. "Some Ecological Aspects of Agriculture in the Prairie." *Ecology* 8:1–17.

539. Weaver, J. E. 1931. "Who's Who among the Prairie Grasses." *Ecology* 12:623–32.

540. Weaver, J. E., and Evan L. Flory. 1934. "Stability of Climax Prairie and Some Environmental Changes Resulting from Breaking." *Ecology* 15:333–47.

541. Weaver, J. E., and F. W. Albertson. 1936. "Effects of the Great Drought on the Prairies of Iowa, Nebraska and Kansas." *Ecology* 17:567–639.

542. Weaver, J. E., and F. E. Clements. 1938. *Plant Ecology*. 2nd ed. New York: McGraw-Hill Co.

543. Weaver, J. E. 1943. "Replacement of True Prairie by Mixed Prairie in Eastern Nebraska and Kansas." *Ecology* 24:421–34.

544. Webb, W. P. 1931. *The Great Plains*. Boston: Ginn & Co.

545. Weld, Isaac. 1803. *Travels Through the States of North America and the Provinces of Upper and Lower Canada*. Paris: Impr. De Munier, Chez Gerard.

546. Wells, R. W. 1819. "On the Origin of Prairies." *AJS* 1:331–37.

547. Werner, A. 1906. *The Natives of British Central Africa*. London: Constable & Co.

547a. Whipple, A. W. 1854. *Itinerary*. Reports of Explorations and Surveys for a Railroad Route from the Mississippi River to the Pacific Ocean, 1853–1854. 33rd Cong., 2nd Sess. Sen. Ex. Doc. No. 78, Vol. 3: 1856.

548. White, Andrew. 1633. *Narrative of a Voyage to Maryland*. Cited by Maxwell (358), p. 90.

549. White, C. A. 1868. "The Lakes of Iowa—Past and Present." *AN* 2:143–55. Cited by Christy (97), p. 91; and Shimek (458).

550. White, C. A. 1870. *Geological Survey of Iowa* 1. Cited by Christy (97), p. 91; and Shimek (458), p. 218.

551. White, C. A. 1871. "Prairie Fires." *AN* 5:68–69. Cited by Christy (97), p. 83; and Shimek (458), p. 218.

552. White, Donald P. 1941. "Prairie Soil as a Medium for Tree Growth." *Ecology* 22:398–407.

553. Whitfield, Charles J., and Hugh L. Anderson. 1938. "Secondary Succession in the Desert Plains Grassland." *Ecology* 19:171–80.

554. Whitfield, Charles J., and Edward L. Brutner. 1938. "Natural Vegetation in the Desert Plains Grassland." *Ecology* 19:26–38.

555. Whitney, J. D. 1858. *Report*. Geological Survey of Iowa 1. Cited by Christy (97), p. 81.

556. Wied-Neuwied, Maximilian. 1839–41. *Travels in the Interior of North America, 1832–1834*. Early Western Travels, 1748–1846, ed. Reuben Gold Thwaites, vol. 22.

557. Wilde, S. A. 1946. *Forest Soils and Forest Growth*. Waltham, Mass.: Chronica Botanica Co.

558. Wilde, S. A., Philip B. Whitford, and C. T. Youngberg. 1948. "Relation of Soils and Forest Growth in the Driftless Area of Southwestern Wisconsin." *Ecology* 29:173–80.

558a. Wilkes, Charles. 1845. *Narrative of the United States Exploring Expedition during the Years 1838, 1839, 1840, 1841, 1842*. Philadelphia.

559. Williams, E. 1650. "Virginia Richly Valued." In Force's *Collections*, 3, no. 11, p. 11.

560. Willoughby, C. C. 1935. *Antiquities of the New England Indians*. Cambridge, Mass.: Peabody Museum, Harvard University.

561. Winchell, Alexander. 1864. "On the Origin of the Prairies of the Valley of the Mississippi." *AJS* 2(38):332–44.

562. Winchell, N. H. 1880. "Eighth Annual Report." In *Geological and Natural History Survey of Minnesota*. Cited by Shimek (457), p. 218.

563. Winslow, Arthur. 1891. In *Geological Society of America Bulletin* 2:240. Cited by Christy (97), p. 95.

564. Winslow, Arthur. 1892. *Communication from State Geologist of Missouri*. Cited by Christy (97), p. 87.

565. Winthrop, John. 1630. *History of New England*. (ed. by James K. Hosmer, 1908). New York: Scribner.

566. Wislizenus, F. A. 1839. *A Journey to the Rocky Mountains in the Year 1839*. St. Louis: Missouri Historical Society, 1912.

567. Wissler, Clark. 1910. *Material Culture of the Blackfoot Indians*. AMNH-AP 5.

568. Wissler, Clark. 1920. *North American Indians of the Plains*. AMNH Handbook Series No. 1. New York.

569. Withrow, Alice Phillips. 1932. "Life Forms and Leaf Size Classes of Certain Plant Communities of the Cincinnati Region." *Ecology* 13:12–35.

570. Wood, L. K. 1856/1863. L. K. Wood narrative. Humboldt, Calif.: *Humboldt Times*.

571. Wood, William. 1639. *New England's Prospect: A True, Lively, and Experimental Description of That Part of America, commonly called New England*. London: John Dawson.

572. Woodbury, Angus. 1947. "Distribution of Pigmy Conifers in Utah and Northeastern Arizona." *Ecology* 28:113–26.

573. Woodman, C. L. 1941. "Interesting Highlights of the Fire Situation in Massachusetts during April." *JF* 39:780–84.

574. Woodward, John. 1924. "Origin of Prairies in Illinois." *BG* 77:241–59.

575. Wooton, E. O. 1916. *Carrying Capacity of Grazing Ranges in Southern Arizona*. USDA Dept. Bulletin 367.

575a. Worden, William L. 1952. "They're Setting Fire to California." *Saturday Evening Post* 225(14) (October 4): 284.

576. Wright, John C., and Elnora A. Wright. 1948. "Grassland Types of South Central Montana." *Ecology* 29:449–60.

577. Yearbook. 1938. *Soils and Men*. Washington, D.C.: USDA.

578. Yearbook. 1948. *Grass*. Washington, D.C.: USDA.

579. Yearbook. 1949. *Trees*. Washington, D.C.: USDA.

580. Young, Vernon A. 1943. "Changes in Vegetation and Soil of Palouse Prairie caused by Overgrazing." *JF* 41:834–38.

581. Zobel, Bruce J. 1948. "Forestry on a Military Reservation." *JF* 46:188–90.

582. Zon, Raphael, F. A. Silcox, F. A. Hayes, J. H. Stoeckeler, et al. 1935. *Possibilities of Shelterbelt Planting in the Plains Region*. USDA—Lake States Forest Experiment Station. Washington, D.C.: Government Printing Office.

583. Zon, Raphael. 1905. *Loblolly Pine in Eastern Texas*. USDA-FS-B 64.

References Cited

Henry T. Lewis and M. Kat Anderson

Abrahamson, W. G., and D. C. Hartnett. 1990. Pine flatwoods and dry prairies. In *Ecosystems of Florida*, ed. R. L. Myers and J. J. Ewel, pp. 103–49. Orlando: University of Central Florida Press.

Abrams, M. D. 1992. Fire and the development of oak forests. *BioScience* 42(5):346–53.

Agee, J. K. 1993. *Fire Ecology of Pacific Northwest Forests*. Washington, D.C.: Island Press.

Anderson, M. K. 1991. California Indian horticulture: Management and use of redbud by the Southern Sierra Miwok. *Journal of Ethnobiology* 11(1):145–57.

———. 1993a. The experimental approach to assessment of the potential ecological effects of horticultural practices by indigenous peoples on California wildlands. Ph.D. dissertation, Department of Environmental Science, Policy, and Management, University of California, Berkeley.

———. 1993b. The mountains smell like fire. *Fremontia* (Journal of the California Native Plant Society) 21(4):15–20.

———. 1993c. Native Californians as ancient and contemporary cultivators. In *Before the Wilderness: Environmental Management by Native Californians*, ed. T. C. Blackburn and K. Anderson, pp. 151–74. Menlo Park, Calif.: Ballena Press.

———. 1996a. The ethnobotany of deergrass, *Muhlenbergia rigens* (Poaceae): Its uses and fire management by California Indian tribes. *Economic Botany* 50(4): 409–22.

———. 1996b. Tending the wilderness. *Restoration and Management Notes* 14(2): 154–66.

———. 1997a. California's endangered peoples and endangered ecosystems. *American Indian Culture and Research Journal* 21(3):7–31.

———. 1997b. From tillage to table: The indigenous cultivation of geophytes for food in California. *Journal of Ethnobiology* 17(2):149–69.

———. 1999. The fire, pruning, and coppice management of temperate ecosystems for basketry material by California Indian tribes. *Human Ecology* 27(1):79–113.

———. 2001. The contribution of ethnobiology to the reconstruction and restoration of historic ecosystems. In *The Historical Ecology Handbook: A Restorationist's Guide to Reference Ecosystems*, ed. D. Egan and E. Howell, pp. 55–72. Washington, D.C.: Island Press.

Anderson, M. K., and M. J. Moratto. 1996. Native American land-use practices and ecological impacts. In *Sierra Nevada Ecosystem Project: Final Report to Congress,* vol.

2, *Assessments and Scientific Basis for Management Options*, pp. 187–206. Davis: University of California, Centers for Water and Wildland Resources.

Anderson, M. K., and D. L. Rowney. 1999. The edible plant *Dichelostemma capitatum:* Its vegetative reproduction response to different indigenous harvesting regimes in California. *Restoration Ecology* 7(3):231–40.

Anderson, R. C. 1990. The historic role of fire in the North American grassland. In *Fire in North American Tallgrass Prairies*, ed. S. L. Collins and L. L. Wallace, pp. 8–18. Norman: University of Oklahoma Press.

Anderson, R. S., and S. L. Carpenter. 1991. Vegetation change in Yosemite Valley, Yosemite National Park, California, during the protohistoric period. *Madrono* 38(1):1–13.

Anderson, W. L., and R. W. Storer. 1976. Factors influencing Kirtland's warbler nesting success. *Jack Pine Warbler* 54:105–15.

Arno, S. F., and K. M. Sneck. 1977. *A Method for Determining Fire History in Coniferous Forests of the Mountain West*. USDA Forest Service General Technical Report INT-42. Intermt.

Axelrod, D. I. 1985. Rise of the grassland biome, Central North America. *Botanical Review* 51:163–201.

Baisan, C. H., and T. W. Swetnam. 1997. *Interactions of Fire Regimes and Land Use in the Central Rio Grande Valley*. Rocky Mountain Forest and Range Experiment Station Research Paper RM-RP-330. Fort Collins: United States Department of Agriculture, Forest Service.

Barbour, M. G., J. H. Burk, and W. D. Pitts. 1980. *Terrestrial Plant Ecology*. Menlo Park, Calif.: Benjamin/Cummings Publishing Co.

Barrett, S. W. 1981. Indian fires in the pre-settlement forests of western Montana. In *Proceedings of the Fire History Workshop, University of Arizona, Tucson, October 20–24, 1980*. Intermountain Forest and Range Experiment Station, USDA Forest Service. Tucson: University of Arizona.

Barrett, S. W., and S. F. Arno. 1982. Indian fires as an ecological influence in the northern Rockies. *Journal of Forestry* 8:647–51.

Barth, F. 1956. Ecological relationships of ethnic groups in Swat, North Pakistan. *American Anthropologist* 58:1079–89.

Bean, L. J., and H. W. Lawton. 1973. Some explanations for the rise of cultural complexity in Native California with comments on proto-agriculture and agriculture. In *Patterns of Indian Burning in California: Ecology and Ethnohistory*, by H. T. Lewis, pp. i–xlvii. Ramona, Calif.: Ballena Press.

Bicknell, S. H. 1989. Strategy for reconstructing presettlement vegetation. *Supplement to Bulletin of the Ecological Society of America* (Program and Abstracts) 70(2):62.

Bicknell, S. H., A. T. Austin, D. J. Bigg, and R. Parker Godar. 1992. Late Prehistoric vegetation patterns at six sites in coastal California. *Supplement to Bulletin of the Ecological Society of America* (Program and Abstracts) 73(2):112.

Biswell, H. H. 1989. *Prescribed Burning in California Wildlands Vegetation Management*. Berkeley: University of California Press.

Blackburn, T. C., and M. K. Anderson (eds.). 1993. *Before the Wilderness: Native Californians as Environmental Managers*. Menlo Park, Calif.: Ballena Press.

Bonnicksen, T. M. 2000. *America's Ancient Forests: From the Ice Age to the Age of Discovery*. New York: John Wiley and Sons.

Bonnicksen, T. M., M. K. Anderson, H. T. Lewis, C. E. Kay, and R. Knudson. 2000. American Indian influences on the development of forest ecosystems. In *Ecological Stewardship: A Common Reference for Ecosystem Management*, ed. N. C. Johnson, A. J. Malk, W. T. Sexton, and R. Szaro, pp. 439–70. Oxford: Elsevier Science.

Bonnicksen, T. M., and E. C. Stone. 1985. Restoring naturalness to national parks. *Environmental Management* 9:479–86.

Borowski, O. 1998. *Every Living Thing: Daily Use of Animals in Ancient Israel*. Walnut Creek, Calif.: AltaMira Press.

Botkin, D. B. 1994. Ecological theory and natural resource management. In *Ecological Prospects: Scientific, Religious, and Aesthetic Perspectives*, ed. C. K. Chapple, pp. 65–82. Albany: State University of New York Press.

Bowman, D. M. J. S. 1998. The impact of Aboriginal landscape burning on the Australian biota. *New Phytologist* 140:385–410.

Boyd, R. 1986. Strategies of Indian burning in the Willamette Valley. *Canadian Journal of Anthropology* 5:65–86.

———— (ed.). 1999. *Indians, Fire and the Land in the Pacific Northwest*. Corvallis: Oregon State University Press.

Braidwood, R. J. 1975. *Prehistoric Men*. Glenview, Ill.: Scott, Foresman.

Brown, J. K. 1991. Should management ignitions be used in Yellowstone National Park? In *The Greater Yellowstone Ecosystem: Redefining America's Wilderness Heritage*, ed. R. B. Keiter and M. S. Boyce, pp. 137–48. New Haven: Yale University Press.

Buell, M. F., H. F. Buell, and J. A. Small. 1954. Fire in the history of Mettler's woods. *Bulletin of the Torrey Botanical Club* 81(3):253–55.

Burch, E. S., and L. J. Ellanna (eds.). 1994. *Key Issues in Hunter-Gatherer Research*. Oxford: Oxford University Press.

Burcham, L. T. 1959. Planned burning as a management practice for California Wild Lands. In *Proceedings, Society of American Foresters, Division of Range Management*, pp. 180–85.

Bye, R. A. 1979. Incipient domestication of mustards in Northwest Mexico. *Kiva* 44:237–56.

California State Board of Forestry. 1892. *Fourth Biennial Report of the California State Board of Forestry for the Years 1891–1892*. Sacramento: A. J. Johnston, Supt. State Printing.

Cane, S. 1989. Australian Aboriginal seed grinding and its archaeological record: A case study from the Western Desert. In *Foraging and Farming: The Evolution of Plant Exploitation*, ed. David R. Harris and Gordon C. Hillman, pp. 99–119. Boston: Unwin Hyman.

Chase, A. 1986. *Playing God in Yellowstone: The Destruction of America's First National Park*. San Diego: Harcourt Brace Jovanovich, Publishers.

Christensen, N. L. 1985. Shrubland fire regimes and their evolutionary consequences. In *The Ecology of Natural Disturbance and Patch Dynamics*, ed. S. T. A. Pickett and P. S. White, pp. 86–100. San Diego: Academic Press.

————. 1988. Succession and natural disturbance: Paradigms, problems, and preservation of natural ecosystems. In *Ecosystem Management for Parks and Wilderness*, ed. J. K. Agee and D. R. Johnson, pp. 62–86. Seattle: University of Washington Press.

————. 1991. Wilderness and high intensity fire: How much is enough. In *Proceedings of the High Intensity Fire in Wildlands Management Challenges and Options 17th*

Tall Timbers Fire Ecology Conference, May 18–21, 1989, pp. 9–24. Tallahasse, Fla.: Tall Timbers Research Station.

Clar, C. R. 1959. *California Government and Forestry: From Spanish Days until the Creation of the Department of Natural Resources in 1927*. Sacramento: Division of Forestry, Department of Natural Resources, State of California.

Clark, J. S. 1990. Fire and climate change during the last 750 years in northwestern Minnesota. *Ecological Monographs* 60(2):135–59.

———. 1995. Climate and Indian effects on southern Ontario forests: A reply to Campbell and McAndrews. *Holocene* 5(3):371–79.

Clark, J. S., and P. D. Royall. 1995. Transformation of a northern hardwood forest by aboriginal (Iroquois) fire: Charcoal evidence from Crawford Lake, Ontario, Canada. *Holocene* 5(1):1–9.

———. 1996. Local and regional sediment charcoal evidence for fire regimes in presettlement north-eastern North America. *Journal of Ecology* 84:365–82.

Clements, F. E. 1904. *The Development and Structure of Vegetation*. Botanical Survey Nebraska 7. Lincoln: Bot. Seminar, University of Nebraska.

———. 1936. Nature and structure of the climax. *Journal of Ecology* 24:252–84.

Clemmer, R. O., L. D. Myers, and M. E. Rudden (eds.). 1999. *Julian Steward and the Great Basin: The Making of an Anthropologist*. Salt Lake City: University of Utah Press.

Coe, M. 1980. African wildlife resources. In *Conservation Biology: An Evolutionary-Ecological Perspective*, ed. M. E. Soulé and B. A. Wilcox, pp. 273–302. Sunderland, Mass.: Sinauer Associates.

Collins, S. L. 1990. Introduction: Fire as a natural disturbance in tallgrass prairie ecosystems. In *Fire in North American Tallgrass Prairies*, ed. S. L. Collins and L. L. Wallace, pp. 3–7. Norman: University of Oklahoma Press.

Connell, J. H. 1978. Diversity in tropical rain forests and coral reefs. *Science* (Washington D.C.) 199:1302–10.

Connor, R. N., and D. C. Rudolph. 1989. *Red-Cockaded Woodpecker Colony Status and Trends on the Angelina, Davy Crockett and Sabine National Forests*. Res. Paper SO-250. U.S. Forest Service, Southern Forest Experiment Station.

Cooper, C. F. 1961. The ecology of fire. *Scientific American* 204:150–60.

Cooper, W. S. 1913. The climax forest of Isle Royale, Lake Superior, and its development. *Botanical Gazette* 55:1–44, 115–40, 189–235.

Cornett, J. W. 1985. Reading fan palms. Natural History 94(10):64–73.

———. 1989a. The desert fan palm—Not a relict. Abstract in *Mojave Desert Quaternary Research Center Third Annual Symposium Proceedings*, ed. J. Reynolds, pp. 56–58. Redlands: San Bernardino County Museum Association.

———. 1989b. *Desert Palm Oasis*. Santa Barbara, Calif.: Palm Springs Desert Museum Companion Press.

Costa, R., and R. E. Escano. 1989. *Red-Cockaded Woodpecker Status and Management in the Southern Region in 1986*. Technical Publication R8-TP12. U.S. Forest Service, Southern Region.

Costa, R., and J. L. Walker. 1995. Red-cockaded woodpeckers. In *Our Living Resources: A Report to the Nation on the Distribution, Abundance, and Health of U.S. Plants, Animals, and Ecosystems*, ed. E. T. LaRoe, G. S. Farris, C. E. Puckett, P. D. Doran, and M. J. Mac, pp. 86–89. Washington, D.C.: U.S. Department of the Interior, National Biological Service.

Covington, W. W., R. L. Everett, R. Steele, L. L. Irwin, T. A. Daer, and A. N. D. Auclair. 1994. Historical and anticipated changes in forest ecosystems of the inland west of the United States. In *Assessing Forest Ecosystem Health in the Inland West*, ed. R. N. Sampson and D. L. Adams, pp. 13–63. New York: Food Products Press.

Cowan, C. W. 1978. The prehistoric use and distribution of maygrass in eastern North America: Cultural and phytogeographical implications. In *The Nature and Status of Ethnobotany*, ed. R. I. Ford, M. F. Brow, M. Hodge, and W. L. Merrill, pp. 263–88. Museum of Anthropology, University of Mchigan, No. 67. Ann Arbor: Museum of Anthropology, University of Michigan.

Cowles, H. C. 1899. The ecological relations of the vegetation on the sand dunes of Lake Michigan. 1. Geographical relations of the dune floras. *Botanical Gazette* 27:95–117.

Cox, P. A. 1989. Preface. In *Islands, Plants, and Polynesians: An Introduction to Polynesian Ethnobotany*, ed. P. A. Cox and S. A. Banack, pp. 7–9. Portland: Dioscorides Press.

Cronon, W. 1983. *Changes in the Land: Indians, Colonists, and the Ecology of New England*. New York: Hill and Wang.

———. 1995. The trouble with wilderness; or, getting back to the wrong nature. In *Uncommon Ground: Toward Reinventing Nature*, pp. 69–90. New York: W. W. Norton and Co.

Crumley, C. L. 1994. Historical ecology: A multidimensional ecological orientation. In *Historical Ecology: Cultural Knowledge and Changing Landscapes*, ed. C. L. Crumley, pp. 1–16. Santa Fe: School of American Research Press.

Dale, V. H., S. Brown, R. A. Haeuber, N. T. Hobbs, N. Huntly, R. J. Naiman, W. E. Riebsame, M. G. Turner, and T. J. Valone. 2000. Ecological principles and guidelines for managing the use of land. *Ecological Applications* 10(3):639–70.

Daubenmire, R. F. 1959. *Plants and Environment: A Textbook of Plant Autecology*. New York: John Wiley Sons.

Day, G. M. 1953. The Indian as an ecological factor in the northeastern forest. *Ecology* 34:329–46.

DeBano, L. F., G. E. Eberlein, and P. H. Dunn. 1979. Effects of burning on chaparral soils. I. Soil nitrogen. *Soil Sci. Soc. Am. Proceedings* 43:504–09.

Delcourt, H. R., and P. A. Delcourt. 1997. Pre-Columbian Native American use of fire on Southern Appalachian landscapes. *Conservation Biology* 11(4):1010–14.

Denevan, W. M. 1992. The pristine myth: The landscape of the Americas in 1492. *Annals of the Association of American Geographers* 82:369–85.

Dobyns, H. F. 1981. *From Fire to Flood: Historic Human Destruction of Sonoran Desert Riverine Oases*. Menlo Park, Calif.: Ballena Press.

Dragoo, D. W. 1976. Some aspects of eastern North American prehistory: A review, 1975. *Antiquity* 41(1):3–27.

Driver, H. E. 1962. *The Contribution of A. L. Kroeber to Culture Area Theory and Practice*. Baltimore: Waverly Press.

Egan, D., and E. Howell (eds). 2001. *The Historical Ecology Handbook: A Restorationist's Guide to Reference Ecosystems*. Washington, D.C.: Island Press.

Ellis, B. A., and J. Kummerow. 1989. The importance of N2 Fixation in *Ceanothus* seedlings in early postfire chaparral. In *The California Chaparral: Paradigms Reexamined*, ed. S. C. Keeley, pp. 115–16. Los Angeles: Natural History Museum of Los Angeles County.

Faegri, K., and J. Iversen. 1975. *Textbook of Pollen Analysis*. 3rd ed. New York: Hafner.

Ferraro, G. P. 1992. *Cultural Anthropology: An Applied Perspective*. Saint Paul, Minn.: West Publishers.

Flood, J. 1990. *The Moth Hunters: Aboriginal Prehistory of the Australian Alps*. Canberra: Australian Institute of Aboriginal Studies.

Ford, J., and D. Martinez (eds). 2000. Traditional ecological knowledge, ecosystem science, and environmental management: Invited feature. *Ecological Applications* 10(5):1249–1341.

Ford, R. I. (ed.). 1978. *The Nature and Status of Ethnobotany*. Anthropological Papers No. 67. Ann Arbor: University of Michigan, Museum of Anthropology.

———. 1981. Ethnobotany in North America: An historical phytogeographic perspective. *Canadian Journal of Botany* 59(11):2178–89.

———. 1985. The patterns of prehistoric food production in North America. In *Prehistoric Food Production in North America*, ed. R. I. Ford, pp. 341–67. Anthropological Papers No. 75. Ann Arbor: Museum of Anthropology, University of Michigan.

Fowler, C. S. 1996. Historical perspectives on Timbisha Shoshone land management practices, Death Valley, California. In *Case Studies in Environmental Archaeology*, ed. E. J. Reitz, L. A. Newsom, and S. J. Scudder, pp. 87–101. New York: Plenum Press.

Fox, S. 1985. *The American Conservation Movement: John Muir and His Legacy*. Madison: University of Wisconsin Press.

Franklin, J. F. 1988. Pacific Northwest Forests. In *North American Terrestrial Vegetation*, ed. M. G. Barbour and W. D. Billings, pp. 103–30. Cambridge: Cambridge University Press.

Frost, C. C. 1993. Four centuries of changing landscape patterns in the longleaf pine ecosystem. In *Proceedings, 18th Tall Timbers Fire Ecology Conference—The Longleaf Pine Ecosystem: Ecology, Restoration and Management*, ed. S. M. Hermann, pp. 17–44. Tallahassee, Fla.: Tall Timbers Research Station.

Frost, E. 1997. *Columbiana: Ecology and Culture in the Pacific Northwest*. Oroville, Wash.: Greater Ecosystem Alliance.

Geertz, C. 1963. *Agricultural Involution: The Processes of Ecological Change in Indonesia*. Berkeley: University of California Press.

Goin, P. 1992. *Stopping Time: A Rephotographic Survey of Lake Tahoe*. Albuquerque: University of New Mexico Press.

Gómez-Pompa, A., and A. Kaus. 1992. Taming the wilderness myth. *BioScience* 42(4):271–79.

Gottesfeld, L. M. Johnson. 1994. Conservation, territory, and traditional beliefs: An analysis of Gitksan and Wet'suwet'en subsistence, Northwest British Columbia, Canada. *Human Ecology* 22(4):443–63.

Gould, R. A. 1971. Uses and effects of fire among the Western Desert Aborigines of Australia. *Mankind* 8:14–24.

Graber, D. M. 1995. Resolute biocentrism: The dilemma of wilderness in national parks. In *Reinventing Nature?: Responses to Postmodern Deconstruction*, ed. M. E. Soule and G. Lease, pp. 123–35. Washington, D.C.: Island Press.

Gruell, G. E. 1983. *Fire and Vegetative Trends in the Northern Rockies: Interpretations from 1871–1982 Photographs*. United States Forest Service General Technical Report INT-158. Ogden, Utah: Intermountain Forest and Range Experiment Station.

————. 1991. Historical perspective: A prerequisite for better public understanding of fire management challenges. In *Proceedings of the High Intensity Fire in Wildlands Management Challenges and Options 17th Tall Timbers Fire Ecology Conference*, May 18–21, 1989, pp. 25–41. Tallahassee, Fla.: Tall Timbers Research Station.

Grumbine, R. E. 1994. What is ecosystem management? *Conservation Biology* 8(1): 27–38.

Guntenspergen, G. R. 1995. Plants. In *Our Living Resources: A Report to the Nation on the Distribution, Abundance, and Health of U.S. Plants, Animals, and Ecosystems*, ed. E. T. LaRoe, G. S. Farris, C. E. Puckett, P. D. Doran, and M. J. Mac, pp. 189–210. Washington, D.C.: U.S. Department of the Interior, National Biological Service.

Gunther, E. 1973. *Ethnobotany of Western Washington: The Knowledge and Use of Indigenous Plants by Native Americans*. Seattle: University of Washington Press.

Guyette, R. P. 1995a. *Determining Fire History from Old White Pine Stumps in an Oak-Pine Forest in Bracebridge, Ontario*. Forest Research Report No. 133. Ontario Forest Research Institute.

————. 1995b. *A History of Fire, Disturbance, and Growth in a Red Oak Stand in the Bancroft District, Ontario*. Forest Research Information Paper No. 119. Ontario Forest Research Institute.

————. 1995c. *A Presettlement Fire History in an Oak-Pine Forest near Basin Lake, Algonquin Park, Ontario*. Forest Research Report No. 132. Ontario Forest Research Institute.

Guyette, R. P., and B. E. Cutter. 1991. Tree-ring analysis of fire history of a post oak savanna in the Missouri Ozarks. *Natural Areas Journal* 11(2):93–99.

Guyette, R. P., and D. C. Dey. 1995. *A Dendrochronological Fire History of Opeongo Lookout in Algonquin Park, Ontario*. Forest Research Report No. 134. Ontario Forest Research Institute.

Hallam, S. J. 1975. *Fire and Hearth*. Canberra: Australian Institute of Aboriginal Studies.

————. 1989. The history of aboriginal firing. In *Fire Ecology and Management in Western Australian Ecosystems*, ed. J. R. Ford, pp. 7–20. WAIT Environmental Studies Group Report No. 14. Perth: Western Australia Institute of Technology.

Hammett, J. E. 1992. The shapes of adaptation: Historical ecology of anthropogenic landscapes in the southeastern United States. *Landscape Ecology* 7(2):121–35.

Hardesty, D. L. 1977. *Ecological Anthropology*. New York: John Wiley and Sons.

Hardison, J. R. 1976. Fire and disease. In *Proccedings Annual Tall Timbers Fire Ecology Conference*, October 16–17, 1974, Portland, Oregon, pp. 223–34. Tallahassee, Fla.: Tall Timbers Research Station.

Harlan, J. R., and J. M. de Wet. 1973. On the quality of evidence for origin and dispersal of cultivated plants. *Current Anthropology* 14(1–2):51–55.

Harper, J. L. 1987. The heuristic value of ecological restoration. In *Restoration Ecology: A Synthetic Approach to Ecological Research*, ed. W. R. Jordan III, M. E. Gilpin, and J. D. Aber, pp. 35–45. Cambridge: Cambridge University Press.

Harris, D. R. 1989. An evolutionary continuum of people-plant interaction. In *Foraging and Farming: The Evolution of Plant Exploitation*, ed. D. R. Harris and G. C. Hillman, pp. 11–26. Boston: Unwin Hyman.

Harris, D. R., and G. C. Hillman (eds.). 1989. *Foraging and Farming: The Evolution of Plant Exploitation*. Boston: Unwin Hyman.

Harris, M. 1968. *The Rise of Anthropological Theory*. New York: Thomas Y. Crowell.

Haufler, J. B. 1999. Strategies for conserving terrestrial biological diversity. In *Practical Approaches to the Conservation of Biological Diversity*, ed. R. K. Baydack, H. Campa III, and J. B. Haufler, pp. 17–30. Washington, D.C.: Island Press.

Haynes, C. D. 1982. Man's firestick and God's lightning: Bushfire in Arnemland. Paper presented to the 52nd Australian and New Zealand Association for the Advancement of Science (ANZAAS) Congress, Sydney, New South Wales.

———. 1985. The pattern and ecology of Munwag: Traditional Aboriginal fire regimes in North Central Arnemland. *Proceedings of the Ecological Society of Australia* 13:203–14.

Heady, H. F. 1972. Burning and the grasslands in California. In *Proceedings: Annual Tall Timbers Fire Ecology Conference*. Tallahassee, Fla.: Tall Timbers Research Station.

Hough, W. 1926. *Fire as an Agent in Human Culture*. Smithsonian Institution, Bulletin 139. Washington, D.C.: Government Printing Office.

Houston, D. B. 1982. *The Northern Yellowstone Elk: Ecology and Management*. New York: Macmillan.

Howell, C. L. 1998. *Cannibalism Is an Acquired Taste and Other Notes from Conversation with Anthropologist Omer C. Stewart*. Boulder: University Press of Colorado.

Huston, M. A. 1994. *Biological Diversity: The Coexistence of Species on Changing Landscapes*. Cambridge: Cambridge University Press.

Ingold, T., D. Riches, and James Woodburn (eds.). 1988. *Hunters and Gatherers*. Oxford: Oxford University Press.

Johnson, L. M. 1999. Aboriginal burning for vegetation management in Northwest British Columbia. In *Indians, Fire and the Land in the Pacific Northwest*, ed. R. Boyd, pp. 238–54. Corvallis: Oregon State University Press.

Johnson, N. B. 1952. The American Indian as conservationist. *Chronicles of Oklahoma* 30(3):333–40.

Johnson, N. C. 1999. Humans as agents of ecological change—overview. In *Ecological Stewardship: A Common Reference for Ecosystem Management*, vol. 2, ed. R. C. Szaro, N. C. Johnson, W. T. Sexton, and A. J. Malk, pp. 433–37. Oxford: Elsevier Science.

Jones, R. 1969. Fire-stick farming. *Australian Natural History* 16:224–28.

———. 1980. Cleaning the country: The Gidjingali and their Arnhemland environment. *BHP Journal* (Broken Hill Proprietary Co.) 1:10–15.

Jordan, W. R., M. E. Gilpin, and J. D. Aber (eds.). 1987. *Restoration Ecology: A Synthetic Approach to Ecological Research*. Cambridge: Cambridge University Press.

Jorgensen, D. L. 1989. *Participant Observation: A Methodology for Human Studies*. Applied Social Research Methods Series 15. Newbury Park: Sage Publications.

Kalisz, J. P. 1982. The longleaf pine islands of the Ocala National Forest, Florida: A soil study. Dissertation. University of Florida, Gainesville, Florida.

Kauffman, J. B., and R. E. Martin. 1987. Effects of fire and fire suppression on mortality and mode of reproduction of California black oak (*Quercus kelloggii* Newb.). In *Proceedings of the Symposium on Multiple-use Management of California's Hardwood Resources*, November 12–14, 1986, San Luis Obispo, California, pp. 122–26. Berkeley: Pacific Southwest Forest and Range Experiment Station.

Kay, C. E. 1997. Is aspen doomed? *Journal of Forestry* 95:4–12.

Kayll, A. J. 1974. Use of fire in land management. In *Fire and Ecosystems*, ed. T. T. Kozlowski and C. E. Ahlgren, pp. 483–511. New York: Academic Press.

Keeley, J. E., and S. C. Keeley. 1989. Allelopathy and the fire-induced herb cycle. In *The California Chaparral: Paradigms Reexamined*, ed. S. C. Keeley, pp. 65–72. Los Angeles: Natural History Museum of Los Angeles County.

Keesing, F. M., and R. M. Keesing. 1971. *New Perspectives in Cultural Anthropology.* New York: Holt, Rinehart and Winston.

Kehoe, A. B. 1992. *North American Indians: A Comprehensive Account.* Englewood Cliffs, N.J.: Prentice-Hall.

———. 1998. *Humans: An Introduction to Four-Field Anthropology.* New York: Routledge.

Kilgore, B. M. 1973. The ecological role of fire in Sierran conifer forests: Its application to national park management. *Journal of Quaternary Research* 3:396–513.

———. 1985. What is "natural" in wilderness fire management? In *Proceedings: Symposium and Workshop on Wilderness Fire*, tech. coord. J. E. Lotan, B. M. Kilgore, W. C. Fischer, and R. W. Mutch, pp. 57–67. U.S. Forest Service General Technical Report INT-182. Missoula, Mont.: U.S. Forest Service.

Kilgore, B. M., and D. Taylor. 1979. Fire history of a Sequoia–mixed conifer forest. *Ecology* 60(1):129–42.

Kimber, R. G. 1993. Learning about fire: Western Desert Aborigines. In *Traditional Ecological Knowledge: Wisdom for Sustainable Developement*, ed. N. M. Williams and G. Baines, pp. 121–25. Canberra: Centre for Resource and Environmental Studies, Australian National University.

Knapp, A. K., J. M. Briggs, D. C. Hartnett, and S. L. Collins (eds.). 1998. *Grassland Dynamics: Long-term Ecological Research in Tallgrass Prairie.* Oxford: Oxford University Press.

Knapp, A. K., and T. R. Seastedt. 1986. Detritus accumulation limits productivity of tallgrass prairie. *Bioscience* 36:662–68.

Komarek, E. V. 1963. Letter dated January 17 to Omer Stewart. Omer Stewart Collection, University of Colorado.

Kottak, C. 1999. The new ecological anthropology. *American Anthropologist* 101:23–35.

Kroeber, A. L. 1952. *The Nature of Culture.* Chicago: University of Chicago Press.

Kutiel, P., and A. Shaviv. 1992. Effects of soil type, plant composition and leaching on soil nutrients following a simulated forest fire. *Forest Ecology and Management* 53:329–43.

La Barre, W. 1942. Folk medicine and folk science. *Journal of American Folklore* 55(218):197–203.

LaRoe, E. T., G. S. Farris, C. E. Puckett, P. D. Doran, and M. J. Mac (eds.). 1995. *Our Living Resources: A Report to the Nation on the Distribution, Abundance, and Health of U.S. Plants, Animals, and Ecosystems.* Washington, D.C.: U.S. Department of the Interior, National Biological Service.

Latham, R. E. 1993. The serpentine barrens of temperate eastern North America: Critical issues in the management of rare species and communities. *Bartonia* 57: 61–74.

Latz, P. K., and G. F. Griffin. 1978. Changes in Aboriginal land management in relation to fire and to food plants in central Australia. In *The Nutrition of Aborigines in Relation to the Ecosystem of Central Australia*, ed. B. S. Hetzel and H. J. Frith, pp. 77–86. Melbourne: CSIRO.

Lee, R. B., and I. DeVore. 1966. *Man the Hunter.* Chicago: University of Chicago Press.

Leopold, A. 1924. Grass, brush, timber, and fire in southern Arizona. *Journal of Forestry* 22(1):2–10. Reprinted in *The River of the Mother of God*, ed. S. L. Flader and J. B. Callicott, pp. 114–22. Madison: University of Wisconsin Press.

———. 1991a. Conservationist in Mexico [1937]. In *The River of the Mother of God*, ed. S. L. Flader and J. B. Callicott, pp. 239–44. Madison: University of Wisconsin Press.

———. 1991b. "Paiute Forestry" vs. forest fire prevention [1920]. In *The River of the Mother of God*, ed. S. L. Flader and J. B. Callicott, pp. 68–70. Madison: University of Wisconsin Press.

Leopold, A. S., S. A. Cain, C. M. Cottam, I. N. Gabrielson, and T. L. Kimball. 1963. Wildlife management in the national parks: The Leopold Report. Submitted to Stewart Udall, Secretary of the Interior, March 4. Washington, D.C.

Leverett, R. 1996. Definitions and history. In *Eastern Old-Growth Forests: Prospects for Rediscovery and Recovery*, ed. M. B. Davis, pp. 3–17. Washington, D.C.: Island Press.

Lewis, H. T. 1972. The role of fire in the domestication of plants and animals in southwest Asia: A hypothesis. *Man* 7:195–222.

———. 1973. *Patterns of Indian Burning in California: Ecology and Ethnohistory.* Ramona, Calif.: Ballena Press.

———. 1977. Maskuta: The ecology of Indian fires in northern Alberta. *Western Canadian Journal of Anthropology* 7:15–52.

———. 1978. Traditional uses of fire by Indians in northern Alberta. *Current Anthropology* 19:401–2.

———. 1980. Indian fires of spring. *Natural History* 89:76–83.

———. 1981. Hunter-gatherers and problems for fire history. In *Proceedings of the Fire History Workshop*, pp. 115–19. General Technical Report RM-81. Salt Lake City: Rocky Mt. Forest and Range Experiment Station, U.S. Forest Service.

———. 1982a. Fire technology and resource management in Aboriginal North America and Australia. In The *Regulation of Environmental Resources in Food Collecting Societies*, ed. E. Hunn and N. Williams, pp. 45–67. American Association for the Advancement of Science Selected Symposium Series No. 67. Boulder, Colo.: Westview Press.

———. 1982b. *A Time for Burning: Traditional Indian Uses of Fire in the Western Canadian Boreal Forest.* Edmonton: Boreal Institute for Northern Studies, University of Alberta.

———. 1985a. Burning the "top end": Kangaroos and cattle. In *Fire Ecology and Management in Western Australian Ecosystems*, ed. J. Ford, pp. 21–31. Environmental Studies Group Bulletin No. 14. Bentley: Western Australian Institute of Technology (WAIT).

———. 1985b. Why Indians burned: Specific versus general reasons. In *Proceedings: Symposium and Workshop on Wilderness Fire*, tech. coord. J. E. Lotan, B. M. Kilgore, W. C. Fischer, and W. R. Mutch, pp. 75–80. Ogden, Utah: Intermountain Forest and Range Experiment Station, USDA Forest Service.

———. 1989a. Ecological knowledge of fire: Aborigines vs. park rangers in northern Australia. *American Anthropologist* 91:940–61.

———. 1989b. Non-agricultural management of plants and animals. In *Wildlife Production Systems*, ed. R. J. Hudson, K. R. Drew, and L. M. Baskin, pp. 54–74. Cambridge: Cambridge University Press.

———. 1990a. Reconstructing patterns of Indian burning in southwestern Oregon. In *Living with the Land: The Indians of Southwestern Oregon*, ed. N. Hannon and R. K. Olmo, pp. 80–84. Medford: Southern Oregon Historical Society.

———. 1990b. Traditional ecological knowledge of fire in northern Alberta: Something old, something new, something different. In *Proceedings of the Fort Chipewyan and Fort Vermilion Bicentennial Conference*, ed. R. G. Ironside and P. A. McCormack, pp. 222–27. Edmonton, Alberta: Boreal Institute for Northern Studies.

———. 1991a. A parable of fire: Hunter-gatherers in Canada and Australia. In *Traditional Ecological Knowledge: A Collection of Essays*, ed. R. E. Johannes, pp. 9–16. Gland, Switzerland: World Conservation Union (IUCN).

———. 1991b. Technological complexity, ecological diversity, and fire regimes in northern Australia: Hunter-gatherer, cowboy, ranger. In *Profiles in Cultural Evolution*, ed. A. T. Rambo and K. Gillogly, pp. 261–88. Anthropological Papers No. 85. Ann Arbor: Museum of Anthropology, University of Michigan.

———. 1993. In retrospect. In *Before the Wilderness: Environmental Management by Native Californians*, ed. T. C. Blackburn and K. M. Anderson, pp. 389–400. Anthropological Papers No. 40. Menlo Park, Calif.: Ballena Press.

———. 1994. Management fires vs. corrective fires in northern Australia: An analogue for environmental change. *Chemosphere* 29:949–63.

Lewis, H. T., and T. M. Ferguson. 1988. Yards, corridors, and mosaics: How to burn a boreal forest. *Human Ecology* 16:57–77.

Loewen, D. L. 1998. Ecology, ethnobotany, and nutritional aspects of yellow glacier lily, *Erythronium grandiflorum* Push (Liliaceae) in Western Canada. Thesis, University of Victoria, Victoria, British Columbia, Canada.

Lofland, J. 1974. Styles of reporting qualitative field research. *American Sociologist* 9:101–11.

Lovegrove, B. G., and J. U. M. Jarvis. 1986. Coevolution between mole-rats (Bathyergidae) and a geophyte, *Micranthus* (Iridaceae). *Cimbebasia* (Windhoek, South Africa).

Marshall, A. G. 1999. Unusual gardens: The Nez Perce and wild horticulture on the Eastern Columbia Plateau. In *Northwest Lands, Northwest Peoples Readings in Environmental History*, ed. D. D. Goble and P. W. Hirt, pp. 173–87. Seattle: University of Washington Press.

Marshall, R. 1998. The problem of the wilderness. In *The Great New Wilderness Debate*, ed. J. B. Callicott and M. P. Nelson, pp. 85–96. Athens: University of Georgia Press.

Martin, R. E., and D. B. Sapsis. 1992. Fires as agents of biodiversity—pyrodiversity promotes biodiversity. In *Proceedings of the Symposium on Biodiversity of Northwestern California*, October, 1991, ed. R. R. Harris and D. C. Erman, pp. 150–57. Division of Agricultural and Natural Resources, University of California, Berkeley.

McBride, J. R., and H. T. Lewis. 1984. Occurrence of fire scars in relation to the season and frequency of surface fires in eucalypt forests of the Northern Territory, Australia. *Forest Science* 30:970–76.

McCabe, T. L. 1995. The changing insect fauna of Albany's pine barrens. In *Our Living Resources: A Report to the Nation on the Distribution, Abundance, and Health of U.S. Plants, Animals, and Ecosystems*, ed. E. T. LaRoe, G. S. Farris, C. E. Puckett, P. D. Doran, and M. J. Mac, pp. 166–68. Washington D.C.: U.S. Department of the Interior, National Biological Service.

McCarthy, H. 1993. Managing oaks and the acorn crop. In *Before the Wilderness*, ed. T. C. Blackburn and K. Anderson, pp. 213–28. Menlo Park, Calif.: Ballena Press.

MacCleery, D. 1994. Understanding the role the human dimension has played in shaping America's forest and grassland landscapes: Is there a landscape archaeologist in the house? Eco-Watch; available at www.lib.duke.edu/forestusfscoll/landscapes.htm.

McDougall, W. B. 1949. *Plant Ecology*. Philadelphia: Lea and Febiger.

McPherson, G. R. 1995. The role of fire in desert grasslands. In *The Desert Grassland*, ed. M. P. McClaran and T. R. Van Devender, pp. 130–51. Tucson: University of Arizona Press.

Merchant, C. 1993. What is environmental history? In *Major Problems in American Environmental History*, ed. C. Merchant, pp. 1–31. Lexington, Mass.: D. C. Heath and Co.

Miller, N. F. 1992. The origins of plant cultivation in the Near East. In *The Origins of Agriculture: An International Perspective*, ed. Wesley Cowan, pp. 39–58. Washington, D.C.: Smithsonian Institution Press.

Minnich, R. A. 1983. Fire mosaics in southern California and northern Baja California. *Science* 219:1287–94.

Mitsch, W. J., and J. G. Gosselink. 1993. *Wetlands*. 2nd ed. New York: Van Nostrand Reinhold.

Muir, J. 1944. *My First Summer in the Sierra*. Boston: Houghton Mifflin Co.

Myers, R. L., and P. A. Peroni. 1983. Approaches to determining aboriginal fire use and its impact on vegetation. *Bulletin of the Ecological Society of America* 64(3):217–18.

Nabhan, G. P., A. M. Rea, K. L. Reichhardt, E. Mellink, and C. F. Hutchinson. 1982. Papago influences on habitat and biotic diversity: Quitova Oasis ethnoecology. *Journal of Ethnobiology* 2:124–43.

National Research Council. 1992. *Science and the National Parks*. Washington, D.C.: National Academy Press.

Norse, E. A. 1990. *Ancient Forests of the Pacific Northwest*. Washington, D.C.: Island Press.

Norton, H. 1979. The association between anthropogenic prairies and important food plants in western Washington. *Northwest Anthropological Research Notes* 13:175–200.

Noss, R. F., E. T. LaRoe III, and J. M. Scott. 1995. *Endangered Ecosystems of the United States: A Preliminary Assessment of Loss and Degradation*. Biological Report No. 28. Washington, D.C.: U.S. Department of Interior, National Biological Service.

Núñez Cabeza DeVaca, A. 1972. *The Narrative of Alvar Núñez Cabeza DeVaca*. Trans. F. Bandelier. Barre, Mass.: Imprint Society.

Nuzzo, V. A. 1986. Extent and status of Midwest oak savanna: presettlement and 1985. *Natural Areas Journal* 6(2):6–36.

Olmsted, F. E. 1911. Fire and the forest—the theory of "light burning." *Sierra Club Bulletin* 8(1):43–47.

Packard, S. 1988. Just a few oddball species: Restoration and the rediscovery of the tallgrass savanna. *Restoration and Management Notes* 6(1):13–20.

Packard, S., and C. F. Mutel. 1997. *The Tallgrass Restoration Handbook for Prairies, Savannas, and Woodlands*. Washington, D.C.: Island Press.

Parker, K. W. 1945. Juniper comes to the grasslands: Why it invades southwestern grassland—suggestions on control. *American Cattle Producer* 27:12–14, 30–32.

Parsons, D. J., D. M. Graber, J. K. Agee, and J. W. van Wagtendonk. 1986. Natural fire management in national parks. *Environmental Management* 10(1):21–24.

Patterson, W. A., III, and K. E. Sassaman. 1988. Indian fires in the prehistory of New England. In *Holocene Human Ecology in Northeastern North America*, ed. G. P. Nicholas, pp. 107–35. New York: Plenum Press.

Peacock, S., and N. J. Turner. 2000. Just like a garden: Traditional plant resource management and biodiversity conservation on the British Columbia Plateau. In *Biodiversity and Native North America*, ed. P. Minnis and W. Elisens, pp. 133–79. Norman: University of Oklahoma Press.

Pearsall, D. M. 1989. *Paleoethnobotany: A Handbook of Procedures*. San Diego: Academic Press.

Peoples, J., and G. Bailey. 1997. *Humanity: An Introduction to Cultural Anthropology*. Belmont, Calif.: West/Wadsworth.

Perry, C. 1999. *Pacific Arcadia: Images of California 1600–1915*. New York: Oxford University Press.

Phillips, W. S. 1963. *Vegetational Changes in the Northern Great Plains*. Report 214. Tucson: University of Arizona Agricultural Experiment Station.

Pickett, S. T. A., V. T. Parker, and P. L. Fiedler. 1992. The new paradigm in ecology: Implications for conservation biology above the species level. In *Conservation Biology: The Theory and Practice of Nature Conservation*, ed. P. L. Fiedler and S. K. Jain, pp. 65–88. New York: Chapman and Hall.

Piperno, D. R. 1988. *Phytolith Analysis: An Archaeological and Geological Perspective*. San Diego: Academic Press.

Purdy, B. A. 1981. *Florida's Prehistoric Stone Technology*. Gainesville: University Presses of Florida.

Pyne, S. J. 1982. *Fire in America: A Cultural History of Wildland and Rural Fire*. Princeton: Princeton University Press.

———. 1991a. *Burning Bush: A Fire History of Australia*. New York: Henry Holt.

———. 1991b. Sky of brass, earth of ash: A brief history of fire in the United States. In *Global Biomass Burning: Atmospheric, Climatic, and Biospheric Implications*, ed. J. S. Levine, pp. 504–11. Boston: MIT Press.

———. 1997a. *Vestal Fire: An Environmental History, Told through Fire, of Europe and Europe's Encounter with the World*. Seattle: University of Washington Press.

———. 1997b. *World Fire: The Culture of Fire on Earth*. Seattle: University of Washington Press.

Pyne, S. J., P. L. Andrews, and R. D. Laven. 1996. *Introduction to Wildland Fire*. 2nd ed. New York: John Wiley and Sons.

Risser, P. G. 1988. Diversity in and among grasslands. In *Biodiversity*, ed. E. O. Wilson, 176–80. Washington, D.C.: National Academy Press.

Robbins, L. E., and R. L. Myers. 1992. *Seasonal Effects of Prescribed Burning in Florida: A Review*. Miscellaneous Publication No. 8. Tallahassee, Fla.: Tall Timbers Research Station.

Ronaasen, S., R. O. Clemmer, and M. E. Rudden. 1999. Rethinking cultural ecology, multilinear evolution, and expert witnesses: Julian Steward and Indian Claims Commission proceedings. In *Julian Steward and the Great Basin: The Making of an Anthropologist*, ed. R. O. Clemmer, L. D. Myers, and M. E. Rudden, pp. 170–202. Salt Lake City: University of Utah Press.

Russell, E. W. B. 1980. Vegetational change in northern New Jersey from precolonization to the present: A palynological interpretation. *Bulletin of the Torrey Botanical Club* 107:432–46.

———. 1981. Vegetation of northern New Jersey before European settlement. *American Midland Naturalist* 105(1):1–12.

———. 1983. Indian-set fires in the forests of the northeastern United States. *Ecology* 64(1):78–88.

Sampson, R. N., and D. L. Adams (eds.). 1994. *Assessing Forest Ecosystem Health in the Inland West*. New York: Food Products Press.

Sampson, R. N., D. L. Adams, S. S. Hamilton, S. P. Mealey, R. Steele, and D. Van De Graaff. 1994. Assessing forest ecosystem health in the inland West. In *Assessing Forest Ecosystem Health in the Inland West*, ed. R. N. Sampson and D. L. Adams, pp. 3–10. New York: Food Products Press.

Sauer, C. O. 1950. Grassland climax, fire, and man. *Journal of Range Management* 3:16–22.

———. 1956. The agency of man on the earth. In *Man's Role in Changing the Face of the Earth*, ed. William L. Thomas, Jr., vol. 1, pp. 49–69. 2 vols. Chicago: University of Chicago Press.

Scupin, R. 1998. *Cultural Anthropology: A Global Perspective*. Saddle River, N.J.: Prentice-Hall.

Sears, W. H. 1982. *Fort Center: An Archaeological Site in the Lake Okeechobee Basin*. Gainesville: University Presses of Florida.

Seymour, R. S., and M. L. Hunter, Jr. 1999. Principles of ecological forestry. In *Maintaining Biodiversity in Forest Ecosystems*, ed. M. L. Hunter, Jr., pp. 22–61. Cambridge: Cambridge University Press.

Shipek, F. C. 1989. An example of intensive plant husbandry. The Kumeyaay of southern California. In *Foraging and Farming: The Evolution of Plant Exploitation*, ed. D. R. Harris and G. C. Hillman, pp. 159–70. Boston: Unwin Hyman.

———. 1993. Kumeyaay plant husbandry: Fire, water, and erosion control systems. In *Before the Wilderness: Environmental Management by Native Californians,* ed. T. C. Blackburn and K. Anderson, pp. 379–88. Menlo Park, Calif.: Ballena Press.

Skinner, C. N., and C. R. Chang. 1996. Fire regimes, past and present. In *Sierra Nevada Ecosystem Project: Published Final report to Congress*, vol. 2, *Assessments and Scientific Basis for Management Options*, pp. 1041–69. Davis: University of California, Centers for Water and Wildland Resources.

SNEP (Sierra Nevada Ecosystem Project) Science Team. 1996. Fire and fuels. In *Sierra Nevada Ecosystem Project: Published Final Report to Congress*, vol. 1, *Assessment Summaries and Management Strategies*, pp. 61–71. Davis: University of California, Centers for Water and Wildland Resources.

Snyder, G. 1995. A note on "Before the Wilderness." *Tree Rings Journal* (Yuba Watershed Institute) 8:9–11.

Soulé, M. E. 1986. *Conservation Biology: The Science of Scarcity and Diversity*. Sunderland, Mass.: Sinauer Associates.

Sousa, W. P. 1985. Disturbance and patch dynamics on rocky intertidal shores. In *The Ecology of Natural Disturbance and Patch Dynamics*, ed. S. T. A. Pickett and P. S. White, pp. 101–24. San Diego: Academic Press.

Spurr, S. H., and B. V. Barnes. 1980. *Forest Ecology*. 3rd ed. New York: John Wiley and Sons.

Stahle, D. W. 1996. Tree rings and ancient forest history. In *Eastern Old-Growth Forests: Prospects for Rediscovery and Recovery*, ed. M. B. Davis, pp. 321–43. Washington, D.C.: Island Press.

Stegner, W. 1961. Letter: The wilderness idea. In *Wilderness: America's Living Heritage*, ed. D. Brower, pp. 97–102. San Francisco: Sierra Club.

Sterling, E. A. 1905. Attitude of lumbermen toward forest fires. In *Yearbook of the United States Department of Agriculture 1904*, pp. 133–40. Washington, D.C.: Government Printing Office.

Steward, J. S. 1940. Native cultures of the intermontane (Great Basin) area. In *Essays in the Historical Anthropology of North America Published in Honor of J. R. Swanton*, pp. 445–502. Smithsonian Miscellaneous Collections No. 100. Washington, D.C.: Smithsonian Institution.

———. 1951. Levels of sociocultural integration: An operational concept. *Southwestern Journal of Anthropology* 7:374–90.

———. 1955. *Theory of Culture Change: The Methodology of Multilinear Evolution.* Urbana: University of Illinois Press.

Stewart, O. C. 1943. *Notes on Pomo Ethnogeography.* University of California Publications in American Archaeology and Ethnology 40:2. Berkeley/Los Angeles: University of California Press.

———. 1951. The effect of Indian burning and natural vegetation in the United States. *Geographic Review* 41:317–20.

———. 1954. The forgotten side of ethnogeography. In *Method and Perspective in Anthropology*, ed. R. F. Spencer, pp. 221–48. Minneapolis: University of Minnesota Press.

———. 1955a. Fire as the first great force employed by man. In *Man's Role in Changing the Face of the Earth*, ed. W. L. Thomas, pp. 115–33. Chicago: University of Chicago Press.

———. 1955b. Forest and grass burning in the Mountain West. *Southwestern Lore* 21:5–9.

———. 1955c. Why were the prairies treeless? *Southwestern Lore* 20:59–64.

———. 1963. Barriers to understanding the influence of use of fire by aborigines on vegetation. *Annual Proceedings, Tall Timbers Fire Ecology Conference* 2:117–26.

———. 1987. *Peyote Religion.* Norman: University of Oklahoma Press.

Stewart, O. C., and M. Knack. 1984. *As Long as the River Shall Run: An Economic Ethnohistory of Pyramid Lake Indian Reservation, Nevada.* Berkeley: University of California Press.

St. John, T. V., and P. W. Rundel. 1976. The role of fire as a mineralizing agent in a Sierran coniferous forest. *Oecologia* 25:35–45.

Stoffle, R. W. 1992. Epitaph for Omer Call Stewart. *High Plains Anthropologist* 11(2): ix–xxiii.

Swetnam, T. W., and C. H. Baisan. 1996. Historical fire regime patterns in the Southwestern United States since a.d. 1700. In *Proceedings of the Second La Mesa Fire Symposium, 29–30 March, 1994, Los Alamos, N.M.*, pp. 11–32. USDA Forest Service Gen. Tech. Rep. RM-GTR-286.

Taylor, A. R. 1974. Ecological aspects of lightning in forests. *Tall Timbers Fire Ecology Conference* 13:455–82. Tallahassee, Fla.: Tall Timbers Research Station.

Thomas, J. W. 1994. Concerning the health and productivity of the fire-adapted forests of the western United States. Statement of Dr. Jack Ward Thomas, Chief, Forest Service, United States Department of Agriculture, before the Subcommittee on Agricultural Research, Conservation, Forestry, and General Legislation Committee on Agriculture United States Senate.

Timbrook, J., J. R. Johnson, and D. D. Earle. 1982. Vegetation burning by the Chumash. *Journal of California and Great Basin Anthropology* 4:163–86.

Turner, N. J. 1991. "Burning mountain sides for better crops": Aboriginal landscape burning in British Columbia. *Archeology in Montana* 32:57–73.

————. 1999. "Time to burn": Traditional use of fire to enhance resource production by aboriginal peoples in British Columbia. In *Indians, Fire and the Land in the Pacific Northwest*, ed. R. Boyd, pp. 185–218. Corvallis: Oregon State University Press.

Turner, N. J., M. B. Ignace, and R. Ignace. 2000. Traditional ecological knowledge and wisdom of aboriginal peoples in British Columbia. *Ecological Applications* 10(5): 1275–87.

Vale, T. R. 1998. The myth of the humanized landscape: An example from Yosemite National Park. *Natural Areas Journal* 18(3):231–36.

Vayda, A. P., and R. Rappaport. 1968. Ecology, cultural and noncultural. In *Introduction to Cultural Anthropology*, ed. J. Clifton, pp. 477–97. Boston: Houghton Mifflin.

Watts, W. A. 1975. A late Quaternary record of vegetation from Lake Annie, south-central Florida. *Geology* 3:344–46.

Watts, W. A., and M. Stulver. 1980. Late Wisconsin climate of northern Florida and the origin of species-rich deciduous forest. *Science* 210:325–27.

Weatherspoon, C. P., S. J. Husari, and J. W. van Wagtendonk. 1992. Fire and fuels management in relation to owl habitat in forests of the Sierra Nevada and southern California. In *The California Spotted Owl: A Technical Assessment of Its Current Status*, ed. J. Verner, K. S. McKelvey, B. R. Noon, R. J. Gutierrez, G. I. Gould, Jr., and T. W. Beck, pp. 247–60. General Technical Report PSW-GTR-133. Berkeley: USDA Forest Service.

Weaver, J. E., and F. E. Clements. 1938. *Plant Ecology*. New York: McGraw-Hill Book Co.

Wells, P. V. 1970a. Historical factors controlling vegetation patterns and floristic distributions in the Central Plains region of North America. In *Pleistocene and Recent Environments of the Central Great Plains*, ed. W. Dort, Jr., and J. K. Jones, pp. 211–21. Department of Geology, University of Kansas Special Publication 3. Lawrence: University Press of Kansas.

————. 1970b. Postglacial vegetational history of the Great Plains. *Science* 167:1574–82.

White, L. A. 1949. *The Science of Culture: A Study of Man and Civilization*. New York: Farrar, Straus and Giroux.

White, P. S., and S. T. A. Pickett. 1985. Natural disturbance and patch dynamics: An introduction. In *The Ecology of Natural Disturbance and Patch Dynamics*, ed. S. T. A. Pickett and P. S. White, pp. 3–13. San Diego: Academic Press.

Whittaker, R. H. 1973. Climax concepts and recognition. *Handbook of Vegetation Science* 8:137–54.

Williams, G. W. 1994. References on the American Indian use of fire in ecosystems. Unpublished paper, available at http://wings.buffalo.edu/academic/department/anthropology/Documents/firebib.txt.

Wills, R. D., and J. D. Stuart. 1994. Fire history and stand development of a Douglas-fir/hardwood forest in northern California. *Northwest Science* 68:205–12.

Winterhalder, B., and E. A. Smith. 1981. *Hunter-Gatherer Foraging Strategies*. Chicago: University of Chicago Press.

Worster, D. 1977. *Nature's Economy: A History of Ecological Ideas*. New York: Cambridge University Press.

Wuerthner, G. n.d. Forest fire as an endangered ecosystem process: The ill legacy of Smokey the Bear. In *Wildfire: An Endangered Ecosystem Process*. Eugene, Ore.: Cascadia Fire Ecology Education Project.

Yen, D. E. 1989. The domestication of environment. In *Foraging and Farming: The Evolution of Plant Exploitation*, ed. D. R. Harris and G. C. Hillman, pp. 55–75. Boston: Unwin Hyman.

Index

Aginsky, B., 290, 307
Agriculture, origins of, 25–27
Aikman, J. M., 132, 134
Alabama, 79, 102
Alaska, 190
Alberta, Canada, 217
Albertson, F. W., 156, 163–64
Aldous, A. E., 155–56, 157
Algonquian-speaking tribes, 10, 74, 80, 112
Anthropology: economic, 23; Stewart's approach to, 21, 29–31
Apache, 139–40, 218, 220
Appalachian region, 41, 49, 87, 107, 112
Arizona, 54, 61, 218, 219, 221–24, 230, 237, 242, 243, 247
Arkansas, 102, 107, 139
Ash Wednesday Fires (Australia, 1983), 13, 15
As Long as the River Shall Run (Stewart and Knack), 6
Aspens, 43–44, 184, 186–88, 191–92, 200, 217, 226, 236
Athabascan-speaking tribes, 10
Atlantic coastal plain, 87, 102
Atsugewi, 292, 293
Atwater, Caleb, 88–89, 113, 120, 206
Australia, 12–15, 24, 31
Australian Aborigines, 13, 15, 16n.4, 24, 31

Balance of nature, 38–39, 44
Bancroft, H. H., 229, 232, 233, 306
Barnett, H. G., 252

Barrens, 88–92, 107
Barrett, S. A., 288–89
"Barriers to Understanding the Influence of Use of Fire by Aborigines on Vegetation" (Stewart), 11
Bartram, William, 97
Basketry, 56, 58, 60, 273, 277, 283
Bates, Carlos G., 154–55, 166
Bauer, H. L., 268, 309
Beaglehole, Ernest, 220
Beals, Ralph A., 291
Benson, Lyman, 147, 152, 154
Bessey, C. E., 159–60
Beverley, R., 72, 82, 83
Bicknell, Susan, 49
Bigelow, T. A., 254
Big trees. *See* Sequoias
Billings, W. D., 102, 121, 127, 208
Biodiversity, 15, 35, 43, 44, 46, 51, 55, 61
Bird, Ralph D., 191–92
Bison (buffalo), 39, 50, 67–68, 115–16, 120, 153, 159, 193, 198, 199, 201
Black Friday Fires (Australia, 1939), 13
Black Hills, South Dakota, 62, 175
Blizzard, Alpheus W., 108, 109
Blumer, J. C., 235–36
Boas, Franz, 252
Bonnicksen, Thomas M., 3, 9, 34
Borowski, Odad, 26
Botkin, Daniel, 38
Bourne, A., 78, 89, 118, 136
Box elders, 162
Bradbury, J., 158–59
Braidwood, Robert, 25

Brandegee, T. S., 234–35, 266, 270–71
Braun-Blanquet, J., 237–38, 247
Bray, William L., 140, 145, 147, 152, 154
Brickell, J., 72–73
"Brief Relations of New England," 74
British Columbia, Canada, 232, 242
Broad-sclerophylls, 266, 271
Brown-spot disease, 96–97, 99
Bruce, David, 100, 102
Brush, 14, 69
Bryant, E., 226–27, 306
Buckbrush, 155–56, 157, 165
Buffalo. *See* Bison
Buffalo grass, 214, 216
Bullock, William, 81–82
Bunchgrass, 42, 165, 166, 209, 225, 243,
    248, 266, 307–10
Burcham, L. T., 42
Burnaby, Andrew, 76–77, 85
Burn preclimax forest, 107
Bush fires, 13
Bushmen, 24
Byrd, William, 73–74

Cahuilla, 10, 62
California, 12, 13, 18, 40, 49, 62, 217, 218,
    231, 242, 256–59, 310–12; Central Valley,
    300–310; lightning fires in, 105, 284–85,
    297–300, 311; northern Coastal Range,
    269–86; Sierra Nevada, 286–300;
    southern Coastal Range, 259–69
Canada, 10, 62, 110, 112; prairies of,
    178–92, 211
Cascade Range, 51, 253
Catlin, George, 116–17
Cedars, 62, 147, 154, 160, 177, 250, 253,
    294, 295
Cemeteries, relict vegetation in, 249
Central Valley, California, 300–310
Chaney, Ralph W., 148, 161, 164, 174,
    197–201
Chaparral, 143, 145, 162, 258, 259, 271, 279,
    286, 294, 300–301, 312; in forests, 297;
    and grasslands, 264–70, 308, 309, 310
Chapman, F. M., 140
Chapman, H. H., 97–100, 103–105, 107
Chavennes, Elizabeth, 128–29
Cherokee, 80

Chestnut-chestnut oak-yellow poplar
    region, 83
Cheyenne, 38
Christy, Miller, 140, 178–91, 208
Clark, H. W., 269–70
Clark, Jim, 54
Clements, F. E., 8, 38, 39, 95, 98, 102,
    106, 107, 113, 125–26, 148, 161–64,
    172–74, 192–94, 196–201, 204, 233,
    236, 241–45, 265, 296, 301–302, 307,
    309, 310
Climate, 39; of Central Valley, California,
    301, 308; and grasslands, 114, 202–206,
    307; of Great Basin and Plateau, 226,
    242; and prairie-plains formation, 113,
    123, 126, 134, 152, 153, 154, 162–63,
    176, 177, 200, 201
Climax forests, 111
Coastal prairies, 49, 143
Coast Range, 253, 255; northern, 269–86;
    southern, 259–69
Cobb, F. E., 174, 175
Coffey, G. N., 102, 206
Colorado, 168–72, 196, 197, 203, 210,
    211, 217, 225, 229, 230, 233–36, 238,
    242, 243, 245
Conifers, 44, 48, 51, 62, 108, 176–77, 212,
    216, 294
Connaughton, C. A., 93, 126
Connell, J. H., 46
Conservation biology, 43, 55
Controlled burning, 9, 12, 14, 34, 35, 99
Cook, O. F., 140–43
Cooper, W. S., 38, 266–68, 271, 308–309
Cornett, James, 48
Cottam, Grant, 127, 129
Cottam, W. P., 245–47
Cottle, H. J., 147
Cowles, H. C., 38, 125
Cox, Ross, 228, 233
Creosote bush, 218, 222
Cro-Magnons, 25
Cultural ecology, Steward's theory of,
    22–25
Culture area concept, 71
Culture element surveys (CED), 29–30,
    220, 221, 229–32, 252, 262, 281, 282,
    290, 292, 303, 307

Dana, James D., 113, 264
Darrah, W. C., 229
Daubenmire, R. F., 240–41, 247–50, 294
Davis, Wilfred S., 167
Day, Gordon M., 7, 17, 18, 22, 31, 71–72, 74
Delaware, 76, 85
Desert fan palm, 10, 48
Deserts, 218, 224–25, 226, 240, 241, 301
"Digger Indians," 258, 270, 305–306
Disturbances in ecosystems, 39, 44, 46, 51–52, 58, 60, 61
Dixon, Roland B., 291–92, 293
Dodge, R. I., 153–54
Douglas, David, 252
Douglas firs, 8, 48, 51, 54, 226, 235–36, 238, 250–55, 285, 294
Drew, William B., 138–39
Driver, H. E., 30, 231, 282, 290, 303, 307
Droughts, 163, 177, 213, 223, 245, 255
Drucker, P., 221, 230, 252, 262
Dwight, T., 77, 85–87

Eastern woodlands, 10, 62, 70–113
Ecological Applications, 40
Ecological niche, Barth's idea of, 35n.5
Ecological restoration, 28, 34–35, 44, 55–61
Ecological sciences: contemporary context of, 42–49; historical context of, 37–42
Ecosystems, 8, 55; decline of, 43–44; disturbances in, 39, 44, 46, 51–52, 58, 60, 61; Indian influences on, 38–39; restoration of, 44
Elias, M. R., 199–200
Endangered species, 35, 43
Environmental determinism, 22
Ernst, Emil F., 286–89, 298
Erosion, 152, 245
Essene, Frank, 281–82
Ethnobiology, 55
Ethnobotany, 54
Ethnoecological studies, 32, 46, 55–61
Ethnogeography, 31
Ethnographic studies, 31
Evaporation, and prairie-plains formation, 132, 134

Farnham, T. J., 228, 306
Faye, Paul Louis, 291
Finley, J. B., 78
Firebreaks, 167
Fire forests, 251, 252
Fire grass, 86
Fireguards, 180, 184, 185
Fire hazards, 12, 14, 15, 16, 107, 109
Fire prevention and protection, 14, 15, 103, 152; by burning, 284, 291
Fires, 3, 5; of Australia, 13–15; of Canadian prairies, 179–92; Colorado grass fires, 171–72; grasslands and, 212–16, 244, 307–308; ill effects of, 102–103; as land management tool, 3–4, 39–40, 48, 50–51; of U.S. prairies, 192–99. *See also* Forest fires; Lightning fires
Fire scars, 54
Fire suppression, 43–44, 50, 51, 240
Fire technology, of indigenous people, 32
Fisher, C. E., 147–48
Flatheads, 229, 232
Flint, James, 79, 90
Flint, Timothy, 88, 136
Florida, 49, 105
Flory, Evan L., 202, 214, 215, 216
Folklore, Native American knowledge as, 42
Folsom culture, 63, 67, 68, 201
Fontaine, James, 82
Foote, W. H., 84
Forage, 101, 152
Forbs, effect of fire on, 43
Fordham, E. P., 118
Forest fires, 14, 69, 142; Euro-American uses of, 28; in Minnesota, 130; Native American uses of, 27–29, 32; in Northeast, 112; in Pennsylvania, 110; in the South, 105, 107
Forests, 69; disturbances in maintenance of, 44; fire in management of, 39–40, 46–47; fire suppression and changes in, 51; indigenous influences on, 41, 50
Forest Service, U.S., 29, 99
"Forgotten Side of Ethnogeography, The" (Stewart), 31

Foster, George M., 282
Fowke, Gerard, 74, 84
Fritz, Emanuel, 283–85, 298
Fuel accumulation, in over-aged vegeta-
tion, 12, 14–16, 35, 50

Game management. *See* Hunting and
game management
Garth, T., 292
Gates, Frank C., 157–58, 162
George, Ernest J., 176, 177
Gerhard, Frederic, 119
Gianella, Bill, 283, 293, 296
Gibbs, George, 272–73
Gifford, E. W., 220, 221, 229, 276–77,
281, 288–89, 292
Glaciers, and prairie formation, 124–25,
135, 175, 200
Gleason, H. A., 117, 121–23, 127, 152,
154, 193, 196–97, 215
Gosiute, 227
Government fire practices and views, 27,
29, 34
Grasshoppers, 265, 278–82, 290, 292,
293, 305–306, 307
Grasslands, 8, 38, 41, 43, 44, 49, 50, 51,
63, 69; of California, 301, 307–308;
chaparral and, 264–69, 270, 308, 309,
310; climate and, 114, 202–206, 307; of
eastern woodlands, 84, 87, 101–102,
108, 113; fire and, 212–16, 244, 307–308;
sagebrush and, 242–50; shelterbelt
and, 210–12; soil and, 206–10. *See also*
Prairies and plains
Grazing, 69, 152, 165, 166, 169–71, 173,
174, 197–99, 223, 224, 239, 244–48,
250, 255, 265, 283, 297, 309, 310, 312
Greasewood, 218, 241, 266
Great Basin and Plateau, 217, 218,
224–50
Great Plains, 32, 200, 205, 210, 211, 214
Great Salt Lake Desert, 241
Great Smoky Mountains, 106
Greene, S. W., 95–97, 98, 101
Gregg, Josiah, 150–51, 153
Griggs, Robert F., 238, 253
Grubs, 127
Gruell, George, 48

Gustafson, R. O., 107–108
Guthrie, John D., 251, 253, 255

Hackberry, 154, 165, 166, 200, 212, 216
Haig, Irvin T., 98, 237
Hallowell, A. Irving, 10–11
Hanson, H. C., 161–63, 170–71, 173, 196,
198–99, 245, 247
Hardpan, 209, 210
Hardwood forests, 9, 107–108; mixed, 111
Harrington, J. P., 275–76
Hartmann, C. W., 139–40, 218, 220
Harvey, LeRoy Harris, 174–75
Haufler, J. B., 61
Hayes, F. A., 210–12
Hazel, 275–76, 277, 282
Heady, Harold, 41
Hemlocks, 62, 235, 250, 253
Hennepin, Louis, 77–78, 115
Hensel, R. L., 155, 156, 157, 223
Heyward, Frank, 98–99, 102, 121, 127,
208
Hickories, 127, 216
Hilgard, E. W., 102, 120–21
Hill, W. W., 219–20
Historical ecology, 48, 61
Hoffman, C. F., 109, 126–27
Holt, Catharine, 293
Hopi, 220
Hopkins, Harold, 156, 163–64
Houck, Louis, 135, 137
Hough, Walter, 219, 221
Hulbert, Archer B., 207–208
Hunter-gatherers, 4–7, 18, 21–24, 26–27,
44
Hunting and game management, 28, 42,
72, 73, 74, 76–79, 85, 103, 115–16, 120,
150, 152; in California, 257, 260, 262,
263, 274–75, 277–78, 281, 282, 289–93,
300, 303, 311; in Great Basin, 227–33;
in Northwest, 252, 253; in Southwest,
218–22
Hupa, 274–75
Hursh, C. R., 93, 126
Hussey, John, 79, 91–92

Idaho, 215, 227–28, 230, 233, 234, 238,
242, 243, 245, 248, 255

Iguace (Yguace), 139
Illinois, 115, 117–26
Illinois (Indians), 10, 115
Indiana, 121, 196
Indians, American. *See* Native Americans
Indigenous burning practices, 3–6, 9, 10, 12, 13, 15, 23–24, 33–34; anthropologists' attitude toward, 17, 21, 23–25; and Euro-American uses of fire, 28–29; plant ecologists' view of, 49–55; Stewart's interest in, 7–8
Interdisciplinary research, 48–49, 52–54, 59
Interviews, 30, 31, 55–56
Iowa, 131–35
Iowa (Indians), 131
Iroquois, 62, 77, 80
Irving, Washington, 150
Isaac, Leo A., 252–53

Jepson, W. L., 273–74, 295
Jones, A. D., 118–19
Jones, Burle J., 310, 312
Jones, Rhys, 24
Julian Steward and the Great Basin (Ronaasen), 21
Junipers, 41, 51, 212, 217, 223–26, 245, 246, 247

Kalm, Peter, 76
Kansas, 153–58, 196, 210, 215, 216, 217
Karok, 275–77, 283
Kato, 278, 281
Keen, F. P., 233, 238, 239
Keesing, Felix, 25–26
Keesing, Roger, 25–26
Kehoe, Alice B., 4–5, 24
Kellogg, Charles E., 206–207
Kellogg, R. S., 154, 160–61, 162, 167
Kelly, Isabel, 231
Kelting, R. W., 156, 163–64
Kentucky, 79, 88, 90–93, 104, 107, 108
Klimek, S., 292
Kluckhohn, Clyde, 21
Knack, Martha, 6
Kniffen, F. B., 279
Knopf, Alfred, 10

Komarek, E. V., 8
Koppen, W., 113, 203–204, 241, 301
Kotok, E. I., 295–96, 298–99
Kotzebue, Otto von, 262
Kroeber, A. L., 7, 18, 19, 21, 29–30, 31, 69, 229, 257, 258, 277, 281, 292, 306, 311

Land management, fire as tool of, 3–4, 39, 41, 50–51
Larsen, J. A., 245
Larson, Floyd, 176, 199
Leopold, Aldo, 223
Leopold Report, 9
Le Page du Pratz, A. S., 115
Lesquereaux, Leo, 113, 119
Lewis and Clark expedition, 176
Lightning fires, 8, 32–34, 39, 46, 48–50, 54, 63, 68, 105, 110, 112, 214–17; of California, 105, 284–85, 297–300, 311; of Mountain West, 233–34, 237–39, 252; of Northwest, 253–55
Lindstrom, P., 76, 85
Little, E. L., 153
Little, S., 106–107
Livingston, Burton E., 83, 113, 132, 144, 146, 194–95, 203, 216, 225, 241, 271, 301
Loblolly pine, 43, 98
Lodgepole pine, 9, 63, 226, 236, 238, 294
Loeb, E. M., 278–79
Logging practices, 54
Longleaf-loblolly-slash pine forest, 94
Longleaf pine, 28, 51, 94–106, 112, 208
Loomis, Chester, 118
Loud, L. L., 275
Louisiana, 99, 100, 102, 107
Love, R. M., 310, 312
Lowie, Robert H., 230, 252
Lutz, H. J., 106, 109–110
Lyell, Charles, 79, 80

McClure, David, 79
McGee, W. J., 129–30, 174
McIntosh, Arthur C., 175
Maidu, 290–92, 306, 307
Maine, 110, 111, 112
Maissurow, D. K., 110–12
Manitoba, Canada, 182–92, 217

Man the Hunter (Lee and DeVore), 6
Manzanita, 223, 266, 276, 279, 291
Marbut, Curtis Fletcher, 206
Marquette, Jacques, 151
Marryat, Frank, 270
Marsh, G. P., 89–90, 119, 120, 192–93
Massachusetts, 75–76, 109
Massey, E. de, 271–72
Matthews, Washington, 218, 219
Mattoles, 272, 282
Maxwell, H., 71, 80–84
Menomini, 10
Mesquite, 51, 141–48, 152, 154, 198, 210,
    217, 220–23
Mexico, 242
Miami (Indians), 10
Michaux, F. A., 90, 98
Michel, F. L., 72, 82
Michigan, 79, 109, 111, 196
Minnesota, 129–30, 182
Mississippi, 96
Miwok, 257, 288–90, 306, 307
Modoc, 293
Moerenhout, Jacques Antoine, 303–305
Mohave, 10, 222
Montana, 177–78, 211, 217, 235, 242,
    243, 245
Montane meadows, 9, 43–44
Mooney, James, 79–80, 305–306
Morgan, L. H., 77
Morris, W. G., 254
Morton, Thomas, 74–75
Mountain West, 217–18; California,
    256–312; Great Basin and Plateau,
    224–50; Northwest, 250–56; South-
    west, 218–24
Muir, John, 90, 120, 127, 294–95
Munns, E. N., 211–12
Muskogee, 80
Myers, Ronald, 49

National and state parks, management
    of, 10, 40
Native Americans, 9, 32, 42; burning
    practices, in historical ecological con-
    texts, 37–42, 48; contemporary knowl-
    edge of fire regimes, 49–55; fire used
    by, 4, 5, 7–10, 13, 24, 27–29, 32–34,

61–63; land claims of, 18–22; vegetation
    influenced by, 67–69. *See also specific
    tribes and geographic areas*
Navajo, 38, 218, 219, 220, 224
Neanderthals, 24–25
Nebraska, 158–68, 196, 211, 213, 215,
    216, 217
Nebraska National Forest, 164, 166–68
Nevada, 225, 227, 230, 231, 234, 242, 243
New Brunswick, Canada, 112
New England, 61, 77, 87
New Jersey, 77; pine barrens, 41, 49, 106
New Mexico, 12, 14, 48, 54, 61, 63, 67,
    217, 218, 222–24, 242
New South Wales, Australia, 14
New York, 76, 77, 85–87, 108
Nez Perce, 229, 232
Nitrification, fire and, 43
North Carolina, 72–73, 98
North Dakota, 211, 216, 217
Northeast, 49–50
Northern desert shrub. *See* Sagebrush
Northern Paiutes, 230–31; Owens Valley
    land claims, 18, 19–20
Northern woodlands, 85
Northwest, 217, 250–56; lightning fires
    in, 105
Northwest Territories, Canada, 189–90
Nuttall, Thomas, 149–50

Oak barrens, 44
Oak-chestnut forests, 62, 107, 108
Oak-dominated forests, 38, 50
Oak-hickory forests, 9, 10, 44, 48, 62,
    107, 109, 139, 216
Oakland Hills, California, 13
Oak-openings, 129
Oak-pine forests, 83, 106, 107, 139
Oaks, 138, 160; of California, 258, 264,
    274, 276, 278, 279, 303; of Texas
    prairies, 142, 143; of Wisconsin
    prairies, 127
Oak savannas, 9, 43–44
Ohio, 78, 79, 88–89, 107, 193, 196
Ojibway, 38
Oklahoma, 149–53, 210, 215, 217
Old-growth forests, 38, 50
Olmsted, F. E., 40

Omaha (Indians), 159
Ontario, Canada, 54
Oregon, 12, 62, 215, 225, 228–29, 233–34, 239, 242–43, 250–55
Overgrazing. *See* Grazing
Owen, David Dale, 90–91
Owens Valley Paiute, 18, 19–20
Ozark region, 138, 139, 149

Pacific Northwest, 8, 51, 54, 62
Pacific states, 63
"Paiute Forestry," 27
Paleoindians, burning practices of, 34
Paleontology, prairies and, 199–202
Palm oases, 10
Papago, 220–21, 222
Parker, K. W., 223, 259
Patwin, 281
Pearson, G. A., 197, 224, 237
Peat deposits, 112, 237
Peattie, Donald Culross, 67
Pechanec, J. F., 245, 247
Penfound, William T., 156, 163–64
Pennsylvania, 76, 109–10
Peroni, Patricia, 49
Perrot, Nicolas, 120, 131
Peyote Religion (Stewart), 6, 21
Pickford, G. D., 244, 245, 247
Pierce, R. A., 154–55, 166
Pima, 10, 221
Pines, 8, 9, 46, 48, 51, 106, 110–12, 157–58, 160, 161, 165–67, 169, 170, 174–76, 200, 212, 216, 217; of California, 294–96, 299; of Great Basin, 225, 226, 235–40, 245; of Texas, 139
Piñon, 225, 226
Plains. *See* Prairies and plains
Plains Indians, 67
Plains Shelterbelt Project, 210, 211
Plant ecology, 38; disturbances and, 46; fire as factor in maintenance of, 42–43; Indians' shaping of, 41; indigenous influences on vegetation, 49–50; and perturbations in vegetation patterns, 39
Plant Ecology (Weaver and Clements), 95, 106, 161, 197, 244
Plummer, F. G., 112, 215, 233–34, 237, 254, 255, 297

Pomo, 7, 278–81
Pool, Raymond John, 164–66
Poplars, 183, 184, 185
Potash deposits, 167
Pound, Roscoe, 164, 173, 192
Prairie peninsula, the, 117, 120, 122, 126, 144, 196
Prairies and plains, 8–9, 32, 38, 39, 41, 44, 68–69, 113–17, 192–99; of Arkansas, 139; Canadian, 178–92, 211; climate and, 202–206; coastal, 49; of Colorado, 168–72; of eastern woodlands, 88–93, 102, 108, 109; with fire, 212–16; without fire, 216–17; of Illinois, 117–26; of Iowa, 131–35; of Kansas, 153–58; of Minnesota, 129–30; of Missouri, 135–39; of Montana, 177–78; of Nebraska, 158–68; of Oklahoma, 149–53; paleontology and, 199–202; Shelterbelt Project, 210–12; soil and, 206–10; of South Dakota, 174–77; of Texas, 139–49; of Wisconsin, 126–29; of Wyoming, 172–74
Precipitation-evaporation (P/E) ratio, 83, 146, 202, 203, 225
Pre-climax forest, 107, 108
print/silent
Pueblo Indians, 220
Pyne, Stephen J., 5, 9, 12, 14, 33
Pyro-dendrochronology studies, 9, 48
Pyrophytic environments, 12, 14

Railroad rights-of-way, relict vegetation in, 123–25, 133, 138, 146, 173–74, 191, 310
Rainfall, 134, 154, 156, 164, 176; and grasslands, 203, 205; of Great Basin, 225, 226, 242; of prairie regions, 195, 200; in Southwest, 224
Ramaley, Francis, 168–69, 172, 237
Ranch management, 155
Rapraeger, E. F., 233, 238
Rattlesnakes, 276, 278, 282
Reciprocal causality, in cultural ecology, 22
Redwoods. *See* Sequoias
Restoration ecology. *See* Ecological restoration

Riegel, Andrew, 163–64
Roach, Archibald W., 169–70
Rocky Mountains, 48, 105, 217, 234, 237, 238
Ronaasen, Sheree, 21
Russell, R. J., 241, 301
Ryan, W. R., 262, 305

Sacramento Valley, California, 301, 306, 307
Sagebrush, 41, 156, 170–74, 198, 210, 217, 218, 225, 226, 240–50
Saint-Amant, P.-C. de, 228–29, 232
Salt desert shrub. *See* Greasewood
Sampson, A. W., 148–49, 256–59, 261, 262, 265, 266, 268–69, 271, 272, 286, 289, 299, 303, 310–11
Sampson, H. C., 123–24
Sandhills, 154–55, 164, 166, 167, 168, 189
Sandia Mountains, 48
Sand pine-scrub vegetation, 51
San Ildefonso, 220
San Joaquin Valley, California, 301, 302, 305, 307, 309
Santa Clara Valley, California, 264, 267, 268
Saskatchewan, Canada, 192, 217
Sauer, Carl O., 7, 12, 69, 88, 90, 93, 135, 137, 200–202, 205–206, 208, 214, 215
Savannas, 50, 82
Schaffner, John H., 124, 156–57, 202–203
Schmidt, Karl P., 108
Schoolcraft, H. R., 126, 136
Scrub, 69, 144. *See also* Grubs
Sears, P. B., 134–35, 152, 153, 201
Seed growing and collecting, 220, 224, 230, 231, 246, 272, 273, 275, 280, 282, 290, 292, 293, 300, 307, 311
Selke, Arthur C., 177
Sequoia-mixed conifer forests, 9, 48
Sequoias, 271–73, 278, 283–85, 295, 298–99
Shaler, N. S., 79, 84, 90, 92–93, 120, 207, 208
Shantz, H. L., 83, 94, 110, 135, 136, 143, 144, 149, 168, 173, 174, 195–96, 209–10, 214–16, 218, 225, 226, 241, 248, 250–51, 255, 266, 271, 294, 300, 307–10

Shawnee, 72
Shear, Cornelius L., 144–45, 222
Shelterbelts, 177, 210–12
Shenandoah Valley, Virginia, 83–84
Shimek, B., 131–34, 190–91
Shoshoni, 230, 231, 232
Show, S. B., 295–96, 298–99, 300
Shreve, Forest, 83, 113, 132, 144, 146, 194–95, 203, 216, 225, 241, 271, 301
Shrublands, 43, 44, 58
Sierra Nevada, 9, 48, 51, 62, 63, 257, 286–300
Silcox, F. A., 210–12
Sioux (Dakota), 38, 129, 174
Skykomish, 62
Smith, Jared G., 140, 144
Smith, John, 72, 81
Snow, 177
Soil, 43, 49; of Canadian prairies, 179, 182, 183, 184; and grasslands, 92, 102–3, 114, 206–10; and prairie-plains formation, 113, 119–21, 123, 127–28, 131, 132, 156
South, forest fires in, 105
South Dakota, 174–77, 215, 216
Southeast, 8, 79, 94, 103, 105–107, 204, 212, 251
Southern desert shrub. *See* Creosote bush
Southern Paiute, 230, 246
Southwest, 51, 62, 217, 218–24
Spanish explorers and settlers, 28, 114–15, 135, 140, 226, 259–64, 302–3
Species dominance, shift in, 53
Spelman, H., 72
Spier, Leslie, 221, 232, 262
Spokanes, 229, 232
Spruce-fir forests, 294
Spruces, 235, 285
Stahelin, R., 238
Stanislaus National Forest, California, 298
Stefansson, Vilhjalmer, 189–90
Stegner, Wallace, 40
Steward, Julian, 18–22, 32, 35n.6, 230–33; cultural ecology theory of, 22–25
Stewart. G., 245–47

Stewart, Omer C.: and advocates of prescribed burning, 34; approach to
  anthropology, 29–31, 39; Clements
  challenged by, 39; efforts to publish
  manuscript, 10–12, 17, 21; importance
  of studies of, 32; and indigenous interactions with nature, 40–42; influence
  of, 14–15; and Kroeber's studies, 30;
  Malinowski Award, 35n.4; and Native
  American land claims, 18–22; Native
  American uses of fire, interest in and
  studies of, 5–9, 22, 28, 29, 41; and
  Steward, 18–22; support for ideas of,
  8–9; weaknesses in manuscript of,
  61–63
Stoddard, Herbert L., 103, 135–36
Stoeckeler, J. H., 177, 210–12
Stoffle, Richard, 19, 20–21
Storer, T. I., 268
Sumac, 156, 157, 160, 164

Tall Timbers Fire Ecology Conference,
  Proceedings (1972), 41
Tall Timbers Research, Inc., 11
Tamalpais, Mount, California, 270–71
Tasmania, Australia, 24
Taylor, A. R., 63
Tennessee, 93–94, 107, 108
Terry, Elwood I., 101
Texas, 115, 139–49, 210, 218, 222, 223
Tharp, B. C., 139, 143–44, 145–46, 148
Theory of Culture Change (Steward),
  22–23
Thomas, Jack Ward, 46–47
Thorp, James, 208
Tillamook fire, Oregon (1933), 255
Timber, 296
Timberline, 238, 253
Tobacco, 231, 252, 257, 276, 282, 290,
  292, 307, 311
Tolowa, 252, 282
Topography, fires and, 213, 214
Trait distributions, study of, 30
Transeau, E. N., 117, 123, 126, 132, 144,
  146, 202
Trees, 43; of California, 294, 295; of
  Canadian prairies, 183–89, 191–92; of
  Coastal Range, 274; Shelterbelt Project,

210–12; of U.S. prairies, 193, 195; with-
  out fires, 216–17
Tules, 300, 303, 307
Turner, Frederick Jackson, 40

University of Oklahoma Press, 12
Urbanized bush, Pyne's notion of, 14
Utah, 226–27, 229, 230, 234, 242, 243,
  246, 247
Ute, 229–30

Vallejo's Treaty (1836), 270, 281
Van Der Donck, Adrian, 76
Vestal, Arthur G., 95, 103, 123
Viking Fund Publications in Anthropol-
  ogy, 11
Virginia, 71–73, 80–84, 104
Voegelin, E. W., 290, 292–93, 307
Vorhies, C. T., 170, 173, 198–99

Wackerman, A. E., 102, 105, 139
Wappo, 270, 281
Washington, 215, 225, 228, 234, 239,
  241–43, 248–53, 255
Water conservation, 152
Weakley, Harry E., 167, 213
Weaver, H., 239–40
Weaver, J. E., 95, 98, 102, 106, 107, 156,
  161–63, 196–98, 202, 209, 210, 214–16,
  296
Webb, W. P., 204
Weld, Isaac, 77, 85
Wells, R. W., 78, 89, 118, 131, 136
Wenner-Gren Foundation, 11
Western larch, 46, 48
Western Mono, 9, 38
Wetlands, 44
Wheeler, H. N., 99, 100
Whipple, A. W., 151
White, Andrew, 81
White, C. A., 131, 133
White, Leslie, 25, 26
Whitman, Warren, 176
Whitney, J. D., 113, 131
Wied-Neuwied, Maximilian, 131, 159
Wilde, S. A., 102, 128
Wilderness areas, 34, 38, 40
Wildfires, 12–15, 35, 46, 51, 109

Wildlands management, 9, 37–38, 47, 51
Wildlife management, 9, 10, 42, 103
Willoughby, C. C., 77
Willows, 184, 186
Wind, fires and, 213
Wintun, 306, 307
Wiregrass, 101
Wisconsin, 111, 126–29
Wissler, Clark, 120, 131
Withrow, Alice Phillips, 126, 132
Wiyot, 275, 282, 283
Wood, William, 75–76
Woodlands, 51
Woodman, C. L., 109
Wooton, E. O., 222, 223
Worden, William L., 312
Wright, Elnora A., 177–78
Wright, John C., 177–78

Wyoming, 172–74, 198, 210, 211, 217, 230, 237, 238, 242, 243

Yana, 292, 306
Yellow pine-sugar pine forests, 286, 294
Yellowstone National Park, 50
Yguace (Iguace), 139
Yokuts, 9, 290, 303, 306, 307
Yosemite National Park, 6, 286
Yosemite Valley, California, 286–90, 298
Yuki, 282
Yurok, 277, 282

Zon, Raphael, 83, 94, 110, 135, 136, 139, 143, 144, 149, 166–68, 173, 174, 177, 195–96, 209–12, 218, 225, 226, 241, 248, 250–51, 255, 266, 271, 294, 300, 307, 309–310